LAND-TO-THE-TILLER IN THE MEKONG DELTA

Economic, Social and Political Effects of Land Reform in Four Villages of South Vietnam

Monograph Series No. 23

Charles Stuart Callison

Center for South and Southeast Asia Studies
University of California
Berkeley, California

UNIVERSITY
PRESS OF
AMERICA

LANHAM • NEW YORK • LONDON

Copyright © 1983 by
The Regents of the University of California

University Press of America,™ Inc.

4720 Boston Way
Lanham, MD 20706

3 Henrietta Street
London WC2E 8LU England

Printed in the United States of America

Library of Congress Cataloging in Publication Data

Callison, Charles Stuart.
    Land-to-the-tiller in the Mekong Delta.

    Bibliography: p.
    Includes index.
    1. Land reform—Vietnam. 2. Land reform—Mekong
River—Delta. 3. Agriculture—Economic aspects—Vietnam.
4. Agriculture—Economic aspects—Mekong River—Delta.
5. Vietnam—Rural conditions. 6. Mekong River—Delta—
Rural conditions, I. Title.
HD1333.V5C34   1983   333.3'1'597   83-6745
ISBN 0-8191-3252-7
ISBN 0-8191-3253-5 (pbk.)

Co-published by arrangement with the
Center for South and Southeast Asia Studies
University of California, Berkeley

FOREWORD

The passionate disputes that wracked the American academic community over Vietnam at long last have begun to dissipate. Events have forced "hawks" and "doves" alike to recognize that neither ever possessed the monopoly of truth implied by the noisy, but often none-too-knowledgeable, debates of the 60's and 70's. Hawks were humbled by the defeat of South Vietnam; doves have been no less disconcerted by the devastation wreaked by Pol Pot in Cambodia, the Vietnamese occupation of Cambodia, the pedagogical war of China against Vietnam, and the exodus of refugees from Vietnam.

Stuart Callison's monograph on the Land-to-the-Tiller program in South Vietnam is an important example of the new willingness to give sober consideration to both past and contemporary events in Indochina. The Land-to-the-Tiller program of the early 1970's was a remarkable success, distributing titles of ownerships to virtually all tenant farmers in the Mekong Delta. The political and economic power of the landlords had been sapped by the activities of the NLF in the countryside, and the war itself had increased the power of the professional military and other non-landowning classes who backed land reform. The South Vietnamese military's acceptance of the importance of land reform combined with foreign resources and increased internal administrative capacity to carry through the most extensive land reform program yet witnessed in any non-communist country in Asia. Like the land reform programs previously initiated in Japan and Taiwan, the transfer of land ownership from landlords to tenants in South Vietnam led to agricultural innovation and substantial increases in agricultural production. In addition, local support for the NLF declined in response to this and other government programs. The depth of the socio-economic transformation brought about by the Land-to-the-Tiller program meant that the post-1975 government of Vietnam faced an altered social fabric for which collectivization and class struggle had scant appeal because middle landholding peasants had become the preponderant class.

As a result, six years after coming to full power government plans for collectivization have not been implemented in the Mekong Delta area and the "rational" peasants of southern Vietnam seem to be withholding their labor and initiative thereby insuring a continuous crisis in rice production in post-war Vietnam.

iii

Those interested in understanding the economic problems of post-war Vietnam and comprehending the possibilities for land reform in other parts of the developing world would be well served by giving careful consideration to Callison's work.

Karl D. Jackson
Editor, Monograph #21

iv

PREFACE

The institutional requirements for successful modernization and economic development are often assumed to have been already met as "essential preconditions" in academic writings on the subject. Many students of the development process are beginning to realize, however, that obtaining the institutional changes required for successful, broadly-based development is the most difficult and vulnerable part of the task, especially when economic development is itself defined, as it increasingly is these days, to include not only rising per capita (average) real incomes but employment, income distribution, and other equity goals as well. Despite cries that "social engineering" is somehow a bad thing for development advisors to engage in, field researchers and practitioners are becoming increasingly aware that to achieve the goals of modernization in any less-developed country the behavior patterns of large numbers of people and institutions must change, that this often requires social, cultural, and political changes of significant magnitude, and that such changes must be themselves "institutionalized" and not mere temporary experiments.

This study focuses on the need for major surgery in the institution of land tenure in the Mekong Delta of South Vietnam: the ways in which the cultural, social, political, and legal aspects of the pre-reform landlord-tenant relationship together inhibited rural development and created unacceptable · inequalities between two classes of people, and on the ways in which the implicit "assumption" of modern economic attitudes toward land prevented many Western analysts from understanding the perverse economic consequences of the existing situation.

Following a brief summary of two earlier land reform programs in Taiwan and Japan for comparison and an historical sketch of land tenure in South Vietnam, the 1970 Land-to-the-Tiller (LTTT) Program in South Vietnam is described as an attempt to complete a major institutional reform with far-reaching economic, social, and political implications.

The major portion of this study reports analytical research efforts to obtain a preliminary assessment of the probable long-run effects of the LTTT Program and to determine whether those apparent effects tend to confirm or deny theoretical expectations. The analysis relies on an extensive field survey comprised of 1) a comparative sample of 180 rice farmers divided equally among three land-tenure categories, on the one hand, and among four different villages in four different provinces of the Mekong Delta, on the other hand,[1] 2) a stratified sample of 40 expropriated landlords, and 3) an opinion poll of 35 village leaders and a few provincial officials. Related evidence from other research is summarized in Chapter IX. The final chapter summarizes the major conclusions to be drawn from the evidence reported here under the two main headings, "Economic Effects" and "Socio-Political Effects."

The purpose of this research endeavor was two-fold. It was designed primarily to test certain theoretical expectations about the effects of a land reform such as the LTTT Program in the "traditional" Vietnamese cultural and institutional context. In keeping with this objective, the farmer sample surveyed was limited to those residing in relatively "secure" and pro-government areas where effective landlord-tenant relationships had remained intact prior to the LTTT Program and where rents had still been collected. These restrictions, required to achieve the primary goal, obviously limit the extent to which the study can achieve its secondary purpose of portraying pre-LTTT land tenure conditions, their change and the effects of that change as representative of the whole Mekong Delta, since the old landlord-tenant relationship had already been severed and rents had not been collected for several years over much of it.

Viewed more broadly, however, even the secondary goal has been achieved in the sense that the landlord-tenant relationships and rent collections still effective in the four relatively more "secure" villages surveyed are themselves watered-down versions of the tenure conditions prevalent over the whole Delta not too many years ago. To the extent that the more recent tenure reforms in the four villages studied represent a telescoped version of what has happened over a longer period of time elsewhere, with the legal reforms of the LTTT Program formally institutionalizing the prior extra-legal chain of events, the study can be viewed as representing some of the probable effects of that whole chain of events.

Obviously, now that the communist government is in charge and is placing its own stamp on land tenure arrangements in the Delta, the "representativeness" of this research becomes a moot point, except for a very brief historical period. Future historians and analysts will no doubt attempt to measure the relative success or failure of the communist approach to agricultural and economic development and to the overall goals of modernization, however, and this study should help form a benchmark for such

---

[1]Plans to include two additional villages along the Central Coast Lowlands, one near Hue and one near Qui Nhon, had to be cancelled due to the Spring Offensive of 1972.

analysis and help indicate the probable course such development might have taken under an alternative approach.

The question of representativeness does not detract from the primary purpose of performing some empirical, if preliminary, tests of theoretical expectations about one kind of land reform in one kind of Asian landlord-tenancy context, and it is hoped that this study will contribute toward a better understanding of the role of land reform in agricultural and economic development.

Charles Stuart Callison

ACKNOWLEDGMENTS

Financial support for this research came from three different sources. Preliminary background research and research design was completed in residence at Cornell University with the support of a Foreign Language Fellowship under Title VI of the National Defense Education Act. Thirteen months of field research in South Vietnam (August 1971-September 1972) was funded by the Foreign Area Fellowship Program of the Social Science Research Council and the American Council of Learned Societies, administered under a grant from the Ford Foundation, which also financed the first six months of the write-up phase. The final four and one-half months of the write-up effort, through the summer of 1973, was supported by a Southeast Asia Program Fellowship of Cornell University.

My wife and I are indebted to the Can Tho University in Can Tho and the Hoa Hao University in Long Xuyen for providing us pleasant quarters in an academic environment during our stay in Phong Dinh and An Giang Provinces. Dr. Nguyen Duy Xuan, Rector, Can Tho University, granted us affiliate status as research associate (tham-van), for myself, and research assistant (phu-khao), for my wife, that greatly facilitated our efforts. We are grateful to Dr. Xuan for his friendly advice and moral support throughout our stay in Vietnam, stemming in part from his own professional and personal interest in the effects of the Land-to-the-Tiller (LTTT) Program and in the course of rural development in Vietnam.

Members of the Land Reform Division of the U.S. Agency for International Development (USAID) in Saigon and in Can Tho provided much relevant information verbally, from their files and in personal correspondence before and after our stay in Vietnam; and they introduced us to appropriate national and local officials of the Vietnamese government. The entire list of USAID officials who assisted us is too long, but special thanks must go to Mr. Keith W. Sherper, whose knowledge of the origins of the LTTT Program runs far deeper than we could present in this thesis, and to Mr. Stephen Klaus, who was very helpful during the pre-testing phase of our field research in Bien Hoa Province and who also provided some valuable comments on an early draft of "The Landlord Side," Chapter VII.

Dr. Henry C. Bush, his two research assistants, Mr. Gordon H. Messegee and Mr. Roger V. Russell, and the staff of the Control Data Corporation, under contract to USAID to study the political effects of the LTTT Program, were very generous of their time and research materials. Our separate research efforts were

ix

complementary in nature, and we spent many fruitful hours comparing notes and discussing research design, methodology, and field experiences. Frequent references are made to their publications in this thesis and portions of their major research effort, **The Impact of the Land-to-the-Tiller Program in the Mekong Delta,** are summarized in Chapter IX.

On the government side, Mr. Bui Huu Tien, Director General of Land Affairs, introduced us to his Province Land Affairs Service (PLAS) chiefs and requested their cooperation in our research efforts, expressing a keen interest in the results of our research. Invaluable assistance was provided by the PLAS chiefs and their personnel in the provinces of Long An, Dinh Tuong, Phong Dinh and An Giang. National Assembly records were of very limited availability and were obtained only through the good offices of Senator Tran Van Qua, Chairman of the Senate Committee on Agriculture, and Mr. Nguyen Hoang Linh, Special Assistant to the Secretary General, House of Representatives.

A word of special thanks is due to the chairman of my Special Committee at Cornell University, Prof. Frank H. Golay, the other two committee members, Prof. Henry Y. Wan, Jr., and Prof. Franklin E. Huffman, and Visiting Professor David G. Marr, for their advice, assistance and moral support during this long and sometimes tedious project.

Several typists, including my wife, typed portions of the draft, but the only one who suffered through the whole thing, from beginning to end, including all the tables of statistics, was Miss Vicky Palmiano of Naga City, Camarines Sur Province, The Philippines, who patiently and painstakingly retyped the original manuscript in final form.

Some of the statistical tables, maps, graphs, and other material included herein were published in 1974 in a short monograph by the author, "The Land-to-the-Tiller Program and Rural Resource Mobilization in the Mekong Delta of South Vietnam," Papers in International Studies, Southeast Asia Series No. 34, printed by the Ohio University Center for International Studies, Athens, Ohio, who have kindly granted permission to republish this copyrighted material here.

Saving the most important acknowledgments until last, I shall never miss an opportunity to express my deep indebtedness and gratitude to my wife, Michelle My-Dung Callison, for not only surviving the whole six-year operation, from its conceptualization in 1970 to its completion in 1976, but also for herself interviewing more than half of the farmers in our sample and generating most of the warm and friendly rapport we enjoyed among the farmers and their communities. And finally, neither my wife nor I shall ever forget the warm and generous reception we met wherever we went, but especially among the farmers themselves and their families, who seldom hesitated to spend a half-day of their time answering our endless questions and explaining the details of their lives, their problems and their hopes for a better future, in the midst of a bitter war that seriously affected them all. May their desire for peace and their dreams of a better life for their children find fulfillment.

TABLE OF CONTENTS

LIST OF TABLES

LIST OF FIGURES

LIST OF MAPS

Chapter 1

THE ROLE OF LAND REFORM IN THE
MODERNIZATION PROCESS

The Modernization Process

The most urgent and challenging task before us, next to the achievement of a lasting peace among competing nations of the world, is that of modernization—the process of social, political, and economic reorganization along more rational lines in order to take advantage of the more efficient production technology now available and to cope with the unprecedented problems of population growth and natural resource depletion. The population explosion of recent decades, primed by successful developments in the field of medicine and health care, has brought mankind to the limits of available resources, especially in arable land and water used for traditional methods of food and fiber production. Despite the new wealth in modern societies (and modern sectors of traditional societies), vast numbers of people are still living in poverty and ignorance, with little hope for improvement in their condition. Unemployment and hunger remain the life-style for millions who would rather work to eat and feed their families. Some progress is being achieved—per capita incomes are slowly rising in most countries—but distribution skews and unemployment problems are excluding too many people from even these modest gains.

The desirability of modernization is occasionally questioned by those beset with a romanticized notion of the "peaceful peasant life," which would stand to be fundamentally altered in the process. These people fail to comprehend the meaning of poverty and the dire prospects for a future without positive progress, given the current rate of population growth and land area limitations. Poverty means watching your children and other loved ones suffer and die of diseases which could be prevented or cured. It means struggling to put in a hard day's work when your body is racked with dysentery or malaria, fearing to rest lest you lose your job and your children go hungry. It means keeping your older children home from school to take care of the younger ones because both parents must work. It means working for wages barely sufficient to cover daily food costs for your family, living in a dank and dusky shack you built with scrap materials or crawling thatch, living in a world you do not understand and over which you have no control, suffering a political system in which you have no voice and cannot participate because of your lack of education, and, perhaps, worst of all, having little or no hope of a much better life for your children. The peasant farmers the author has met may try to maintain certain religious and cultural practices traditional to their way of life, but they are almost unanimous in their desire for improvement, a higher standard of living and better prospects for their children.

Requirements

To reach the goal of substantial economic improvement, the process of modernization must be sustained over a long period of time. This is an extremely complex process, different in every country and in every historical time frame, and it is only partially understood by the best of our social scientists. There seems to be general agreement, however, that it both requires and induces a considerable amount of change from the old way of doing things. The study of economic development must be concerned with the social, economic, and political changes required in each country and with the way such changes can be sustained.

Speaking generally, the modernizing society must develop the capacity to involve the masses of its population in the effort, since it needs all the human energy, initiative, talent, and enthusiasm it can find. It must mobilize its human resources to the task through education, training, and work experience to develop their productive potential, through economic and social incentives to encourage greater effort and sacrifice, and through broader political participation to insure the institutional flexibility required by constant change. If the society fails in any of these areas, its modernization and development program will falter.[1]

The search for talented and hard-working individuals to lead the complex processes of change and to master the new technologies of organization and production must extend to all strata of the population. The genetic combinations which produce leadership and intellectual potential are found no less frequently among the poor than among the wealthy families, and the poor make up the bulk of the population. If the educational system denies equal opportunity to the poor student, or if the lack of social mobility prevents talent from fulfilling its potential, the society as a whole suffers and progress will be stifled. Educational opportunity and social mobility themselves can provide important incentives for greater individual effort and sacrifice.

---

[1]W. Arthur Lewis discusses the importance of certain institutional characteristics in the development process and the nature of the changes required for sustained progress in **The Theory of Economic Growth,** (London: George Allen and Unwin Ltd., 1955; New York: Harper and Row, 1970), Chapter 3.

Change must be accepted as continual and necessary if modernization is to proceed peacefully. Social, political and economic institutions must be flexible enough to respond to ever-new demands arising out of ever-new conditions. If they cannot respond, development will be slowed and pressures will build into explosive situations. In extreme cases rigidity leads to riots, rebellions and revolution.[2]

Production and distribution activities must be reorganized to incorporate modern scientific and technical knowledge. The goal is to increase output per man, not merely by achieving a "Pareto optimum" position of production and exchange, but by leading the country up onto successively higher production-possibility-curves and by changing employment and resource ownership patterns, income distribution, political power and institutional factors so that they will lead to the moving, continually improving Pareto-optimum possibilities characteristic of a rapidly developing economy.

Figure 1-1: **Production Possibility Curve**

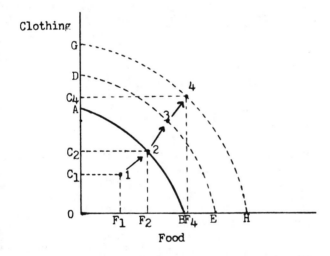

Traditional economics concentrates on static efficiency criteria whereby an economy can raise its total output from some point 1 in Figure 1-1, where it is operating at below full capacity and/or

[2]For an analysis of the inherently revolutionary nature of the modernization process see Chandler Morse, "Becoming versus Being Modern: An Essay on Institutional Change and Economic Development," in Chandler Morse, **et. al., Modernization by Design,** (Ithaca, New York: Cornell University Press, 1969), pp. 238-382.

at less than optimum technical efficiency. Development economics, on the other hand, seeks ways to shift the whole production possibility curve upward from A2B to D3E, G4H and beyond, by increasing productive capacity (especially through the creation of more physical capital and more "embodied capital" in labor) and by steadily improving the state of technology available to individual productive units within the economy.

Figure 1-2:   **Lorenz Curve of Income Distribution**

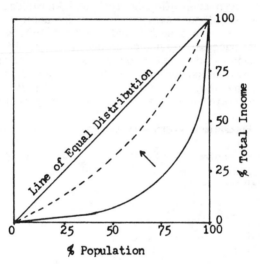

It was once thought that, while the sharply skewed distribution of income found in most less-developed countries might be considered socially unjust, it would nevertheless lead to a higher rate of capital investment and therefore to a higher rate of economic growth for the economy as a whole, due to the supposedly higher average propensity to save of the high income groups. Recent studies have indicated, however, that the rich tend to indulge in a substantial amount of luxurious living, usually supported by a high level of imports, and that when they do accumulate large savings it is often deposited in a "safer" bank abroad.[3] The economy thus loses not only potential funds for domestic investment, but a considerable amount of scarce foreign exchange, as well.

_____

[3]For a summary discussion of some of these studies see Peter Dorner, **Land Reform and Economic Development**,   (Baltimore: Penguin Books, 1972), pp. 82-91.

Many economists now believe that a more equal distribution of wealth and income, as depicted in Figure 1-2, will not only satisfy increasing political demands for greater social justice, but will also reduce the demand for luxury consumption imports, permitting more savings at home for domestic investment projects. In addition, it will mean more income available in rural areas out of which savings can be mobilized for rural development projects—infrastructure investment projects for which the urban rich are notably unenthusiastic—and from which a greater consumer demand for medium quality products can stimulate domestic investment and production in light industry.

The Role of Agriculture in Development

The agricultural sector must play an important role in the modernization process. First of all, it must provide food and industrial crops for the rapidly growing population and industrial sector. Secondly, since in the early stages of development the modern, non-agricultural sectors are too small in size to absorb the annual increment to the labor force resulting from population growth, the agricultural sector must continue to serve for some time as the residual employer, absorbing additional labor every year. Only when industrial development reaches a sufficient rate of growth and the industrial sector achieves a sufficient size relative to the rest of the economy can the farm labor force begin to contract without creating problems of unemployment.[4] This has important implications for the choice between labor- and capital-intensive agricultural development policies, such as the timing of agricultural consolidation and mechanization.

Much can be done to raise the productivity of Asian agriculture, per hectare and per man, through the adaptation of labor-intensive, scientific techniques. Japan and Taiwan are good examples of this approach. Successful agricultural development can improve average incomes and economic welfare for large masses of people, since most of the population of the less developed countries are still farmers. Broader income distribution can improve domestic demand and markets for the fledgling industrial sector, providing an important spur to private investment in domestic industries. Higher agricultural production can save or earn foreign exchange by reducing imports and increasing exports of agricultural goods, thus providing more foreign exchange for the importation of industrial capital goods. Savings and taxes skimmed off rising rural incomes can be

---

[4]An elaboration of this point can be found in John W. Mellor, **The Economics of Agricultural Development,** (Ithaca New York: Cornell University Press, 1966), Chapter 2.

channelled into infrastructure investments, such as education, transportation facilities, agricultural research and water control projects, and into investment funds for more rapid industrial development.

Agricultural development policies can complement efforts to increase the political participation of the masses, to decentralize decision-making authority, and to share political power with local government and new political pressure groups, thereby improving the responsiveness of the political system to changing conditions, needs, and demands of the citizenry. This will enhance the long-run stability of the political system through the turbulent course of modernization.

Socially, raising the incomes and status of the rural masses can help to improve social mobility and enhance the search for talented leadership, especially if the local tax base and parental incentive can be tapped to support a better system of education. Rural development projects can provide forms of status and prestige based on performance and ability as alternatives to traditional, ascriptive forms, thus expanding opportunities and incentives for advancement. Successful development in agriculture can help create a climate of innovation and progress, normalizing modern change and institutional flexibility and making continued development there and elsewhere more readily understood and accepted.

The Role of Land Reform

The diversity of land tenure arrangements worldwide is immense, as are the conditions of the natural environment and the local economic, political, and social systems under which the farmer must work. Economists find it difficult to generalize about the effects of land reform, relating most of their remarks to particular kinds of reforms in particular types of tenure systems—if not to specific country situations as well. Doreen Warriner identifies the three major types of landownership systems subject to reform as the Asian tenancy system, the Latifundian system, and the plantation system.[5]

Depending mostly on the political and economic ideology of the government carrying out reforms, these systems are normally

---

[5]Doreen Warriner, **Land Reform in Principle and Practice,** (London: Oxford University Press, 1969), pp. 45-51.

transformed into private family farms, group farms such as cooperatives or collectives, or state farms.[6]

The economic, social and political effects of reform indicated by theory and historical experience depend not only on what type of pre-reform system is transformed into what type of post-reform system, but also on the host of other conditions peculiar to the country or region involved, on what other political and economic programs are undertaken to complement or counteract the effects of land reform, and, of course, on the detailed provisions of the land reform itself and on how successfully they are actually implemented. Since this study deals with the conversion of an Asian tenancy system into privately-owned family farms, the following discussion will be limited to that part of the theory.[7]

In an Asian tenancy system the owner may own 1,000 hectares or only 5, but he typically "leases his land in small holdings to cultivators who work the land with their own livestock, and he collects rent from them in the form of money or produce" either as a share of the crop or as a fixed amount per hectare.[8] The tenants often have no legal security of tenure and may be evicted at the will of the landlord, while the landlord himself may or may not provide any function related to the production process, such as the provision of credit, seeds, irrigation facilities, or field supervision. Landlords may require their tenants to perform certain tasks of menial labor in and around his own mansion, especially in preparation for festive occasions, and may demand extra gifts of poultry, fruit, or other items from time to time. The pervasive power of the landlord class over the lives and activities of their tenants has led some variants of the Asian tenancy system to be called "feudalistic"

---

[6]See Peter Dorner, **Land Reform & Economic Development,** (Baltimore: Penguin Books, 1972), pp. 49-66.

[7]Economists often find much room for productive improvements beginning with land reform programs in the latifundian and Asian tenancy systems of land tenure, but rarely so in the case of commercially-run plantation estates. It should be emphasized that the discussion below presents a relatively favorable view of land redistribution possibilities in the typical Asian tenancy system. This does not mean the same favorable effects should be expected from similar reforms in a plantation or latifundian context, nor can they be necessarily expected from those Asian tenure systems which depart from the "typical" model. Each case must be carefully analyzed on its own merits, as we shall do with the Vietnam case in this study. The reader is referred to Doreen Warriner, **Land Reform,** for a discussion of the plantation and latifundian cases.

[8]Warriner, **Land Reform,** pp. 45-6.

in nature, although the use of this term in Asia must be understood to refer to the **de facto** enserfment of tenants, and not to any other resemblance to the feudal order of medieval Western Europe.[9]

Details of the South Vietnamese version of Asian tenancy will be presented in Chapter 3. Here we shall consider the theoretical consequences of converting a feudalistic Asian tenancy system into private family farms, while in Chapter 2 we shall take a brief look at the comparable experiences of Japan and Taiwan.

Land reform is a redistributive instrument usually undertaken for political reasons, to break the power of the landlord class and to win broader popular support for the government by reducing the power of a few over many, thus achieving greater equity and social justice in the eyes of larger numbers of people. The change in ownership and control over income-producing resources results in a redistribution not only of income, but also of social status and political power, since the latter two attributes are inherently related to property ownership and to the level and security of one's income, especially in a rural society.

History has demonstrated that the social and political changes accompanying the modernization process can lead to a variety of modern political forms, including democratic capitalism or socialism, fascism, communism, or military dictatorship, depending largely on what social stratum or group controls the process. It is widely believed, however, that the development of a small, family-owned farm system of land tenure should generate broader political participation in rural areas, foster a greater flexibility in local political institutions, and contribute to the growth of a strong middle class with democratic tendencies.

With the growth of a strong middle class to fill the gap between the very rich and the poor, social mobility and the national search for talent will be enhanced while social rigidities inimical to modernization will be reduced. By transferring control of landed wealth from urban landlords to rural farmers, greater support can be expected for rural development projects and rural educational institutions, expanding opportunities for advancement among rural youth.[10] The higher dignity and social status conferred upon new owners can lead them into a higher level of social participation in the community. The sudden change in land tenure laws itself can help create a climate of innovation and progress more favorable to the introduction of new techniques and institutions.

---

[9]Warriner, **Land Reform**, pp. 4-10.

[10]Dorner, **Land Reform and Economic Development**, pp. 130-1.

If tax and repayment policies permit a significant redistribution of income from a wealthy few to the poor farmers, it should have predictable consequences on the pattern of domestic market demand. Demand for the simpler types of consumer goods, food products, and farm inputs should rise, while luxury imports could be expected to fall, resulting in a market stimulus to domestic industry and conserving foreign exchange for developmental purposes.[11]

A number of factors affect the impact that a land reform program will have on agricultural production.[12] Does the program increase the land area under cultivation? Does ownership give former tenants an incentive to work harder and invest more in production, or do they evince a "backward-bending supply curve of labor," choosing to spend their higher incomes on more leisure, working less than before? Do the new owners have access to sufficient credit for investment, or have their incomes been raised sufficiently to provide investment funds? How has the provision of other services—such as marketing, input supply, research and extension, irrigation, transportation, education—been affected by removing the landlords?

In theory, converting a feudalistic Asian tenancy system to a family-farm system should result in higher production, since the landlords were providing no important services and the incentives of land ownership by the cultivators in such societies are reportedly very high, though the latter point is questioned by those who still believe tenant farmers are lazy.

This is in contrast to results obtained with programs redistributing commercial plantation land to tenant-workers, where the loss of efficient management, technical know-how and other services provided by the former plantation owners has usually resulted in a significant drop in production.

---

[11]Dorner, **Land Reform and Economic Development,** pp. 82, 91.
[12]See Mellor, **Agricultural Development,** pp. 253-9 for a good discussion of this point.

Figure 1-3:   **Labor Supply Curve**

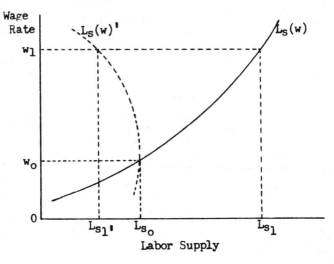

Labor Supply

The normal view of labor supply is that it is positively related to the wage rate within the relevant range, so that the amount of labor offered on the market increases as the wage rate increases, as represented in Figure 1-3 by the $L_S(w)$ curve. The "backward-bending" supply curve of labor argument is that at higher levels of income the amount of labor offered (and therefore total production) actually decreases, as along the $L^S(w)'$ curve, since many workers will choose to enjoy more leisure instead of higher incomes. While this argument may be valid for very high levels of income, such as in the United States (witness the drop in the average work-week over the last century), its validity has never been substantiated for very low levels of income where desirable goods and services were available in local markets.

While this "preference for leisure" line of reasoning is often heard as an argument against land redistribution to peasant farmers, it is really not very relevant to the conversion of Asian tenancy to a family farm land tenure system, since there is no reason to suppose the agricultural wage rate would rise simply because rents were remitted (although it may ultimately rise with an increased marginal productivity of labor due to better farm management and a higher level of agricultural investment, as discussed below). Former tenants do not receive an increase in **wages** when rents are remitted, rather they receive implicit rent on land they now own along with ownership rights to the entire return on their production decisions. They would still maximize their net farm income by performing labor or by **hiring** labor inputs up to the point where the marginal productivity of labor on their farm just equalled the market wage rate for that labor. Claiming they would do otherwise is assuming they are not good farm managers—not merely that they prefer leisure to higher incomes—and there is much evidence to the contrary, especially in comparison with the record of the absentee landlords.

The fact that ownership incentives to invest time, effort and money into farm operations might differ between absentee landlords and owner-cultivators deserves some explanation, since it conflicts with a superficial reading of "conventional" economic theory. The argument is heard that if an investment is profitable to an owner-cultivator, it should be equally profitable to a landlord, if he can collect the resulting incremental output, or to the landlord and tenant acting jointly, if they would normally share the incremental output. Several factors militate against this, however, in the typical Asian tenancy system, especially in the variant found in the Mekong Delta before 1970.

The third-generation landlords typical of most of the Mekong Delta did not make or permit as much productive investment in their riceland as their grandfathers did. There were several reasons for this. First of all, they were highly educated urban-dwellers with very little knowledge or understanding of agricultural operations, and even less interest in bothering with them. Secondly, they often wished to retain the option of evicting their tenants if they should become troublesome or refuse to pay rents, if some relative of the landlord wanted to return to farming, or simply as a means of raising rents in the future; and eviction is more difficult if the present tenants have invested heavily in the land. Thirdly, the only monetary incentive for such investments would be higher rents, and these had been notoriously difficult to collect since World War II and the rise of the Viet Minh, let alone to raise. Fourthly, intimidation of landlords by the Viet Minh and the National Liberation Front of South Vietnam (NLF) tended to prevent or discourage the landlord's active involvement in or supervision of agricultural investment activity, even when he might otherwise have been so inclined.

Tenants, on the other hand, typically lacked access to investment funds except at exorbitant rates of interest, since they had no collateral to offer, and their post-rent incomes were barely more than the subsistence level. Even those tenants with access to investment funds had to receive permission for new ventures from often reluctant landlords; and they hesitated to invest too much in the land for fear of eviction and the loss of their capital. Even where fixed-rent controls were enforced, rents could eventually be raised legally if the productivity of the land were increased, since the legal rent ceiling was stated as a percentage of the average annual crop. It is an accepted economic principle that where a tenant must bear the whole cost and risk of a new investment while receiving only part of its expected future return, total investment will be depressed below the Pareto-optimum level.

Two other factors served to inhibit productive investment on the part of the tenants. One was the psychological effect of the tenant's inferior social position with respect to his landlord, local government officials, and his owner-cultivator neighbors, which inhibited the tenant from active participation in community activities, from communicating with those in-the-know, from learning and even from seeking to learn about new techniques and production possibilities. A tenant was not expected to be a progressive and innovative farmer by those around him, his landlord, nor even by himself.

Secondly, there was in South Vietnam a strong cultural tradition of sumptuary restrictions on the standard of living a tenant should enjoy, the violation of which could be counted on to alienate one's landlord and result in increasing demands for higher rent, in no tolerance for crop failures and in possible eviction. By trying to raise his standard of living the tenant was considered to be stepping out of place, presuming to be the landlord's equal and thereby insulting him. This sumptuary tradition had a profound effect on the tenant's incentive to invest and increase production, simply by denying him the right to enjoy the fruits of any significant, long-run improvement in productivity.

A textbook economist might argue that, if there are competitive forces at work in the rental market, pushing rents up as population pressure on the land grows, it matters not who receives the "Ricardian rent," the landlord or the farmer, since Pareto efficiency in the economy will be achieved so long as the division of labor among various economic activities is such as to keep the marginal productivity of labor everywhere equal.

For example, if the total labor force were divided up completely between the two sectors, agriculture and manufacturing, as in Figure 1-4, assuming both sectors are subject to declining average and marginal productivities of labor, then the maximum economic production would be achieved at point P, where O_aP labor worked in agriculture and O_mP Labor worked in manufacturing, and where the marginal productivity of labor in agriculture (MP_{La}) equalled that in manufacturing (MP_{Lm}). Total production at point P is indicated by the area under the two MP_L curves, which is equal to the average productivity of labor in agriculture and in manufacturing above point P times the respective amounts of labor in each sector, summed ($O_aABP + O_mDCP$). Any deviation from this division of labor will result in a net loss of output, such as at point P', where $MP_{La} < MP_{Lm}$ and $w_a < w_m$, the loss of output is represented by the triangle EFG.

If the economy is operating under competitive equilibrium conditions at point P, so the argument goes, Pareto efficiency of production obtains in the sense that output cannot be increased, regardless of who receives the Ricardian-rent portion of agricultural production represented by the rectangular area w_aABF. (Farm labor receives the wage rate w_a in this example, equal to its marginal productivity at P, and the total agricultural wage bill is represented by the rectangle O_aw_aFP.

Figure 1-4: **Pareto–Optimum Division of Labor between Agriculture and Manufacturing**

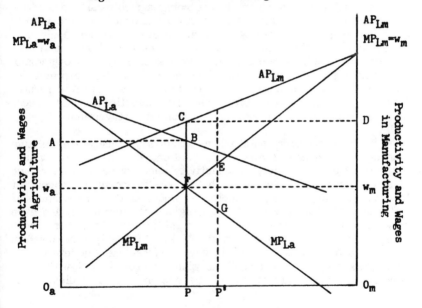

This argument is based on a static analysis of point efficiency and is irrelevant to the major task of economic development, which is to **raise** the marginal and average productivity of labor in both sectors through investment (increasing the stock of capital per worker) and technological change—and for this task it surely **does** matter who receives the Ricardian rent if incentives to invest and to adopt risky innovations are greater among owner-cultivators than among tenants and landlords, as discussed above.

Furthermore, an increase in agricultural investment takes the form not merely of financial resources alone, but also of labor and management inputs. The theory of land redistribution in an Asian tenancy context tells us that the latter two forms of investment can often be significantly increased, as well as financial inputs. Ownership incentives operate so as to inspire greater efforts and longer hours from owner-cultivators than from tenants. Where this is true it again takes us outside the static Pareto-efficiency framework of Figure 1-4, both by expanding the total supply of labor offered by farmers[13] (lengthening the O_aO_m axis) and by raising the AP_{La} and MP_{La} curves (through better farm management), both of which will increase total production. This is primarily a motivational phenomenon, similar to the "X-efficiency" factor in industrial firms believed by Harvey Leibenstein to be a more important problem than allocative efficiency factors.[14]

A final point to be made regarding agricultural productivity concerns the land market. According to Western economic theory, even if the above factors were true, Pareto efficiency could still be achieved by the competitive transfer of land from inefficient landlord ownership to more productive owner-cultivator ownership, since the owner-cultivators would be able to bid higher prices for the land than the landlords, based on their higher expected returns from it. Thus desirable land redistribution would occur automatically, without requiring government intervention.

Such a transfer mechanism assumes a freely competitive market for land as a factor of production, with its market values determined by its expected productivity under different owners and different uses. The trouble is that a purely economic concept of land value is alien to Asian societies, where land acquires much of its value from social, cultural and religious considerations, and even as a route to political power. It is safe to say that there is no competitive market for land in the Mekong Delta, in the Western sense of a market, since land is **never** offered for sale by private owners except under extreme hardship conditions, and where the necessity of such sale is viewed by one and all as indicative of

---

[13]This would occur if a farmer is more willing to work hard on his own land, since he feels happier and more secure as an owner than as a tenant. In other words, his indifference curves between farm work and leisure may shift when he becomes an owner such that his "offer curve" of labor shifts right. He is willing to work for a lower marginal return on his own land than on someone else's land.

[14]Harvey Leibenstein, "Allocative Efficiency vs. 'X-Efficiency,'" **American Economic Review**, (1966), pp. 392-415.

personal and family tragedy and disgrace, even if the price is exorbitant as compared with expected productivity.

Under Asian socio-cultural conditions, even on those rare occasions when land is sold, it is seldom sold to cultivators who could make the most productive use of it, partly because they can rarely afford the "cultural" prices asked and partly because a landlord feels further disgraced if he is forced to sell his family inheritance to his "inferiors" (his tenants).   The transfer, instead, is usually from one absentee landlord to a more fortunate absentee landlord, or from an unfortunate owner-cultivator to a landlord (the seller often becoming a tenant on his own land).   And so the   Asian tenancy system, with all its production inefficiencies, perpetuates itself.

In economic jargon, this means the ownership of riceland is desired not merely as a productive asset which will yield a future stream of economic income, but also as a cultural, social, and political asset which will yield social status and political power and will satisfy important religious and cultural needs. Snob consumer behavior, as defined by H. Leibenstein,[15] is strongly present in **both** the demand and the supply sides of the land market, causing both the demand and the supply curves to be less elastic with respect to price than if land were valued for its economic productivity alone, and resulting in far less land marketed each year at far higher prices.

This can be illustrated as in Figure 1-5. D_p and S_p represent riceland   demand   and   supply   curves   based   on   productivity considerations, and they would result in Q_p hectares of land being sold each year at a price of P_p per hectare. D_s and S_s, on the other hand, represent the actual, restricted and inelastic supply and the inelastic demand for land based on the snob behavior discussed above, resulting in only Q_s hectares sold each year at the much higher price of P_s. This will prevent the "automatic" redistribution of land **via** the free market to its most productive economic users.

Even if total production does increase, or at least does not fall, due to land redistribution, the government must still be concerned about the marketable surplus. The income elasticity of demand for food products of low income families is thought to be fairly high, close to 1.0, while that of landlords is considerable less. This could mean an overall reduction in the amount reaching the

[15]H. Leibenstein, "Bandwagon, Snob, and Veblen Effects in the Theory of Consumers' Demand," **Quarterly Journal of Economics,** (1950), pp. 183-207.

unless the farmers are taxed or required to make annual payments for their land equal to the cancelled rents.[16]

The diffusion of land ownership among many small farmers may make the collection of agricultural land taxes more difficult administratively, but often easier from a political point of view, especially if such taxes are clearly designated for use in local rural development projects. Land taxes themselves are usually kept at low levels because of the political power of large owners residing in the urban administrative centers; and the use of general revenue funds for rural infrastructure investment—schools, transportation facilities, medical clinics, etc.—is often blocked by the same group of people, who are more interested in improving their urban infrastructure than that of the remote, rural villages.   The redistribution of landed wealth among small farmers, if coupled with decentralized rural taxation and development programs, can have a stimulating effect on public economic development efforts.[17]

Figure 1-5: **Snob Behavior in Asian Land Markets**

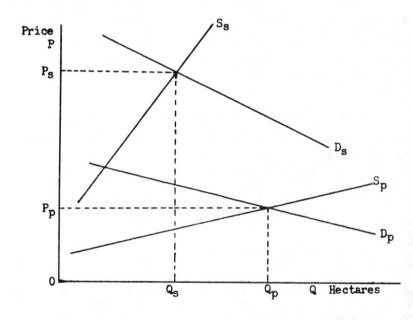

[16]See Mellor, **Agricultural Development**, pp. 258-9.
[17]Dorner, **Land Reform and Economic Development**, pp. 127-

Another important by-product of land reform can be its effect of rural employment.[18]   If higher incentives to produce are translated into more intensive cultivation of the land, especially if it leads to multiple crops each year instead of single cropping, for example, the demand for farm labor will rise, helping to solve the problem of unemployment in a growing population.   Industrial employment will also rise if, as noted above, the income redistribution stimulates demand for the products of and investment in domestic industries.

On the unfavorable side of the ledger, such a reform could introduce new rigidities into the land market, tying former tenants more tightly to their holding and forbidding sale for a number of years, the latter a provision often written into land reform legislation in an effort to prevent the re-accumulation of large holdings by land speculators or the old landlords.[19] Some people express concern about the perpetuation of a system of small, uneconomical farms and its effect on future agricultural development efforts. The added burden of landlord compensation on an already overloaded budget will increase inflationary pressures as well, especially if tenants are not required to pay for their land, and this can hamper developmental efforts.

Politically, of course, land reform programs are expected to generate additional support for the government from the farmers. There is also concern, however, that it might cause such conflict between resident landlords and their tenants at the local level as to become a destabilizing influence, especially if corruption and other irregularities in the distribution process become widespread. Would the social discord created overwhelm the beneficial consequences of greater social equity and justice?   And what effect will it have on local leadership?   Will the power and prestige of local landlords be so greatly reduced as to create a vacuum of local leadership, will other able leaders step in to fill the gap, or will the relative position of leading families remain unchanged?

The major socio-political and economic effects to be expected from land redistribution in a typical Asian tenancy system are listed in Table 1-1, along with the various factors affecting each effect which can be scrutinized by field research.   This volume reports research efforts into the case of South Vietnam that attempt to determine how the Land-to-the-Tiller Program affected each contributory factor and whether its major effects were favorable or not favorable for long-run economic development.   A point-by-

---

[18]Ibid., pp. 92-109.
[19]Mellor, **Agricultural Development**, p. 259.

point summary of the research results, using Table 1-1 as an outline, is presented in the concluding chapter.

Table 1-1

Theoretical Effects of Land Redistribution in an Asian Tenancy System

<u>Major Effects</u>

Contributory factors affected by land redistribution and subjects of present research/analysis effort

A. Economic Effects

1. <u>Agricultural Production</u>
  a. Incentives to invest labor and capital?
  b. Credit and access to investment funds?
  c. Agricultural services: marketing, input supply, research & extension, irrigation, transportation, education & training?
  d. Fragmentation of land or perpetuation of suboptimal farm sizes?
  e. Land area under cultivation?

2. <u>Marketable Surplus</u>
  f. Income elasticity of demand for food of tenants vs. landlords?
  g. Amount of tenant payments for land received?
  h. Level of agricultural taxation?
  i. Availability of desirable non-agricultural consumer and capital goods?
  j. Rate of growth of agricultural production?

3. <u>Distribution of Income</u>
  k. Level of pre-reform rents cancelled?
  l. Extent of land redistribution?
  m. Nature and amount of compensation to landlords (and tenant's share of it)?
  n. Rate of inflation?
  o. Level of agricultural taxation?

4. <u>Employment</u>
  p. Labor- or capital-intensive development of agriculture?
  q. Increased demand for domestically manufactured goods?
  r. Increased investment in domestic industries?

5. <u>Industrial Development</u>
  s. Increased farm income spent on domestic goods?
  t. Landlord compensation invested in domestic industries?
  u. Increased agricultural production to provide food, fiber, foreign exchange and capital savings for the industrial sector?

6. <u>Infrastructure Development</u>
  v. Rural taxation for local development projects?
  w. Local participation in self-help projects?
  x. Local Initiative encouraged?

Table 1-1

(Continued)

7. Inflation
        y. Nature of compensation arrangements?
        z. Consumption or investment of compensation funds?

B. Socio-Political Effects

  1. Political Stability
        a. Greater equity and social justice?
        b. Broader political support for government?
        c. Level of conflict between landlords and tenants?
        d. Local leadership change or gap?
        e. Corruption and irregularities in implementation?
        f. Security and level of income?

  2. Distribution of Social Status and Political Power
        g. Reduction in landlord power?
        h. Extent of redistribution of land ownership?
        i. Extent of income redistribution?

  3. Institutional Flexibility
        j. Broader political participation?
        k. Larger middle class?
        l. Economic and political control retained by
           landlords and/or traditional elites?
        m. Economic and political control obtained by
           modern elite?

4. National Talent Search
        n. Class distinctions between rich and poor reduced?
        o. Social mobility enhanced, rigidities reduced?
        p. Increased political support for rural development
           and education projects/Expanded opportunities for
           rural youth?

  5. Social Attitudes Toward Change Innovation

        q. Favorable results and reception of changes in
           land tenure laws?

Chapter II

LAND REFORM IN JAPAN AND TAIWAN:
A COMPARATIVE STUDY

Background: Prior Conditions of Land Tenure

In Japan

The 1946 land reform legislation was passed in Japan following World War II under pressure from the American Occupation, whose leaders were convinced that prewar land tenure conditions had caused widespread economic distress and had fostered authoritarian political tendencies, together leading to aggressive policies and war. While the reforms were no doubt more sweeping due to Occupation pressure, R. P. Dore seems convinced that substantial land tenure reforms would have been legislated in any case and that the basic initiative for this postwar program lay with the Japanese themselves.[1]

The Meiji Restoration of 1868 had formally abolished hereditary class distinctions and declared the legal equality of all Japanese. Universal systems of male suffrage, conscription and public education, all legally ignoring class distinctions and rewarding individual performance more often based on ability rather than birth, went far to break down traditional attitudes of deference to social status.[2]

High-handed landlord treatment of tenants became less and less palatable as the land tenure system, characterized by a high proportion of tenancy and high rents, became increasingly anachronistic in a social context of high and rising literacy, industrialization, egalitarianism, and commercial possibilities. In 1941 some 68 percent of all farm families were full or part tenants, renting 46 percent of the total cultivated area at an average rent of 48 percent of their annual rice harvest. A mere 7.4 percent of the landowners held title to 43.4 percent of all agricultural land.[3]

---

[1]R. P. Dore, **Land Reform in Japan,** (London: Oxford University Press, 1959), pp. 147-8.

[2]Ibid., p. 54.

[3]Part tenants are those renting more than 10 percent of the land they cultivate. **Ibid.,** pp. 175-6, and Elias H. Tuma, **Twenty-six Centuries of Agrarian Reform** (Berkeley: University of California Press, 1965), pp. 130-1.

In Taiwan

The Nationalist Chinese government too pursued a land reform program under outside pressure, but a pressure different in nature from an occupation army. Concentration of land ownership on the Chinese mainland, together with high rents and feudalistic landlord control over tenants and local governmental machinery, had created conditions of social unrest easily exploited by the communist insurgents against the Nationalist government. Communist reforms on the mainland, despite the brutality and social injustice that accompanied them, provided propaganda effectively used against the Nationalists, who were forced to retire to exile on Taiwan in 1949. Belated efforts at land reform were continued on the island, mostly to deny the communists the use of the land issue there. It was imposed on the native Taiwanese landlords by an authoritarian government controlled by the mainlander minority.[4]

By 1948 concentration of land ownership was similar to the Japanese case, although not quite so bad: 67 percent of all farming families were either landless laborers (7 percent) or rented all (36 percent) or part (24 percent) of their land, while 39 percent of all private farmland was under tenant operation.   Rents reportedly averaged around 50 percent of the total harvest, and they often went to 60 or 70 percent.   Advance rent and rent deposits equal to one year's rent were often demanded.   Contracts were normally mere verbal agreements which could not be enforced, and the landlord could thus raise rents or evict his tenants at will.[5]

Much work had been accomplished before World War II, however, while the island was under Japanese control (1895-1945), which greatly facilitated the land reform measures of 1949-53. Infrastructure investment in road and harbor construction, irrigation, and water conservation projects had been made.   Agricultural research and extension work had resulted in notable technical improvements in rice and sugar cane production.   And cadastral surveys conducted between 1898 and 1925 had established clear land ownership records.[6]

---

[4]Martin M. C. Yang, **Socio-Economic Results of Land Reform in Taiwan,** (Honolulu: East-West Center Press, 1970), pp. 3-17.

[5]Anthony Y. C. Koo, **The Role of Land Reform in Economic Development: A Case Study of Taiwan,** (New York: Praeger, 1968), p. 39, and Yang, **Land Reform in Taiwan,** pp. 9-11 and 83.

[6]Koo, **Role of Land Reform,** pp. 12 and 25.

Comparison of Land Reform

Objectives

Both Japan and Taiwan sought important political objectives through their land reform programs, as well as economic improvement. In Japan the law was designed to promote "democratic tendencies in rural communities" and thereby to aid in the "pacification of a warlike people." As the program got underway it assumed another political goal—to create "a bulwark against the spread of Communism in Japanese rural areas."[7]

The Nationalist government in Taiwan pursued their land reform policy in the shadow of the Communist Chinese domination of the mainland and their mounting threat to the freedom of Taiwan as well. Their purpose was to eliminate a key issue successfully exploited by the insurgents and to counter the worldwide propaganda efforts of the Red Chinese regarding their land reform program.[8]

In addition, both countries announced goals of social and economic justice and modernization, such as the redistribution of income in favor of the cultivator, the wider and more equal distribution of land ownership among farmers, the relief of overcrowding and rural unemployment, and the improvement of agricultural productivity. In Japan the reforms were specifically designed to "destroy the economic bondage which has enslaved the Japanese farmers for centuries of feudal oppression," and to eliminate heavy farm indebtedness, high interest rates, and discriminatory government control over farmers without regard for their interests. In Taiwan landlord interests were to be protected by helping them to convert their landholdings into industrial holdings, as land titles were transferred to the tenant cultivators.[9]

Programs

The first postwar land reform legislation passed by the Japanese Diet was rejected by the American Occupation as being too mild. On October 21, 1946, the second measure was passed and accepted, in the form of an amendment to the Agricultural

---

[7]Dore, **Land Reform in Japan**, p. 315.

[8]Yang, **Land Reform in Taiwan**, p. 15.

[9]Dore, **Land Reform in Japan**, pp. 134 and 315, Koo, **Role of Land Reform**, pp. 31-7, and Yang, **Land Reform in Taiwan**, pp. 15-21. Quotation is from December 1945 memorandum from the Supreme Commander to the Japanese government, quoted in Dore, p. 134.

Land Adjustment Law of 1938 and a separate Owner-Farmer Establishment Special Measures Law. The government was to purchase cultivable land held in excess of 12 **cho** in Hokkaido and an average of 3 **cho** in the rest of Japan.[10] Of the acreage retained, landowners could lease out only 4 **cho** in Hokkaido and an average of one **cho** elsewhere, and the rest must either be cultivated by the owner or relinquished. Land values were calculated at 1945 prices and worked out to be about half the annual harvest. Landlords were paid in cash and bonds, the latter redeemable in cash within 30 years at 3.6 percent interest. Inflation quickly wiped out most of the real value of the compensation and permitted most land recipients to complete their payments within one or two years after purchase. The purchase price was the same as that paid to the former landlords, and payments could be made in cash and spread over 30 years at 3.2 percent interest.[11]

The land transferred under this program was at first made inalienable to prevent speculative buying and resurgency of landlordism, but this provision was modified in 1950. Village and town Land Committees were established to administer the transfer of land from landlord to tenant. Extension programs, credit facilities, credit and marketing cooperatives were promoted, and written contracts were required to protect all remaining tenancy agreements, in which rent was limited to cash payments no greater than 25 percent of the annual harvest.[12]

In Taiwan the land reform program consisted of three major steps: farmland rent reduction in 1949, sale of public land in 1951, and the Land-to-the-Tiller Act of 1953. Rents were limited to 37.5 percent of the main crop; advance payments and security deposits were prohibited; and all leases were to be renewed for a minimum of 6 years. Farm tenancy committees were set up in 1951 to supervise these provisions.[13]

Publicly owned land in Taiwan, much of it repossessed from Japanese nationals, was to be sold at a price 2.5 times the annual main crop yield, which was about 10 times the annual rent collected on public farmland. The purchase price could be paid over 10 years in 20 equal semi-annual installments (at harvest seasons) expressed in kind as a hedge against inflationary depreciation of their real

---

[10]One **cho** = .99174 hectares = 2.45072 acres. Dore, **Land Reform in Japan,** p. 473.
[11]Ibid., pp. 138-40.
[12]Tuma, **Agrarian Reform,** p. 138.
[13]Koo, **Role of Land Reform,** pp. 31-4, and Yang, **Land Reform in Taiwan,** pp. 55-6.

value. Annual installments were thus 25 percent of the main crop, and with a 4.5 to 7.5 percent land tax, total payments to the government were 29.5 to 32.5 percent of the annual harvest, or somewhat less than the 37.5 percent rent ceiling.[14]

The Land-to-the-Tiller Act required government purchase of all farmland owned in excess of 3 **chia** for resale to the actual cultivators.[15] The purchase price was set at 2.5 times the annual harvest and was payable in 20 equal semi-annual installments over 10 years, in kind, at 4 percent interest. Landlords received their compensation 70 percent in land bonds, redeemable in kind, and 30 percent in government enterprise stocks. The land bonds earned 4 percent interest.[16]

A lesser part of the Taiwan land reform was a voluntary land redemarcation program to achieve more rational land use, to consolidate fragmented holdings, to permit better irrigation and drainage facilities and road construction, and to allow more economical use of machinery.

Implementation

The success of both programs in converting tenants into owner-cultivators is evident from the statistics, especially, for time-comparative purposes, those data showing the changed proportions of land rented and of tenant farm families. In Japan the percentage of all cultivated land leased to tenants dropped from 46 to 10 between 1941 and 1950, while in Taiwan it fell from 45 to 15 between 1948 and 1956. The percentage of farm households owning 90 percent or more of the land they cultivated doubled from 31 to 62 between 1941 and 1950 in Japan, while it rose from 33 to 57 in Taiwan between 1948 and 1956. Those listed as renting more than 50 percent of their land in Japan dropped from 48 percent to 12 percent, and the tenant-farmer category in Taiwan shrunk from 36 percent to 15 percent, during the same periods.[17]

The Japanese program was naturally much larger, involving the transfer of some 1,933,000 **cho** of land from 2,341,000 landlords to 4,748,000 tenants. The Taiwan program resulted in the compulsory purchase of 143,568 **chia** from 106,049 landlords for resale to 194,823 recipients. In addition, 28,960 farming families in Taiwan purchased

---

[14]Koo, **Role of Land Reform**, pp. 35-7.
[15]One **chia** = .9699 hectare = 2.3968 acres. **Ibid.**, p. xvii.
[16]**Ibid.**, 37-41, 44.
[17]Dore, **Land Reform in Japan**, pp. 175-6, and Koo, **op. cit.**, p. 39.

15,646 **chia** directly from landlords, many of whom chose to sell out to avoid the government program, and 63,000 **chia** of public land were sold to 121,953 households.[18] To add the land purchasers in Taiwan would involve double-counting, since many farmers purchased land in two or more ways, but the total acreage transferred comes to 222,214 **chia**, (or 215,525 hectares), as compared with 1,933,000 **cho** (1,917,033 hectares) in Japan.

In Japan the total cultivated land area was around 5,200,000 **cho** (5,156,840 hectares) in 1950, including 2,914,000 **cho** of riceland and 2,286,000 **cho** of upland, of which 37.2 percent had been redistributed by that date.[19] In Taiwan, "cultivable land totals about 880,000 hectares, almost all of which has been fully cultivated,"[20] and of this area the ownership of 24.5 percent was transferred from landlords to farmers during the land reform program.

Economic Effects

Farmer Income

A substantial increase in farmer income following the land reform programs has been reported for both countries. R. P. Dore reported a 36 percent increase in rural per capita consumption in Japan from 1934-6 to 1954, while urban consumption per head declined by 6 percent.[21] Between 1950 and 1960 total real consumption in the farm sector of Taiwan rose by 102 percent, while the rural population grew by only 34 percent.[22] This means a rise in real, per capita rural consumption at 51 percent over the decade.

Martin M. C. Yang has studied other indicators in rural Taiwan, all of which tend to confirm statistical reports of a general rise in rural income in recent years—indicators such as food consumption, sources of drinking and cooking water, housing, clothing,

---

[18]Dore, **Land Reform in Japan**, p. 174, and Yang, **Land Reform in Taiwan**, pp. 59, 71-5.

[19]Redistributed land included 1,137,000 **cho**, or 39.0 percent of total Japanese riceland and 796,000 **cho**, or 34.8 percent, of total upland. Dore, **Land Reform in Japan**, pp. 174-5.

[20]Koo, **Role of Land Reform**, p. 131, Table 2.

[21]Dore, **Land Reform in Japan**, p. 202.

[22]Calculated from tables in Koo, **Role of Land Reform**, pp. 59 and 138.

transportation and communication facilities and their use, health care, and education services.[23]

There were many factors contributing to rising farm incomes, of which land reform was only one. Koo notes that cultivators in Taiwan benefitted directly, however, both from rent reduction and from rent stabilization as a fixed cash charge in a period of inflation, which reduced its real value as time went on. Currency depreciation benefitted owner-cultivators as well, since the land tax was stated as a fixed cash charge.[24] Although land reform recipients had to pay for their land in kind, increasing productivity reduced the burden of these payments, since land values had been calculated at the beginning of the reform and were not revised upward as yields improved.

The ratio of agricultural produce sold to that consumed on the farm decreased during and immediately following the period of land redistribution in Taiwan, however, as a result of the rapid increase in per capita consumption of self-produced foods coupled with the high rate of population growth in the rural sector.[25]

Dore cites a long list of factors responsible for rising rural incomes in Japan. Reduction of rent payments (from 16.6 percent to 0.2 percent of total agricultural income between 1934-6 and 1953),[26] higher productivity per acre, and better land utilization can all be attributed in whole or in part to land reform. The postwar inflation and food shortages helped to wipe out rural indebtedness, and this was followed by continued high prices for agricultural products and lower input costs as Japanese industry advanced. Agricultural taxes were reduced after 1950, while government aid to the rural sector and social services in general increased, the former taking such forms as an expanded agricultural extension service, subsidies and grants for drainage, irrigation and reclamation projects, agricultural research and experimentation, agricultural scholarships, credit and marketing assistance, crop insurance and the like.[27]

---

[23]Yang, **Land Reform in Taiwan**, pp. 276-385.

[24]Koo, **Role of Land Reform**, p. 61.

[25]Teng-hui Lee, **Intersectoral Capital Flows in the Economic Development of Taiwan, 1895-1960**, (Ithaca, New York: Cornell University Press, 1971), p. 78.

[26]Dore, **Land Reform in Japan**, p. 213.

[27]Ibid., pp. 202-38.

Occupation and Income of Former Landlords

Landlords in both countries suffered a decline in income, but those in Japan were hurt worse due to the effect of the inflation on the real value of their cash compensation, which was nominally much less than in Taiwan in the first place. In Taiwan, 70 percent of the compensation due a landlord was paid in "land bonds" stated in kind, but many suffered losses on the remaining 30 percent paid in stocks. Koo reports that much of the loss was unwarranted and resulted from scare-selling. Only one of the three former government enterprises, the Taiwan Cement Corporation, showed a profit in the early years after the land reform; and the other shares, which comprised 20 percent of the landlord compensation, declined in value.[28] Even with all their compensation in land bonds, however, the landlords would still have experienced a decline in income. Land values were based on a fair capitalization of land ownership under the new rent limitation of 37.5 percent of the average harvest, which was already less than its value under the traditional 50 percent or more rent level.

Most "resident" landlords merely lost part of their land, remaining in their communities as prosperous owner-cultivators of still larger-than-average farms and retaining their traditional leadership roles in social and political affairs. Others, along with most of the absentee landlords, were forced to seek other means of livelihood, or else to see their fortunes quickly worsen as they consumed their capital. Many were already pursuing other occupations or business activities and merely switched all their attention to it, using their compensation payments to expand or improve an existing business or previous sideline. Large landlords usually had more education and better connections in the business world, and thus were better able to make successful investments with their large sums of compensation. Many of the small landlords, however, were unable to make such a drastic change.[29]

Investment

A higher level of investment in agriculture was reported for both Japan and Taiwan following the land reform program, and this greater capital input is given a major share of the credit for the increased agricultural productivity experienced during this period. Koo reports that the average agricultural output for 1956-60 in Taiwan was 18 percent higher than in 1953, and that more than

---

[28]Koo, **Role of Land Reform**, p. 44.
[29]Yang, **Land Reform in Taiwan**, p. 244.

half of the increase can be attributed to larger capital inputs.[30]
Yang reports that of 1,250 former tenant farmers interviewed 80
percent said they had been making more improvements on their
farms because the land had become their own, and 85 percent of
the 250 original-owner farmers interviewed claimed that even they
had increased labor and capital inputs since the land reform, "because
they noticed that most other farm households were working harder
than before."[31] Those who remained tenants were similarly affected
by the rent reduction and the new security and incentives provided
by written-contract and fixed-rent requirements—80 percent said
they put in more work and 59 percent said they invested money
saved from reduced rents on farm improvements.[32]

Dore reports increased mechanization on Japanese farms and
other investment due to the greater incentives to invest.
Restrictions against land alienation and tenant evictions, size
limitations on land ownership and land rented, and rent limitation
to an unprofitable 25 percent of harvest—all combined after land
reform to change the investment propensities of farmers from the
purchase of more land to the improvement of land already owned.[33]

Koo noted that, as Taiwanese agricultural production increased,
investment funds began, in the late 1950's, to flow out of agriculture
into the industrial and service sectors, and that the increased
agriculture production also saved or earned foreign exchange needed
for industrial investment.   In addition, noticeable increases in
expenditure on rural education and in the proportion of farm children
reaching higher grade levels in school were made possible by higher
farm incomes and should be counted as valuable investment in human
capital.[34]

Agricultural Productivity

Farm production increased by 18 percent in Taiwan from 1953
to 1956-60, as noted above, and by 13 percent in Japan from 1933
to 1955 with roughly the same area under cultivation. Koo attributes
the increase in Taiwan to greater capital and labor input (75 percent)

---

[30]Of the 18 percentage points, one can be accounted for by
increased land area under cultivation, 3.9 by increased labor input,
9.8 by the growth in capital investment, and the residual, or 4.4,
by technological change. —See Koo, **Role of Land Reform**, pp. 68-9.

[31]Yang, **Land Reform in Taiwan**, pp. 211-12.

[32]**Ibid.**, pp. 217-18.

[33]Dore, **Land Reform in Japan**, pp. 205-6, 216-7.

[34]Koo, **Role of Land Reform**, pp. 78-87, 107, 117-8, and Yang,
Land Reform in Taiwan, pp. 373, 414.

and improved technology (24 percent), both of which were no doubt influenced by the incentive effect of fixed rent and new land ownership. He cites evidence that the rate of technological change during the 1951-60 period was higher than the historical trend.[35] Other writers have come to the same conclusion:[36]

> "The increase of agricultural production was due in substantial part to the enthusiasm for work and incentive for higher incomes generated among farmers by the land-reform program.[37] The four-year agricultural development plans provided an additional boost to production."

Dore notes similar factors at work in Japan, but assigns increased labor input a much smaller role. He cites mechanization, better land utilization due to irrigation and drainage works, consolidation of holdings, road construction, improved production technology such as the use of more fertilizer, improved crop strains and pest control methods, and the more rapid diffusion of knowledge and techniques already available. While better farmer incentives and more available capital can be expected to result in an increase of the factors requiring capital investment, Dore also assigns the land reform a major role in making the last item on this list important—the more rapid diffusion of knowledge and techniques. Land reform eliminated landlord restraints on crop diversification and on the use of new and more costly inputs and new techniques.[38]

---

[35]Dore, **Land Reform in Japan**, p. 213, and Koo, **Role of Land Reform**, pp. 68-9. See footnote 30 on page 29 above.
[36]The following quotation and its footnoted reference are found in Teng-hui Lee, **Capital Flows in Taiwan**, p. 44.
[37]H.S. Tang and S.C. Hseih, "Land Reform and Agricultural Development in Taiwan," **The Malayan Economic Review**, vol. VI, no. 1, April 1961, pp. 49-54.
[38]Dore gives a detailed example of a "paternalistic landlord," whose permission had to be obtained to grow anything but the accustomed crop and who was very reluctant to grant such permission. His "tenants were threatened with dispossession if they used too much fertilizer, since though it often improved yields it also increased the risk of a crop failure due to winds and early frosts—and while custom dictated a reduction in rent in bad years, it did not allow an increase in rent after a good year. Nor was the landlord interested in improving irrigation and drainage systems on a large scale, since the resurveying necessary would reveal the true size of land plots sometimes 20 to 30 percent larger than the registered area, and this would result in higher tax assessments and more trouble from tenants if he subsequently tried to raise their

It gave the farmer more economic and psychological incentives to try new ideas as well as the risk capital to use for new inputs. It fostered a sense of self-reliance in the cultivator, inspiring him to learn better ways to do his job, and it eliminated a stifling, conservative landlord domination of local affairs, giving control of the villages and community projects over to the owner-cultivator class, whose natural interests cause it to direct village activities more toward projects that will help it in its business of agricultural production.[39]

Social Effects

The land reform in both Japan and Taiwan has altered the group relationships of rural society: (1) former landlord influence and power has been reduced, (2) former tenants have been elevated to the landowner class, (3) absentee landlord control over village affairs has been eliminated in favor to local landowner control, the latter simultaneously being made a much larger group, and (4) feudalistic relationships of nearly total dependence of many men on the whims of a few have been broken. Higher social status and income have induced many more farmers to send their children to school and to become more active in community affairs. Freedom of choice and decision about farm crops and methods of cultivation has given them greater interest in agricultural extension organizations and activities. Greater control over their own success or failure has had an important incentive effect, inspiring more diligence and greater efforts. The demise of landlord control has weakened the rigidity of the social structure and allowed greater social mobility among social classes and toward positions of leadership.[40]

According to Dore, "One of the chief functions of the land reform has been to reduce the dependence of one man on another in Japanese villages."[41] Hereditary status has been weakened in favor of present wealth and individual accomplishment; there is less

---

(cont.)
rents appropriately. These landlords took few positive measures to educate their tenants into higher productivity. They played safe; devoting their energies to preventing any reduction in their income, rather than either to increasing it or to improving the lot of their tenants. Their interference was mostly negative." —Dore, **Land Reform in Japan**, pp. 36-7.

[39]**Ibid.**, pp. 213-18.

[40]See Tuma, **Agrarian Reform**, pp. 141-2, and Yang, **Land Reform in Taiwan**, pp. 411-6.

[41]Dore, **Land Reform in Japan**, p. 371.

economic dependence between low and high status families; and less overt deference is required among persons of different status, resulting in greater ease of social discourse, intermarriage, etc. The income redistribution has broadened the "middle class" of landowners and widened the stratum of potential leadership.[42]

Dore reports that former landlords still hold significant advantages in the contest for social and political leadership, due to their greater experience, self-confidence, wealth, education, wider social connections, and to traditional social attitudes of loyalty and respect. Their former dominance has been seriously weakened, however, and most of these remaining advantages are transitory in nature, since the former tenants and small landowners are rapidly catching up in most of these areas. In fact, Dore and Yang both conclude that the widened stratum of owner-farmers now dominate village counsels and win most of the elective offices of the village.[43]

Political Effects

This brings us to the political effects of land reform. Yang finds not only an increase in the percentage of public office held by new landowners, as compared with when they were still tenants, but also a general increased participation in local politics by all tenure classes.[44] Dore notes the process of land reform itself, by requiring that 50 percent of the Village Land Committee membership be tenants, gave many former tenants experience in local politics which led to later political careers.[45]

Land reform was only one of several factors responsible for political change, however. It cannot be considered in isolation from more democratic election systems, increased education, a rising standard of living, and the natural attrition of the older, more conservative generation. These "continuing and accelerating factors" were behind the significant attitudinal changes, while land reform was only a one-shot contributor.[46]

Once completed, the new land regime created powerful vested interests in the new political climate which effectively blocked landlord attempts to regain their old positions. While the reforms have denied the land issue to extreme left-wing political groups, it

---

[42]Ibid., p. 378.
[43]Ibid., pp. 327-36, 379, and Yang, **Land Reform in Taiwan**, pp. 492-3.
[44]Yang, **Land Reform in Taiwan**, pp. 490-3.
[45]Dore, **Land Reform in Japan**, pp. 325.
[46]Ibid., p. 404.

has resulted in new farmer cooperative organizations with strong political clout in favor of agricultural interests and in rural voter constituencies carefully courted by national politicians.[47]

Conclusion: The Contribution of Land Reform to the Modernization Process

Land reform, as conducted in Japan and Taiwan, can be credited with significant contributions toward the achievement of economic development, greater social egalitarianism and more active political participation by ordinary farmers.   There is no need to repeat the details of this conclusion.   It should be emphasized, however, that the wider distribution of land ownership and the levelling of rural incomes, which were the primary results of the reforms, can help achieve these social, economic and political goals only in appropriate combination with other processes and policies directed toward the same ends.

Land tenure reform constituted major social surgery to create a new socio-economic and political structure within which people were to live and conduct their daily activities.   For this new structure to be better than the old, however, its inhabitants had to learn many new roles and attitudes in order to fill it with the required functional activities.   The learning process is difficult, it takes much time and effort, and it results in many emotional conflicts between traditional and new attitudes and values.

Successful functioning of small-owner, commercially-operated, agricultural "businesses," of participatory political systems, whether local or national, and of egalitarian, grassroots social organizations to achieve desirable cultural, educational, health, and economic objectives all require the development of many individual and collective   attributes   besides   the   dignity   and   security   of landownership and the wealth of higher incomes.   More widespread and pertinent education must give the farmer the intellectual tools and the scientific attitudes necessary for modern farming methods. Agricultural research, experimentation, and extension efforts must produce useful information and make it available to the farmer in acceptable forms.   Credit facilities must permit the purchase of new inputs and reduce the financial risk of failure.

Marketing organizations and transportation facilities must be streamlined to provide inputs at appropriate times and locations and to assure product markets at reasonable cost. Water control projects are often essential to the profitable introduction of new seed

---

[47]Ibid., pp. 430-1, 470-2.

varieties and techniques.   They require cooperative organizational skills and attitudes. Government fiscal, taxation, pricing, and foreign trade policies must be devised so as to maintain and foster appropriate farmer incentives to invest and to improve productivity. Land tenure reform has a legitimate claim to importance as a necessary structural change in cases similar to Japan and Taiwan, but it is only one step on the road to modernization.

Chapter III

HISTORY OF LAND TENURE IN SOUTH VIETNAM

Pre-French History

Virginia Thompson, in criticism of French colonial policy, stated that "The native government had never been so imprudent as to create an independent landed class."[1] This belief was echoed by Joseph Buttinger in 1967 in his assertion that French land policies in Indochina had created two new classes of Vietnamese—large landowners and landless peasants—that "had not existed in pre-colonial Vietnam."[2] John T. McAlister followed the same theme in 1969.[3] However, this view was contradicted in an earlier work by Buttinger himself, who wrote in 1958 of

" . . . a basic conflict in Vietnamese society: its survival required a progressive and centralized state, but its essentially agrarian economy allowed for no ruling class free of feudal economic interests and feudal political aspirations. No matter how often the monarchy dispossessed the factious lords and smashed the power of ambitious local administrators, within the limits of Vietnam's agrarian economy the social basis of a local type feudalism was constantly reproduced.

" . . . Ly Thai Thong (1028-1054) paid his officials for their services and rewarded his servants for their loyalty with large domains of rice land.

" . . . the growth of these landholdings, in addition to transforming a great number of peasants into serfs, made many of them landless."[4]

---

[1]Virginia Thompson, **French Indo-China,** The Macmillan Company, London, (citations from reprint edition, New York: Octagon Books, 1968), p. 233.

[2]Joseph Buttinger, **Vietnam: A Dragon Embattled,** (New York: Praeger, 1967), pp. 161-4.

[3]John T. McAlister, Jr., **Viet Nam: The Origins of Revolution,** (New York: Knopf, 1969), p. 70.

[4]Joseph Buttinger, **The Smaller Dragon,** (New York: Praeger, 1958), pp. 145-7.

The Vietnamese throne followed a vacillating policy down through the centuries, with some kings rewarding their supporters with control over large areas of land or its revenue and some kings instituting land reform measures and attempting to reduce the power of the feudal landlord class.

In 1397 Ho Qui Ly limited landholdings of everyone but royalty to no more than 10 **mau** (8.8 acres), distributing excess land to landless peasants, in order to reduce landlord power and to encourage a village economy.[5]

The great Le Loi (Le Thai To) (1428-1433) "ordered a general repartition of land among the whole population."[6] His redistribution was unequal, with the amount of land received varying according to the recipient's station in life. Many peasants were left without land.

Le Thanh Tong (1461-1497) moved to protect remaining communal lands from acquisition by large landowners by declaring them inalienable and untransferable. In 1471 he opened new lands for settlement along the Central Coast, through the conquest of Champa, and protected the rights of small landowners in new Vietnamese villages. Large holdings grew equally as fast, however, and Tong rewarded officials with lands that could, for the first time in Vietnamese history, be kept in the family of the recipient through inheritance.[7]

The last great reformers before the arrival of the French were the Nguyen emperors. Gia Long (1802-1820) "abolished all large landholdings by princes, nobles and high officials."[8] He also gave up an eight-century-old practice of paying officials and rewarding nobles with tax claims. Minh Man decreed in 1839 that all salaries, pensions and other awards be paid only in money and rice, thus ending completely all feudal rights to collect taxes. Permanent ownership of new lands given to the landless was legalized.[9]

Still, even though the reforms of Gia Long and Minh Mang broke the feudal threat to imperial power, feudal exploitation of landless peasants and small-holders by rich landowners remained. Execution of the new decrees was left to the village councils, which constituted local oligarchies usually controlled by the mandarins and

---

[5]**Ibid.**, pp. 155 and 189 (footnote 41).
[6]**Ibid.**, p. 159.
[7]**Ibid.**, p. 160.
[8]**Ibid.**, p. 279.
[9]**Ibid.**, pp. 279-80.

the rich, and "As had always been the case with Vietnamese agrarian reforms, quite a few of these measures remained on paper."[10]

The French Period

While the view that French policies created the landlord-tenant system in Vietnam is incorrect, it can be said that they reversed the latest trend of the throne, which was to encourage small-owners and to reduce the power of large landlords, and that they permitted the development of a far more powerful landlord class in Cochinchina than existed at the time in Tonkin and Annam.

The French administration sold large "concessions" of land cheaply to Frenchmen and to cooperative Vietnamese. While in Tonkin this took the form of outright expropriation of land temporarily abandoned by peasants fleeing areas ravaged by fighting (with unfortunate social consequences later), in the South concessions normally involved only new, uncultivated lands. Unequal land distribution increased in all areas under the French regime, but became most pronounced in the South, where 6,300 out of a total 6,800 large Indochinese landowners were located before World War II.[11]

Small landholders comprised 72 percent of all landowners in Cochin-china, but held only 15 percent of the total private and communal land area, while only 2.5 percent of the landowners held 45 percent of this land.[12] The large estates grew not only because

---

[10] Ibid., p. 281.

[11] Buttinger, **Vietnam: A Dragon Embattled**, p. 167.

[12] Le Thanh Khoi, **Le Viet-Nam**, (Paris: Les Editions de Minuit, 1955), p. 422. In the interest of accuracy it should be emphasized that large landholdings in the South included much unoccupied, virgin land which would have required large investments in water and salinity control systems before cultivation. If the land area relevant to this discussion is taken to be cultivated and readily cultivable land, then these figures must be considered rather skewed. For example, of 681,541 hectares of land "expropriated" from large Vietnamese landowners under the Ngo Dinh Diem land reform (Ordinance 57) and purchased from French landowners with French aid funds, 223,436 hectares, or 30 percent, were listed as "uncultivated, uncultivable or unclassified" in 1968. It is doubtful that so much of the small holdings would fall into this category. (See William Bredo, et. al., **Land Reform in Vietnam: Summary Volume**, (Menlo Park, California: Stanford Research Institute, 1968), pp. 9-11.)

Even if we could correct for this inaccuracy, however, which

of the concession policies of the French, but also through the practice of usury and the ability of the wealthy to foreclose on the property of debtors who could not repay loans burdened with exhorbitant interest rates.[13]

Robert Sansom tags their permissive policy toward large landholdings as one of the two great failures of French economic efforts, the other being the static technology they perpetrated in agriculture.[14] His economic analysis of the Mekong Delta, however, indicated that the landlord-tenant system played an important role "for over fifty years as an efficient mechanism for development."[15] It allowed persons with working capital and entrepreneurial ability to clear, dike, and bring under cultivation vast new land areas in the Delta at a far faster pace than had previously been possible. The area under rice cultivation in Cochinchina was increased by more than four times between 1880 and 1930, and the "essence of the land question . . . changed from country-wide shortage to unequal distribution."[16] Sansom found that wages and average rice incomes in the Mekong Delta rose between 1880 and 1929, so long as the settlement of new lands continued and labor was scarce relative to land.[17]

The frontier had all but vanished by 1930, however, when practically all the readily cultivable land had been occupied and subjected to the plow. More land was and still is available, but it will require heavier investment in drainage, irrigation and flood and salinity control than the French were prepared to make at that time.[18] In fact, the French regime has been severely criticized by some writers for not investing more in this productive area rather than so much in poorly planned and uneconomic railroads, highways, and splendid theaters.[19]

(cont.)
is impossible with the available data, a very pronounced inequality in land distribution would still be evident.

[13]Buttinger, **Vietnam: A Dragon Embattled**, p. 165.

[14]Robert L. Sansom, **The Economics of Insurgency in the Mekong Delta of Vietnam**, (Cambridge, Massachusetts: M.I.T. Press, 1970), pp. 50-1.

[15]**Ibid.**, p. 25.

[16]Buttinger, **Vietnam: A Dragon Embattled**, p. 163.

[17]Sansom, **Economics of Insurgency**, p. 39.

[18]See Joint Development Group, **The Postwar Development of the Republic of Vietnam**, (New York: Praeger, 1970), pp. 426-46, 470-5, 495-500, 517-9, and 523-9.

[19]See Buttinger, **Vietnam: A Dragon Embattled**, pp. 26-40, and Thompson, **French Indo-China**, pp. 205-19.

After 1930 tenancy became, rather than a positive force for progress, a "mechanism for widespread economic exploitation and social abuse."[20]   Second and third generation landlords preferred urban life and conspicuous consumption to the more rigorous life of managing farm operations. Absentee landlordism grew, while competition for the now fixed supply of land to farm among a growing number of potential tenants pushed rents up to between 40 and 60 percent of the annual rice harvest.[21]   Around 80 percent of the cultivated land area in the Mekong Delta was farmed by tenants.[22] Landlord wealth was not reinvested in land development as had been the case earlier, since these landlords-by-inheritance knew or cared little about agricultural matters and provided almost no technical direction of capital investment assistance to their tenants. "Their only concern was to collect rents."[23]

Based on his study of rice exports and internal consumption, wage trends and harvesting techniques in the Mekong Delta, Sansom concluded that, while rural economic conditions improved throughout the period of settlement, they declined after 1930 until World War II interrupted the export trade. By 1945-6 the Viet Minh had gained enough influence in the rural areas to force rent reductions and some land redistribution. Many landlords fled to the cities to join those already there, and rural conditions again improved.[24]

Thanks largely to the landlord-tenant system rice exports were maintained at high levels throughout the 1930's and until 1943, despite steadily increasing population pressures on domestic consumption.   Using three-year averages, Sansom calculated estimates of per capita paddy consumption in the Mekong Delta as having risen from 107 kilograms in 1879-80 to 217 in 1899-1901 and 202 in 1920-22, only to fall back to 127 kilograms in 1935-37. It rose again to 207 kilograms in 1950-52.[25]

---

[20]Sansom, **Economics of Insurgency**, p. 25.

[21]Ibid., p. 31.

[22]Bredo, **Summary Volume**, p. 3.

[23]Sansom, **Economics of Insurgency**, pp. 31 and 52.

[24]Ibid., 34-45.

[25]Ibid., pp. 36-8. About 240 kilograms of paddy per person per year is considered the required minimum in South Vietnam. This is roughly equivalent to 156 kg. of milled rice, which would provide 1,530 calories per day. It must be supplemented by other foods to reach the general Asian standard of 2,100 to 2,300 calories per day. Both the government and the Viet Cong use the 240 kg. of paddy figure as an annual per capita requirement. (See Note 22, pages 37-8, in Sansom.) Less than this must be supplemented to a larger extent with less favored coarse grain and root crops, such

Viet Minh Reforms

The Viet Minh revolutionary coalition was organized to win independence from French colonial rule, and it sought the widest possible support from all classes of Vietnamese. The Indochinese Communist Party (ICP) had, in 1941, "resolved to create 'an enlarged National Front to include not only workers and peasants...but also patriotic landowners;'" and it adopted a mild stance toward agrarian reform, typified by the slogan, "'Confiscation of the land owned by traitors for distribution to the poor farmers.'"[26]

In practice, this nationalistic policy meant that only land owned by Frenchmen and by the largest Vietnamese landlords (those who owned more than 50 hectares of land and who were identified with the French) was confiscated for redistribution, while attempts were made to win the support of and financial assistance from lesser landowners.[27] This policy remained in effect until 1953, when Viet Minh victory seemed assured and continued support from middle-landowners was no longer considered necessary.[28]

Various means of persuasion were used against French and "traitor" landlords, including the use of terror and assassination, to obtain their removal from the scene and to induce the lesser and "loyal" landlords to lower rents, to agree to some redistribution, and to pay Viet Minh taxes.[29] Many landowners fled to the cities in the 1946-48 period to escape Viet Minh threats to their lives, joining the growing class of absentee landlords already living there. Their lands "were immediately confiscated and redistributed."[30] In fact land redistribution was carried farther in the South than the Viet Minh leadership desired at that time, and they had to issue

---

(cont.)
as barley, corn, wheat, tubers, manioc, and sweet potatoes, if these are available, in order to avoid undernourishment.

[26]Bernard B. Fall, **The Two Viet-Nams,** (New York: Praeger, 1963), p. 62, quoting from Nguyen Giang, **Les Grandes Dates du Parti de la Classe Ouvriere du Viet Nam,** (Hanoi: Foreign Languages Publishing House, 1960), p. 42.

[27]William Bredo, et. al., **Land Reform in Vietnam: Working Papers** (4 vol.), (Menlo Park, California: Stanford Research Institute, 1968), v. 3, p. 40-1.

[28]Fall, **The Two Viet-Nams,** p. 62.

[29]Sansom, **Economics of Insurgency,** pp. 55-6.

[30]**Ibid.,** p. 55, and Bredo, **Working Papers,** V. 3, p. 41, quoting from Bredo.

strong reprimands and instructions to hold their southern activists in check.[31]

The amount of land available for redistribution in areas under Viet Minh control and the number of potential recipients determined the actual size of the reallocated holdings. An attempt was made to give each peasant enough riceland to provide a little more than subsistence for himself and his family. Peasants who owned very small plots were often given more to bring them up to the subsistence-plus standard. Reallocated plots were usually less than one hectare, but families in some areas received 2 or 3 hectares.[32]

Sansom reports that the Viet Minh reforms had lasting effect. Most of the landlords never returned to their villages after independence, but remained in absentee status and tried to collect rents through hired agents or government officials. Former landowners were seldom able to repossess land redistributed by the Viet Minh, nor to collect rents above 25-40 percent of the harvest (as compared with the pre-1946 era of 40-60 percent rents).[33]

While the primary goal of the Viet Minh was no doubt to obtain stronger popular support from rural areas in their struggle against the French and their collaborators, most writers agree in describing the land tenure situation as one in which the peasantry saw grave injustices, which they naturally blamed on the French colonial regime. To ask whether the Viet Minh redistributed land to gain peasant support or the peasants supported the Viet Minh to obtain a redistribution of land (as well as independence)—in other words, to ask whether the Viet Minh rebellion was inspired and directed by a revolutionary elite whose chief strength was organization or was essentially a peasant uprising based on popular grievances—is merely to confuse the issue.[34] Both were undoubtedly true, the revolutionary elite and the discontented peasants each drew strength from the existence of the other, and one group could probably not have succeeded alone.

---

[31]Milton I. Sacks, "Marxism in Vietnam," in Frank N. Trager (ed.), **Marxism in Southeast Asia,** (Stanford, California: Stanford University Press, 1959), pp. 154 and 326 (note 158). Also discussed in Douglas Pike, **Viet Cong,** (Cambridge, Massachusetts: M.I.T. Press, 1966), p. 29.

[32]Bredo, **Working Papers,** v. 3, p. 41.

[33]Sansom, **Economics of Insurgency,** p. 56.

[34]For a discussion of these two "opposing" views see **Ibid.,** pp. 241-45.

Land Reform under Ngo Dinh Diem

Emperor Bao Dai proclaimed the need for land reform throughout Vietnam in 1951, but little was done until June 4, 1953, when Prime Minister Nguyen Van Tam issued land reform decrees. The provisions of these decrees are of interest only in that they show the recognition of land reform as an important issue, since they were not implemented. They included:[35]

"Distribution of concession lands for cultivation...

"Establishment of maximum rental ratios of 15 percent of the total annual crop on rice fields or other annually cropped agricultural land.

"Limitation of large scale ownership of land by restricting retention to 12 to 36 hectares in North Vietnam, 15 to 45 hectares in Central Vietnam, and 30 to 100 hectares in South Vietnam. The area of land retained would vary with the family size of the owners...

"Establishment of usufruct rights for farmers who squatted on private land that was left uncultivated...."

Prime Minister Ngo Dinh Diem attempted to reduce rents and to provide greater security of tenure with his first land reform decrees in 1955. Ordinance 2, January 8, 1955, restricted rents to between 15 and 25 percent of the average harvest and required 3-year,[36] written contracts. The latter provision was intended to reduce competitive evictions. Ordinance 7, February 5, 1955, gave additional protection to tenants on new and abandoned land to encourage its cultivation. These decrees also limited rental payments after a crop failure and gave a tenant the first right of refusal to purchase the land he tilled should his landlord decide to sell it.[37]

The following year, after Diem had become President, he promulgated his major land reform measure, Ordinance 57, October

---

[35]Bredo, **Summary Volume**, pp. 4-5.

[36]Extended to 5 years in 1964. Bredo, **Working Papers**, v. 1-2, p. D-7.

[37]Sansom, **Economics of Insurgency**, p. 57, and Bredo, **Summary Volume**, p. 4.

22, 1956.[38] This law limited riceland ownership to no more than 100 hectares, with 15 hectares additional allowed for ancestral worship land. Of total land retained, however, owners were allowed to cultivate no more than 30 hectares themselves and were thus "required" to rent out up to 74 percent of their land. Expropriated landlords were paid by the government for their land with 10 percent cash and 90 percent in non-transferable bonds, bearing 3 percent interest and amortized within 12 years. Tenants tilling the land were given first priority in land redistribution. A land recipient was required to pay the government the same value received by the former landowner, less the interest, but in 6 annual installments instead of 12.[39] The recipient received a temporary title registration until all payments were completed, the actual title remaining with the government in the interim.

A Ministry of Land Reform was organized to implement the program and a National Land Reform Council was established to supervise and coordinate the effort in all branches of the government. Stiff penalties were authorized for any person interfering with the implementation of the program.

Article 1 of the ordinance listed only the economic goals of the law, but its political nature was obliquely recognized near the end:[40]

"ARTICLE 1. The Land Reform established by this Ordinance aims at an equitable distribution of the land to help tenant farmers become small landowners for the development of agricultural production, and the orientation of large landlords toward industrial activities."

. . .

"ARTICLE 31. All provisions set forth in this Ordinance are of a public security nature."

---

[38]See Bredo, **Working Papers,** v. 1-2, pp. E-5-11, for an English translation of this document.

[39]The monetary value of the land expropriated was determined by regional committees, subject to the approval of the National Land Reform Council. It averaged 3 to 4 times the value of the annual production of the land. MacDonald Salter, **Land Reform in South Vietnam,** Spring Review Country Paper, (Washington, D.C.: Agency for International Development, June 1970), pp. 64-5.

[40]Bredo, **Working Papers,** v. 1-2, pp. E-5 and E-11.

Ta van Nho, an agricultural engineer in the Land Reform Office, lectured on "The Meaning of Land Reform" in 1955, after Ordinance 2 and 7 but while Ordinance 57 was still in the planning stage. He spoke of the need "to create more suitable conditions for the increase of agricultural production" and to raise the standard of living of society. This was to be accomplished by changing the social status of cultivators with respect to the land—eliminating the large landowner class and transforming tenants and squatters into small landowners. Rural living standards were also to be improved by regulating remaining land rental arrangements, limiting the alienation of land to non-farmers and foreigners, establishing first rights of purchase and protecting squatters' rights.[41]

J. P. Gittinger reported the major policy objectives of the Diem program were 1) "achieving greater political stability" and 2) "laying the foundation for increased production and productivity." Writing in 1959, he stated that "It would appear . . . (these objectives) . . . have been in substantial measure achieved." He described the conditions the program was intended to alleviate in these words:[42]

> "When the Diem government came to power, it inherited a land tenure system seriously out of harmony with the times and which had been effectively exploited by the Communist Viet Minh to gain peasant support. About 40 per cent of the riceland areas was held by some 2,500 individuals—0.25 per cent of the rural population. Many large owners were French. Rent rates were commonly 50 per cent of the crop or even more. The tenant had virtually no security, and depended upon the whim of his landlord for his future. For nearly a decade many landowners had been afraid to visit their holdings, so normal economic relationships had been completely disrupted. Most large landowners had ceased loaning money to their tenants. The introduction of new agricultural techniques was seriously blocked by the tenure structure . . . "

---

[41]Ta van Nho, "Dinh-Nghia Danh-tu Cai-cach Dien-dia" (The Meaning of Land Reform), in Nha Cai-cach Dien-dia (Land Reform Office), **Nhung Bai Giang ve Cai-Cach Dien-dia** (Lectures on Land Reform), Bo Dien-Tho va Cai-Cach Dien-dia (Ministry of Land and Land Reform), Saigon: 1955, pp. 36-7.

[42]J. P. Gittinger, **Studies on Land Tenure in Viet Nam** (U.S. Operations Mission to Vietnam, December 1959), p. 1.

Reduced rents were to be computed on the basis of the average yield of the tenant's land as of the date of the contract, so that the tenant would keep the higher income resulting from investment or improved techniques.   Special inducements were provided for the cultivation of virgin or abandoned land.   Tenure security provisions were designed to assure the tenant would receive the benefits from permanent improvements on the land in succeeding years without being forced to compete with others by paying higher rents. Thus it was expected that farmer incentives to invest would be enhanced.

The land transfer program was expected to improve incentives to invest among its recipients even more. Since the redistribution of ownership did not change the pattern of cultivation, but merely gave land titles to the farmers who were already farming the land, Gittinger did not anticipate a reduction in production. He admitted the possibility of a reduction in rice marketing, as the peasant's family was able to consume more of its own output instead of selling it to meet rental obligations; but he did not expect this effect to be important, since "the South Vietnamese peasantry already has among the highest per capita levels of rice consumption in Asia."[43]   He continued:

"The most important effect of the transfer will come later when the economic incentives of ownership and fixed produce rentals are felt by individual peasant farmers.   The land transfer program does not break up management units: peasants make their own management decisions. Large absentee landlords have not been important in the rural credit market for over a decade, since they have been unable to collect their loans 'in the face of local insecurity. (Credit has been supplied through relatives, small landowners living in the village, and by local merchants.) As to extensively exploited holdings growing rice, although several existed before World War II in the Mekong Delta, by the time of the land transfer ordinance, only one continued to be operated as a large-scale unit. All the rest had broken up their land into tenant-sized individual holdings . . . . there is no impressive evidence that large-scale exploitation in rice is more efficient

_____

[43]Ibid., p. 14. According to Sansom (**Economics of Insurgency,** p. 39) this was due to previous Viet Minh efforts.

than peasant agriculture under Vietnamese conditions."[44]

Landowners were to be encouraged to exchange their government bonds, received in compensation for expropriated land, for shares of stock in four new industries, purchasing government equity in those companies.[45] Government funds thus released could be used for other economic development projects. Additional investment funds were expected to accrue to the government as the peasants paid for their land more rapidly than the government was to pay the landlords.[46]

To summarize, four main political, economic, and social objectives were targeted by the Diem land reform program:

1. Greater political stability by a) reducing landlord exploitation of peasants and b) creating a larger class of small landowners.

2. Redistribution of income from wealthy landowners to poor farmers.

3. Increased agricultural production by a) improving farmer incentives to invest and to adopt new production techniques and b) encouraging cultivation of new and abandoned land.

4. Increased investment in industry by former landlords.

The success of the Diem program in achieving these objectives is questionable. While the reforms were important steps against the power of the landlords, their total effect was apparently small.

[44]Ibid., p. 14. In another place Gittinger had this to say about the efficiency of large-scale farms: "To be economically justified in a peasant economy, a large-scale mechanically operated enterprise must not only be able to produce more cheaply than the present farmer—a formidable challenge in itself—but must in addition be more efficient to compensate for what might be termed the social opportunity cost of any peasant labor left unemployed...this cost cannot be eliminated from the social account nor ignored in assessing relative efficiencies." Besides this consideration, he notes that the few large-scale, mechanized, French rice farms that did exist (before World War II) "were profitable not because of labor saving techniques but largely because they had access to low cost government-sponsored credit not available to small farmers and because they were able to control the quality of the rice they produced through seed selection." —Ibid., pp. 48-9.

[45]Ibid., p. 7.

[46]Ibid., p. 5.

The program probably had only a minimal effect on **political stability,** for several reasons. Although a large percentage of the tenants did sign the required contracts with their landlords,[47] none of which could specify a rent of more than 25 percent of the total annual harvest,[48] in actual fact subterfuge of the law was widespread. In a 1967 Hamlet Resident Survey conducted by the Stanford Research Institute (SRI) actual fixed rents paid in kind by 102 landless tenants in 1966 were found to average 34.5 percent of the total crop, ranging from an average of 57.1 percent in Hoa Hao areas to 27.3 percent in peripheral areas. (It was 35.0 percent in densely populated, non-Hoa Hao areas.) Altogether, 61 percent of

---

[47]By 1959 a total of 781,899 contracts covering 1,365,423 hectares were reportedly in effect, but by 1964 this had dropped to 658,237 contracts for 1,326,678 hectares. Privately owned riceland rented to tenants was reported to total 1,313,644 hectares in 1964. That these figures are not consistent is typical of statistical problems in dealing with Vietnam. In this case it probably results from duplication in the contract figures due to failure by local clerks to report cancellation of expired contracts as renewals were registered. Bredo, **Working Papers,** v. 1-2, p. 43, and v. 1-1, p. 68. Nevertheless, a sizeable portion of tenants apparently felt that signing the contracts might give them some bargaining leverage against their landlords. Sansom estimated one million tenants in the Delta in 1960-61, while Wolf Ladejinsky reported a 1955 estimate of 600,000 tenants in the Delta, 400,000 in the Coastal Lowlands. Sansom, **op. cit.,** p. 54, and Wolf Ladejinsky, "Agrarian Reform in Free Vietnam," in **Vietnam in World Affairs,** Special Issue, **Studies on National and International Affairs.** Vietnam, 1960, pp. 154-73, reprinted in Bredo, **Working Papers,** v. 1-2, pp. B-17-36. See p. B-19.

[48]"A major restriction of the rent limitation provisions arises out of administrative reinterpretation of the ordinance itself. While the ordinance provides for the rent to be paid on 'the value of the annual harvest of the principal crop' (Ordinance 2, Article 13), a series of interpretive circulars provides that: (1) the land rent is based on the total amount of the annual income from the principal type of cultivation; (2) for two-crop riceland the rent is based on the total production from the two harvests; (3) for land giving one rice crop and one crop other than rice, the rent **is still** based on the income from rice **plus** the income from the other crop; and (4) the rent does not apply where a second crop, rice or otherwise, is 'secondary,' i.e., 'is to satisfy the (food) needs of the tenant family.' Hence, the term 'annual harvest' is interpreted to mean 'total yearly harvest' rather than 'main yearly harvest,' and the meaning of 'principal crop' includes two totally different kinds of crops." Bredo, **Summary Volume,** pp. 60-1.

the landless tenants interviewed paid rents above the legal rate.[49] Sansom reported 1967 rents of 25 to 40 percent in the secure—and Hoa Hao—province of An Giang.[50]

While these figures are subject to question, the personal interviews conducted by both Sansom and SRI provide ample evidence that landlords have not hesitated to demand illegal rents if they could get away with it. Where lower rents did exist they could not be attributed to the Diem regulations, which were not enforced, but rather to pressure from the Viet Cong. In secure areas the landlords would feign compliance with the law by signing a contract for the legal rent, but would simultaneously obtain an unwritten agreement outside the law for whatever rent the market would bear. Rent reductions for crop failures are required by the law in legal contracts, but SRI found that landlords were notably reluctant to grant tolerance after the 1966 floods. They estimated the tenants as a group obtained only about 50 percent of the reductions they were entitled to receive.[51]

If landlord exploitation was reduced by the Diem reforms it was reduced very little; nor was a large, new class of small landowners created. By 1968, under both Ordinance 57 and the French land purchase program together, only 132,208 farmers had received title to their land or could expect it someday.[52] This was about 10 percent of the number of tenants in the country.

It is difficult to see how unenforced rent regulations and such a small redistribution program could have had much effect on

---

[49]Bredo, **Working Papers**, v. 4-1, p. 73. It should be noted that these rental rates, based on 1966 production figures and rents-in-kind reported by the tenants tend to overstate the case, since legal rents are based on 5-year average yields and 1966 was a very bad year due to severe floods. That an exaggeration has occurred is corroborated by a look at the actual survey table (HRS table #309, **Working Papers**, v. 4-2, p. C-197.), in which 10 respondents out of 102 are listed as having paid 100 percent or more of their crop as rent, one of them 225 percent. Flood damage was worst in the Hoa Hao provinces, with the densely populated areas on down the river also badly affected—and these rental figures reflect that damage. A general tendency on the part of tenants to understate production—but not rental—figures must also be taken into account here.

[50]Sansom, **Economics of Insurgency**, p. 61.

[51]Bredo, **Working Papers**, v. 4-1, p. 70.

[52]Bredo, **Summary Volume**, p. 11. They received 294,453 hectares, or an average of 2.2 hectares each. See Table 3-1.

Table 3-1

Status of Expropriated and Former French Lands as of July 15, 1968

Distributed or Allocated Lands[1]	Ordinance 57		Former French		Total	
	Farmers	Hectares	Farmers	Hectares	Farmers	Hectares
General Recipients	116,741	250,563	7,562	21,860	124,303	272,423
Land Development Centers						
Cai San I	2,870	8,608	1,905	5,715	4,775	14,323
Cai San II	1,130	2,823	--	--	1,130	2,823
Other	2,000	4,884	--	--	2,000	4,884
Sub-total	6,000	16,315	1,905	5,715	7,905	22,030
TOTAL DISTRIBUTED OR ALLOCATED	122,741	266,878	9,467	27,575	132,208	294,453
Undistributed or Unallocated Lands[1]						
Cultivated	21,000	63,227	--	100,425	--	163,652
Uncultivated[2]	--	121,896	--	51,300	--	173,196
Status Unknown[2]	--	--	--	50,240	--	50,240
TOTAL UNDISTRIBUTED OR UNALLOCATED	21,000	185,123	--	201,965	--	387,088
GRAND TOTALS - Land Acquired		452,001		229,540		681,541

[1] Allocated means applications for purchase have been received, approved at village level and being processed further.

[2] Both categories are estimates reflecting a condition of uncertainty but present a reasonably accurate picture.

Source: "Activities of Land Reform Directorate," July 16, 1968 (Monthly Activities Report) by Directorate General of Land Affairs and "Abstracts from the 1967 Annual Report, Directorate General of Land Affairs, GVN" by Land Reform Staff, USAID.

Reprinted from William Bredo, et. al., Land Reform in Vietnam, Summary Volume, (Menlo Park, Calif., 1968), Stanford Research Institute, p. 11.

political stability. In fact about half the Vietnamese-owned riceland expropriated and all the French land was retained by the government (until 1967-8) and rented out by local administrative officials to provide government revenue, instead of being redistributed as promised. Along the Central Coast, where political disaffection with Saigon has been historically more intense than in the Mekong Delta, the Diem reforms had virtually no effect whatsoever. Metayage sharecropping agreements, which were and still are the rule in this region, were specifically excluded from the rent control laws and remained operative on a normal 50 percent-share basis. With only minor exceptions, moreover, there were no large landholdings along the Central Coast to be redistributed.[53]

The amount of **income redistribution** from landlords to poor farmers was also minimal, in view of the ineffectiveness of rent control provisions and the small number of actual land recipients. Since the latter had to make annual payments for the land roughly equal to the 25 percent rent level,[54] they would have apparently enjoyed higher incomes only in "secure" areas where rents had remained higher than that. Only one third of the new owners had made any payments to the government at all, however, before subsequent payments were cancelled by the LTTT Law in 1970, and only 22 percent of all payments due had been collected.[55]   This indicates that some income redistribution did occur, although it cannot all be attributed to the intended Diem program. Inflation in the late 1960's greatly diminished the real value of these payments, as well, so about 10 percent of South Vietnam's tenants should have been made better off than before. This change can hardly be called revolutionary, but at least it reversed previous trends.

If tenant incentives to invest in **increased agricultural production** were to be improved by reducing his rents and fixing them to a prior average yield, the Diem program again was not very successful.

The land recipients had been placed in a slightly healthier economic situation, but their numbers were small, as discussed above.

---

[53]A total of 148 hectares were expropriated along the Central Coast under Ordinance 57, all of it in Binh Thuan Province; and 4,405 hectares were purchased from French owners in the four southernmost Central Coast provinces, most of them (3,545 ha.) in Ninh Thuan. Bredo, **Summary Volume,** p. 8.

[54]Gittinger, **Studies on Land Tenure,** p. 5.

[55]Bredo, **Summary Volume,** p. 73.

Agricultural production does seem to have been encouraged by special contract inducements to bring virgin and abandoned lands into cultivation. Type B and C contracts for abandoned and uncultivated land were registered for a nationwide total of 452,387 hectares by 1959.[56] Rice area cultivated in the Delta rose from 1,572,000 hectares in 1954 to 1,810,000 in 1959, and Cochinchinese rice exports, after falling to zero in 1956, climbed back up to 246,000 metric tons in 1959.[57]

Regarding **increased investment in industry** by former landlords, SRI has this to say:[58]

"This (1967 Absentee Landlord) survey . . . reveals that some of the absentee landlords have either sold all their land or some of it and have transferred their wealth to other business endeavors. Commerce, particularly, and industry seem to be capturing the interest of these landowners in preference to agriculture.

"As a result of the expropriation of holdings of large landowners under Ordinance 57, landlords are no longer able to accumulate great wealth. Today the merchant appears to be succeeding the landlord as the wealthy investor, and the landlords appear to be moving into commerce and industry. In this case, it means a transfer of wealth from agriculture or from the land to commerce, industry, and real estate development."

In summary, it seems that the Diem land reform program had little effect on political stability, only a small role in redistributing income, a moderate effect on agricultural production by increasing the cultivated area (and by improving incentives for 10 percent of the tenant farmers), but perhaps greater success in encouraging wealthy landlords to invest in non-agricultural pursuits. Most of its shortcomings resulted from the high retention rate of 100 hectares, leaving too little land as excess to be redistributed and leaving the feudal landlord-tenant agricultural system basically unchanged, with all its social and political consequences, as well as from a lack of enforcement of rent controls. The second failure followed from the first, since effective enforcement of provisions against landlord interests was unlikely so long as the landlords themselves remained in control of the rural political structure.

---

[56]Bredo, **Working Papers**, v. 1-2, p. D-110.
[57]Sansom, **Economics of Insurgency**, p. 262.
[58]Bredo, **Working Papers**, v.4-1, p. 80.

Viet Cong Reforms

The prime importance of political objectives on the land reform efforts of the Viet Cong was openly admitted and clearly stated. Considerations of economic efficiency in production were secondary—as was no doubt true of government (GVN) reforms, although the GVN prefered to talk more about economic aspects. To quote from Douglas Pike:[59]

"Around land and on the solution of land tenure problems, the NLF built its indoctrination system.

" . . . Declared a Red Flag editorial, 'satisfactorily sol-ving the land problem of the peasants . . . is a way of mobilizing the people in the liberated area to participate in the struggle for, and protection of, the Revolution, . . . a means of mobilizing the masses in the oppressed areas to rise up . . . and liberate themselves.' Cadres were instructed to turn every issue into land terms."

The SRI study asserts that the Viet Minh land reform program, continued later by Viet Cong, was " a way to destroy the traditional social organization in the villages" by eliminating the landlord class, in order to gain support from and control over the much larger peasant class.[60] The need to maintain and increase rice production exerted a moderating influence on these efforts, since too much rural disturbance adversely affected production and since the wealthier peasants could be taxed more heavily to support the VC effort.[61]

Nevertheless, SRI concluded that[62]

"For the Viet Cong, the overriding consideration in the implementation of land reform has been its usefulness in seeking to gain the commitment of the rural population to the revolution . . .

---

[59]Pike, **Viet Cong**, p. 276.

[60]Bredo, **Summary Volume**, pp. 24-5.

[61]**Ibid.**, pp. 30-5. Apparently Viet Cong redistribution of land belonging to middle peasants created such serious problems in the early 1960's that the policy was reversed in 1965, previous NLF directives on land reform were suspended, and the VC returned to the Viet Minh policy of seeking "solidarity with middle farmers."

[62]Bredo, **Summary Volume**, p. 31.

"The ultimate goal of Viet Cong land policy is to create a communist society based on a dictatorship of the proletariat. The terminal acts of Communist land reform are the collectivization of land and the final elimination of private ownership as a social incentive . . . . (but) the beneficiaries of Viet Cong land reform are deluded into thinking that some form of private ownership will be retained in the future Communist society."

Sansom reported a marked landlord preference for the Viet Minh over the Viet Cong. "They recalled that the Viet Minh struggle was simply a resistance movement against the French and not a conflict with the landlords, whereas for the Viet Cong, according to one landlord, 'it is a class struggle and no landlord dares live in his home village'"[63] A 1965 NLF document on agrarian policy stated its goal was to "reinforce the peasants' support for the patriots' fight for rural unification."[64]

The land policies of the VC fell into three main categories: land redistribution, rent reduction, and higher farm wages. The implementation of these reforms was carried out with much flexibility, with decision-making decentralized to the village and hamlet level, in contrast to the highly centralized administration and relative inflexibility of the GVN program.[65] This enabled the VC to adapt their policies to the local conditions in each village to achieve the maximum political effect, a capability the GVN did not have.

On the other hand, Viet Cong land distribution policies appeared to many to be piecemeal and discriminatory, with preference given to members of the National Liberation Front, producing an uneven effect.[66]

There seems to be a general consensus of opinion on the relative success of the NLF reforms in the Mekong Delta as compared with the GVN efforts. Sansom found rents falling markedly the more distant were the tenants from a secure road or guardpost. He estimated that 1966-67 rents for the Delta region as a whole averaged between 5 or 10 percent, while it was still 25-40 percent in secure areas:[67]

---

[63]Sansom, **Economics of Insurgency**, p. 56.
[64]Quoted in **Ibid.**, p. 64.
[65]**Ibid.**, pp. 63-5, and Bredo, **Summary Volume**, pp. 147-8.
[66]Bredo, **Summary Volume**, p. 151, and Sansom, **op. cit.**, p. 56.
[67]Sansom, **op. cit.**., pp. 60-1.

"By 1966 the benefits of the Viet Cong land program, initiated with the 1960 General Uprising Campaign, were manifest. Approximately 817,000 tenants in the Delta were apprised of a single overriding fact: Rents paid on land in the Delta were determined by the Viet Cong and the market; they were not affected by Vietnamese government regulations or laws."

Regarding land redistribution, SRI concluded that:[68]

". . . it would appear that in Viet Cong-controlled areas, most of the land has been redistributed—which is interpreted to mean that in these areas, landlordism has been abolished by the Viet Cong. In the portion where Viet Cong land redistribution is not yet complete, it may reasonably be assumed that the landlord has been rendered politically ineffective as a force in the society and that tenure security is guaranteed by the Viet Cong.

". . . It is clear that Viet Cong intimidation of the landlord is a common and effective practice in contested areas as well as in many areas defined as secure. It appears likely that the Viet Cong has achieved a greater impact on the landlord-tenant relationship than has the GVN."

Other economic policies used by the VC encouraged land redistribution. They raised agricultural wage rates with boycotts against large-scale farmers. Viet Cong tax policies were highly progressive above a subsistence exemption, leaving the wealthier farmers with little incentive to keep more than the average amount of land.

The overall effect of VC land policies on the peasant's welfare was quite favorable. In addition, while the selective use of terror against landlords and uncooperative rich peasants was a widely used tactic, Sansom concluded from his landlord interviews that the "impetus behind the Viet Cong land reform was not in the general case terror but the sanction of implied force supported by the general will."[69]

The Viet Cong reforms were naturally illegal as far as the government was concerned, and the GVN found itself in "the position of having to protect the landlord from Viet Cong terrorism, help him recover his land, and otherwise defend his right to collect

---

[68]Bredo, **Summary Volume**, pp. 142-4.
[69]Sansom, **Economics of Insurgency**, p. 65.

rents."[70]   The GVN attempted to extricate itself from this corner by granting certain occupancy rights to beneficiaries of VC land distribution; but the laws regarding "confused lands" remained ambiguous and of limited application, retaining provisions for the ultimate eviction of the VC beneficiary by the original owner and tenant. In addition, with the retention of 164,000 cultivated hectares expropriated under Ordinance 57 or purchased from French nationals, the government itself became the largest landlord in many villages. Malpractice and corruption in the administration of this land on the part of local officials continued to alienate farmers and provided juicy propaganda themes for Viet Cong efforts to discredit the GVN in rural areas.[71]

Land Tenure in the 1960's

Extent of Tenancy

In 1970-71 the Republic of Vietnam reported 2,510,700 rice crop-hectares, producing an average of 2.28 metric tons of paddy per hectare.   The Southern Region accounted for 81 percent of the rice-crop area and 84 percent of the paddy production, even though only 65 percent of the country's 18 million people lived there. Another 30 percent of the population is strung out along the Coastal Lowlands on only 17 percent of the rice-crop area.   The remainder is in the Central Highlands.[72]

---

[70]Bredo, **Summary Volume**, p. 144.
[71]Ibid., **Summary Volume**, pp. 142-46.
[72]The rice-crop area reported here refers to crop-hectarage and **not** to the actual amount of land under annual cultivation. The **Report of the Agricultural Census of Vietnam, 1960-61** made a clear distinction between the two and reported both figures, where we can determine that 62 percent of the paddy land in the Coastal Lowlands was double-cropped, while less than 2 percent in the Southern Region was.   The distinction was dropped by 1970-71, however, and the "cultivated area" referred to in recent statistical yearbooks is evidently crop-hectarage, and not annual-cultivation-hectarage, though nowhere is it labelled as either. (This conclusion is based on a comparison of the historical series with the 1960-61 Census Report.)   The reported "cultivated area" of rice production increased by 18 percent in the Southern Region between 1967-68 and 1971-2, but by only 1.5 percent in the Coastal Lowlands. While some of this increase may be due to a resumption of cultivation on temporarily abandoned land, much of it can be attributed to the rapid growth of double-cropping with Miracle Rice, especially in the Southern Region where double-cropping had previously been rare and where 24 percent of the 1971-2 crop-hectarage was reported

The pressure of the population upon the cultivated land area was evident in the results of the 1960-61 Agricultural Census, which indicated an average operating ricefarm size of 2.08 hectares in the Southern Region and only 0.53 hectare in the Coastal Lowlands.[73] The first figure is comparable with the average riceland area cultivated per rice farmer in the SRI Hamlet Resident Survey of 2.21 hectares (Southern Region), which varied from 1.38 in the most densely populated provinces to 3.11 in the Hoa Hao, floating-rice provinces.[74]

The land tenure reported in the 1960-61 Census is summarized in Table 3-2. In the Southern Region 72.9 percent of all farmers rented all or part of their land, while along the Central Coast the figure stood at 68.7 percent. Most of the tenants along the Coast also owned some land as well, whereas most of those in the Southern Region did not. In terms of area, 62.5 percent of all farmland in the Southern Region and 39.3 percent in the Coastal Lowlands was rented. More than half the rented land along the Coast was publicly

----

(cont.)
to be in Miracle Rice. The statistical practice of reporting only crop-hectarage makes it impossible to say, from these official published statistics, how much land is currently under rice cultivation, and it also causes considerable confusion. For example, the Stanford Research Institute used crop-hectarage figures for paddy cultivation as reported in the **1966 Agricultural Statistics Yearbook** and called them "Total Agricultural Area" and "Ricelands Area," apparently not realizing the double-counting included in those figures, especially in the Coastal Lowlands.—**Phuc Trinh ve cuoc Kiem Tra Canh Nong tai Viet Nam, 1960-61 (Report on the Agricultural Census of Vietnam),** Agricultural Economics and Statistics Service, (Saigon: 1964), p. 48; **Nien Giam Thong Ke Vietnam, 1971,** (Viet Nam Statistical Yearbook), National Institute of Statistics, (Saigon: 1972), p. 353; **Nien Giam Thong Ke Vietnam, 1971,** (Viet Nam Statistical Yearbook), National Institute of Statistics, (Saigon: 1972), p. 353; **Nien Giam Thong Ke Nong Nghiep, 1970,** (Agricultural Statistics Yearbook), Agricultural Economics and Statistics Service, (Saigon: 1971), p. 31; **Nguyet-San Thong-Ke Nong Nghiep,** So 3, 1972 (Dac Biet), (Monthly Bulletin of Agricultural Statistics), No. 3, 1972 (Special Issue), Agricultural Economics and Statistics Service, (Saigon: 1972), p. 10; and William Bredo, et. al., **Land Reform in Vietnam, Summary Volume,** p. 36 and **Working Papers,** Vol 4-1, p. 131.

[73]Calculated from **Report on the Agricultural Census of Vietnam, 1960-61,** (Saigon: 1964), Table 25, p. 49.

[74]Bredo, **Working Papers,** Vol. 4-1, p. 19.

Table 3-2

A. PERCENTAGE OF TOTAL AREA OF HOLDINGS BY TENURE IN 1960-61

	Owner-operated	Rented, privately -owned	Rented, publicly -owned	Other tenure	Total hectares
Coastal Lowlands[1]	57.2%	18.5%	20.8%	3.6%	464,911
Southern Region[2]	35.2	54.9	7.6	2.3	2,046,872
All 27 Provinces	39.3	48.1	10.1	2.5	2,511,783

B. PERCENTAGE OF NUMBER OF HOLDINGS BY TENURE IN 1960-61

	Owner-operated only	Rented only	Other tenure only	Mixed tenure	Total number of holdings
Coastal Lowlands[1]	27.4%	10.7%	3.9%	58.0%	695,981
Southern Region[2]	21.9	44.4	5.3	28.5	1,175,829
All 27 Provinces	23.9	31.8	4.8	39.5	1,871,810

SOURCE: Phuc Trinh Ve cuoc Kiem Tra Canh Nong tai Viet Nam, 1960-61
(Report on the Agricultural Census of Vietnam), (Saigon: Agricultural Economics and Statistics Service, 1964), Tables 7-9
and 14-16, pp. 31-3 and 38-40.

---

[1] The Coastal Lowlands included 9 provinces: Binh Dinh, Binh Thuan, Khanh Hoa, Ninh Thuan, Phu Yen, Quang Nam, Quang Ngai, Quang Tri and Thua Thien. The same area included 10 provinces in 1970.

[2] The Southern Region included 18 provinces: An Giang, An Xuyen, Ba Xuyen, Bien Hoa, Binh Duong, Dinh Tuong, Gia Dinh, Kien Hoa, Kien Giang, Kien Phong, Kien Tuong, Long An, Long Khanh, Phong Dinh, Phuoc Tuy, Tay Ninh, Vinh Binh and Vinh Long. The same area included 24 provinces in 1970.

owned (communal land), but in the Southern Region most of it was privately owned.

The Ordinance 57 and French Land Reforms were being implemented at the same time the Agricultural Census of 1960-61 was underway. In fact, of all Ordinance 57 land redistributed between 1958 and 1968, 21 percent had been transferred to new owners before the beginning of 1960 and 91 percent had been by the end of 1961, or 70 percent during the two years of the Census.[75] Census results in the Coastal Lowlands could not have been much affected, since by 1968 total Ordinance 57 and French land redistributions there involved only 0.2 percent of all farmers and 0.4 percent of all farmland. In the Southern Region, however, total redistributions by 1968 involved 11 percent of all (1961) farm operators and 14 percent of all (1961) farmland. This redistribution amounted to between 19 and 23 percent of all rented land, depending on how much of it (the redistribution) was included in the census count, and it made new owners out of 13-15 percent of the tenants (in the Southern Region).[76]

In their 1967-68 Hamlet Resident Survey (HRS) the Stanford Research Institute and the Center for Vietnamese Studies conducted a total of 854 (usable) interviews of randomly selected residents in 54 hamlets of 22 provinces of the Southern Region. Of those respondents 62.4 percent were farm households (not counting 2.5 percent non-farming landlords), including 10.9 percent landless farm workers and 51.5 percent farm operators. Of the 440 farm operators interviewed, 46.6 percent were owner-operators, 10.7 percent owner-tenants, and 42.7 percent tenants.[77]

Their results place at least 13.3 percent more farmers in the owner-operator category than the 1960-61 Census plus the Ordinance 57 and French land reforms would lead us to expect, even adopting the extreme assumptions that the Census reported none of the land recipients as owners and that all recipients had become pure owners (not part-owner, part-tenants). The HRS bias toward owner-operators (as compared with the Census) is even more pronounced in terms of land area, since it reported only 37.6 percent of all land as rented.[78] The most favorable adjustment of the Census data (subtracting the total amount of land redistributed between

[75]Ibid., **Summary Volume**, p. 15.

[76]Ibid., **Summary Volume**, p. 8, 11, **Working Papers**, Vol. 1-2, p. B-72, 73; and **Report on the Agricultural Census of Vietnam, 1960-61**, pp. 27, 34.

[77]Bredo, **Working Papers**, Vol. 4-1, p. 13.

[78]Ibid., **Summary Volume**, p. 198.

1958 and 1968) would still leave us with 48.2 percent of all land rented. Given the alternative assumption that half the redistributed land had been processed to half the eventual recipients (all of the latter entering the owner-operator slot, which, of course, is itself an extreme assumption) and had been so reported in the Census, then 55 percent of the farmland would still have been rented to 67 percent of the farmers in 1968 (in the Southern Region).[79]

The explanation for this divergence probably lies in the fact that the HRS sample selection process was more restricted by conditions of insecurity than was that of the Census. In the HRS 48 percent of the hamlets chosen were dropped as inaccessible, as were 10 percent of the households selected in the remaining hamlets.[80] The Census report indicated that only 21 percent of their original list of 1,700 hamlets were dropped or replaced for security reasons.[81] The GVN has always maintained that conditions of insecurity prevented the implementation of its land redistribution program in many areas, meaning that redistributed land was more or less concentrated in the same set of more secure hamlets in which the HRS was also concentrated (the Edward J. Mitchell analysis notwithstanding[82]), and probably producing an HRS bias toward owner-operated farms. Another factor could be that larger areas of formerly tenanted land lay abandoned due to insecurity and military action than areas of owner-operated land, the former tending to be on large tracts of former concession lands owned by absentee landlords in the more remote regions of each province.

If we use the last extent-of-tenancy estimate above as the most nearly correct for the Southern Region we can say that in 1968 there were still at least 787,805 tenants (67 percent of 1,175,829) in that area, who were renting approximately 1,125,780 hectares (55 percent of 2,046,872) (ignoring the effects of both population growth since 1961 and the military conflict). Along the Central Lowlands there were still some 476,517 tenants (68.5 percent of 695,981) renting 180,669 hectares (38.9 percent of 464,911)

---

[79]The 1960-61 Agricultural Census itself was a random survey, but since its sample included some 54,000 questionnaires from 1,434 hamlets (994 in the Southern Region), its reliability is fairly high. See **Report on the Agricultural Census of Vietnam 1960–61**, pp. 8 and 186.

[80]Bredo, **Working Papers,** vol. 4-2, pp. A-14-17.

[81]**Report on the Agricultural Census of Vietnam, 1960–61**, p. 17-18.

[82]See footnote 118, below.

(ignoring land abandoned due to the hostilities).[83]   The grand total for these two key regions of South Vietnam (we are excluding the Central Highlands for lack of data, which held 5 percent of the population and only 2 percent of the riceland area[84]) comes to roughly 1,264,322 tenants renting 1,306,449 hectares, or 68 percent of the farm operators renting 52 percent of the farmland.[85]

Gini Indices of Inequality

Two devices frequently used to measure and compare degrees of inequality in the distribution of land ownership are the graphic Lorenz curve and the Gini index of concentration derived from it.[86] Lorenz curves are plotted on a graph by connecting the points relating the cumulated percentage of owners, ranked along the horizontal axis in order from the smallest to the largest, to the cumulated percentage of area owned, measured along the vertical axis.   A 45 degree line bisecting the graph from the zero to the hundredth percentiles is called the "line of equal distribution," and it represents the locus of a Lorenz curve in the hypothetical situation where the total land area is divided equally among all owners.   The farther the actual Lorenz curve deviates from the line of equal

---

[83]These tenant estimates include both "pure" tenants and those owning part of their holding.   The figures on land area rented, however, include only the amount of land rented and not the part which is owned.

[84]Bredo, **Summary Volume**, p. 36.

[85]Of the total farmland area estimated by the Census of 1960–61 (2,511,783 ha.) for these two regions, 91.8 percent was cultivated and 80.0 percent was under rice cultivation.   The percentage under rice cultivation was 83.2 percent for the Southern Region and 66.4 percent for the Coastal Lowlands.   But of all farm operators, 69.4 percent of those in the South produced rice paddy, while 83.3 percent of those along the Coast did.   Calculated from **Report of the Agricultural Census of Vietnam, 1960–61**, pp. 50, 48, 27.

[86]See Bruce M. Russett, et. al., **World Handbook of Political and Social Indicators** (New Haven, Connecticut: Yale University Press, 1964), pp. 237–40, and Bruce M. Russet, "Inequality and Instability, The Relation of Land Tenure to Politics," **World Politics**, (April, 1964), pp. 442–54.   Using the Gini Index and the percentage of farms rented as measures of inequality in making multi-country comparisons, Russet found a clearly "negative relationship between unequal distributions of land, and especially of income, and economic development" (**World Handbook...**, p. 292) and "within certain ranges, a one-point (out of 100) decrement in the Gini Index has the effect of decreasing domestic violence by 3 percent" (**World Handbook...**, p. 321).

distribution, the higher is the degree of inequality and concentration in land ownership. Such curves can be used to compare the degree of ownership inequality among countries or to demonstrate its change over time within a single country or region.

The Gini index[87] is a numerical summary of the same information used to construct a Lorenz curve. It is simply the ratio of (1) the area between the actual Lorenz curve and the hypothetical, 45 degree, line of equal distribution to (2) the total area under the line of equal distribution, or one-half of the entire graph. If distribution were perfectly equal and the two lines coincided, the Gini index number would be zero. The more concentrated land ownership becomes, the more nearly the actual Lorenz curve approaches the number one. The larger the Gini index, the less equal and more concentrated is the ownership distribution; the smaller it is, the more equal is the distribution.

Figure 3-1 contains two Lorenz curves plotted from the cumulative percentage data (columns 4 and 7) of Tables 3-3 and 3-4, comparing the distribution of land ownership in the Southern Region of Vietnam in 1955 with that of 1966 and demonstrating the effects of the Ordinance 57 land reform in the interim. The lower part of the 1955 curve suffers from insufficient detail in the data. It would probably remain below the 1966 curve, instead of crossing it, if the first size category of Table 3-3 were broken up into the same four components as in Table 3-4.

To derive the Gini index, one must first rank the data in order of size categories as in columns (1) of these two tables, small to large. Let n represent the rank order of each category. Moving down the list, calculate the percentage of owners (column 3) and of area (column 6) in each category and, starting from the top (smallest size category), add to obtain the cumulative percentages (as in columns 4 and 7), which are the coordinates to be used in plotting the Lorenz curve.

If X_n is the cumulative percentage of owners for each category n (column 4) and Y_n is the corresponding cumulative percentage of area (column 7), the area between the Lorenz curve and the 45-degree line of equal distribution is algebraically equal to:

---

[87]The fundamental article on the Gini index, also called the "coefficient of concentration," is in Italian: C. Gini, "Variabilita e Mutabilita," **Studi Economico-Giuridici della R. Universita di Cagliari**, anno 3, part 2, (1912), p. 80. It is discussed in Maurice G. Kendall, **The Advanced Theory of Statistics**, (New York: Hafner Publishing Co., 1943), Vol. 1, p. 47.

$$\sum_{X_n=Y_n=0}^{X_n=Y_n=100} (X_n-X_{n-1}) \left[(X_{n-1}+ \frac{X_n-X_{n-1}}{2}) - (Y_{n-1}+ \frac{Y_n-Y_{n-1}}{2}) \right] \qquad (1)$$

which can be reduced to:

$$.5 \sum_0^{100} (X_n-X_{n-1}) \left[(X_n+X_{n-1}) - (Y_n+Y_{n-1}) \right] . \qquad (2)$$

Since the Gini index equals the ratio of this area to half of the 100x100 graph, the

$$\text{Gini Index} = (.5/5000) \sum_0^{100} (X_n-X_{n-1}) \left[(X_n+X_{n-1}) - (Y_n+Y_{n-1}) \right]$$

$$= .0001 \sum_0^{100} (X_n-X_{n-1}) \left[(X_n+X_{n-1}) - (Y_n+Y_{n-1}) \right]$$

$$= .0001 \sum_0^{100} \left[(X_n^2-X_{n-1}^2) - (X_n-X_{n-1})(Y_n+Y_{n-1}) \right] . \qquad (3)$$

But since $\sum_0^{100} (X_n^2-X_{n-1}^2) = 10,000,$ the

$$\text{Gini Index} = 1-.0001 \sum_0^{100} (X_n-X_{n-1})(Y_n+Y_{n-1}). \qquad (4)$$

Equation (4) is easily calculated from ownership distribution data as normally tabulated. The term (X_n-X_{n-1}) is simply the percent of owners in each size category (columns 3 of Tables 3-3 and 3-4); and (Y_n+Y_{n-1}) (see columns 8) can be calculated from the cumulative percentage of area figures (in columns 7) as the sum of the cumulative percentage of area for each category plus the one immediately preceding it. The product $(X_n-X_{n-1})(Y_n+Y_{n-1})$ is then obtained by multiplying the entry in column (3) times the entry in column (8) for each category, as has been done in columns (9). Subtract from 1.0 the sum total of column (9) times .0001 (or divided by 10,000) to obtain the Gini index.

Figure 3-1

**Lorenz Curves of Land Ownership Distribution
Among Owners in the Southern Region,
South Vietnam, 1955 and 1966**

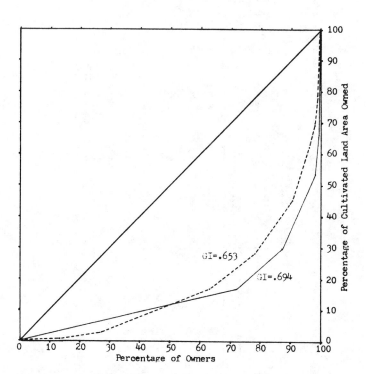

Legend: —— 1955 Distribution (Gini Index = .694)
---- 1966 Distribution (Gini Index = .653)

Sources: See Tables 3-3 and 3-4.

Table 3-3

Land Ownership Distribution in the Southern Region, 1955, Including Owners Only

Republic of Vietnam

(1) Size Category (n) (hectares)	(2) Number of Owners	(3) Percent of owners $(X_n - X_{n-1})$	(4) Cumulative % of owners (X_n)	(5) Area owned (hectares)	(6) Percent of area $(Y_n - Y_{n-1})$	(7) Cumulative % of area (Y_n)	(8) $(Y_n + Y_{n-1})$ from col.(7)	(9) $(X_n - X_{n-1}) \times (Y_n + Y_{n-1}) =$ Columns (3)x(8)
1. 0.1-4.9	183,670	72.44	72.44	360,000	16.44	16.44	16.44	1190.9
2. 5.0-9.9	37,110	14.64	87.08	284,000	12.97	29.41	45.85	671.2
3. 10.0-49.9	26,840	10.59	97.67	526,000	24.02	53.43	82.84	877.3
4. 50.0-99.9	3,550	1.40	99.07	273,000	12.47	65.90	119.33	167.1
5. 100.0- up	2,330	0.92	99.99	747,000	34.11	100.01	165.91	152.6
TOTALS	253,500	99.99		2,190,000	100.01			3059.1

Gini Index = $1 - .3059 = .6941$ Average per owner = 8.64 hectares

SOURCE: Columns (1) through (7) are obtained from William Bredo, et. al., Land Reform in Vietnam, Working Papers, (Menlo Park, Calif.: Stanford Research Institute, 1968), Vol. IV, Part I, Annex Table A-2, and are from a 1955 study of 14 provinces in the Southern Region by the Directorate of Land Administration.

Table 3-4

Land Ownership Distribution in the Southern Region, 1966, Including Owners Only

Republic of Vietnam

(1) Size Category (n) (hectares)	(2) Number of Owners	(3) Percent of Owners $(X_n - X_{n-1})$	(4) Cumulative % of owners (X_n)	(5) Area owned (hectares)	(6) Percent of area $(Y_n - Y_{n-1})$	(7) Cumulative % of area (Y_n)	(8) $(Y_n + Y_{n-1})$ from col. (7)	(9) $(X_n - X_{n-1}) \times (Y_n + Y_{n-1}) =$ Column (3) x (8)
1. 0.1-0.4	24,185	13.1	13.1	6,046	0.6	0.6	0.6	7.9
2. 0.5-0.9	24,972	13.5	26.6	18,729	1.9	2.5	3.1	41.9
3. 1.0-2.9	68,001	36.7	63.3	136,003	13.9	16.4	18.9	693.6
4. 3.0-4.9	27,681	14.9	78.2	110,722	11.3	27.7	44.1	657.1
5. 5.0-9.9	22,850	12.3	90.5	171,378	17.6	45.3	73.0	897.9
6. 10.0-19.9	10,592	5.7	96.2	158,869	16.3	61.6	106.9	609.3
7. 20.0-29.9	2,931	1.6	97.8	73,261	7.5	69.1	130.7	209.1
8. 30.0-49.9	2,043	1.1	98.9	81,710	8.4	77.5	146.6	161.3
9. 50.0-99.9	1,389	0.8	99.7	104,140	10.7	88.2	165.7	132.6
10. 100.0-114.9	143	0.1	99.8	15,443	1.6	89.8	178.0	17.8
11. 115.0- up	419	0.2	100.0	92,449	10.2	100.0	189.8	38.0
TOTALS	185,206	100.0		975,750	100.0			3466.5

Gini Index = 1 - .3467 = .6533   Average per owner = 5.27 hectares

SOURCE: Columns (1) through (7) are obtained from William Bredo, et. al., Land Reform in Vietnam, Working Papers, (Menlo Park, Calif.: Stanford Research Institute, 1968), Vol. IV, Part I, Annex Table A-2, and are based on 1966 land tax records sampled from 15 Provincial Tax Offices in the Southern Region.

The Gini index for the 1955 land distribution is .694, while for 1966 it is .653. This implies a 5.9 percent decline in ownership concentration, as measured by the index, during the intervening period, presumably due primarily to the Diem land reform measures. It should be noted, however, that the same lack of detail in the data in the first size category of the 1955 table that causes the Lorenz curves to cross also biases the Gini 1955 index downward, since with the smaller categories the 1955 curve would probably stay below the 1966 curve and its index number would be larger. These Lorenz curves are only approximations of the true curves, and the smaller the size brackets used, the closer will the approximation be to reality.

The traditional usage of Lorenz curves and Gini indices to represent land ownership distribution, as discussed above, does not adequately tell the story of a land reform program, however, since it demonstrates the skew of inequality at each period of time only among owners, ignoring the number of landless tenants on the land. The two Lorenz curves in Figure 3-1 are not really comparable, since the number of people they represent as owners varies considerably in absolute terms and in proportion both to the total amount of land and to the total number of people who have a vital interest in how the land is used (the farmers). The 1955 ownership titles averaged 8.64 hectares per owner, while in 1966, after the Ordinance 57 land reform, the average had been reduced to 5.27 hectares per owner. Furthermore, the proportion of landless farmers, those who rented all the land they tilled, was reduced by probably around 10 percent. The 1960-61 Census reported 44.4 percent of the farmers in the Southern Region as landless tenants.[88] Since the census was conducted about half-way through the Diem land reform, this would suggest that about 46.7 percent of the farmers "rented only" in 1955, and that approximately 42.0 percent remained landless in 1966.

In this case the land reform had a limited, though measurable, impact on the skew of ownership distribution. It is entirely conceivable, however, for a significant land redistribution program (such as the Land-to-the-Tiller Program studied below) to result in an ownership distribution skew, as measured by the traditional Lorenz curve and Gini index techniques, identical with that of the pre-reform period, even though it drastically reduces the average size of plots owned, greatly increases the total number of landowners, and significantly reduces the proportion of landless tenants.

---

[88]See Table 3-2.

Lorenz curves can be derived to give a more complete picture of the actual inequalities existing before and after a land reform program by simply including as the first size category all those farmers owning no land at all. If, during a land reform program, any landlords were completely dispossessed they would revert to this zero landownership category, while their tenants would move into the ownership brackets. In this way the number of contemporary individuals represented on the horizontal axis can be held constant, just as a constant land area is represented on the vertical axis, rendering before-and-after curves logically comparable.

The effect and usefulness of this technique will become clearer in Chapter 5, below, when before-and-after data from the LTTT Program is analyzed. The more comprehensive curves for 1955 and 1966 are approximated in Figure 3-2, however, based on the estimated percentage of tenancy discussed above. (See Tables A-1 and A-2.)* When we include landless tenants in the first ownership bracket, the Gini index becomes .838 in 1955 and drops by only 4.6 percent to .799 in 1966.[89] For comparison, Figure 3-2 includes a curve representing the distribution of operating farm sizes,[90] irrespective of ownership, in 1968, which has a Gini index of .587. A pure "Land-to-the-Tiller Program," abolishing landlordism completely, with no retention limit for owner-operators and no distribution limit for tenant-recipients, would cause the ownership distribution curve to approach this latter one.

Conditions of Tenancy

Sample surveys conducted by the Stanford Research Institute and others in the late 1960's revealed a record of poor enforcement of the rent control and tenancy regulations decreed in the mid-1950's.[91] Five-year written contracts were required by law to end the practice of competitive evictions, but only 36.2 percent of the HRS tenants had written contracts in 1967.[92] Landlords confirmed this: only 33.3 percent of the HRS landlords[93] and 33.1 percent

*For "A" Tables, see Appendix C.

---

[89]This 4.6 percent figure is again too small, since the 1955 data still suffers from the same lack of detail noted above, giving its Gini index a downward bias.
[90]Based on Table A-3.
[91]See pages 45 and 46, above.
[92]Bredo, **Working Papers**, Vol. 4-2, Table 119, p. C-72.
[93]**Ibid.**, Vol. 4-2, Table 115, p. C-70.

Figure 3-2

**Lorenz Curves of Land Ownership Distribution
Among Owners and Tenants in the Southern Region,
South Vietnam, 1955 and 1966,
and Compared With Operating Farm Size in 1968**

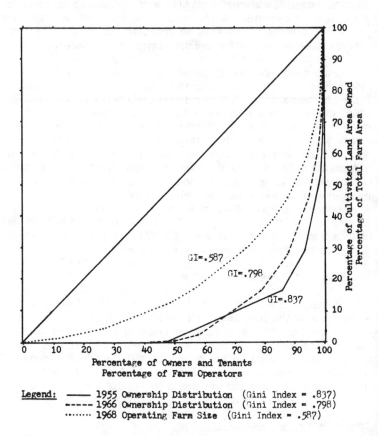

Legend: ——— 1955 Ownership Distribution (Gini Index = .837)
         – – – 1966 Ownership Distribution (Gini Index = .798)
         ······· 1968 Operating Farm Size (Gini Index = .587)

Sources: See Tables A-1, A-2 and A-3.

of the Absentee Landlord Survey (ALS)[94] respondents claimed to have signed written contracts with any of their current tenants. The eviction rate was very low and most tenants reported long-term or indefinite right of tenure,[95] but, as noted above, this was due more to the generally weakened positions of the landlords in the rural areas, thanks to the insurgency, than to the effectiveness of legal contract requirements.

The pre-emption rights reserved for tenants had little effect simply because Vietnamese landowners rarely sold land to anyone and were most reluctant to sell to their tenants, whom they regarded as their social inferiors. Culturally ingrained attitudes toward land and social status prevented the development of a land market following normal economic principles. Land was considered a sacred family possession, a heritage to be passed on from father to son and grandson. Each generation perceived it a religious duty to preserve its heritage intact—expanded, if possible, but never diminished—so that succeeding generations would have the strength to continue the family line and to maintain the prescribed altars and religious ceremonies in honor of the venerable ancestors. As is typical of a pre-modern society, land was the only form of wealth and security considered permanent.

Socially, considerations of status made land transactions between landlord and tenant extremely difficult, even if the former had been willing to sell. SRI put it this way:[96]

". . . even now a tenant would not approach his landlord directly concerning the purchase of land, because it would be a grave insult to the landlord. One reason is because an 'inferior' would be approaching a 'superior' with such an offer. A second reason is that the request would imply that the landlord had to sell his land because he was too poor to keep it. Conversely, a landlord cannot approach a tenant with an offer to sell land, because it would imply that he was in desperate financial stress and he would be demeaning himself to an 'inferior'. Therefore, in any case, an intermediary would have to

---

[94]Ibid., Vol. 4-2, p. B-35. Also conducted in 1967-8 by the Stanford Research Institute and the Center for Vietnamese Studies, the ALS included 187 interviews (162 in Saigon and 25 in Long Xuyen) with landlords who had lost land under the Ordinance 57 land reform.

[95]Ibid., **Summary Volume**, p. 22-23.

[96]Ibid., **Working Papers**, Vol. 4-1, p. 87-8.

be used, and the transaction would have to be handled with great delicacy."

Robert Sansom, in commenting on the absence of a land market, noted that in the two villages he studied no more than 7 land transactions had occurred in the previous 20 years (he was obviously excluding those occurring under the Ordinance 57 land reform). "Inquiries regarding the price of land brought puzzled expressions, an occasional reserved smile or chuckle, but usually no reply."[97]

Although rents were legally limited to 25 percent of the annual harvest, landlords continued to collect whatever the rental market and local security situation would allow, as discussed above.[98] The HRS found 16 percent of the tenants queried paid a certain share of the crop as rent, while 82 percent operated under fixed-rent agreements.[99] The landless tenants in the HRS paid an average of 34.5 percent of their total crop in 1966 rents (a bad year due to flood damage). The sharecropping arrangements in the Coastal Lowlands remained exempt from legal control; landlords typically received a 50 percent share of the harvest, while the proportion of operating expenses they shared varied.[100]

Finally, the law required landlords to grant tolerance to their tenants for crop failures, reducing rents on a graduated scale depending on the extent of the failure. Again the HRS suggested a dismal record of compliance, with 25 percent of the fixed-rent tenants who suffered a complete crop failure (due to floods) receiving no tolerance at all, and 37 percent of those who had suffered at least partial losses receiving no tolerance (79 percent of all tenants reported partial or total losses that year).[101]

Of all land estimated as rented after the 1960-61 Census, 17.3 percent was publicly owned land. Public land comprised 12.2 percent of all rented land in the Southern Region, but 52.9 percent in the Coastal Lowlands.[102] Most of this was classified as communal lands, which in 1960 totalled 284,340 hectares, or 8 percent of the cultivated area of South Vietnam.[103] Sixty-five percent of the

[97]Sansom, **Economics of Insurgency**, p. 74.

[98]See page 47-8, above.

[99]Bredo, **Working Papers**, Vol 4-2, Table 131, p. C-79.

[100]**Ibid., Summary Volume**, pp. 21-22.

[101]**Ibid., Summary Volume**, p. 22.

[102]Calculated from **Report of the Agricultural Census of Vietnam, 1960-61**, Table 10, p. 34.

[103]Bredo, **Working Papers**, Vol. 1-1, p. 107.

communal land area was under rice cultivation, and this represented 5.4 percent of the total riceland area in the Southern Region plus 28.3 percent of that in the Coastal Lowlands. A few provinces along the Central Coast had high ratios of communal land. Quang Tri led the field with communal land containing 90.2 percent of its riceland area, while Thua Thien and Binh Dinh followed with 49.6 percent and 38.5 percent, respectively.[104] In a more recent (1970) study of communal land use in the 5 northernmost provinces of South Vietnam, village officials reported 62 percent of all riceland as communal in Quang Tri, 64 percent in Thua Thien and 50 percent in the new Quang Nam.[105]

Most communal land plots in the South and about 25 percent of those along the Coast had been rented to the highest bidder, on leases ranging from 1 to 3 years, to provide village revenue. Official circulars issued in 1965 extended the Ordinance 2 rent and tenure controls to these lands, prohibiting competitive bidding, subleasing, and rental rates higher than 25 percent of the annual harvest, while exempting the other 75 percent (known as **quan cap dien**) along the coast. Despite these measures, competitive bidding and subleasing continued and illegally high rents were still collected by many village officials, who relied on them for their salaries and operating expenses.[106]

Quan cap dien (literally, "land to be distributed equally"), estimated as 75 percent of all communal land in the Coastal Lowlands and found by Fitzgerald and Bush to be about 80 percent in their 5 provinces, has traditionally been leased at token rental rates to village natives and/or residents for social welfare purposes. The land was either assigned to all eligible adults in equal shares or by periodic lotteries, or it was reserved for hardship families according to a system of welfare priorities, which varied somewhat from place to place, but which normally placed families of deceased

---

[104]Calculated from data in **Report of the Agricultural Census of Vietnam, 1960–61, Summary Volume**, p. 81.

[105]Quang Tin reported 10 percent, Quang Ngai 28 percent. In the old (1960) Quang Nam Province 16.9 percent of all riceland was communal, but it had been split into 2 smaller provinces by 1970—Quang Nam and Quang Tin—Edward T. Fitzgerald and Henry C. Bush, **Village Use of Communal Rice Land in Quang Tri, Thua Thien, Quang Nam, Quang Tin and Quang Ngai Provinces, Vietnam.** (Saigon: Control Data Corp., December 1970), p. 10.

[106]Ibid., p. 4, and Bredo, **Summary Volume**, pp. 80-3, 128, and **Working Papers**, vol. 1-2, p. H-54.

or disabled war veterans and other victims of war at the top. Subleasing was permitted in some cases.[107]

Another category of public domain was "concession land," essentially undeveloped land for which title had never yet been granted to a private individual or had reverted back to the state due to non-compliance with the law (that a concession must be brought under cultivation within a specified period after the grant). By 1967 some 33,852 squatters had been identified as occupying 274,945 hectares, about 119,000 ha. of it cultivated, and had filed claims for an even larger area, averaging more than 10 hectares each. A nationwide total of around 180,000 squatters was estimated, however, composed mostly of refugees occupying both public and private land. By definition, squatters were people occupying land without legal status and without paying rents. Laws decreed in 1964 established procedures for granting ownership titles to those on public domain without compensation, but by July 1968 titles for only 3,052 ha. had been approved.[108]

The Role and Contribution of the Landlord

Both of the two major surveys conducted in 1967-68, one with hamlet residents and the other with absentee landlords, confirmed the conclusions of earlier studies that Mekong Delta landlords were making almost no contribution to agricultural production, providing no significant services or financial support to their tenants.[109] For example, only 4 percent of the tenants interviewed had borrowed money from their landlords.[110] It was also evident that landlords had not only suffered declining revenues from their land in recent years, but they had lost their once considerable clout in political and social affairs, as well. Both resident and absentee landlords remarked on their loss of influence with and respect from their tenants over the last 10 years, and no one at hamlet level thought the landlords still exerted much influence in the village council.[111]

According to another survey conducted in December 1969-January 1970, only 10 percent of the village and hamlet officials in the Mekong Delta were landlords, while 29 percent of them were

---

[107]Fitzgerald & Bush, **Village Use of Communal Riceland**, p. 10-15.

[108]Bredo, **Summary Volume**, p. 79, 127; **Working Papers**, Vol. 1-1, p. 105, and Vol. 1-2, p. G-14.

[109]Ibid., **Summary Volume**, p. 176.

[110]Ibid., **Working Papers**, Vol. 4-1, p. 78.

[111]Ibid., **Summary Volume**, pp. 175-7.

tenants.[112] This survey did not inquire into the tenure status of relatives of village officials—an important omission in Vietnam, where families are large and even distant kinship ties are important, and where wealthy landlords seldom cared to bother themselves with direct administrative responsibilities at village level anyway, but would instead use their influence to obtain key positions for their younger kinsmen. It did indicate, however, that relatively few local officials would suffer direct losses from a program to redistribute land to the cultivators, and that landlord influence over local affairs, if it still existed, was at least indirect. The sample of local officials included a high proportion (47 percent) of tenants and owner-operators, although some of these would have been related to and sympathetic with landlords.

In former times many villages were controlled by large, absentee landlords, who concerned themselves with the politics of the district seat or province capital of their residence, and who assured the appointment of, not their own relatives, but their own more "trusted" tenants to key positions in the village government. Since in those days tenants lived in almost mortal fear of their landlords, this simple expedient assured that the landlord's wishes would be followed in village affairs.[113] So even the appearance of unrelated tenants on the village councils could not have been construed as proof of landlord impotence.

This survey demonstrated that the self-interest of local officials was not strongly biased against the radical Land-to-the-Tiller Program they were about to be asked to administer. Even if a tenant-official were a "trusted" (fearful?) representative of his landlord's interests, he would nevertheless have a strong self-interest in seeing that a Land-to-the-Tiller Program was successfully implemented and that it not be thwarted. The landlords' hold over their tenants and over the village councils had already suffered a drastic decline, as discussed elsewhere in this volume, a fact that this survey of local officials confirmed.

---

[112]A total of 697 village officials and hamlet chiefs were interviewed in 131 villages in five Delta provinces: Chau Doc, Chuong Thien, Go Cong, Long An and Phong Dinh. Of these, 10 percent were landlords, 18 percent owner-operators, 29 percent tenants, 37 percent neither landlords nor farmers, and 7 percent owners of abandoned land.   Edward T. Fitzgerald, Henry C. Bush, E. Eugene Dayoff and Vilis Donis. **Land Ownership and Tenancy Among Village and Hamlet Officials in the Delta.** (Saigon: Control Data Corp., March, 1970), pp. i-ii.

[113]As explained to the author by elderly village residents in 3 different villages.

Pressures for More Land Reform

Land-based grievances alone did not cause the South Vietnamese peasants to rise up in revolt, but they were undoubtedly one more element in the nationalistic, anti-colonialist appeal of the Viet Minh and their successors, the National Liberation Front (NLF). The latter, lacking the clear-cut colonialist issue of the earlier Viet Minh, placed more emphasis on the faults of the Saigon regime. The exploitative, oppressive nature of the landlord-tenant system, as it operated in the Southern Region, was an issue of immense emotional appeal among the rural population, and its propaganda value was appreciated by the insurgents.

The GVN found itself backed into the landlord's corner, upholding the legal rights of the wealthy few, while the NLF championed the cause of the numerous, downtrodden tenant-farmers. Local government officials, supported by military units, became rent-collectors both for absentee landlords, so that they could in turn collect the land tax (plus a 30 percent commission on rents) from the landlords, and for the government itself on vast tracts of undistributed former-French and Ordinance 57 land (the provincial treasury retained 40 percent of these rents, with 60 percent due Saigon).[114]   The NLF could easily include corruption among their charges, for everyone could see government officials collecting rent on public land that was supposed to have been distributed.[115]

In 1965 the government decided to distribute former French land in accordance with Ordinance 57 procedures,[116] and thus took another small step toward meeting these complaints.   Land tenure problems and their possible solutions remained on the back burner in Saigon, however, in part because the American establishment, whose blessing and money were needed for any new program of major emphasis,[117] "did not believe that land-based grievances were important," deluding themselves with, among other things, a specious statistical study by a Rand Corporation analyst purporting to show that land-related issues were not important sources of insurgent

---

[114]None of the former-French land was distributed until 1966, and distribution of expropriated land under Ordinance 57 all but ceased after 1961, the year province authorities were first permitted to collect rents on it.   Sansom, **Economics of Insurgency**, pp. 66-8; Bredo, **Summary Volume**, pp. 74, 78, and **Working Papers**, vol. 1-2, pp. E-80, F-15.

[115]Bredo, **Summary Volume**, p. 130.

[116]**Ibid.**, p. 78.

[117]No. U.S. funds or advisors were provided to help the land reform effort from 1961 through 1965. **Ibid.**, p. 120.

support.[118] Robert Sansom concluded that high American officials could not understand the dominant role of land in the Vietnamese economic, social, political, and cultural context and that they suffered from "an ideological desire to condemn the Viet Cong," refusing the credit the Viet Cong with a program truly beneficial to the peasants. The lack of understanding was enhanced by bureaucratic ignorance in both Saigon and Washington, perpetuated by the short duration of assignments to Vietnam.[119]

Another writer noted the existence of a "'loyal opposition' which steadfastly argued for a vigorous programme . . . aided . . . by congressional investigations in the United States into American inaction in the area of land reform, by strong lobbying efforts by advocates of land reform outside the government, and by routine transfers out of the American Mission in Saigon of personnel opposed to further efforts in this area."[120] The Stanford Research Institute prefaced part of their study by remarking,[121]

"There has been much controversy as to whether extending more land ownership to farmers in the ricelands of Vietnam would assist in pacification . . .

---

[118]Sansom, **Economics of Insurgency**, p. 229-30, referring to Edward J. Mitchell, "Land Tenure and Rebellion: A Statistical Analysis of Factors Affecting Government Control in South Vietnam," RAND Memorandum 5181-ARPA, Santa Monica, California, June 1967; which was summarized in **Asian Survey**, Vol. VII, (August, 1967): pp. 1577-580; reported in the **New York Times**, (October 16, 1967); and published as "Inequality and Insurgency: A Statistical Study of South Vietnam," in **World Politics**, Vol. XX, no. 3, (April, 1968): pp. 421-438. Mitchell's study was used as a bad example—how **not** to use multiple regression techniques—in a social statistics course at Harvard University in the summer of 1970. It has been attacked both in print and in unpublished papers. The field research of Robert Sansom and the Stanford Research Institute apparently helped turn official positions around, as the resulting Land-to-the-Tiller Program is ample evidence.
Two other published critiques of Mitchell's analysis are: Jeffery M. Paige, "Inequality and Insurgency in Vietnam, A Re-analysis," **World Politics**, Vol. 23, (October, 1970), pp. 24-37; and Dennis Paranzino, "Inequality and Insurgency in Vietnam: A further Re-Analysis," **World Politics**, Vol. 24, (July, 1972): pp. 565-78.
[119]Sansom, **Economics of Insurgency**, pp. 233-6.
[120]Race, Jeffrey, "The Battle Over Land," **Far Eastern Economic Review**, (August 20, 1970), pp. 19-22.
[121]Bredo, **Working Papers**, Vol. 4-1, pp. 81-2.

" . . . Basic to the issue is the peasants' attitude towards land ownership.

"One view is that the farmer of Vietnam, steeped in a long heritage as a tenant, has no understanding of land ownership and what it can mean to him, and that he would therefore be satisfied with tenancy subject to full security of tenure rather than ownership. Another view is that land ownership to the farmer of Vietnam constitutes a vital issue that has great and fundamental meaning to him. According to this view, the Vietnamese farmer's whole idea of social justice is inextricably intertwined with the basic urge to own land, and to him permanent occupancy with security of tenure can never be counted as an adequate substitute for land ownership."

The Hamlet Resident Survey included questions designed to test the desire of farmers to own land and thereby to shed some light on this controversy. Of the 235 tenants and owner-tenants responding, 85 percent would rather purchase land in 12 annual installments than rent it with permanent occupancy.[122]

"The responses to the survey give overwhelming empirical evidence of the desire of the landless farmers in the Southern Region to own land. The overwhelming proportion of those who say they want to own land and the consistency among them in this desire—regardless of conditions of sale—are rarely seen in sample surveys of this type.

"The desire of farmers to own land is closely intertwined with their attachment to the soil where they live. A tenant living in a thatched hut on one-third of a hectare expressed this vividly and simply to an American member of the team. To the initial question: 'Do you want to own the land you till, and to have legal title to it?', the immediate response was, 'Yes'. To the second question, 'Why do you want to own it?', the response was equally unhesitating: 'Because my ancestors lived here and because to own it will secure my future.' With a few words he linked ownership to his past, present, and future.

"This feeling about land has been called by a Vietnamese colleague an obsession of the farmers of the

---

[122]Ibid., **Summary Volume**, p. 172.

Delta. From another point of view, land ownership is a sheer economic necessity. When the farm laborer or the tenant becomes too old to work, he has no source of income since he has no land to rent out and most likely he has accumulated no life savings. He becomes economically dependent on someone else, generally a member of his family. The ownership of land takes care of the past, his ancestors; the present, his livelihood; and the future, his descendants; and provides assurance that his descendants will take care of him and that they will continue to venerate their ancestors."[123]

In another question farmers were asked whether they would prefer to own riceland or to have a job in the city, and again riceland ownership was the overwhelming choice—86 percent of the owners, 100 percent of the owner-tenants, 97 percent of the tenants and 87 percent of the farm workers rejected the city in favor of owning land.[124]

In an open-ended question about "what needed to be done in the village to improve life for themselves and their families" and in other questions comparing different types of governmental assistance, land ownership was always given the highest priority. SRI concluded, "Next to security it seems that the farmer wants ownership above everything else that the government can provide."[125]

A related question asked in what order of priorities should land be distributed to potential recipients. The respondents were practically unanimous—96-97 percent gave the same listing—in assigning first priority to landless farm workers, second to tenants with little land and third to owners with little land. SRI pointed out that this "rural conception of social justice" is consistent with land redistribution policies of the Viet Cong, but not with those of the GVN.[126]

On the opposite side of the field, resident landlords spoke of a reluctance to sell their land equal to the eagerness of tenants to buy—92 percent of the HRS landlords were unwilling to sell for cash at a fair market price.[127] Among large absentee landlords,

---

[123]Ibid., **Working Papers**, vol. 4-1, pp. 83-4.
[124]Ibid., **Summary Volume**, p. 54.
[125]Ibid., **Summary Volume**, p. 173.
[126]Ibid., **Summary Volume**, p. 171-2.
[127]Ibid., **Summary Volume**, p. 172, **Working Papers**, vol. 4-2, p. C-119, Table 204. These were all resident landlords.

however, beset with rent collection difficulties and declining land revenues, the reluctance to sell was waning. Only 17 percent of the ALS landlords declared an unwillingness to sell for any price, and only 20 percent indicated implacable opposition to a new land redistribution program.[128] It is from the latter group of landlords and their wealthy, urban relatives that any effective opposition to renewed land reform efforts would have been expected to come; and in this light these survey results had special significance.

It must be emphasized that the SRI surveys were conducted entirely in the Southern Region of South Vietnam. No one had asked similar questions of tenants and landlords in the Coastal Lowlands before the Land-to-the-Tiller Program.[129] A pair of 1970 studies on communal land (conducted before it was distributed) revealed widely divergent attitudes about it between the two regions, however. Out of 676 villagers interviewed in 5 provinces along the Central Coast, only 24 percent favored the distribution of communal land (which represented 55 percent of all rented land in those provinces in 1960-61) to the current tillers; whereas 76 percent of the 269 villagers interviewed in Long An Province (where 10 percent of all rented land in 1960-61 was communal) were in favor of it.[130]

While communal land provided some village revenue in both regions which would have to be replaced if it were distributed, Dr. Henry C. Bush concluded that the major differences between the two regions lay in the fact that along the Central Coast communal land provided basic welfare security, perpetuated traditional ties to one's birthplace and reinforced religious ties among villagers by symbolizing a common ancestry, thus serving as a considerable factor in the maintenance of social cohesion, whereas in the Southern Region (as represented by Long An) communal land did none of these things. He expressed fears of creating "a social hiatus" in Central Vietnam if communal land were distributed as planned, but not in the Mekong Delta.[131]

---

[128]Ibid., **Working Papers**, Vol. 4-2, pp. 54-55, questions 104 and 110.

[129]For the results of a subsequent study see **Obstacles to the Land-to-the-Tiller Program in Coastal Central Vietnam** by Dr. Henry C. Bush (Saigon: Control Data Corporation, June, 1973).

[130]Fitzgerald and Bush, **Landownership and Tenancy**, pp. 27-8, and Henry C. Bush, **Village Use of Communal Rice Land in Long An Province, Vietnam,** (Saigon: Control Data Corporation, January, 1971), p. 17. (1960-1 percentages calculated from the **Agricultural Census, 1960-61**, p. 34.)

[131]Fitzgerald and Bush, **Land Ownership and Tenancy**, pp. iv-v and 34-5 and Bush, **Village Use of Communal Riceland**, pp. 22-3.

President Nguyen Van Thieu and his newly appointed Minister of Land Reform and Agricultural Development, Cao Van Than, rather suddenly decided to propose a strong program of land redistribution in late 1968.   Due largely to their continued support as the draft made its way through the legislative process, the final law passed by the National Assembly was in much the same form as originally proposed, despite the seriously weakened version initially approved by the Lower House.

The next chapter will discuss details of the new law and its legislative history. It was designed to rely heavily on village officials for implementation and to free rural areas from any remaining domination by urban landlords, reinforcing other measures adopted in 1966 and 1967 to decentralize governmental authority and give greater responsibilities to village officials.   Popular elections of local officials were decreed in December 1966, as a measure of self-government was returned to the villages; and a 1967 tax regulation provided that all garden and riceland taxes were to be retained by the village for local projects and operating expenses, instead of the previous rate of about 8 percent, thus restoring a measure of fiscal autonomy to the village and preparing the way for local developmental projects in the future.[132]

---

[132]Bredo, **Summary Volume**, pp. 77, 108-9, 136, and **Working Papers**, vol. 2, pp. 109-10.

Chapter IV

LAND-TO-THE-TILLER

The Law

On March 26, 1970, President Thieu signed Law No. 003/70 in Can Tho, promulgating a new Land-to-the-Tiller Program for South Vietnam.[1] The provisions of this law went farther than the revolutionary land reform program of the Viet Cong. Where the VC were careful to "seek solidarity with the middle peasants" in many areas, permitting small owners (with less than 25 hectares) to keep their rented land if they reduced rents and paid VC taxes,[2] the government program sought to eliminate tenancy altogether, expropriating and redistributing all land not directly cultivated by the owner (except for small amounts of ancestor worship land). Furthermore, the National Liberation Front granted new ownership rights on a provisional basis only, contingent upon continued, active support for their cause;[3] whereas the GVN Land-to-the-Tiller Program granted definitive titles to all current tillers, regardless of their legal status upon the land or of their alignment in the civil war. As one farmer in Dinh Tuong Province explained the difference, "If a Viet Cong land recipient dies or gets killed, the VC will often redistribute his land to another cadre in reward for services, leaving the widow and children of the deceased cadre landless, while on the GVN side the widow and children would inherit the land."

The new law allowed a retention limit of only 15 hectares, and that only where the owners themselves cultivated the land. No one but religious organizations could retain ownership of any rice or secondary crop land which he did not cultivate himself, except for up to 5 hectares of ancestral worship land and cemetery land already so designated and registered.[4] All government-owned

---

[1] See Appendix A for an English translation of the entire law.

[2] See Pike, **Viet Cong,** p. 278, and Sansom, **Economics of Insurgency,** p. 60.

[3] Jeffrey Race, **War Comes to Long An,** (Berkeley: University of California Press, 1972), p. 272.

[4] This exception included **Huong-Hoa,** land left by parents to their descendants for the worship of ancestors, **Hau-Dien,** land given by an individual to the village/community on the condition that the village/community shall worship him or his parents after his death, and **Tu-Duong** or **Ky-Dien,** land given by an individual to the community to be used for worship. See Bredo, **Working Papers,** v.

riceland, including communal lands, were to be deeded over to cultivators. Unlike the Diem land reform, this law was designed to eliminate tenancy throughout the Republic—even in the sharecropping, small-landlord areas of the Coastal Lowlands, areas untouched by previous reforms.

Ownership of land, for purposes of expropriation and compensation, was to be based only on transfers registered before March 26, 1970, thus reducing opportunities for last minute transfers to one's relatives and close friends.

Recipients were to receive land free of charge to a maximum of three hectares per family in the South, one hectare in central Vietnam. No fee was to be charged for the transfer of land, and recipients were exempted from any land tax for one year. No person was to receive land unless he cultivated it himself, and he was forbidden to resell it for 15 years. The current tillers of the land had first priority to receive title to it, regardless of whether their present occupancy was considered legal. Persons who had already received land under Ordinance 57 or the French purchase agreement were exempted from payment of any balance due.

Former landlords were to be compensated at a rate equal to 2-1/2 times the average annual paddy yield of their land (averaged over the last 5 years). They were to be paid 20 percent in cash and the rest in government bonds bearing 10 percent interest and amortized over eight years. These bonds could be transferred and used to pay land taxes or to buy shares in private or national enterprises.

The President was given wide authority to implement the new law by decree, and stiff penalties were provided for obstructing its implementation or violating its provisions.

Estimates of the number of tenants who would ultimately receive title to land varied from 500,000 to one million, while the amount of land transferred was expected to be close to one million hectares.[5] The cost was estimated as at least US $400 million,

---

(cont.)
1-2, p. E-6.
[5]According to MacDonald Salter, "it could benefit as many as 500,000 tenant farmers by transferring them to some 900,000 hectares of privately owned lands." William Bredo speaks of "the creation of up to a million new land owners," while the **Viet-Nam Bulletin** expects 800,000 recipients of one million hectares of land. MacDonald Salter, "Ther Broadening Base of Land Reform in South

while the amount of outside assistance was uncertain.[6] The announced goal was to complete all administrative tasks connected with the transfer of ownership by the end of 1973, using aerial photography to identify land boundaries and computers to print the titles.

Legislative History

The key provisions of the law differed very little from the original executive proposals, despite a serious attempt by the Lower House to substitute a much weaker version. The Lower House Committee on Agriculture reported its own bill, which was substantially adopted and sent to the Senate, after considering three different land reform proposals.[7]

The first proposal, introduced on January 22, 1969, by 3 senators and 25 representatives, would have merely reduced the Ordinance 57 retention limit from 100 to 30 hectares (10 in the Coastal Lowlands), selling the excess to tenants as before, regularized squatter's rights (which the government was already doing), and organized cooperatives and demonstration farms to speed agricultural development. It was recognized as a very weak and ineffective program, benefiting only about 84,000 families at the most.

A radical proposal was introduced by 3 senators on June 6, 1969, calling for the nationalization of all farmland, private and communal, rented and owner-operated alike, and its free redistribution in plots of equal size to all farmers desiring to cultivate it. Farmer's associations would be organized in every village to supervise cultivation and to supervise the consolidation of small plots for mechanized operations. This bill was considered

---

(cont.)
Vietnam," p. 733, and William Bredo, "Agrarian Reform in Vietnam: Vietcong and Government of Vietnam Strategies in Conflict," p. 750, both in **Asian Survey**, (August, 1970); and "Land Reform in RVN," **Viet-Nam Bulletin** (Washington, D. C.: Embassy of Viet-Nam, Vietnam Information Series 27, March, 1970).

[6]**Viet-Nam Bulletin**, p. 7.

[7]Summaries of these proposals were presented in the "Report of the Lower House Committee on Agriculture" appearing in the **Bien Ban Phien Hop cua Ha Nghi Vien (Session Minutes of the Lower House)**, So: 63/69/H/BB/DB, Ha Nghi Vien, Viet-Nam Cong Hoa (Lower House, Republic of Vietnam), August 25, 1969, (mimeographed), pp. 8-15.

unrealistic, too difficult and too disruptive to implement under present conditions.

The executive proposals were transmitted to the Lower House on July 7, 1969. Its main provisions were: to abolish the landlord-tenant system, declaring the rental of riceland illegal; to transfer ownership of all riceland, including communal and all other publicly-owned riceland, not directly cultivated by its owner to the current tillers, regardless of the latter's legal status on the land, free of charge, up to a limit of 3 or 5 hectares per family; to compensate expropriated owners with 20 percent in cash, 80 percent in rice bonds to be amortized over 8 years with 5 percent interest; and to permit a maximum retention limit of 30 hectares on land directly cultivated by the owner.

After nine days of often stormy debate, the House (on September 9) passed a land reform bill which would have permitted an unconditional retention limit of 15 ha. in the Southern Region and Central Highlands, 5 ha. along the Central Coast, plus another 15 ha. per extended family (**gia toc**) of ancestor worship land (if legally designated as such before the promulgation of the law). Village-owned communal land was specifically exempted, although other public lands were to be distributed.   First priority in distribution was reserved for tenants **legally** tilling the land, and fourth priority for returning refugees, thereby eliminating those placed on the land by the Viet Minh and the Viet Cong unless they had subsequently come to terms with the owner of record. (This would also have raised difficult legal questions for those tenants who held expired leases or only verbal agreements, should their landlords have decided to fight expropriation). Distribution limits were lowered to 3 ha. in the South and Highlands, 1 ha. along the Central Coast. Landlord compensation was to proceed at a much faster pace than the President proposed, with much larger initial cash payments.[8]   Separate chapters, dropped completely by the Senate, dealt with encouraging the cultivation of virgin land in the public domain and the consolidation and subsidized mechanization of small rice farms.[9]

---

[8]Cash payments were to cover 100 percent of the first 10 ha. expropriated, 50 percent of the next 20 ha., and 25 percent of everything over 30 ha., the remainder to be paid in rice bonds bearing 5 percent interest and maturing within 5 years.

[9]The final version of the bill as sent to the Senate by the Lower House can be found in "Report of the Lower House Committee on Agriculture", So: 72/69/H/BT, September 9, 1969, pp. 33-40.

The Senate version, which ultimately became law (since the Lower House lacked the two-thirds majority required to reject it), restored most of the key provisions as originally proposed by the executive, or with only slight modifications, and rejected most of the changes passed by the Lower House. There were four significant differences between the original executive proposal and the final Law No. 003/70: 1) the retention limit for land directly cultivated by the owner was lowered from 30 to 15 ha.; but, 2) each extended family (**gia toc**) was to be allowed to keep up to only 5 ha. of (rented) ancestor worship land, if legally designated as such before the promulgation date of the law, whereas all worship land had been exempted from expropriation in the executive proposal, up to the 15-hectare limit of Ordinance 57 still in effect; 3) redistribution limits to present tillers were reduced from "3 to 5 ha." to 3 ha. in the Southern Region and 1 ha. in Central Vietnam; and 4) the value of compensation bonds was to be stated in cash amounts instead of in terms of rice, thus deleting an important guarantee against the loss of real value due to inflation, although the annual rate payable on the bonds was raised from 5 to 10 percent. The Senate also added a provision specifying that the amount of landlord compensation would be calculated on the basis of 2.5 times the average annual yield of the land expropriated (as averaged over the last 5 years).

The first point of difference listed was not very important, since very few owner-operators in Vietnam were directly cultivating over 15 ha.; but the reduced retention of ancestor-worship-land was a significant defeat for the landlords, even though it still provided a loophole through which some families were able to retain sizeable amounts of land.[10] The conversion of rice bonds into cash bonds was an even bigger blow against landlord interests. Subsequent depreciation (due to inflation) of the real value of cash bonds eased the strain of compensation payments on the national treasury, but it also reduced the real amount of compensation received by the landlords, further decreasing their economic position in the society.

In response to the Lower House version of the bill, the government had indicated its willingness to pay 100 percent cash in compensation for the first 5 hectares in the Southern Region, 3 ha. in the Central Region, then 20 percent in cash and 80 percent

---

[10]See p. 324, below, for further discussion of the **Huong Hoa,** or ancestor-worship land, provision.

in rice bonds for the rest,[11] but the final Senate version contained no provision for full cash payment for small holdings nor for any part of larger holdings.

The reduction of the redistribution limit to 3 hectares in the South, as passed by the House and retained by the Senate, apparently did not seem very important at the time, since few tenant farmers operated more than 3 hectares over most of the Mekong Delta; but it subsequently caused considerable trouble and ill effects in the broadcast-rice areas, where farms did average larger than that.

Objectives and Expectations

In proposing the LTTT Program the GVN had three major goals in mind: 1) social justice, 2) agricultural development, and 3) political pacification.   Greater social justice would be achieved simply by abolishing the landlord-tenant system, thus reducing the exploitative features of the current system and enlarging the class of small, middle-class, owner-cultivator farmers. Land redistribution would enhance agricultural development programs by giving the farmers incentives of ownership to care for their land and enabling them to retain the total product of their labor and investment, which was expected to induce greater efforts to raise production and "provide the basis for a sound agricultural economy." Of more immediate concern, the program was expected to "undercut the Viet Cong land program and gain the farmers' political support," thus shortening the struggle to defeat the communists.[12]

These three basic goals were echoed in the halls of the National Assembly, where the most urgent goal was clearly recognized as

---

[11]From mimeographed comments and recommendations prepared by the Ministry of Land Reform and Agricultural Development for the Senate Committee on Agriculture, undated, titled "Bang Nhan Xet va De Nghi Tu Chinh Du Luat Cai Cach Dien Dia cua Ha Nghi Vien" (Table of Comments and Recommended Amendments for the Lower House Land Reform Bill), p. 12.

[12]"Vietnam Land-to-the-Tiller Plan Unprecedented," **Vietnam Bulletin,** Vol. V, No.15 (Washington, D.C.: Embassy of Viet-Nam, April 12, 1971), p. 3 and **Tai Lieu Giai Thich Luat Nguoi Cay Co Ruong** (Explanation of the Land-to-the-Tiller Law), Ministry of Information, updated pamphlet, p. 1.

the political—"to win the hearts of the people."[13] One Assemblyman cried out, " . . . a red wave is threatening to inundate the South, and here we have a program to block it . . . "[14]

Senator Trinh Quang Quy, the first to speak for the bill after floor debates were opened in the Senate, declared that making tenants into owners would give them economic independence and democratic freedom, leading to more stabilized rural conditions. He listed arguments from tenant spokesmen that the LTTT Program would create greater support for GVN and bring an earlier end to the war, largely **because** it would correct the social injustices of the old landlord-tenant system and give farmers ownership incentives to work harder, to increase production, and to fight to protect their neighborhoods—"leaving the Communists no place to stand."[15]

Senator Hoang Kim Quy echoed most of these sentiments in favor of the program and added that landlords could be encouraged to invest their compensation funds in domestic industry and thus stimulate more rapid economic development on another front.[16] Not all Assemblymen were convinced of the virtues of Land-to-the-Tiller, however. Shortly after Senator Quy called it a "social, democratic, and humanitarian revolution" of which the people would be proud,[17] Senator Tran Canh termed it "unpopular, socially destructive, sowing confusion in the countryside, and moreover uneconomic, immoral and counter-progressive as well."[18] Senator Canh expected strong landlord opposition to the expropriation of

---

[13]"Report of the Lower House Committee on Agriculture," **op. cit.,** p. 15 and 17; speech by Representative Danh Cuong, speaking for the House Committee on Agriculture, **Bien Ban Phien Hop cua Ha Nghi Vien, (Session Minutes of Lower House)** So:63/69/H/DB, (August 25, 1969), p. 19; and speech by Senator Trinh Quang Quy, **Bien Ban Phien Hop cua Thuong Nghi Vien (Session Minutes of the Senate),** So:06/70-TNV/BB, Thuong Nghi Vien, Viet-Nam Cong Hoa (The Senate, Republic of Vietnam), (March 2, 1970) (mimeographed) pp. 7 and 15.

[14]Representative Dang van Phuong, **Bien ban Phien Hop cua Ha Nghi Vien, (Session Minutes of the Lower House),** So: 65/69/H/BB/BT, (August 28, 1969), p. 48.

[15]He also took note of tenant vows to support the re-election of those Assemblymen who voted for the LTTT Program and, conversely, to work for the defeat of those who voted against it. Senator Trinh Quang Quy, **(Session Minutes of the Senate),** pp. 7 and 10.

[16]Senator Hoang Kim Quy, **Ibid.,** pp. 23-26.

[17]**Ibid.,** p. 20.

[18]Senator Tran Canh, **Ibid.,** p. 43.

their land would rise, "probably to the point of more bloodshed," in many rural areas.[19]

Several Assemblymen objected to what they considered negative political effects of the program. One described it as "just a tool to help Mr. Nguyen van Thieu's campaign (for re-election)," and did not think the government had the capability actually to implement it.[20]   Many expressed concern about financing landlord compensation, the political consequences of its inflationary impact and the pitfalls of increased reliance on American support.[21] Describing the manner in which dependence on foreign aid leads to foreign pressure on and influence over governmental activities, one senator groaned, "they will put a ring in our nose and lead us around like water buffalos."[22]   A member of the Lower House suspected the whole proposal was part of a secret plot to cause the Republic either to be overthrown or to fall completely under foreign domination.[23]

Doubts were expressed as to how much social justice would be achieved by a program that would "take land from our friends to give to our enemies."[24]   The Secretary General of the Lower House, Representative Tran Ngoc Chau, argued that to approve the bill at that time would actually cause even more injustice and confusion in the Vietnamese society, since it would take land away from soldiers and pro-government refugees, who fled the Viet Cong and/or were fighting on the government side, and distribute it to the communist sympathizers who remained behind. He wanted the matter postponed until after security had been restored and all who

---

[19]Ibid., p. 42.

[20]Representative Duong van Ba, **Session Minutes of the Lower House,** So:64/69/H/BB/BT (August 26, 1969), pp. 11-13, worries about inflation, p. 19.

[21]The U.S. had earmarked $40 million for direct support of the LTTT Program and had also promised to increase general budgetary support through the Commodity Import Program to help control the rate of inflation.

[22]Senator Vu Minh Tran, **Session Minutes of the Senate,** p. 146.

[23]Representative Le Quang Hien, **Session Minutes of the Lower House,** So:65/69/H/BB/BT, (August 28, 1969), p. 25.

[24]Loosely translated and paraphrased from Senator Tran Ngoc Oanh, **Session Minutes of the Senate,** p. 17.

desired to reclaim their farms could do so.[25]   Of course, there were many complaints about how unjust the program would be to landlords in general, taking away their private property.

In addition to the concern about the inflationary impact of the program, mentioned above, other economic arguments were raised in opposition. It was feared the fragmentation of land and the legal confirmation of the existing small-farm system would interfere with efforts to mechanize farm operations and would perpetuate inefficient farming methods,[26] even though Taiwan had been cited as an actual case where farms averaged smaller in size than in Vietnam, but where mechanization was nevertheless proceeding apace.[27]   Objections were raised (and sustained, in the Lower House) against distributing communal land on the grounds it provided needed revenue for village development projects,[28] despite assurances that there were other ways to raise revenue, such as with the general land tax.[29]   And there were those who disputed assertions that ownership incentives would cause former tenants to work harder and increase production. Senator Le Tan Buu believed to the contrary, that peasant farmers work harder in order to get enough to feed their families if they must pay rent first. He saw the demands of the rental contract as a sort of benign bondage forcing the tenant not to neglect his production activities.[30]

Still other Assemblymen argued that while they were not against the Land-to-the-Tiller Program in principle, they doubted

---

[25]Representative   Chau   estimated   there   were   700,000 government soldiers (70 percent of one million) and up to 4 or 5 million refugees who would lose their land. Representative Tran Ngoc Chau, **Session Minutes of the Lower House,** So: 63/69/H/BB/DB, (August 25, 1969), pp. 37-8 and So: 67/69/H/BB/BT, (September 2, 1969), pp. 7-8.

[26]Senator Tran Ngoc Oanh, **Session Minutes of the Senate,** p. 17.

[27]Representative Nguyen Hoang, Chairman of the Lower House Committee on Agriculture, **Session Minutes of the Lower House,** So: 70/69/H/BB/BT, (September 5, 1969), p. 44.

[28]Representative Dang van Phuong, **Ibid.,** So: 67/69/H/BB/BT, (September 2, 1969), p. 50.

[29]Representative Duong van Ba, **Ibid.,** So: 67/69/H/BB/BT, (September 2, 1969), p. 52.

[30]Senator Buu favored the nationalization of all farmland, the government renting it to farmers, encouraging them to form cooperatives for large-scale, mechanized farming, and using rent revenues for economic development projects. Senator Le Tan Buu, **Session Minutes of the Senate,** pp. 55-6.

the government could implement it effectively at this time and thought it should be postponed. One senator listed six obstacles to land reform: 1) the unstable political and military situation, 2) landlord opposition, 3) confused implementation by subordinate levels of government, 4) limited facilities and capabilities, 5) Viet Cong sabotage and 6) farmers' lack of confidence.[31] To this list another senator added the charge that corruption among government officials would block effective implementation.[32]

In contrast to these pessimistic sentiments, the (new) official American position was one of optimistic enthusiasm. It was succinctly stated by MacDonald Salter, an AID official in Washington:[33]

"The prospects for a successful program are good. Planning for implementation has been undertaken and experimentation has proven the feasibility of decentralized administration to the village level. The major efforts will be focused on the rapid transfer of land ownership, so that the tiller has control of the land and ceases to pay rent, followed by payment of compensation to the former landowner. Administrative simplicity is a major objective. For example, the government uses its authority to expropriate but does not take possession of

---

[31]Senator Hong Son Dong, **Session Minutes of the Senate**, p. 36.
[32]Senator Vu Minh Tran, **Ibid.**, p. 78, 145.   The Stanford Research Institute noted some of these problems in 1968. They cited personnel problems in the Land Affairs Service due to low salaries and per diem, large numbers being drafted, a low education level, excessive routine paperwork and a preoccupation with bureaucratic procedures. Cadastral surveys were being conducted on only 10,000 hectares a year, at which rate it would take 90+ years to complete the required survey work on land already designated for redistribution, to say nothing of a new program. SRI found that only about 1/3 of the villages maintained a land register, another 1/3 relied on the province land register, and the remaining 1/3 had none at all either in the village or at province level. With respect to rented land, only 1/3 of the villages had maintained an up-to-date lease contract register, as well. SRI also noted that "charges of corruption are often leveled at officials at the district and especially at province level, (but) rarely . . . at officials in the village or hamlet." William Bredo, et. al., **Summary Volume**, pp. 106, 109, 112, 119, and **Working Papers**, Vol. 4-1, p. 30.
[33]Salter was the Chief, Local Development Staff, Office of National Development, Bureau for Vietnam, U.S. Agency for International Development. Salter, **Asian Survey** (August, 1970), p. 734.

land. This time the land will be transferred directly to the tiller or other eligible farmer. Because land records are seriously deficient, aerial photography has been accepted as the prime basis for land identification. Title issuance will be expedited by application of computer technology.

"While this new and revolutionary land reform program was taking form a major effort was being carried out in the countryside, both to secure the areas from insurgent forces and influences, and to advance economic conditions. This has been highly successful—the small farmer now has the prospect of owning and controlling his own land, and of being provided with supporting institutions essential to his well-being as a farmer. Since the Vietnamese farmer is a good manager, whether he owns or rents his land, transference of ownership will not change the foci of entrepreneurial capability. Accordingly, land redistribution is a key factor in the complex institutional requirements for successful agrarian reform sought by President Thieu. Land reform will provide a firm foundation for rural development and will demonstrate graphically the Vietnamese Government's interest in providing real improvement in the lives of the rural population."

Writing in the same issue of **Asian Survey,** William Bredo, who directed the major research project on land tenure and reform in Vietnam by the Stanford Research Institute (discussed in Chapter 3, above), and Roy L. Prosterman, Associate Professor of Law at the University of Washington, who had participated in the SRI project as a consultant on land law, both expressed belief that, if implemented properly, the Land-to-the-Tiller Program would have a strong positive effect on the government's struggle to win political support in rural areas.[34]

At least one American observer was not so sure of the ultimate political impact, however, though he did not deny the importance of and the need for the program. Jeffrey Race, after conducting extensive field research into political problems and recent developments in Long An Province, concluded that the LTTT Program was "little more than the Saigon government's stamp of approval on

[34]Bredo, "Agrarian Reform in Vietnam: Vietcong and Government of Vietnam strategies in Conflict," pp. 738-750 and Roy L. Prosterman, "Land-to-the-Tiller in South Vietnam: The Tables Turn," pp. 751-764, both in **Asian Survey,** 10:8, (August, 1970).

a land redistribution already carried out by the (Communist) Party—in many cases a quarter of a century before."[35]

---

[35]Race, **Far Eastern Economic Review** (August 20, 1970), p. 273.

Chapter V

VILLAGE CASE STUDIES

Farmers were interviewed in the villages of **Khanh Hau,** Thu Thua District, Long An Province, **Long Binh Dien,** Cho Gao District, Dinh Tuong Province, **Phu Thu,** Chau Thanh District, Phong Dinh Province, and **Hoa Binh Thanh,** Chau Thanh District, An Giang Province. Khanh Hau represents the progressive and rich Upper-Delta single-transplant region just south of Saigon, where double-cropping with the new Miracle Rice strains has already become commonplace. Long Binh Dien is also in the Upper-Delta, single-transplant region, but it is much poorer and slower to adopt new techniques--Miracle Rice is being tried here, but hesitantly and with less satisfactory results. Phu Thu is in the Lower-Delta double-transplant[1] region and is the most isolated and poorest of the villages visited. Having no roads suitable for even motorbike traffic, it must rely exclusively on water transport; and double-cropping with Miracle Rice is still a new and experimental venture. Hoa

---

[1]The double-**transplant** method of cultivation should not be confused with double-cropping. The latter refers to the raising and harvesting of two complete crops per year, while the former refers to the method of planting a single crop of rice, traditional in a large part of the lower Mekong region, which involved transplanting the rice seedlings twice for each crop instead of once, as elsewhere, first from the initial seedbed into a larger area, and later from there into the whole paddy. Local farmers will tell you they obtain somewhat higher yields this way, although their labor costs are higher. More technical explanations are that it (1) is an important weed control device in an area where tough natural grasses grow rapidly, by giving rice plants a head start in fields which can be flooded to a higher level at the second transplanting; (2) facilitates water control by keeping the seedlings in a smaller area for a longer period, permitting easier irrigation if the rains fail in the early season (in an area where an early start is essential to keep the rice-plant growth above the high-water levels during the mid-rainy season); and (3) serves as a growth-control device counteracting the high organic nitrogen content of the soils in this region, using the shock of the second transplanting to reduce the growth of leaves and thereby permit more grain formation. (I am indebted to Professor Leslie Small, an agricultural economist at Rutgers University who has spent some time in this part of the Mekong Delta, for a discussion of these points, and especially for explaining the last one.)

RICELAND AREAS IN REPUBLIC OF VIETNAM

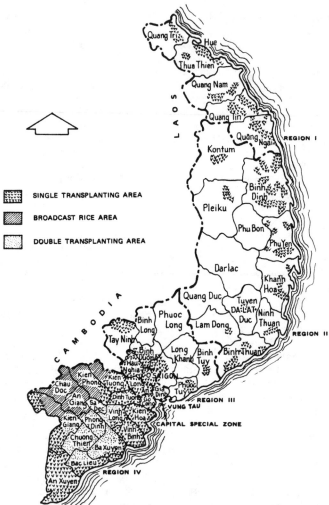

Source: William Bredo, et al., *Land Reform in Vietnam,* Summary Volume, Stanford
Research Institute, Menlo Park, Calif., 1968, p. 35.

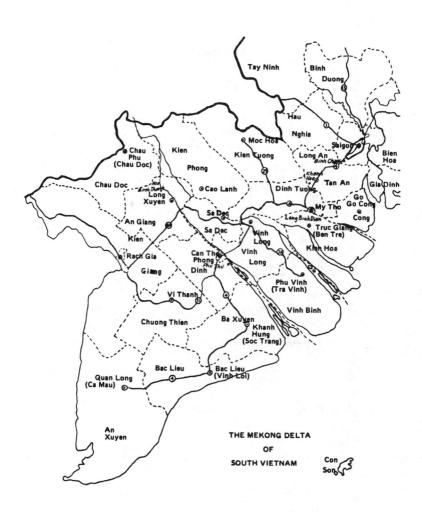

Tay Ninh

Binh
Duong

Hau
Nghia

Moc Hoa

Chau
Phu
(Chau Doc)

Kien

Phong

Kien Tuong

Long An
Binh Chanh

Saigon

Bien
Hoa

Chau Doc

Hoa
Binh Thanh

Long
Xuyen

Cao Lanh

Sa Dec

Dinh Tuong

Khanh
Hoa

Tan An

Gia Dinh

Go
Go Cong
Cong

An Giang

Sa Dec

My Tho

Long Binh Dien

Truc Giang
(Ben Tre)

Kien

Vinh
Long

Can Tho
Phong
Dinh

Phu Thu

Vinh
Long

Kinh Hoa

Giang

Rach Gia

Vi Thanh

Phu Vinh
(Tra Vinh)

Chuong Thien

Ba Xuyen

Khanh
Hung
(Soc Trang)

Vinh Binh

Quan Long
(Ca Mau)

Bac Lieu

Bac Lieu
(Vinh Loi)

An
Xuyen

THE MEKONG DELTA
OF
SOUTH VIETNAM

Con
Son

Table 5-1

Village Statistics

Village	Khanh Hau	Long Binh Dien	Phu Thu	Hoa Binh Thanh
Population	5,599	4,738	6,178	13,163
Number of Households	773	829	1,000	2,144
Residents per household	7.2	5.7	6.2	6.1
Area (ha.)	1,606	1,200	1,486	5,438
Cultivated riceland (ha.)	992	1,005	1,104	5,290
Distance from province capital (km)	4	11	4	9
Province capital	Tan An	My Tho	Can Tho	Long Xuyen
HES Security rating	A	B	B	A
Proportion of hamlets studied	5/5	4/7	2/4	7/7

SOURCE: Village offices.

Table 5-2

Progress of LTTT Program at Time of Visit

Village	Kharh Hau	Long Binh Dien	Phu Thu	Hoa Binh Thanh
Time of visit	11/71 -1/72	1-3/72	4-5/72	6-8/72
Official LTTT Goal (ha.)	500	600	1000	4100
--proportion of cultivated riceland	.50	.60	.91	.78
Land Subject to LTTT according to village officials (ha.)	316	600	600	2419
--proportion of cultivated riceland	.32	.60	.54	.46
LTTT title applications approved (ha.)	274	551	441	2158
--proportion of cultivated riceland	.28	.55	.40	.41
--proportion of land subject to LTTT	.87	.92	.74	.89
LTTT titles distributed (ha.)	247	524	411	1595
--proportion of cultivated riceland	.25	.52	.37	.30
--proportion of ha. approved for distribution	.90	.95	.93	.74
Number of LTTT applicants approved	224	481	464	1352[1]
--proportion of all households	.29	.58	.46	.63
Number of LTTT title recipients	214	428	464	1014[1]
--proportion of all households	.28	.52	.46	.47
--proportion of applicants approved	.96	.89	1.00	.75

[1]These were preliminary estimates, since the number of multiple applications for different plots of land by the same farmer was not known. The DGLA computer print-out for March 1973 listed HBT Village as having approved applications for 2241 ha. for 1197 different farmers and as having distributed titles for 1610 ha. to 877 different farmers.

SOURCE: Village offices.

Binh Thanh, in solid Hoa Hao and floating rice country, was the most secure village in the list, also the largest and the most diverse, but it possessed characteristics unique to this region which apparently caused the Land-to-the-Tiller Program to produce effects contrary to those in the other three villages.

All four villages were chosen for study because they were predominantly rural, far enough from the province capital not to be urban or suburban (but necessarily close enough for our daily journeys back and forth), and representative of different agricultural and economic conditions found in the Mekong Delta region.[2] Security was another necessary criterion, since the author and his wife had to walk unescorted throughout each village daily for about two months. These constraints in the selection of villages impose a decided bias in the study toward relatively secure, easily accessible areas. A sample size of four villages is too small to be representative of the whole Mekong Delta, in the first place, and this, coupled with the bias just mentioned, would make any attempt to generalize from the results of this study alone to the whole Delta rather hazardous.

Khanh Hau, Long An Province

Our first village was studied in depth in 1958-59 by a three-member team from the Michigan State University Advisory Group in Vietnam: anthropologist Gerald C. Hickey, economist James B. Hendry, and government specialist Lloyd W. Woodruff.[3] This previous research provides a basis from which to look for changes over time, in this case an intervening 13 years.

Khanh Hau straddles National Highway 4, the main route from Saigon south into the Delta, and lies about one hour by bus from Saigon, or about 50 km. The capital of Long An Province, Tan An, is about 4 km. up this same highway, and it serves as the main marketplace for Khanh Hau villagers, although a small, informal

---

[2]We deliberately chose villages where the LTTT Program was proceeding fairly well, in order to study its effects on the farmers. We did not focus on problems of implementation. (See Tables 5-1 and 5-2 for basic data on all four villages and on the progress of LTTT at the times of our visits.)

[3]Gerald C. Hickey, **Village in Vietnam**, New Haven, Yale University Press: 1964; James B. Hendry, **The Small World of Khanh Hau,** Chicago: Aldine Publishing Co., 1964; and Lloyd W. Woodruff, **The Study of a Vietnamese Rural Community — Administrative Activities,** 2 Vols., Saigon: 1960; Michigan State University Vietnam Advisory Group.

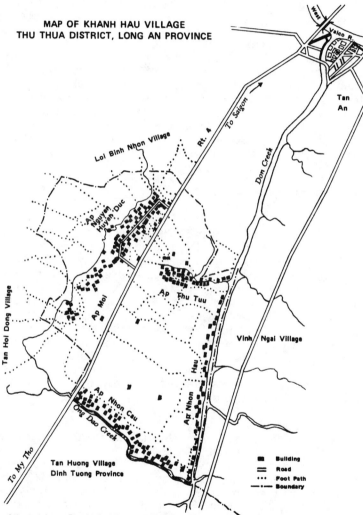

MAP OF KHANH HAU VILLAGE
THU THUA DISTRICT, LONG AN PROVINCE

Adapted from Gerald C. Hickey, *Village in Vietnam*, Yale University Press, New Haven, 1964, p. 2, and James B. Hendry, *The Small World of Khanh Hau*, Aldine Publishing Co., Chicago, 1964, p. 4.

market gathering can be observed in the village itself in the early morning hours.   Khanh Hau is a prosperous, progressive village. Most of its land was double-cropped and it enjoyed relatively greater security than most villages.   It had long been considered a model village, and government officials often used it as a showcase for foreign visitors.

Hendry noted in 1959 that it had better than average educational facilities, due partly to the presence of the Fundamental Education Center, sponsored by UNESCO, on village land.[4]   This Center has become the Long An Normal School, a junior-college-level facility for training elementary school teachers, and its students practice teaching in the Khanh Hau Elementary School.   In addition, new classrooms have been constructed and are in use for the first 2 or 3 grades in three of the outer four hamlets, so that only the older children must make the long walk across the highway to attend the central school.

Demographic Data

Population increased 73 percent (or at a whopping annual rate of 4.3 percent) from 1958 to its 1971 level of 5,595, but the number of households increased by only 31 percent, which means the number of persons residing in each household also rose, from an average 5.5 in 1958 to 7.2 in 1971.   An educated guess, based on observation in many of the homes we visited, is that many war widows and soldiers' wives, and their children, are living with older relatives, usually parents or parents-in-law, but sometimes brothers or sisters, instead of establishing separate homes with their husbands.   There has also been a movement away from peripheral areas, such as Moi and Nhon Hau Hamlets and more isolated neighboring villages, for security reasons, with many people living "temporarily" with relatives in the more secure areas, awaiting the day when they can return to their original homesites.

The statistics show that the number of girls and women increased by 99 percent over this 13-year period, while the male population rose by only 46 percent.   The female percentage of the total population rose from 51.1 percent in 1958 to 58.7 percent in 1971, while the male percentage declined from 48.9 to 41.3. Furthermore, the population of the central hamlet, Nguyen Huynh Duc, grew by 116 percent, while that of Ap Moi and Ap Nhon Hau grew by only 33 percent and 13 percent, respectively, partly as a result of forced relocations due to the now-defunct Strategic Hamlet Program.   (See Table 5-3.)

---

[4]Hendry, **Khanh Hau**, p. 23.

Table 5-3

Population Data - Khanh Hau Village

Hamlet	1958	Proportion of total	1971	Proportion of total	13-year Growth Rate
Nguyen Huynh Duc	1239	.38	2679	.48	1.16
Moi	373	.12	496	.09	.33
Thu Tuu	529	.16	892	.16	.69
Nhon Hau	636	.20	721	.13	.13
Nhon Cau	464	.14	807	.14	.74
Total Village	3241	1.00	5595	1.00	.73
Female	1655	.51	3286	.59	.99
Male	1586	.49	2309	.41	.46
No. of households	590		773		.31
Ave. household size	5.5		7.2		.31

SOURCES: 1958 -- Hendry, Khanh Hau, p. 11. 1971 -- Village office.

Table 5-4

Khanh Hau Interviewee Data

Total		15 present tenants	14 title recipients	15 owner-cultivators	44 Village
Interviewees:	Male	12	8	12	32
	Female	3	6	3	12
Average					
Age of interviewee:	Male	54.8	54.8	47.9	52.2
	Female	45.7	30.7	41.7	37.2
Education (yrs.):	Male	2.8	3.0	4.7	3.6
	Female	0.7	1.3	2.3	1.4
No. of household residents		7.3	7.7	9.7	8.3

The Village Office listed Khanh Hau residents as 42 percent Buddhist, 34 percent Confucian ancestor worship, 20 percent Cao Dai and 3.6 percent Christian (0.1 percent other) in 1971. The farmer sample we interviewed turned out to be 50 percent Buddhist, 14 percent Confucian ancestor worship, and 36 percent Cao Dai.

Sample Selection

Dividing 15 sets of interviews (3 to a set—one tenant, one LTTT-title recipient, and one owner-cultivator) among the 5 hamlets roughly according to their population,[5] we drew 7 farmers in Ap Nhon Cau.[6] By asking each farmer drawn for 2 others nearby (of different land tenure categories) to complete the set, we obtained 3 times this many interviews in each hamlet, plus one extra, for a village total of 46.[7]

Village officials felt it safe enough for us to walk unescorted everywhere in the village except that part of Ap Nhon Hau along the Don Creek (Rach Don), on the far eastern edge of the village. They explained that their concern in that area had nothing to do with the local residents, but that the Viet Cong could slip across the creek from the other side where sentiments were less pro-government. They offered to provide armed escorts so we could go safely, however, saying that the farmers themselves would feel better and worry less about possible trouble if 2 or 3 members of the village Popular Defense Force went along. If a VC did stick his head up out of the water, they said, and saw a couple of rifles, he would just quietly withdraw, whereas if he saw an American alone and unarmed, there might be trouble. Leaving his wife pursuing interviews in the central hamlet, the writer spent 3 days

---

[5]See Appendix B for a complete description of the selection process for our farmer interviews.

[6]The word "**ap**" means "hamlet."

[7]The extra interview occurred when one farmer who had been introduced as a tenant (and who referred to himself as such) turned out to have received title under the LTTT Program. Great efforts had been made to obtain an appointment with this busy farmer, so the interview was continued even though we had already completed enough of them in his category. Two new-owner interviews have been eliminated from most of our calculations as uncertain or mixed cases which reduced the total to 44—one was fighting her landlord in court over whether the land was Huong Hoa worship land and had not yet received title to it, although she had stopped paying rents, and the other worked land fairly equally divided among all 3 land tenure categories (owned, rented and just distributed under LTTT). (See Table 5-4.)

walking paddy dikes escorted by a couple of 15-year-old local kids and a PDF sergeant, each armed with a carbine, interviewing 4 farmers along the Don Creek (no escorts were required for 2 other interviews in Nhon Hau midway between the creek and the highway). There were no incidents and the reception was always friendly; but the rapport seemed more distant than normal in 2 or 3 of the cases, and there was more reason to suspect fudging on some of the answers, especially those involving personal wealth and production levels. Henceforth, we conducted interviews only in those areas where we could go unescorted.

Land Tenure

Before the 1958 Ordinance 57 land reform, Hendry found 73 to 77 percent of all farmers in Khanh Hau were tenants, depending on how many of the 20 resident landlords also farmed. The farmer group themselves comprised 59 to 62 percent of the 590 households, counting only farm operators, and not farm workers, as farmers.[8] The Ordinance 57 reform distributed 223 hectares to 147 tenants,[9] reducing estimated tenancy to 33-35 percent of the farmers. In 1971 village officials estimated 60-70 percent of all households were farmers, or around 500 of the 773 households, and that tenancy had climbed back up to about 60 percent of these, or to about 300 families.

At the time of our visit (Nov. 1971-Jan. 1972) the village had approved title applications from 250 tenants, and expected soon to process 24 more on communal land. Village officials estimated the number of tenants left after the LTTT Program on Huong Hoa worship land, Pagoda land and relative's land (the latter eligible to request title, but not desiring to) would be about 55, or 11 percent of all farmers. This is probably an underestimation of remaining tenancy. Officials were not sure how many tenants were on how much Huong Hoa worship land, since some of it is directly cultivated, but estimated 44 tenants on 125 hectares, or an average holding of 2.8 ha. The 15 tenants we interviewed (a sizeable portion of the 55 they thought remaining) averaged only 1.2 ha. each, as did the 250 former tenants already approved for title distribution (on 300

---

[8]There were in all 130 landowners, 31 of whom were non-residents, and a total of 51 landlords. I am assuming all 31 of the absentee owners rented out their land, but of the remaining 20 resident landlords some were probably direct cultivators as well. There were 267 tenants. Hendry, **Khanh Hau**, pp. 34 and 45-6.

[9]According to current records in the Village Office. Hendry reported 232 ha. distributed to 149 tenants, but his information was probably preliminary. See **Ibid.**, pp. 39-40.

ha.). At this rate there would be 104 tenants on 125 ha. of Huong Hoa land, 1 on pagoda land, and about 10 on relative's land, or 115 altogether, giving us 20 percent of the farmers left as tenants on 13 percent of the riceland, still much reduced from the 69 percent rate of tenancy before LTTT.[10]

In terms of land area, before Ordinance 57 tenants farmed 642 ha., or 69 percent of village riceland. After Ordinance 57 tenanted riceland was reduced to 419 ha., or 45 percent. In 1971 village officials estimated the amount of tenanted land before LTTT as around 457 ha., or 46 percent of village riceland, and this was to be reduced by the LTTT Program by at least 316 ha., so that only 14 percent of village riceland would remain tenanted.[11]

The distribution of ownership became more equal, as a comparison of Lorenz curves will demonstrate. (See Figure 5-1 and Tables A-4 and A-5.) Before Ordinance 57, the smaller 65 percent of the owners held only 13 percent of the land; afterwards, 60 percent of the owners held 18 percent of the land. Twelve years later, before the LTTT Program, the smaller 73 percent of the owners held 29 percent of the land, whereas in 1972, 70 percent held title to 36 percent of the land.[12] Inequalities still existed in Khanh Hau, but they were not so large as before. The Gini index of inequality declined from .717 before 1958 to .573 after the Diem land reform (the latter figure is understated due to insufficient data) and down to an estimated .455 after the LTTT Program, for a total decline of 36.5 percent. The LTTT Program alone reduced it from .582 to about .455, a decline of 21.8 percent.

As discussed in Chapter 3, traditional Lorenz curves do not adequately tell the story of a land reform program, however, since they demonstrate the skew of inequality at each period of time only among owners, ignoring the number of landless tenants on the

---

[10]This estimate would raise the total number of farmers to about 566, or 73% of all households. All these figures are preliminary, since the LTTT Program was still young and several cases from Khanh Hau were awaiting legal decision in the Long An Special Land Court. Village estimates of the number of farmers and tenants in the village and the amount of Huong Hoa land rented out are not based on hard data, either.

[11]The total amount of village riceland was listed as 926 ha. in 1958, but as 992 ha. in 1971. See Hendry, **Khanh Hau**, p. 32.

[12]1972 figures are preliminary and incomplete.

Figure 5-1

**Lorenz Curves of Land Ownership Distribution
Among Owners in Khanh Hau Village,
Before and After Diem's 1958 Land Reform and
Before and After the 1970 LTTT Program**

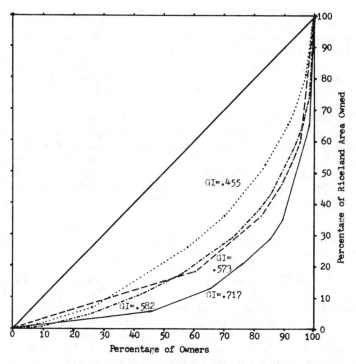

Sources: See Tables A–4a and b and A–5a and b.

land. The before and after curves in Figure 5-1 are not really comparable, although they are frequently compared, since the number of people they represent as owners (of a constant amount of land) varies considerably. The skew of two before and after curves could very well be identical and still represent a considerable redistribution of land (from 288 large landowners to 508 smaller ones, for example).

Lorenz curves can be derived to demonstrate the effects of a land reform program more completely simply by including the number of tenants with the landowners to determine the percentages along the horizontal axis, and by including the number of owners completely dispossessed in the "after" curve. This holds the number of people represented by both curves constant, as well as the hectarage, thus making them truly comparable.

This has been done for Khanh Hau Village in Figure 5-2 for the Ordinance 57 reform of 1958, and in Figure 5-3 for the LTTT Program (based on Tables A-6 and A-7). Figure 5-2 is based on complete and accurate information; but Figure 5-3 relies on preliminary and incomplete data and makes use of two estimates as to the number of tenants remaining on retained land, and it must be understood as a tentative approximation. Changes in land-ownership distribution among all those having a direct interest in village land, whether as absentee or resident landlords or as tenant or owner cultivators, can be much more accurately portrayed on these curves.

Before Ordinance 57, the smaller 89 percent of the owners and tenants owned only 13 percent of the land, whereas later 87 percent of the same group held 36 percent of the land. The proportion of landless tenants and completely dispossessed former owners can be read directly from the horizontal axis, where the percent of paddy land owned goes to zero—it drops here from 67 percent to 30 percent due to the Ordinance 57 reform. The LTTT Program reduced landlessness from a 47-52 percent range of the 1970 owners-plus-tenants group to only 13-22 percent. The lower 86 percent of the group owned only 29 percent of the land before LTTT, but this rose to 51 percent of the land after LTTT.

Superimposing Figure 5-2 on Figure 5-3, as in Figure 5-4, illustrates these changes over time. The LTTT curves represent land-ownership distribution among 50 percent more people than the Ordinance 57 curves, but here the difference is defendable as due to the growth of population over the intervening 12 years and does not produce a logically inconsistent comparison. The effect of population pressure is evident in Figure 5-4, pushing the rate of tenancy from 30 percent in late 1958 up to 50-55 percent in early

Figure 5-2

**Lorenz Curves of Land Ownership Distribution
Among Owners and Tenants in Khanh Hau Village,
Before and After Diem's 1958 Land Reform**

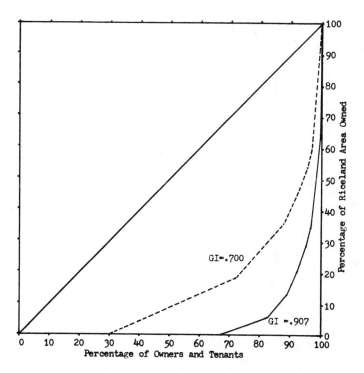

Legend: —— Before 1958 Ord. 57 Reform (397 Owners & Tenants)
- - - - After 1958 Ord. 57 Reform (397 Owners & Tenants)

Source: See Table A-6.

Figure 5-3

**Lorenz Curves of Land Ownership Distribution
Among Owners and Tenants in Khanh Hau Village,
Before and After 1970 LTTT Program**

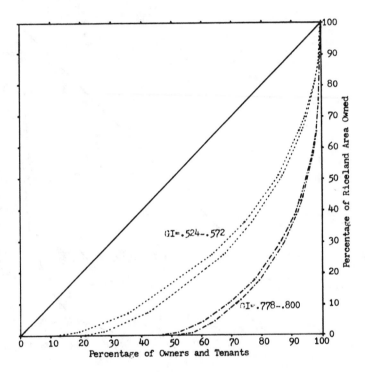

Legend: ≕≕≕ Before 1970 LTTT Program (544-604 Owners & Tenants)
        ∷∷∷∷ After 1970 LTTT Program (544-604 Owners & Tenants)

Sources: See Table A-7a and b.

Figure 5-4

**Lorenz Curves of Land Ownership Distribution
Among Owners and Tenants in Khanh Hau Village,
Before and After Diem's 1958 Ordinance 57 Reform
and Before and After 1970 LTTT Program**

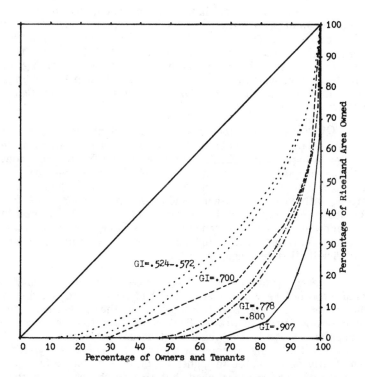

Legend: ─────── Before 1958 Ord. 57 Reform (397 Owners & Tenants)
        ─ ─ ─ ─ After 1958 Ord. 57 Reform (397 Owners & Tenants)
        =:=:=: Before 1970 LTTT Program (544-604 Owners & Tenants)
        :::::: After 1970 LTTT Program (544-604 Owners & Tenants)

Sources: See Tables A-6 and A-7a and b.

1970, during the interim between the two land reform programs. Moreover, the combined effect of population growth and both land reform programs has changed the situation from great inequality of land ownership among 397 households in 1958 to one of much less inequality among 600 or so households in 1972, though a pronounced skew of distribution still exists.

The Gini index of land concentration, based on the data including landless tenants, declined by 22.8 percent (from .907 to .700) during the Ordinance 57 reform and by an estimated 29-33 percent (from the .778-.800 range to .524-.572) during the LTTT Program, depending on the actual number of remaining tenants. The total improvement in the Gini index in Khanh Hau Village from the mid-1950's to the mid-1970's has probably been between 37 and 42 percent.

Other aspects of land tenure arrangements are also of interest. Of the 15 present tenants we interviewed, 14 had landlords residing in the village, and only 5 were protected with written contracts. Of the 16 new owners in the sample, only 5 had had resident landlords and 11 had had written contracts. This indicates continued strong influence of resident landlords. As a matter of fact, the 31 absentee landowners listed by Hendry in 1958 retained 294 ha. of paddy land after the Ordinance 57 reform,[13] so this group could account for most of the 300 ha. of privately-owned land approved for distribution by January 1972.

Average rents were reported to be 40 percent or more of the main crop before World War II, but had declined to between 25 and 30 percent by 1958, a little higher than the 25 percent stipulated in newly required contracts due to the practice of secret verbal agreements outside the legal contractual arrangement.[14] Hendry expected that any permanent increase in annual yields would eventually be reflected in higher rents, as old contracts expired and new agreements were reached, but that in the short run the fixed-amount rents stipulated in the new contracts would permit the tenants to benefit from any productivity gains.[15]

This was relevant to the current situation, where average annual yields were rising rapidly due to extensive double-cropping

---

[13]Hendry, **Khanh Kau,** p. 36.

[14]Ibid., pp. 49-50. See Chapter III, note 48, p. 45, above for the official Vietnamese interpretation of "main crop." Hendry was apparently using it in a different sense here, which I call the "American usage," meaning a single crop of rice on every hectare.

[15]Ibid., p. 165.

with new Miracle Rice varieties. Actual rents paid as reported by
our sample of tenants declined from 16 percent of the annual paddy
harvest in 1969 to 10 percent in 1971. The absolute amount of
rent remained about the same, but annual yields increased by 50
percent. Only 2 tenants in Khanh Hau thought their landlord would
demand more rent if yields were raised. The average stipulated
rent of 34 **gia**/ha. was equal to 22 percent of the 1971 yield per
crop hectare (154 **gia**, which would approximate the "main crop"
yield, American usage), down from 27 percent in 1969 (127 **gia**),
but the actual amount paid was 3 or 4 points lower.[16] Stipulated
rents were far from uniform, ranging from 25 to 53 **gia**/ha. and
from 10 to 67 percent of what tenants claimed was a normal **annual**
yield a few years ago, with a third of them 30 percent or higher.

Hendry found that 36 percent of a 50-tenant sample rented
land from relatives in 1958.[17] We found that 53 percent of our
present tenant sample did in 1971-2, but unfortunately we neglected
to ask this question of former tenants in Khanh Hau (our guess is
that the percentage would be much less for the latter group).

Living Standards

The economic standard of living in Khanh Hau had improved
noticeably since 1958. If it had been a relatively prosperous village
then, it had become a relatively rich village now, and this
improvement had occurred in spite of a shortage of labor due to
military conscription and a steady fragmentation of land due to
population growth.[18]

In rural Vietnam one of the clearest signs of wealth or poverty
is simply the kind of house a family lives in. A house constructed
of more durable materials is not only more comfortable, healthier
and a source of family pride, dignity, and social status, but it is
also highly valued as a religious tribute to the honor of the ancestors
that will stand for generations to come, providing a permanent
shrine of family worship for one's descendents. In addition,

---

[16]A **gia** is a unit of dry measure equal to 40 liters (1.133
bushels). One **gia** of paddy can range from 16 to 24 kilograms in
weight, depending on the variety of rice, its quality and its moisture
content. At an average of 20 kilos per **gia**, 50 **gia** will equal one
metric ton.

[17]**Ibid.**, p. 47.

[18]The village had a per capita hectarage of cultivated paddy
land of .29 in 1958, but only .18 in 1971. If it had been divided
evenly among all resident owners and tenants, each household would
have had 2.5 ha. in 1958, but only 1.6-1.8 ha. in 1971.

government officials were known to be very reluctant to grant agricultural credit to families living in thatched houses, less so if the house was of wood and corrugated metal, and much more agreeable if it were of masonry and tile; so there was economic incentive as well to build a better house. If a farmer could save enough money to build a house of tile and masonry he was considered to have "arrived" in the local community. When asking his way around a hamlet, a stranger was always directed by and to particular houses according to the type of roofs they had—very visible symbols of wealth.

Hickey surveyed housing for the 299 families residing on the west side of Highway 4 in 1958, in Nguyen Huynh Duc and Moi Hamlets, and found only 15 percent of them had tile roofs, while 85 percent lived under thatch.[19] In 1971 village records showed these same two hamlets contained 413 households, of which 42 percent had tile roofing, 33 percent corrugated metal or pressed cement fiber,[20] and only 25 percent thatched. (The percentage for the whole village of 773 households were 29, 32 and 39, respectively.)

Corrugated metal is not necessarily an improvement over thatch because of the intense heat it develops under the sun. Several farmers in Khanh Hau remarked that they preferred thatch but were unable to obtain it as cheaply as before, due to wartime clearing of dense growth by local military units and to defoliation measures in more remote areas. Thatch is cooler and traditionally inexpensive to replace with family labor. Corrugated metal is much more durable and cleaner to live under, but it is unbearably hot in the daytime and requires a larger initial investment. If about half of the middle category was now of pressed cement fiber, however,

---

[19]In 1958 what is now Nguyen Huynh Duc Hamlet was divided into two, known as Ap Dinh-A and Ap Dinh-B. "Ap" means "hamlet." See Hickey, **Village in Vietnam**, p. 27.

[20]The corrugated metal and pressed cement fiber look very much alike from a distance, but the latter is cooler, more expensive (and heavier, requiring stronger and more costly beams and supporting framework) and much preferred among those who can afford it over the metal, but who cannot yet afford the still more expensive tile. The pressed cement fiber roofing was becoming increasingly popular in Khanh Hau, but it was relatively new and village statistics did not yet differentiate it from the corrugated metal. Of the 13 Khanh Hau houses we visited in this category, 6 had cement fiber roofs, 7 corrugated metal.

(as indicated by our sample),[21] which definitely is considered an improvement over thatch, then we can say that about 57 percent of the houses now had tile or pressed-cement-fiber roofs, 43 percent thatch or corrugated metal. Surely this, compared with Hickey's findings, represented an important improvement in living conditions.

Much of this improvement had come very recently, since the introduction of the motor pump and Miracle Rice, which together permitted steady double-cropping with high yields and from which all classes have benefitted to some extent. Miracle Rice was popularly called "Honda Rice" at first, since so many Honda motorbikes were purchased after the first good harvest. In late 1971, though, it was coming to be called "House-Construction Rice" (lua cat nha), since so many farmers were using its proceeds to rebuild their homes. The LTTT Program was accelerating this development—93 percent of the title-recipients in our sample were repairing, remodeling or reconstructing their houses, compared with 73 percent of the tenants and 67 percent of the owner-cultivators.[22]

Owner-cultivators clearly lived in better houses, with 73 percent under tile or pressed-cement-fiber roofs, compared to only 20 percent of the present-tenant houses. The LTTT-title-recipients were leaving the ranks of the tenants and catching up with owner-cultivators, with 50 percent tile and pressed-cement-fiber roofs. (See Table 5-5.)

The ownership of certain consumer durable items was also an indication of the wealth and status position of a family, and of general income trends over time. Again we found noticeable improvement since 1958. In Hendry's sample roughly 18 percent of

---

[21]This probably overstates the proportion, as our sample omits landless labor, shopkeeping and artisan families, the 20-30 percent of the population who were among the lower-income group.—See **Ibid.**, p. 235. On the other hand our sample includes the 3 hamlets on the east side of the highway, where the average farmer was poorer than in Hickey's area and where fewer laborers and shopkeepers lived, and it also includes a disproportionate 34 percent share of present-tenants, compared with a truly random sample of the farmer population in which present tenants should number about 12-20 percent. These two considerations tend to balance the bias of omission to some extent. In our sample of 44 farmers from all 5 hamlets, 48 percent had tile or pressed-cement-fiber roofs, 52 percent thatched or corrugated metal.

[22]The title recipients were more involved with major house reconstruction, as well, rather than with routine repairs, than were the tenants. (See Table 6-7.)

Table 5-5

Type of housing of Khanh Hau Farmer Sample, 1971-72

Type of Housing	Proportions of:			
	15 present tenants	14 Title-recipients	15 Owner-cultivators	All 44 farmers
Roof: Thatch	.53	.43	.13	.36
Corrugated metal	.27	.07	.13	.16
Sub-total	.80	.50	.26	.52
Pressed cement fiber	.07	.14	.20	.14
Tile	.13	.36	.53	.34
Sub-total	.20	.50	.73	.48
Walls: Thatch or bamboo	.60	.43	.13	.39
Wooden		.21	.33	.18
Brick or cement	.40	.36	.53	.43
Floor: Packed earth	.87	.79	.67	.77
Cement	.07	.07		.05
Tile	.07	.14	.33	.18
Proportion repairing, remodelling, or re-constructing in 1971-2	.73	.93	.67	.77

Table 5-6

Ownership of Selected Consumer Durables and Vehicles in Khanh Hau

1971 Sample Compared with 1958

Item	15 present tenants	14 title-recipients	15 owner-cultivators	All 44 farmers	Hendry's[1] 68 farmers in 1958
Wardrobe	.93	.86	1.00	.93	.65
Glass-front cabinet	.20	.43	.40	.34	.47
Chinese character fresco	.27	.29	.60	.39	.43
Sewing machine	.40	.71	.73	.61	.18
Radio	.73	.64	.87	.75	.04
Television	-	-	.07	.02	-
Wall clock	.27	.36	.33	.32	.34
Pressure lamp	.40	.57	.87	.61	.46
Bicycle	.60	.57	.40	.52	.37
Scooter or motorbike	-	.07	.33	.14	.07
Sampan, hand	.07	.07	.13	.09	?
Sampan, motor	.07	-	.07	.05	?
Proportion of households purchasing consumer durables in 1971 or planning to in 1972	.47	.36	.40	.41	

[1]Hendry's findings have been recalculated to make them more comparable with our farmer survey by assuming all 32 of his non-farmers fell into the "lower class," as Hickey reported, and deducting a proportionate number from those in that class listed as owners of each item, then recalculating the "all classes" column from the remainder to produce the estimated 1958 farmer ownership proportions used here. This resulted in slightly higher fractions owning each item than for Hendry's whole sample of 100 households. —See Hendry, Khanh Hau, pp. 203 and 206, and Hickey, Village in Vietnam, p. 235.

the farmers owned sewing machines and only 4 percent owned radios—indeed, Hickey reported there were only 6 radios in the whole village, which would have been less than 2 percent of all farmers, assuming farmers owned them all.[23]   In our sample 61 percent owned sewing machines and 75 percent radios; and one large owner-cultivator owned a television set, as well, with another planning to buy one soon.   Significant increases had also occurred in the ownership of wardrobes, pressure lamps, bicycles and motorbikes.   Land tenure correlations existed in the ownership patterns of the latter three items and of sewing machines.   Bicycles appeared to be an "inferior good"—some of the wealthier, owner-cultivator families dropping them for motorbikes or scooters.   (See Table 5-6.)

Indebtedness

Sixty-four percent of our farmer sample had contracted debts during the preceding year, the same incidence of debt found by Hendry 13 years before.   The three major sources of credit were also the same: relatives, friends and neighbors, and the government agricultural credit program.[24]   (See Table 5-14.)   Landlords and professional moneylenders were insignificant sources of credit in both studies.

Hendry's more thorough study revealed that about 15 percent of the loans came from the **hui** (mutual aid societies or tontine).[25] None of our Khanh Hau respondents named the **hui** as a source of credit, and we did not ask a direct question about it because of time constraints and the difficulty in determining whether a participant is a net debtor or creditor.   Vietnamese farmers apparently consider the **hui** more a way of saving money than of borrowing, though of course it is both.

Thanks to the combined effects of higher crop yields and reduction of rents, more of our sample had decreased their debts over the last two years than had borrowed more, which is a reversal of the trend observed in 1958 and all the more remarkable in the

---

[23]Hickey, **Village in Vietnam**, p. 235, and Hendry, **Khanh Kau**, pp. 203 and 206 (see source note to Table 5-6).
[24]Hendry, **Khanh Hau**, pp. 206 and 218.
[25]See **Ibid.**, pp. 213-16, and Sansom, **Economics of Insurgency**, pp. 114-22, for detailed discussions of the **hui** and how it works.

current era of rapid inflation.[26] The reversal was due entirely to
the LTTT-title-recipient debtor group, of whom only 9 percent
borrowed more, compared with 40 percent of the owner-cultivators
and 42 percent of the tenants who did, and with 52 percent of
Hendry's 1958 sample who were increasing their debts.

The average amount borrowed increased by 32 percent for the
debtor tenants and by 116 percent for the owner-cultivators over
the two years discussed, compared with a fall of 4 percent for the
title-recipients. If we exclude the largest loans in each group as
atypical, we find the average amount borrowed by title-recipients
fell by 39 percent, while it **rose** by an identical percentage for the
other two groups.

Most (86 percent) of those who borrowed money in 1971 did
so at least in part to meet farm operating expenses, while somewhat
fewer (61 percent) did so for consumption purposes (including 46
percent who borrowed for both reasons). More tenants borrowed
than owners; but more of the tenants who borrowed did so to meet
farm expenses, and fewer for consumption, than did the owners.

Agricultural Production

One indication of agricultural investment is the number of
farm implements owned or purchased by each household. In our
sample, 43 percent of the title-recipients had just bought or planned
to buy new farm implements in the coming year, compared with
only 27 percent of the tenants and 40 percent of the wealthier
owner-cultivator group. Wealth counted in the ownership of modern,
gasoline-powered implements like the motor pump and the expensive
rototiller. Some 60 percent of the owner-cultivators owned a motor
pump, as did 36 percent of the title-recipients and only 13 percent
of the tenants. Two members of our sample owned rototillers, and
both of them were owner-cultivators. One more owner and two
new owners planned to buy rototillers in the coming year, which
would raise the total to 11 percent of the sample who owned one.
Ownership of the wooden plow pulled by water buffalo had dropped
from 47 percent of Hendry's 1958 farmer sample to 18 percent of
ours. The new rototillers plowed ground for about a third of our
farmers in 1971, and several more said they planned to switch from
buffalo to mechanical power in 1972, bringing this proportion up to

---

[26]The Consumer Price Index for middle class families in Saigon
actually **fell** by 2.9 percent between 1956 and 1958, compared to
a climb of 65.1 percent between 1969 and 1971. **Nien Giam Thong
Ke Vietnam—1971** (Vietnam Statistical Yearbook), (Saigon: National
Institute of Statistics, 1972), p. 314.

about half. All but two (4.5 percent) said they had made the change
within the last two years. The fees charged by rototiller owners
varied, some farmers claiming plowing by machine was more
expensive per hectare than by water buffalo, some said it was
cheaper, some said the same; but they all agreed it was much faster
and killed the weeds more effectively.

In 1958 there was only one motor pump in the whole village,
and it was considered less efficient than the traditional wooden
waterwheel where the water needed to be raised only one half
meter or less.[27]   About 27 percent of the 66 farmers in Hendry's
sample owned a waterwheel, 45 percent of the owners and 18 percent
of the tenants. Thirteen years later, however, the waterwheel had
disappeared completely. None of our 44 farmers had one, nor did
we see one in operation anywhere. Instead, 36 percent of our
sample owned motor pumps, most of which were the domestically
altered sampan motor (with a tin sleeve over the 2.5-meter shaft
and an impeller replacing the propeller) described as a new innovation
by Robert Sansom.[28]   (See Table 5-7.)

The motor pump and the new Miracle Rice varieties combined
to change double-cropping from a "very risky venture that frequently
fails to cover the marginal costs"[29] to a very profitable, routine
undertaking. The motor pump was first "invented" near My Tho in
1962 and spread rapidly, so that by mid-1966, according to Sansom,
43 percent of the farmers in Than Cuu Nghia Village, just 7-8 km.
south of Khanh Hau on Highway 4, owned one. Miracle Rice (IR-
8) was first planted in Khanh Hau in 1968, unsuccessfully. Despite
the derision of his friends and neighbors, the innovator tried again
the following year, learning from his mistakes and from personal
observations made on trips to other provinces where the new seed
was being used successfully. In 1969 he had 2 bumper crops, and
since then many others in the village had followed his example. In
1971 this same farmer, an owner-cultivator of 9 hectares who prided
himself on being an innovator and on taking (often costly) risks to
improve his productivity and that of the village, was experimenting
with new techniques and a combination of seeds[30] to harvest **three**

---

[27]Hendry, **Khanh Hau**, pp. 58, 70-2.
[28]Sansom, **Economics of Insurgency**, Chapter 8.
[29]Hendry, **Khanh Hau**, p. 80.
[30]These included selecting a third crop variety somewhat
resistant to brackish water, which he brought in from one of the
coastal provinces, using the fast-maturing Miracle Rice varieties
for the first 2 crops, carefully dovetailing harvest and transplant
operations between crops to save time, and, of course, liberal use
of the motor pump.

Table 5-7

Ownership of Farm Implements, Khanh Hau, 1958 and 71, and Proportion Who Hire Labor

Implement	Tenants 1958	Tenants 1971	LTTT title recipients 1971	Owners 1958	Owners 1971	All farmers 1958	All farmers 1971
Hand Plow	.43	.27	.07	.55	.20	.47	.18
Harrow	.39	.27	.14	.45	.27	.41	.23
Roller	.32	.27	.14	.45	.27	.36	.23
Threshing Sledge	.61	.67	.50	.59	.47	.61	.55
Waterwheel	.18	-	-	.45	-	.27	-
Motor Pump	-	.13	.36	-	.60	-	.36
Rototiller	-	-	-	-	.13	-	.05
Proportion of farmers purchasing implements in 1971-72		.27	.43		.40		.36
Proportion of farmers who hire labor		.87	.93		1.00	.43	.93

SOURCES: 1958--Calculated from Hendry, <u>Khanh Hau</u>, Tables 4.1 and 10.2, pp. 57 and 206. Hendry's 6 owner-tenants have been included here in the owner column. (N=66, 44 tenants and 22 owners)

1971--Farmer interviews (N=44, 15 tenants, 14 LTTT-title-recipients and 15 owner-cultivators)

crops of rice.

By 1971, 70 percent of our farmer sample was using one of the Miracle Rice varieties, and almost all of these indicated they had first used it that year or the year before. Another 25 percent said they intended to switch to Miracle Rice in the coming year, bringing the total up to 95 percent. Two farmers thought their land was too low for the new variety, which is sensitive to high water levels. In addition, the proportion of paddy land double-cropped by our sample rose from 48 percent in 1969 to 80 percent in 1971.[31]

These developments raised annual production per hectare from an average of 181 **gia** to 280 **gia,** or by 55 percent, in two years. Average yields per crop hectare also grew from 122 **gia** to 154 **gia,** or by 26 percent, thanks to the higher crop yields of Miracle Rice.[32] (See Table 5-8.)

Hendry found that over two-thirds of the village rice crop was sold for cash in 1958.[33] By 1969 this had dropped to about half of the crop, due no doubt to population pressure within the village, since yields were about the same as in Hendry's day; but by 1971 cash sales had grown back to almost two-thirds again.[34] Another sign of the increasing commercialization of farm operations is the proportion of farmers who hire non-family labor to work in their fields. Hendry reported only 43 percent of all farmers hired labor to some extent in 1958,[35] whereas 93 percent of our sample

---

[31]Only 4 farmers (9 percent) did not double-crop any of their holdings, and 2 of these planned to do so the following year, raising the total hectarage double-cropped to 84 percent. This would leave 8 farmers (18 percent) with all or part of their land still single-cropped, and they cited various reasons for this—land too low for adequate drainage, too high and too far from a canal for proper irrigation, lack of capital, shortage of labor, and insecurity (hard to get workers to go there).

[32]From all reports, 1969 was a fairly normal year for Khanh Hau, so these production increases were real, not illusions produced by a poor base year. Hendry found yields per crop hectare averaging 120 **gia** in 1958, which further supports this conclusion. --Hendry, **Khahn Hau**, p. 85.

[33]**Ibid.,** p. 119.

[34]Cash sales here do not include paddy sold to pay cash rents; but rents amounted to only 7.4 percent of the total crop of our sample in 1969, 2.7 percent in 1971, and perhaps half of them were paid in cash, so the error is not large.

[35]Hendry, **Khanh Hau,** p. 255.

Table 5-8

Rice Production and Disposition
in Khanh Hau Village

Average	15 present tenants	14 title[4] recipients	15 owner cultivators	All 44 farmers
Present holding of paddy land (ha.)	1.2	1.6	4.0	2.3
Ha. received under LTTT		1.5		
Gross paddy production per farm, 1971 (gia)[1]	340	393	1157	635
Annual yield/ha. '71 (gia)	285	244	292	280
Annual yield/ha. '69 (gia)	190	157	187	181
Annual yield/ha., before '69	186	150	195	184
(% increase 1969-71)	(50)	(55)	(56)	(55)
Portion of riceland double-cropped, 1971	.84	.92	.74	.80
Portion of riceland double-cropped, 1969	.49	.46	.48	.48
(% increase 1969-71)	(71)	(100)	(54)	(67)
Yield/crop ha., 1971 (gia)	154	127	166	154
Yield/crop ha., 1969 (gia)	127	107	126	122
(% increase 1969-71)	(21)	(19)	(32)	(26)
Stipulated rent/ha. before LTTT (gia)	34.1	30.4		32.0
Stipulated rent/'69 annual yield/ha.	.18	.19		.18

Percentage increase or decrease in
last 2 years of (rice paddy use):

Gross paddy production	50	56	56	54
Rent	- 3	-94	0	-44
In-kind labor payments	51	63	53	54
Home consumption and feed	4	9	8	8
Paddy sales	104	219	77	97
Disposable paddy[2]	61	91	56	63
(MPC disposable paddy[3])	(.03)	(.06)	(.05)	(.05)

---

[1] A gia is a unit of dry measure equal to 40 liters and to 1.133 bushels. One gia of paddy can range from 16 to 24 kilograms in weight, depending on the variety of rice, its quality and its moisture content. Taking 20 kilos per gia as a good average, 50 gia will equal one metric ton.

[2] Gross paddy production minus both rent and in-kind labor payments.

[3] Marginal Propensity to Consume (and use as feed) disposable paddy equals the change in home consumption and feed divided by the change in disposable paddy. It is calculated from the absolute amounts of change, not from the percentage change figures shown in this table.

[4] Two interviewees omitted as confused or mixed cases. One was still fighting her landlord in court over whether land was Huong Hoa, and the other was 3/8 owner, 3/8 title-recipient, and 1/4 tenant.

did so in 1971. Although this was partly a symptom of the shortage of family labor caused by the military draft, it nevertheless is another indication that the self-sufficient, peasant-farm stereotype was rare in Khanh Hau.

Long Binh Dien, Dinh Tuong Province

Long Binh Dien Village (LBD) is 11 kilometers (6.9 miles) east of the province capital, My Tho, along the route to Go Cong, Provincial Highway 24. This highway was in fairly good condition, but was off the beaten track and carried only light, mostly local traffic. Very few buses traversed this area; the common carrier was the 3 wheeled Lambretta and its 4-wheeled, Japanese-made equivalent, which ran between My Tho and Cho Gao, going through LBD at frequent intervals from dawn to dusk. A person never had to wait longer than 10 or 15 minutes for one, and the 11-km. ride cost about U.S. 7.5 cents (30VN piastres when we were there).

LBD lies astride the Ky Hon River, which links the Upper Mekong River (Vietnamese = **Song Tien Giang**) to the Cho Gao Canal as part of the Mekong Delta waterway system. Residents and visitors crossing the river to Long Dinh Hamlet on its southern bank must dodge the continuous procession of heavily laden canal boats and barges, which can easily swamp a small sampan ferry caught in their wakes. Irrigation canals carry the river water (at high tide) to some of the nearby fields and orchards, allowing the more fortunate farmers to exercise a degree of water control.

This village was one of the two studied in depth by Robert Sansom in 1967, and some of his findings provide useful comparisons with our own. Village officials had completed an unofficial census of the entire village just before our arrival, which provided us with more complete and up-to-date information than we were able to obtain in our other three villages.[36]

---

[36]This door-to-door census was conducted throughout the district at the request and under the guidance of the Cho Gao District chief, Lt. Col. Ly, acting on his own initiative. Although it was planned and executed by professionals and therefore has some obvious shortcomings, it does provide some useful and interesting information, and it could be especially valuable for comparative purposes in later years. Conducted in Long Binh Dien Village between November 1971 and January 1972, it will hereinafter be referred to as the "LBD Census, 1972."

**MAP OF LONG BINH DIEN VILLAGE,
CHO GAO DISTRICT, DINH TUONG PROVINCE**

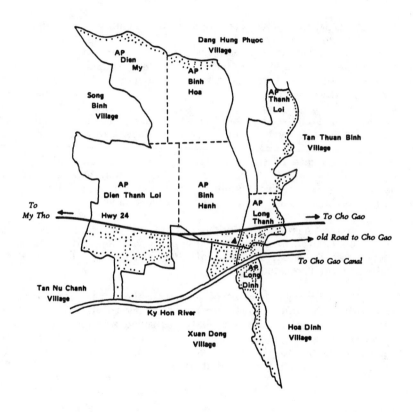

▲ Village Office

Demographic Data[37]

The seven hamlets of LBD contained a population of 4,738 people, 58.6 percent of them female, 41.4 percent male, proportions practically identical with those in Khanh Hau Village. There were 829 households, however, which means each household averaged only 5.7 residents—significantly lower than the current Khanh Hau average of 7.2.

A surprisingly low proportion of the population was listed as gainfully employed—only 15.9 percent. This group together with those listed as housewives comprised only 22.6 percent of the village population. The rest were either small children, students, or the elderly. This tends to confirm the complaints of a local labor shortage heard from so many farmers. Of the 753 individuals listed as gainfully employed, 72.2 percent gave farming as their chief occupation, 18.9 percent gave orchard tending, and 8.0 percent said they worked chiefly as hired labor (0.9 percent other).

A high rate of literacy was reported, with only 1.7 percent of the adults classified as illiterate; 17.5 percent had reached the secondary school level of studies, while the remaining 80.9 percent had received at least some elementary schooling.

On the question of religious orientation 64.1 percent said they practiced Confucian ancestor worship, only 28.8 percent declared themselves Buddhist, 6.3 percent Cao Dai and 0.4 percent each Catholic and Protestant.[38]

The political alignment of each household was also recorded, though it is doubtful it was determined during the interviews. 85.4 percent of the households were listed as supporting the government, 11.5 percent as being neutral, and 3.1 percent as sympathizing with the communists, most of the latter residing in the two northwestern-most hamlets, Dien My and Binh Hoa.

---

[37]From the **LBD Census,** 1972.

[38]In our own sample of 45 farmers, 44.4 percent said they were Confucian and 66.7 percent Buddhist, with 15.6 percent claiming both (4.4 percent were Cao Dai). I suspect the percentage who follow some of both Buddhist and Confucian ancestor worship traditions is fairly high, higher than our 15.6 percent, and that one can get different results on preferences depending on how one poses the question. The **LBD Census** listed no respondents as both, which may indicate their query was not as open-ended as ours. (See Table 5-16.)

Sample Selection

Village officials felt it would be safe enough for us to travel unescorted throughout the four southern hamlets, but thought we should have an escort in the northern three, Dien My, Binh Hoa and Thanh Loi. We therefore limited our selection process to the southern four, Dien Thanh Loi, Binh Hanh, Long Thanh, and Long Dinh, which included 71.2 percent of the total village population. We were more fortunate than Robert Sansom, who in 1967 could visit only the 2 central hamlets, Binh Hanh and Long Thanh, containing (in 1972) only 38.4 percent of the village population.[39]

Since the LBD Census indicated the number of rice farmers in each hamlet, we used that instead of the total population to allocate our interviews.[40] The selection process proceeded as before, by drawing lots out of a hat for each set of three farmers, until we had interviewed a total of 45 farmers, 15 in each land tenure category, divided among hamlets as indicated in Table 5-9.

---

[39]Sansom reported the village had only 6 hamlets, inexplicably omitting the largest one, Dien Thanh Loi, through which he had to travel every day enroute between My Tho and the 2 hamlets he studied. Both village and hamlet officials assured me that LBD has had all 7 hamlets as long as they could remember, and they exhibited an old French map of the village showing the same boundaries as exist today. See Sansom, **Economics of Insurgency**, pp. 12 and 13.

[40]We made one adjustment to compensate for an apparent bias in the census figures. The census indicated an almost equal number of rice farmers in the two largest hamlets, Dien Thanh Loi and Binh Hanh. In the former, however, 122 persons were listed as housewives, while none were in Binh Hanh. When asked why there were no housewives in Binh Hanh, village officials explained that many women are both housewives and farmers and they also work as hired labor. When recording occupations in Dien Thanh Loi Hamlet, the census takers apparently put most of these women down as "primarily" housewives, whereas in Binh Hanh other census takers emphasized the gainful employment. This is typical of the problems encountered in a non-professional census-taking operation. To compensate for this, we assigned one more set of 3 interviews to the larger hamlet, assuming that the number of farmers listed there was understated, while in Binh Hanh it was overstated (as, for example, when both husband and wife are listed as farmers on the same farm). See Table 5-9.

Table 5-9

A. POPULATION DATA - LONG BINH DIEN VILLAGE

Hamlet	(1) 1971 Popu- lation	(2) % of total village popu- lation	(3) % of total population in Hamlets Surveyed	(4) Reported Number of Rice Farmers	(5) Col.4 as % of total rice farmers in Hamlets Surveyed	(6) Number of Farmers Inter- viewed	(7 Col. as % tot. Inte viev
Long Dinh	327	6.9	9.7	22	6.2	3	6.
Dien Thanh Loi	1228	25.9	36.4	129	36.3	18	40.
Binh Hanh	983	20.7	29.1	130	36.6	15	33.
Long Thanh	836	17.6	24.8	74	20.8	9	20.
Sub-totals	3374	71.2	100.0	355	99.9	45	100.
Dien My	446	9.4					
Binh Hoa	434	9.2					
Thanh Loi	484	10.2					
Sub-totals	1364	28.8					
Village Total	4738	100.0					
Female	2778	58.6					
Male	1960	41.4					

Number of Households: 829
Average Household Size: 5.7

B. LONG BINH DIEN INTERVIEWEE DATA

Total:	15 Present Tenants	15 Title Recipients	15 Owner- Cultivators	All Fa
Interviewees: Male	4	4	9	1'
Female	11	11	6	2
Average:				
Age of Interviewee: Male	49.5	63.0	57.2	5
Female	42.4	48.5	52.7	4'
Education (years): Male	4.3	1.3	4.4	
Female	2.6	1.9	1.7	
Number of Household Residents:	8.1	6.8	6.6	

SOURCE: Col. 1-5, Table A: LBD Village Office, Jan. 1972.

Land Tenure

The village land register lists a total cadastral area of 1,198 hectares in Long Binh Dien, with 1,005 hectares identified as riceland and the remainder mostly as orchard land.[41]   The LBD Census reported its 544 rice farmers cultivated only 674 hectares of paddy land, however, including the land they worked in other villages. This means that 1/3 or more of the riceland in LBD was cultivated by non-residents, farmers living in neighboring villages who worked fields in LBD.[42] By applying the average ricefarm size as indicated by the LBD Census (1.24 ha.) to the total riceland area, we can determine that approximately 810 farmers are working paddy fields in LBD. By March 26, 1973, three years after the LTTT Program was launched, titles had been printed for distribution to 507 farmers, or 63 percent of the estimated 810 farmers on village riceland, transferring ownership of 590 ha., or 59 percent of all LBD riceland.[43] Some 95 percent of these applications had been approved and 84 percent of the titles distributed at the time of our visit in January to March, 1972.

Unfortunately, no questions regarding land tenure were included in the LBD Census, but village officials reported that 158 ha. were exempt from distribution as Huong Hoa land, and they estimated that about 100 of these hectares were farmed by about 100 tenants, the remainder being directly cultivated by the owners. In addition, they reported 6 tenants farming 7 hectares of religious land and that approximately 30 tenants were farming 20 ha. of land owned by relatives and did not wish to request title.   Thus, about 17 percent of all farmers (136/810) would remain tenants, unaffected by the LTTT Program, on roughly 13 percent of the LBD riceland area.   This represented a substantial reduction from around 79

---

[41]Small amounts are designated as cemetery plots and residential areas, but most residential plots are included in the "orchard" category. —Village Office, August 1972.

[42]This also means that while the proportions of village riceland area affected by the LTTT Program indicated in Table 5-2 are correct, the proportions of "all households" listed as affected are overstatements, since the 829 households of LBD include only 2/3 of the rice farmers who would be receiving their titles through the village office.   Village boundaries divide or exclude several residential areas adjacent to large areas of included riceland.

[43]All but 3 titles for a total of 3 hectares had been received by the farmers by this date.   1973 data is from the computer printout, "Bao Cao Tinh Trang Cap Phat Dat Thuoc Chuong Trinh NCCR, Ngay 26-03-73" (Progress Report on Land Distribution under the LTTT Program, 26 March 1973), for Long Binh Dien Village.

percent tenancy on 71 percent of the riceland area before the program.

Again, traditional Lorenz curves of land ownership distribution, such as presented in Figure 5-5, tell only a small part of the story. Looking at the curve, one sees that whereas the upper 17 percent of the owners held title to 57 percent of the land before the LTTT Program, redistribution had progressed by August 1972 to the point where the same **proportion** of owners still held 44 percent of the land. The actual **number** of owners represented by that 17 percent ratio increased, however, from 51 to 115, or by 125 percent, and this important change is hidden by traditional curves, although it can be easily calculated from the tables on which they are based. We can see from Table A-8 that holdings of less than 3 ha. included 68 percent of the owners and only 25 percent of the land before the program, but 92 percent of the owners and 71 percent of the land by August 1972. The average size of holding owned fell from 3.3 to 1.5 hectares.

A modified set of Lorenz curves, such as presented in the preceding section for Khanh Hau, appears in Figure 5-6, based on the LBD data as of August 1972 tabulated in Table A-9. Both of the curves in Figure 5-6 represent the same number of people, including all former and present owners and an estimated 136 remaining tenants.

The "before" curve is based on fairly accurate data, having been derived directly from a 1969 land register maintained by the Village Office; but the "after" curve is based on incomplete and preliminary data, since the work of expropriation and redistribution was still underway and land records were understandably in a state of flux. Records for LBD were more complete than for any of the other 3 villages we studied, however; of the 1,198-hectare cadastral area listed in the pre-LTTT land register, we could account for 1195 hectares in the August 1972 records at our disposal. A small amount of land had been reclassified from riceland to orchard land or the other categories (residential plots, roadway, cemetery land), so that the total riceland figure is smaller by 14 ha. than before.

A slight adjustment of the "after" data was required to compensate for multiple titles issued to 22.2 percent of the recipients, since the data we obtained was by titles and not by owner.[44]   The procedure we followed has resulted in a slightly

---

[44]Not realizing the extent of the problem until later, we failed to obtain the names and identifying numbers of each new owner when we reviewed copies of their titles, rendering us unable to

larger bulge in the 1.00-1.49 ha. ownership stratum than it actually should have, but it is a closer approximation of the actual situation than the unadjusted figures.

When these data were collected there were copies of 518 new LTTT titles on file, indicating the redistribution of 509 hectares; and records indicated 106 landlords had lost a total of 523 hectares. These figures, upon which Tables A-8 and A-9 and Figures 5-5 and 5-6 are based, represent 85 percent of the 3-year totals reported in March 1973.[45]

Despite these deficiencies the modified Lorenz curves (Figure 5-6) demonstrate a significant redistribution of land ownership among all parties directly concerned with the land, either as owners or as cultivators, by the LTTT Program, even though it was only 85 percent complete. Landlessness fell from 65 percent to 23 percent of the entire group, the first percentage including only tenants, the latter including 16 percent tenants and 7 percent completely dispossessed landlords. Whereas the lower 80 percent of this owner-plus-tenant group held title to only 9.7 percent of the riceland in 1969, by August 1972 the lowest 79 percent of the same group held 45 percent of the riceland. At the upper end of the curves, we see that while the wealthiest 11 percent of the group held title to 75 percent of the riceland in 1969, the upper 13 percent held only 44 percent of it in 1972.

(cont.)
combine those titles issued to the same person. To compensate for this error we have deducted 33.6 percent of the LTTT titles proportionately from the 2 lowest ownership strata, .01-.49 ha. and .50-.99 ha., and added 16.8 percent to the average stratum, 1.00-1.49 (distribution has averaged 1.16 ha. per recipient in LBD), along with an appropriate amount of land. In addition to the problem of multiple LTTT titles distributed to new owners, there were also a number of cases in which part-owner, part-tenants received LTTT titles to add to their previous holdings (permitted so long as each combined holding did not exceed the upper limit of 3 ha.). We were unable to correlate the new titles with the old ownership records, for the same reason indicated above, and we have not attempted to adjust for this problem, since we do not know the extent of it (although we believe that only a small proportion of holdings are involved in this village).

[45]By March 1973, 609 titles for 590 hectares had been distributed to 507 recipients. Compare this in magnitude with the earlier Ordinance 57 land reform program, in which, according to one of its participants, a total of 54 hectares was distributed to 36 tenants in this village.

Figure 5-5

**Lorenz Curves of Land Ownership Distribution
Among Owners in Long Binh Dien Village,
Before and After 1970 LTTT Program**

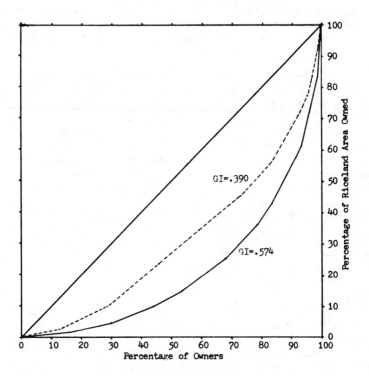

Legend: ———— Before LTTT Program (301 Owners)
           ----- After LTTT Program (667 Owners)

Source: See Table A-8a and b.

Figure 5-6

**Lorenz Curves of Land Ownership Distribution
Among Owners and Tenants in Long Binh Dien Village,
Before and After 1970 LTTT Program**

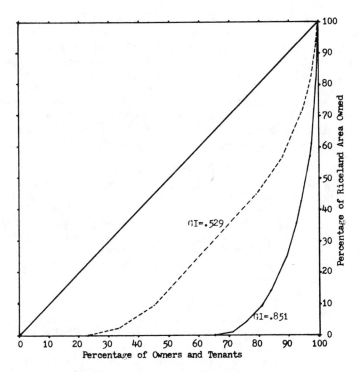

Legend: ———— Before LTTT Program (868 Owners & Tenants)
        ----- After LTTT Program (868 Owners & Tenants)

Source: See Table A-9.

The Gini index of the more traditional Lorenz curves in Figure 5-5 dropped from .574 to .390, or by 32.1 percent, due to the LTTT Program. When we include all the landless tenants who received titles and an estimated 136 who remained landless, the index drops by 37.8 percent, from .851 to .529, indicating a much more severe state of inequality prior to and a more significant improvement as a result of the LTTT Program.

Robert Sansom concluded that a significant fragmentation in the size of landholdings owned occurred in LBD Village between 1931 and 1962, with the percentage of holdings of more than 5 hectares declining from 18.3 percent to 3.0 percent.[46] The data we obtained from the Village Land Register for 1969, which had been copied by village officials from the records of the Provincial Land Service, Dinh Tuong Province (the same source cited by Sansom), differ substantially from Sansom's data and support a conflicting conclusion—that very little fragmentation of ownership had occurred, despite the intervening Ordinance 57 land reform.

Our information on all land owned, presented in Table 5-10 in a form compatible for comparison with Sansom's data, indicates that 12.2 percent of all holdings were still 5 hectares or more in 1969, a third down from 1931, but four times the ratio Sansom reported in 1962. When we consider only riceland, as in Table A-8, we find that 16.9 percent of the holdings were 5 hectares or more. Only in 1972, with the LTTT Program 85 percent completed, does the 5 ha. or more proportion of holdings drop (to 3.3 percent) near Sansom's level.[47]

_____

[46]Sansom, **Economics of Insurgency**, p. 72. Sansom used 1931 data from Yves Henry, **Economie Agricole de l'Indochine**, (Hanoi: Imprimerie d'Extreme-Orient, 1932), p. 164.

[47]One plausible explanation for this is that Sansom might have neglected to combine the numerous entries in the land register of small plots owned by the same person or family. Only one of the larger holdings was listed all in one piece, and that was a 40-ha. orchard. The largest holding, 58 ha., was divided among 8 separate entries, all under the same name. Another holding of 35 ha. was divided among 9 entries. This practice was common even on small holdings of only a few hectares—they were often divided among multiple entries. We were able to identify enough multiple entries to reduce the 619 main entries in the 1969 land register (and many of these were subdivided) to 458 owners.

To make matters even worse, as discussed in Chapter 6, landlord families commonly owned land in several villages and had often split legal ownership among immediate family members, though still administering the property as a single unit. Both of these

Table 5-10

**Historical Trends in Ownership Distribution of Land,
Long Binh Dien Village, 1931-1972**

Ownership Stratum (hectares)	Percentage of Individuals Owning All Land				Percentage of Individuals Owning Riceland Only	
	1931	1962	1969	1972	1969	1972
0-1	43.1	63.0	45.6	38.9	29.9	28.3
1-5	38.5	33.1	42.1	57.8	53.2	68.2
5-10	12.1	2.9	7.2	2.8	9.6	3.0
10-50	5.9	0.1	4.8	0.5	7.0	0.4
50-100	0.3	0	0.2	0	0.3	0
100-500	0.01	0	0	0	0	0
Totals	99.91	99.1	99.9	100.0	100.0	99.9
Number of Individuals Listed as Owners:	1787	414	458	936	301	667

SOURCES: 1931 and 1962: Sansom, Economics of Insurgency, p. 72.
1969 and 1972: Village Land Register, LBD Village Office.

NOTE: Sansom's 1931 figures are from Yves Henry, Economie Agricole de l'Indochine, (Hanoi: Imprimerie d'Extreme-Orient, 1932), p. 164, and are for the whole district of which LBD Village comprised over one-third. His 1962 figures came from Dinh Tuong Province Land Service records, but are believed to be uncorrected for multiple parcels of land owned by the same individuals, and thus seriously biased downwards.

(cont.)

practices would tend to make a comparison between 1931 district and 1962 village data overstate the actual fragmentation which had occurred.

There also appears to be either a misprint or miscalculation in his tabulation, since his 1962 percentages total only 99.1 and the last entry on the 1962 row (0.1 percent) is an impossibility, since 1/414 = .0024. That last entry should probably be 1.0 percent, and this alone would raise his 1962 "5 ha. or more" proportion from 3.0 to 3.9 percent.

Thirteen of the 15 tenants we found for interview were farming land registered as Huong Hoa ancestor worship land, one was renting land from a Catholic Church, and one was simply unaware of the paperwork requirements for land redistribution until our visit.[48] One third of the tenants were renting land belonging to relatives (one giving this as the reason he had not requested title on the portion of this farm which was not Huong Hoa), compared with only 13 percent of the LTTT-title-recipients who had been renting from relatives.

Not much difference can be discerned between the tenant and title-recipient groups in landlord location and type of contract. About 28 percent of them had or had had landlords residing in the same village, 31 percent in the same district, 34 percent in the same province, and only 6 percent elsewhere. The same proportion of both groups, 47 percent, held or had held written contracts with their landlords, while the other 53 percent operated or had operated under verbal agreements.

Stipulated rents averaged 26 **gia** per hectare before the LTTT Program, which would have required 19 percent of the 1969-70 crop. The LTTT recipient group claimed to have paid the full amount required that year, but the present tenants reported paying a slightly smaller amount, coming to 16 percent of the annual crop.[49] The proportion of a "normal" annual yield paid in rents ranged from 6 percent to 50 percent, but with only 4 out of 29 tenants or former tenants paying more than the 25 percent legal limit, compared with a third of the Khanh Hau tenants who were paying more.

Living Standards

The average standard of living in LBD is lower than in Khanh Hau. Of the LBD households, 66 percent live under roofs of thatch, while only 7 percent have roofs of tile or concrete, compared with 39 percent and 29 percent, respectively, in Khanh Hau.[50] Our sample of farmers was wealthier than the village average, as one should expect, since we excluded the landless laborers and probably have a higher proportion of owner-cultivators—the wealthiest group—

---

[48]The hamlet chief introducing us expressed his surprise at this and made arrangements on the spot to help this lady farmer with her title application form.
[49]See Tables 5-11 and 5-28.
[50]See Table 5-12.

Table 5-11

Rice Production and Disposition in Long Binh Dien Village

Average	14 Present Tenants[4]	15 Title recip- ients	15 owner culti- vators	All 44 Farmers
Paddy land holding (ha.)	1.3	1.3	1.9	1.5
Ha. received under LTTT		1.3		
Gross Paddy Production per farm,				
1971-2 (gia)[1]	184	167	259	203
Annual yield/ha. 1971-2 (gia)	136	130	133	133
Annual yield/ha. 1969-70(gia)	157	138	147	147
Annual yield/ha.before '69(gia)	159	138	156	152
(% increase last 2 years)	(-13)	(- 6)	(-10)	(-10)
Portion of riceland double-cropped,				
1971-2	.27	.35	.32	.31
Portion of riceland double-cropped,				
1969-70	.25	.20	.38	.29
(% increase 1969-71)	(6)	(78)	(-18)	(6)
Yield/crop ha., 1971-2 (gia)	107	97	101	101
Yield/crop ha., 1969-70(gia)	125	115	107	114
(% increase in 2 years)	(-14)	(-16)	(- 6)	(-11)
Stipulated rent/ha. before LTTT(gia)	26.9	24.9		25.8
Stipulated rent/1969-70 annual				
yield	.17	.19		.19
Percentage increase or decrease in last 2 years of (rice paddy use):				
Gross paddy production	-13	- 5	-11	-10
Rent	- 6	-100	0	-53
In-kind labor payments	-18	-10	-12	-13
Home consumption and feed	- 4	21	- 4	5
Paddy sales and debt repayment	-19	21	-15	-11
Disposable paddy[2]	-14	21	- 7	- 2
(MPC disposable paddy[3])	(.09)	(.56)	(.20)	(-.86)

---

[1]See Note 1, Table 5-8.

[2]Gross paddy production minus both rent and in-kind labor payments.

[3]See Note 3, Table 5-8.

[4]One tenant was omitted from production, investment, rent and yield calculations because she had been farming for only two years.

than would a truly random sample.[51]   Of the 45 farmers we interviewed, 29 percent had tile or concrete roofs on their homes, only 44 percent thatch.

Differences in housing between owner-cultivators and the other two groups were marked, as in Khanh Hau; but, except for the fact the 2/3 of the LTTT beneficiaries were repairing, remodelling, or reconstructing their houses, while only 40 percent of the remaining tenants were, there was little to indicate the new owners of LBD were fast catching up with the "old" owner-cultivators. Sixty percent of the "old" owner-cultivators had tile roofs, compared with only 13 percent of the present and former tenants. Fifty-three percent of the former had brick or cement walls, only 17 percent of the latter did. Only 40 percent of the owner-cultivators lived on packed-earth floors, while an even 80 percent of the other two groups did.[52]

Table 5-13 indicates the proportions of our farmer sample owning selected vehicles and consumer durables and compares our results with the findings of the LBD Census. Our farmer sample again proves to be richer than the average village resident, 67 percent of them owning at least one bicycle, 24 percent owning motorbikes, 76 percent radios and 52 percent sewing machines, to mention the more important "modern" items.   Land tenure correlations exist in the ownership statistics of all four of these items, but show up most strongly in the ownership of a fifth—the wall clock, which was apparently considered by many to be a prestigious luxury. Some of the new owners were using their higher incomes to purchase consumer durables—6 of them did so in 1971, compared with only 2 tenants and one owner-cultivator.   Among the items purchased the favorites were table and chair sets and worship tables or cabinets.

---

[51]Our sample contained 33 percent owner-cultivators by design. While they were selected within that tenure category in a semi-random manner, their proportion in the total sample was pre-determined.   Robert Sansom, **Economics of Insurgency**, p. 72, reported that 54 percent of his sample were owner-cultivators; but since he was limited exclusively to the two central, more secure hamlets, where the wealthier families have long concentrated their homes, his sample is not representative of the whole village, either. Estimates used above would place the number of owner-cultivators farming LBD land at 167, or 21 percent of all 810 farmers, and they would be tilling 288 ha., 29 percent of the LBD riceland area.

[52]See Table 5-12.

Table 5-12

Type of Housing in Long Binh Dien Village, 1971-72

Percentages of:

Type of Roofing	15 Present Tenants	15 Title recip- ients	15 Owner culti- vators	All 45 Farmers Inter- viewed	593 Houses of the 4 Southern Hamlets	829-House Village Total
Tile or concrete	13.3	13.3	60.0	28.9	9.8	7.0
Corrugated metal	40.0	26.7	13.3	26.7	28.0	27.4
Thatch	46.7	60.0	26.7	44.4	62.2	65.6
Walls						
Brick or cement	20.0	13.3	53.3	28.9		
Wood	53.3	60.0	40.0	51.1		
Thatch or bamboo	26.7	26.7	6.7	20.0		
Floors						
Tile	0	6.7	53.3	20.0		
Cement	20.0	13.3	6.7	13.3		
Earth	80.0	80.0	40.0	66.7		
Percentages Re- pairing, Remodel- ling or Reconstruct- ing in 1971-72	40.0	66.7	66.7	57.8		

SOURCE of last two columns: LBD Village Census, 1971-2.

Table 5-13

Ownership of Selected Vehicles and Consumer Durables
in Long Binh Dien Village, 1971-72

| | Percentage owning at least one: | | | | Average Number Owned per Household, Sample of 45 Farmers | Village Census Results | |
Item	15 Present Tenants	15 Title Recipients	15 Owner-cultivators	All 45 Farmers		Total Number Owned in Village	Average Number Owned per Household
Chinese-character fresco	40	60	53	51	.93		
Glass-front cabinet	40	33	47	40	.53		
Wardrobe cabinet	73	93	93	87	1.38		
Wall clock	13	33	53	33	.33		
Pressure lamp	33	40	33	36	.36		
Sewing machine	40	53	60	51	.51	199	.24
Radio	67	67	93	76	.78	512	.62
Television	0	0	13	4	.04	9	.01
Bicycle	53	73	73	67	.91	284	.34
Motorbike	20	13	40	24	.36	61	.07
3-wheeled Lambretta	0	0	0	0	0	8	.01
Light truck	0	0	0	0	0	2	.002
Bus	0	0	0	0	0	1	.001
Automobile	0	0	0	0		0	0
Sampan, motor	0	0	7	2	.02	2	.002
Sampan, hand	0	7	0	2	.02	21	.03
Percentage of households purchasing consumer durables in 1971 or planning to in 1972:	13	40	13	22			

SOURCE of last two columns: 1971-2 LBD Village Census, Village Office. Total number of households reported in the census was 829.

Indebtedness

Of our sample of 145 farmers, 53 percent had borrowed money during the year preceding our interviews, excluding debtors of the **hui** associations.[53]   Over half of those borrowing (54 percent) did so only to meet farm operating expenses or to make agricultural investments, 8 percent borrowed for purely consumption purposes, while the remaining 38 percent used the money for both production and consumption expenditures.

The major source of credit in LBD was the government Agricultural Development Bank (ADB), which provided 61 percent of the loans and 79 percent of the funds reported by our sample. Next came relatives, who provided 29 percent of the loans and 20 percent of the funds, with friends and neighbors trailing in a very poor third and last place, providing only 1 percent of the amount borrowed. This contrasts with the situation in Khanh Hau Village, where friends and neighbors provided more of the funds than any other source. None of our LBD sample mentioned a moneylender, merchant or landlord as a source of credit. (See Table 5-14.)

Owner-cultivators were still (as in 1966-67[54]) obtaining the lion's share of government loans. While comprising only a third of our sample this group received 54 percent of the ADB funds reported by all 45 farmers. 53 percent of the owner-cultivators interviewed had borrowed from the ADB within the last year, compared to 40 percent of the LTTT-title-recipients and only 20 percent of the remaining tenants.

We visited LBD Village after a couple of bad harvests due to insect damage. Annual production had fallen 10 percent over the last 2 years for those in our sample, despite a 6 percent increase in the amount of land double-cropped. The remission of rents nevertheless allowed the LTTT beneficiaries to experience a rise in income, since their disposable paddy (after rents and in-kind labor payments) rose by 21 percent. Both of the other two groups were

---

[53]We did not ask questions about **hui** participation due to limitations of time and the difficulty of determining a member's net debtor or creditor status. This makes our findings on indebtedness in LBD not quite comparable with those of Robert Sansom, who did include the **hui** and took the time to study it in great detail. Sansom found that 76 percent of his 50-farmer sample in LBD were debtors in 1966-67, and of the 127 loans reported in the 2 villages he studied, 41 percent were from **hui** associations. Sansom, **Economics of Insurgency**, pp. 105-22.

[54]See **Ibid.**, p. 112 .

Table 5-14

Sources of Cash Credit by Village, 1971-72

Source	28 debtors in Khanh Hau		24 debtors in LBD		23 debtors in Phu Thu		30 debtors in HBT	
	% of loans	% of amount	% of loans	% of amount	% of loans	% of amount	% of loans	% of amount
Government	28	28	61	79	9	10	9	11
Relatives	28	33	29	20	39	27	47	40
Friends & neighbors	33	21	11	1	48	62	44	50
Landlords	3	3						
Moneylenders	3	1			4	1		
Pawn shops	3	2						
Commercial credit	3	14	—	—	—	—	—	—
	101	102	101	100	100	100	100	101

Total

Number of loans	36	28	23	32
--% of total	30%	24%	19%	27%
Amount of loans (1000's)	1474.5$	1142$	411$	1418$
--% of total	33%	26%	9%	32%
--% of total gov't. credit	27%	60%	3%	10%

having to tighten their belts, however; the owner-cultivators suffered a 7 percent drop in disposable paddy, the tenants 14 percent.

Of those borrowing in 1969, 88 percent of the owner-cultivators were able to increase their debts in 1971-72, in response to the fall in their incomes, while only 14 percent of the tenants were able to do so. Rent remission helped a fourth of the new-owner debtors to reduce their debts, but 63 percent of them borrowed more than before, mostly for farm expenses and investments.[55] This evidence supports the observation that land ownership makes it easier for a farmer to obtain credit and to obtain more credit in times of greater need.

Agricultural Production

The farmers of LBD are proving to be much slower in adopting some of the modern methods of production that are sweeping Khanh Hau. In 1971 only 2 percent of our LBD sample plowed their fields with mechanical power, the rest still using the water buffalo; and only 7 percent more planned to make the switch in 1972, bringing the total to 9 percent, compared with 50 percent in Khanh Hau. Sansom found 38 percent of his LBD sample were double-cropping rice in 1966-67.[56] This had risen to only 42 percent of our sample[57] in 1971-72, compared with 91 percent in Khanh Hau. The new Miracle Rice seeds were not introduced into the Mekong Delta until 1968.[58] While in Khanh Hau 95 percent of our sample planned in 1972 to plant this new, high yield variety, in LBD only 27 percent had such plans and only 20 percent had planted it in 1971.

---

[55]See C. Stuart Callison, **Land-to-the-Tiller in the Mekong Delta,** Ph.D. Dissertation, Cornell University, Ithaca, N.Y., 1976, Table 5-24.

[56]Sansom, **Economics of Insurgency,** p. 78.

[57]Our sample was double-cropping 31 percent of its riceland area, compared with 80 percent for the Khanh Hau sample. The LBD Census, in 1972, however, reported that 48 percent of the riceland area was double-cropped and that not quite half of this (23 percent of the total area) was planted in Miracle Rice.

[58]IR-8 rice was first harvested outside a government experimental station in Vo Dat Village, Binh Tuy Province, in February 1968, and it was distributed for planting throughout the Mekong Delta in succeeding months. "Miracle Rice Comes to Vietnam," **Viet-Nam Bulletin,** Viet-Nam Info Series 15, Agriculture: Miracle Rice (11-69), (Washington, D.C.: Embassy of Vietnam), p. 6.

A slightly higher proportion of our LBD sample (44 percent)[59] owned a motor pump than in Khanh Hau (36 percent), but no rototillers were reported in the whole village.[60]   As in Khanh Hau, the ownership distribution of motor pumps was highly skewed toward landowner-cultivators, of which 60 percent owned at least one pump, compared with 47 percent of the LTTT owners and only 27 percent of the remaining tenants.   (See Table 5-15.)

As noted above, LBD rice yields dropped 10 percent in the last 2 years.   In 1971-72 they averaged only 48 percent of the annual per-hectare yield in Khanh Hau, 66 percent of the latter's crop-hectare yield.   (See Table 5-11.)   The proportion of the total rice harvest sold remained steady at 48 percent, however, while the portion consumed rose from 30 to 35 percent, thanks to the remission of rents.   The proportion sold was up from Sansom's reported 32 percent (with 43 percent consumed) in 1966-67,[61] but was considerably lower than the 64 percent sold by Khanh Hau farmers in 1971.   (See Table 5-24.)

[59]Up from 38 percent in Sansom's 1967 sample, and with a smaller proportion of owner-cultivators than his sample.   The LBD Census, 1972, reported 150 motor pumps in the whole village, or an average of one for each of 27 percent of the farmers.   Sansom, **Economics of Insurgency,** p. 169.

[60]In neither the LBD Census nor our sample interviews.   The census did report 29 pressure insecticide sprayers on hand, enough for 5.3 percent of the farmers, up from 2 percent of Sansom's sample.   **Ibid.,** p. 84.

[61]Sansom reported an average crop-hectare yield of 1.99 MT in LBD in 1966-67, which was apparently another bad year.   At 50 **gia** per metric ton our sample averaged 2.28 MT per crop-ha. in 1969-70, 2.02 MT in the "bad year" of 1971-72.   Calculated on an annual basis, our LBD sample averaged 2.66 MT/ha. in 1971-72, 2.94 MT two years before, and they claimed to average 3.04 MT/ha. before that (and before anyone had Miracle Rice).   **Ibid.,** p. 186, and our Table 5-11.

Table 5-15

Ownership of Farm Implements in Long Binh Dien Village, 1972,

And Percentage of Farmer Sample Who Hired Labor

| Implement | Percentages owning of: | | | |
	15 Present Tenants	15 Title Recipients	15 Owner-Cultivators	All 45 Farmers
Hand Plow	7	33	20	20
Harrow	7	27	20	18
Roller	7	33	20	20
Threshing Sledge	60	47	40	49
Motor Pump	27	47	60	44
Rototiller	0	0	0	0
Percentage purchasing new implements in 1971-2	20	27	27	24
Percentage who hire labor:	100	93	100	98

Note: The 1971-2 Village Census counted a total of 150 motor pumps, 29 insecticide sprayers, and no rototillers owned by village residents.

Phu Thu, Phong Dinh Province

The Village of Phu Thu stretches back from the southwest bank of the Lower Mekong or Hau Giang River (the French call it the Bassac River) between 3 and 5 kilometers downstream from Can Tho, the capital of Phong Dinh Province and the largest city in the Delta. Despite its proximity to a large urban area, Phu Thu was the least accessible village of the four under study. It had no roads whatsoever. All transportation to and from Can Tho was by water, the trip to the Village Office taking about 30 minutes by motorized sampan (**ghe may**) water-taxi, depending on the direction and speed of the tide, and costing 150$ VN ($.38 U.S.). Renting a **ghe may** or **tac ran** (the latter a faster boat, long and narrow, but more expensive) is a luxury only the richer could afford, but the wait for a **do may** to depart the market was often a long one.

The **do may** were motorized, wooden water-buses constructed with a roof on top and a row of windows along each side. They could be seen plying the rivers in various sizes, the larger ones handling the more distant traffic. The Phu Thu **do** could seat about 24 passengers on the inside and more up on the roof, and they charged 30 piasters ($.08 U.S.) each for the Phu Thu—Can Tho trip. A **do may** would pass about once every 30 minutes in the morning, but only two or three trips would be made all afternoon, at irregular times, and if one missed the last one to Can Tho, which usually left Phu Thu between 4 and 4:30 PM, he would be stranded. The **ghe may**, easy to obtain at the Can Tho market, were seldom to be seen along the local streams of Phu Thu, especially in late afternoon. (On several afternoons, a Popular Defense Force soldier had to fire his carbine in the air as a signal to a boatman passing far out in the Mekong River to pick us up.)

The ebb and flood of the tide causes the water level in Phu Thu to fluctuate commonly 9 or 10 feet at irregular intervals,[62] creating special transportation problems for some areas of the village. Three sets of our interviews (9 interviews) drawn were in the upper reaches of the (**Rach**) Cai Doi Creek, 3 or 4 km. upstream from its mouth on the Hau Giang (in an area called Ngon Chua of Phu Hoa Hamlet), accessible only at high tide. If the tide was high only at midday we could not interview in this hamlet, as we would have been stranded at low tide in the late afternoon. We

---

[62]Tidal schedules were published daily in the local Can Tho newspapers, but they seemed to have little relation to the timing of high and low tides we observed in Phu Thu, nor could we discern a regular variation between the observed and printed timing. There seemed to be an irregular whiplash effect in the upstream tributaries.

MAP OF PHU THU VILLAGE,
CHAU THANH DISTRICT,
PHONG DINH PROVINCE

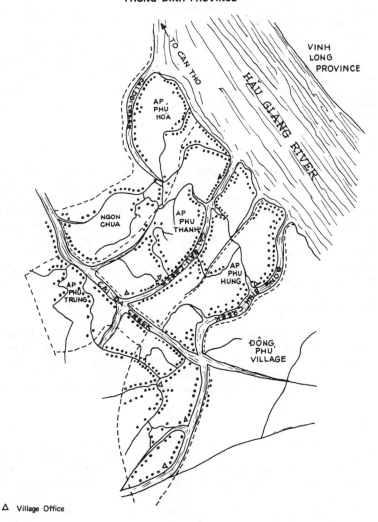

△ Village Office

had to watch for a high morning tide on which to go in, conduct our interview(s) and eat lunch while the tide went out, and wait for the waters to rise again in the afternoon to return home.[63]

Unpaved footpaths line the banks of the local streams. During the rainy season they become muddy and slippery, and they are often submerged at high tide. One can cross most of the smaller creeks and canals via appropriately named bamboo "monkey bridges" (**cau khi**), rickety constructions high over the water (so sampans can pass underneath), with one bamboo pole to walk on and one or two smaller ones between knee and waist high to hang on to.[64] The main streams are far too wide and deep for the monkey bridges, however, and must be paddled across in tiny canoe-like boats or the larger sampans.

Demographic Data

The four hamlets of Phu Thu Village contained a population of 6,178 people. There were exactly 1,000 households on record in May, 1972, indicating an average household size of 6.2 persons. The village is predominantly (61 percent) of the traditional Buddhist faith, but with a sizeable minority (29 percent) of Hoa Hao and a sprinkling of those who call themselves Confucian, Cao Dai or Christian. (See Table 5-16.) Very little other information on the sociological characteristics of the population was available at the time of our visit.

Sample Selection

We were cautioned not to go to the two more distant hamlets unescorted, Phu Trung and Phu Hung; so our selection process was limited to the two central hamlets—Phu Hoa along Rach[65] Cai Doi and Phu Thanh along Rach Cai Sau—which contained 61 percent of the village population. Household numbers were selected out of a

---

[63]Fortunately, we were befriended by a young man, a slightly disabled veteran from Saigon who had married a young lady from this hamlet and had settled there near her family. He went by the nickname Tam Tho Den (Tho Den means "the lampmaker"), since he made decorative bamboo lanterns for sale through a Can Tho novelty and gift shop. Mr. Tam resided near the mouth of the Cai Doi Creek and was always ready to retrieve us from upstream with his **ghe may** and small son as soon as the tides would permit.

[64]Their users are frequently dunked, to which the local residents and my wife will attest.

[65]**Rach** means creek or small river.

Table 5-16

Religious Preferences Among Farmer Sample and All Village Residents, By Village, 1971–72

(Percentages)

Religion	Khanh Hau Sample N=44	Khanh Hau Village N=837	Long Binh Dien Sample N=45	Long Binh Dien Village N=4798	Phu Thu Sample N=45	Phu Thu Village N=1256	Hoa Binh Thanh Sample N=46	Hoa Binh Thanh Village N=13478	Total Sample N=180
Buddhist: Traditional	50	42	51	29	73	61	2		44
Hoa Hao					13	29	83	91	24
Cambodian							7		2
Confucian (ancestor worship)	14	34	29	64	2	3			11
Buddhist & Confucian			16	6					4
Cao Dai	36	20	4		11	5		0.2	13
Christian: Catholic		4		0.4		1.3	9	9	2
Protestant				0.4		0.7			
Other		0.1							
	100	100.1	100	99.8	99	100.0	101	100.2	100

SOURCE: Village statistics were provided by the respective village offices during the period of our survey in 1971–72. Khanh Hau kept religious preferences by household, LBD and HBT by person, and Phu Thu officials said their figures included only adults, although the total seems too small to have included all adults (12% is only 20% of the total village population and is only 26% greater than the total number of households). The HBT data includes an obvious error, since 4.3% of its population are of Cambodian descent and practice their own brand of Buddhism, but are apparently included here as Hoa Hao, which they certainly are not. In addition, one of our HBT sample said he was Buddhist, but disclaimed being of the Hoa Hao sect, while the village Office does not list any in that category, either.

Table 5-17

Population Date — Phu Thu Village

Hamlet	(1) Population	(2) Percentage of total Village Population	(3) Percentage of total population in hamlets surveyed	(4) Number of Farmers Interviewed	(5) Col. 4 as percentage of total interviewed
Phu Thanh	2712	43.9	71.5	33	73.3
Phu Hoa	1083	17.5	28.5	12	26.7
Sub-total	3795	61.4	100.0	45	100.0
Phu Trung	868	14.0			
Phu Hung	1515	24.5			
Sub-total	2383	38.6			
Total	6178	99.9			

Number of Households: 1000
Average of Household size: 6.2

SOURCE: Village Office, May 1972

Table 5-18

Phu Thu Village Interviewee Data

Total		15 Present Tenants	16 Title Recipients	14 Owner-Cultivators	All 45 Farmers
Interviewees:	Male	9	11	8	28
	Female	6	5	6	17
Average					
Age of Interviewee:	Male	56.0	54.4	57.1	55.7
	Female	42.2	51.4	43.3	45.3
Education (years):	Male	1.7	1.6	2.1	1.8
	Female	0.3	0.8	0.7	0.6
Number of Household Residents		7.8	7.3	6.8	7.3

hat, as before, and divided proportionately between the two hamlets according to their population, as indicated in Table 5-17.[66]

Land Tenure

The total cadastral area of Phu Thu is 1,485.5 hectares, with about 74 percent of that in rice, 13 percent in orchard and residential land, and 7 percent classified as planted to vegetables in 1972 (about 50 hectares, or 3.4 percent of the total village hectarage were reported as abandoned, uncultivated land in Phu Hung Hamlet). From the best estimates that could be derived, with the help of the village agricultural commissioner, it appears that approximately 69 percent of the farmers were tenants before the LTTT Program, renting 58 percent of the cultivated land. Land expropriation and redistribution statistics gathered in May 1972 were again preliminary and incomplete; but it was estimated that the LTTT Program would reduce tenancy to no more than 128 farmers, or to around 13 percent of all farmers,[67] renting 189 hectares, or 13 percent of the cultivated land.[68]

---

[66]See Table 5-17 for sex, age, level of education and household size of the Phu Thu sample.

[67]The base number of all farmers, 993, derived by adding different groups of farmers separately estimated, is undoubtedly too high in a village with only 1,000 households. While we were able to reduce the multiple-LTTT-titles received to an appropriate number of recipient farmers with statistical adjustments similar to those described earlier in this chapter, there are other sources of duplication we were unable to eliminate, especially since we are here counting all land, and many residential orchard plots and paddy fields owned by the same farmers would be listed and counted separately. Fully 36 percent of the farmers we interviewed in this village were of mixed tenure status, about half of these owning plots of orchard or vegetable land as well as renting (or receiving LTTT title to) riceland, the other half of mixed tenure on riceland itself. Village officials had no occupational data to show us, but they estimated the proportion of farmers in Phu Thu would be high, between 80 percent and 90 percent of total households.

[68]Since we were unable to separate the orchard land from the riceland areas in some of the statistics obtained, these figures include all land instead of just the riceland area as in the discussions above of Khanh Hau and LBD. Most of the "orchard land" in Phu Thu is in reality residential area, subdivided among owners and tenants into tiny household plots, which were not redistributed under the LTTT Program but remain under the names of the original owners. Because of the obvious duplication involved, we did not include estimates of tenants on this retained orchard land, since

Traditional and modified Lorenz curves of landownership distribution in Phu Thu show the same lessening of inequality as in the two villages discussed above. The effects of the LTTT Program demonstrated in Figures 5-7 and 5-8 have been dampened by the necessary inclusion of all cultivated land, instead of using the riceland area alone. The numerous, small residential plots of "orchard land" and the duplication of owners counted (as mentioned in footnote 67) increase the skew of both curves and decrease the observed differences between them, since these plots are unaffected by the Program.

Taken as rough approximations, however, the statistics show that the number of landowners increased from 452 to 872, or by 93 percent, and that the proportion of them owning less than 3 ha. increased from 67 to 90 percent.[69] The proportion to total land area in holdings of less than 3 ha. increased from 25 to 63 percent. Considering all tenant farmers and landowners together, the upper 14 percent of them owned 75 percent of the land area before the LTTT Program, whereas the upper 15 percent owned only 50 percent of the land in May 1972.

The traditional Gini index of inequality in ownership distribution declined from .558 before the LTTT Program to .475 with redistribution 85 percent complete, for a decline of 14.9 percent. The more comprehensive index obtained by including landless tenants in the data, as in the Lorenz curve of Figure 5-8, declined from .810 to .563, however, or by 30.5 percent, indicating that a very significant reform toward greater equality in land ownership was indeed underway in Phu Thu Village.

(cont.)
most of them are already counted as LTTT-title recipients or Huong Hoa tenants of riceland. The orchard plots themselves are included in the land area figures, however, 90 ha. of them rented. Deducting orchard land would leave an estimated 98.6 ha. of riceland still rented after the LTTT Program, or about 9% of the total riceland area.

[69] As of May, 1972, with distribution 85 percent complete as compared with the 3-year mark of March 26, 1973. By the latter date 700 LTTT titles for a total of 581 ha. had been printed for distribution to 553 farmers. In the earlier Ordinance 57 and French purchase land reform program, only 104.36 ha. had been distributed to 90 former tenants, according to village data. (See Tables A-10 and A-11.)

Figure 5-7

**Lorenz Curves of Land Ownership Distribution
Among Owners in Phu Thu Village,
Before and After 1970 LTTT Program**

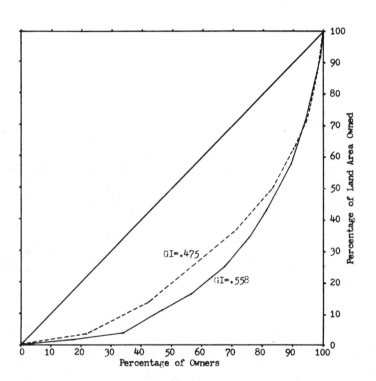

Legend: —— Before LTTT Program (452 Owners)
        ---- After LTTT Program (872 Owners)

Source: See Table A-10a and b.

Figure 5-8

**Lorenz Curves of Land Ownership Distribution
Among Owners and Tenants in Phu Thu Village,
Before and After 1970 LTTT Program**

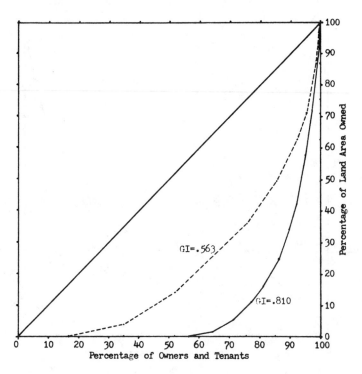

Legend: ——— Before LTTT Program (1045 Owners & Tenants)
         ---- After LTTT Program (1045 Owners & Tenants)

Source: See Table A-11.

Thirty-five percent of the 43 landlords discussed by our sample resided in the same village, and 51 percent resided outside the village but within the same district (which included the province capital, Can Tho). The remaining 14 percent were scattered to more distant locations, including 7 percent in Saigon. All 5 of the landlords reported as residing outside the province had had their land expropriated, but the tenant and title-recipient groups reported similar proportions of landlords residing in the village as opposed to elsewhere in the province.

A majority of the LTTT beneficiaries (55 percent) reported having had written contracts with their landlords, whereas only a third of the remaining tenants did. The proportion of landlords reported as relatives was only slightly higher for the tenant group (28 percent, as opposed to 19 percent for title recipients). All 15 of the remaining-tenant groups were renting Huong Hoa land and gave that as the reason they could not request title. Of the 3 title-recipients who still rented part of their holding, however, one held a parcel of orchard land, one some land inside the city limits of Can Tho (which had within the last 2 years been extended to engulf the village adjacent to Phu Thu), and one also rented a small amount of Huong Hoa worship land, all three of which categories were exempt from redistribution.

Stipulated rents averaged 11.5 **gia** per hectare in this village, or 14 percent of the 1969-70 paddy yield from rented land.[70] Actual paddy rents paid that year averaged only 12 percent of total production, however.[71] The agreed and actual rents were significantly lower in Phu Thu than in any of our other three villages, both in absolute paddy per hectare and as percentages of gross production. This could be a reflection of the more labor-intensive nature of the double-transplant cultivation practices here; but it probably also reflects the more isolated conditions of the village and its inherent "less secure" nature in the eyes of the absentee landlords, few of whom have dared to visit their tenants for years.

---

[70]See Table 5-23. The 1969-70 year was a bad year; production was off 16 percent from what the tenants considered normal and down 7 percent in the eyes of the new owners. As proportions of a "normal" year's harvest, stipulated rents averaged .113 for the present tenants, .143 for the former tenants, for an overall average of 13 percent.

[71]Actual paddy rents paid (Table 5-28) have been calculated for only 10 tenants and 14 title recipients, omitting those paying in cash. All but one of the whole sample reported stipulated rents in paddy figures, however (Table 5-23).

Stipulated rents ranged from 3 percent to 47 percent of the "average" yield before 1969 (as reported by the farmers), but only 4 out of 33 were over the legal 25 percent limit. Of these 4, two were just barely over (26 percent and 27 percent) and must be considered in the ballpark, especially since one was high merely because the tenant was cultivating only about two-thirds of the land for which he was paying rent. The other two (28 and 48 percent) were high mostly because the farmers claimed extremely low average yields. If divided by the former yield average for the whole sample (86/**gia**), the 38 percent rent reduces to a legal 24 percent, and the 47 percent rent becomes 33 percent, leaving us with only one clear case of illegally high rent in the whole Phu Thu sample.[72]

Living Standards

Our Phu Thu Sample of farmers had the smallest average farm size (1.16 ha.), coupled with the lowest yields per hectare anywhere but in HBT, where low-yielding floating-rice farms averaged almost 5 times as large in size. Gross paddy production averaged only 108 **gia** per farm, compared with 203 in LBD, 456 in HBT and 635 in Khanh Hau. One would expect these facts to lead to a lower standard of living in Phu Thu, and this is most apparent in the housing data.

Only 4 percent of the entire Phu Thu sample had houses with roofs of tile and walls of bricks or concrete, compared with 29 percent in LBD, 34-43 percent in Khanh Hau and HBT.[73] A higher

---

[72]That particular former tenant had had a landlord who resided in the village, a non-relative with whom he had only a verbal rental agreement, who permitted him no freedom to try new crops or techniques (refusing to grant permission to build better irrigation dikes, for example), and who, the tenant believed, would have raised his rent demands if the tenant had succeeded in raising his yields. The landlord did grant tolerance for crop failures: the former tenant reported he only paid half his normal rent in 1969-70, when he suffered a 42 percent crop failure; but his rent that year still amounted to 40 percent of his gross production. Since receiving an LTTT title, this farmer was beginning to build water control dikes in order to double-crop Miracle Rice, and he spoke enthusiastically about his future.

[73]In the HBT sample, 35 percent of the roofs were of tile but only 4 percent of the walls were brick or cement. Houses there are built on stilts several feet above the ground to stay above the annual high-water mark, and they are normally made with light-weight walls of either wood or thatch. The wealthiest landowners

proportion of Phu Thu farmers had walls and roofs of thatch than in any of the other three. (See Table 5-19.)

Except for the numbers of farmers repairing, remodelling or rebuilding their houses, which were higher for the owner-cultivator and title-recipient groups than for the tenants, the housing statistics in Phu Thu show no significant correlations with land tenure status. This is partly because there were no significant differences in average farm size among the three groups of the sample, with the owner-cultivators in fact having slightly smaller operating farm units than the tenants and former tenants. In part, however, it was due to the insecure and turbulent conditions of recent years, which affected Phu Thu more than our other three villages.[74] Even the farmer who could afford to build a better house feared to do so lest it become a casualty of war. Some of those who were now in the process of or planning reconstruction explained that only during the last two or three years had they begun to feel safe enough to risk it. Others intended to wait longer still.

Although slightly fewer Phu Thu farmers owned some of the consumer durable items on our list than those in the other villages, the difference was not as noticeable as with housing. Eighty percent of them had a radio, 60 percent a sewing machine. One of our sample owned a motorbike, which he had to cart to Can Tho by boat in order to use very much; but no one we interviewed had a bicycle, not surprising in view of the nature of the present land routes. Ninety-three percent of all households surveyed owned a sampan or boat of some kind, and 73 percent of them had motors for their boats. (See Table 5-20.)

A reverse correlation between land tenure status appears in the ownership data for sewing machines, wall clocks and motor sampans, with a larger proportion of tenants and former tenants owning these items than owner-cultivators, while the more traditional brass altar fixtures were owned by more owner-cultivators than the other two groups. More owner-cultivators were making consumer durable purchases than title-recipients, while present

---

(cont.)
in HBT typically had houses with wooden floors and walls and tile roofs, as discussed below.

[74]Local residents told us they were at the mercy of the communist guerrilla bands until after 1968, when they were finally given arms to defend themselves (in the Popular Defense Force Program). They had often witnessed small-scale skirmishes in and around their village and reported that a Viet Cong unit moved in and took over the whole village during the 1968 Tet Offensive, holding it for some time until they were driven out.

Table 5-19

Type of Housing in Phu Thu Village, 1972

(Percentages of Sample)

Roofing	15 Present Tenants	16 Title Recipients	14 Owner Cultivators	All 45 Farmers
Tile or concrete	0	6.3	7.1	4.4
Corrugated metal	60.0	37.5	35.7	44.4
Thatch	40.0	56.3	57.1	51.1
Walls				
Brick or cement	0	6.3	7.1	4.4
Wood	46.7	37.5	28.6	37.8
Metal sheets	0	0	14.3	4.4
Earth	0	0	7.1	2.2
Thatch or bamboo	53.3	56.3	42.9	51.1
Floors				
Tile	20.0	12.5	21.4	17.8
Cement	20.0	12.5	14.3	15.6
Earth	60.0	75.0	64.3	66.7
Percentages repairing, remodelling, or reconstructing in 1971-2	33.3	56.3	57.1	48.9

Table 5-20

Ownership of Selected Consumer Durables and Vehicles Among Phu Thu Sample, 1972

Item	Percentage owning at least one: 15 Present Tenants	16 Title Recipients	14 Owner Cultivators	All 45 Farmers
Chinese-character fresco	13	19	21	18
Brass Altar fixtures	27	31	57	38
Glass-front cabinet	13	13	7	11
Wardrobe cabinet	53	69	57	60
Wall clock	27	25	7	20
Pressure lamp	20	50	38	36
Sewing machine	73	69	38	60
Radio	80	75	86	80
Television	0	0	0	0
Bicycle	0	0	0	0
Motorbike or scooter	7	0	0	2
Sampan, motor or hand	93	94	93	93
Sampan, motor	80	75	64	73
Sampan, hand	13	31	36	27
Percentage of households purchasing consumer durables in 1971 or planning to in 1972:	0	19	38	18

tenants were making none; but, rather than the more modernistic items and machines, both groups were purchasing more items of basic furniture—clothes closets, worship cabinets, tables and chairs and the heavy wooden bed (**bo van**).

Indebtedness

In Phu Thu all nine of the title-recipient debtors interviewed had increased their debts over the last two years, six of them borrowing for the first time.[75] Among the other two groups, however, it was the tenants who increased their debt status and their average debt more than the owner-cultivators. Debt levels averaged lower in Phu Thu than anywhere else, only one third to one half the average cash amounts borrowed in the other three villages; and they increased by only 1 percent over the last two years. Phu Thu had the largest percentage increase in the number of farmers borrowing, though by 1971-72 the proportion of all farmers borrowing (51 percent) was still lower than elsewhere.

The chief sources of loans and loan funds here were friends and neighbors, who provided 62 percent of the cash amounts borrowed. Relatives followed by providing 27 percent and the government placed a poor third with 10 percent (see Table 5-14). Only one person out of 23 debtors had borrowed from a moneylender and not one had borrowed from a landlord.

About half of the debtor-farmers borrowed solely to meet operating expenses and to make farm investments, while only 22 percent said they borrowed for purely consumption needs. A quarter of them admitted to using the money for both types of expenses.

Agricultural Production

A very few farmers in Phu Thu had ever used water buffalo to plow their fields. The grass in this region grows so thick and strong between seasons that buffalo must strain to pull a plow through it. Traditionally most of the farmers here had to chop the grass off as close to the roots as they could swing a long, machette-like blade (with a 90-degree crook near the handle and the cutting edge on the outside), rake it and then grub up the sod by hand. It was hard, back-breaking work, a very labor-intensive process, which may help account for the small size of the farms here, even among owner-cultivators. Not one of our Phu Thu sample owned a water

---

[75]Meaning they had borrowed the year of our interview, but had not done so two years before. See Callison, **Land-to-the-Tiller**, Table 5-36.

buffalo nor any of the farm implements associated with them (the hand plow, the harrow or the roller), although 3 of them (7 percent) did hire at least part of their plowing done by buffalo (one or two explaining that his ground was too low and wet for the new machines).

The new rototillers imported from Japan have relieved these farmers of this great annual drudgery, and 89 percent of our sample hired or used their own machine plows in 1971. Only 2 out of 45 farmers (4 percent) still did all the work by hand, though 3 others still did or hired part of their land by hand, as well. Three of the owner-cultivators and 1.14 title-recipients owned rototillers (one of the latter having 14 percent interest in one), but none of the tenants did.[76]

Miracle Rice is almost synonymous with double-cropping in Phu Thu (as, indeed, it was in the first 2 villages). Out of 22 farmers who planted Miracle Rice seed in 1971-72, only one used it as a single crop. The other 21, or 47 percent of our sample, had double-cropped at least a portion of their land—17 of them obtaining 2 crops for the first time ever that year or the year before. Some were planting both crops to the new MR varieties, but many were using it as an early crop, harvested in time to plant traditional varieties as the second crop. Eight additional farmers planned to try the double-cropping techniques the next year, bringing the total to 64 percent of the sample.[77]

While Phu Thu experienced the largest increase in the proportion of farmers switching from single to double-cropping between 1969-70 and 1971-72 (9 to 47 percent) **and** the largest percentage increase in the mount of land double-cropped (270 percent), the actual amount of land double-cropped remained small, rising from only 5 percent to 19 percent of the riceland farmed by the sample. Farmers here were proceeding slowly and on an experimental basis, partly because of the risk factor in trying new varieties and familiar techniques, and partly because the initial capital investment to prepare the land and obtain the necessary equipment for Miracle Rice was higher here—in the poorest village—than elsewhere. It was amazing that they were adopting the new techniques as fast as they were, and that they were doing so with such great enthusiasm, in view of the difficulties they faced.

---

[76]See Table 5-21 for ownership of farm implements in Phu Thu. Sixty percent of the sample said they would like to buy a rototiller for themselves, if only they had enough money.

[77]Actually, 9 more farmers were going to try double-cropping for the first time, but another one was giving it up as too much work, leaving a net increase of 8. See Table 5-22.

Table 5-21

Ownership of Farm Implements in Phu Thu Village, 1972

And Percentage Who Hire Labor

Implement	Percentages owning of: 15 Present Tenants	16 Title Recipients	14 Owner-Cultivators	All 45 Farmers in Sample
Hand Plow	0	0	0	0
Harrow	0	0	0	0
Roller	0	0	0	0
Threshing Sledge	87	63	64	71
Power Weed Cutter	0	0	7	2
Motor Pump	0	19_1	7	9
Rototiller	0	7	21	9
Percentage purchasing new implements in 1971-2	0	13	14	9
Percentage who hire labor:	93	100	86	93

[1] One title-recipient farmer owns a rototiller jointly with 6 other farmers (each having an equal 14% interest in it), in a cooperative venture called a to hop, encouraged with a government loan, while another owns one by himself. The two are counted here as 1.14 farmers, or 7% of 16.

Table 5-22

Proportion of Farmers Double-Cropping At Least Part of Their Riceland or Planning to in the Coming Year

Number of Farmers & Village	1969-70	1971-2	Planning to in 1972-73	% increase in number of farmers double-cropping from 1969-70 to 1972-3
44 Khanh Hau	.59	.91	.95	62
44 Long Binh Dien	.36	.41	.48	31
45 Phu Thu	.09	.47	.64	625
46 Hoa Binh Thanh	.17	.41	.46	163
1st Three Villages				
44 tenants	.32	.55	.61	93
45 title-recipients	.29	.62	.73	154
44 owner-cultivators	.43	.61	.70	63
133 Total	.35	.59	.68	98
Hoa Binh Thanh				
15 tenants	.27	.73	.73	175
15 title-recipients	.07	.13	.20	200
16 owner-cultivators	.19	.38	.44	133
46 Total	.17	.41	.46	163

The land in Phu Thu is uneven. Tractors must be hired to level it before the first planting of Miracle Rice. Paddy dikes must be constructed to keep irrigation water in for the first crop—and larger ones to keep flood waters out of the second, if MR is to be planted both crops (local varieties can take the high water, but MR cannot). Canals and ditches must be dug or constructed (above ground level in some cases) to carry sufficient water inland at high tide. Large motor pumps must be purchased; the small sampan motor (with a sleeve over the propeller shaft and a reversed propeller), in such wide use in the upper Delta, is insufficient here.[78] The farmers explained that the soil here was somewhat sandy and water seeped through it rapidly. You pumped enough water into the paddy today only to see it gone tomorrow. The constant pumping required during dry weather was too much for the smaller motors; it wore them out too fast. So one had to have the larger, more efficient (and more expensive) motor pump.

One expenditure was smaller for Miracle Rice than for traditional varieties—that of transplanting. The new rice was transplanted only once, not twice, for each crop, as are the traditional varieties in this region.[79] On the other hand, MR requires higher cash outlays for fertilizer and insecticides, which were seldom used at all on local varieties; and pulling off two crops means a higher overall use of labor throughout the year.

Eighty-one percent of the respondents thought they could still improve their yields significantly by adopting the new seeds and techniques, if they had not already done so, or by expanding the area under two crops. The chief reason given for not doing so was a shortage of labor, generally meaning both a shortage of family labor **and** the high cost of hiring non-family labor (for which they had insufficient funds). Secondly, they cited a lack of either capital or credit to make the heavy initial investment required. Most of the farmers who were double-cropping with Miracle Rice had started out on a small part of their land, leaving the rest in the traditional single-crop, and they planned to expand the double-cropped area little by little each year by investing the proceeds from the year before.

Our Phu Thu sample had improved their yields over the last 2 years by 18 percent on an annual basis, but by only 4 percent

---

[78]Although 73 percent of our sample had the small motors for use on their sampans, only 9 percent claimed to have a motor pump. In the upper Delta the two are synonymous.

[79]See explanation in Chapter V, footnote 1, page 93.

per crop-hectare.[80]   Most of the annual improvement was due to the additional 14 percent of riceland double-cropped, since the total proportion of crop-hectarage in Miracle-Rice was still too small for its higher yields to make much difference. It is also worth noting, for purposes of this study, that the production performance of the LTTT-title-recipients in this village greatly surpassed that of the owner-cultivators and the remaining tenants. They increased their gross paddy production more than twice as much as the owner-cultivators and more than 6 times as much as the tenants, in percentage terms. (See Table 5-23.)

The remission of rents alone, by suddenly raising the income level of the former tenants and increasing the owned funds out of which they could invest,[81] especially coming as it did just after the introduction of Miracle Rice, must undoubtedly be given much of the credit for the increased level of investment by the LTTT beneficiaries. The income effect was less in Phu Thu than elsewhere, however, partly because rents had been lower and partly because the required lump-sum initial investments, which had to be undertaken as a package program, were higher and constituted a bigger discontinuity with the past.

The pure incentive effect of ownership on investment cannot be statistically measured, but we have reason to believe it was higher in Phu Thu than in the other three villages. This is a more isolated, "traditional" part of the Delta, where legal rights of the land and sumptuary mores about consumption still affected the attitudes of the tenant farmers, perhaps more strongly than in the other three villages (although they were still operative there, as well). This is especially true when combined with ignorance of the economics, technical requirements and modern possibilities of farming and the feudalistic attitude toward the rental relationship on the part of some of the landlords in this area.

Some 63 percent of the LTTT-title-recipients plus two beneficiaries of the Ordinance 57 land reform (interviewed as owner-cultivators) said they lacked the freedom under their former

---

[80]The 1969-70 harvest was slightly poorer than average for most of the respondents, however, averaging 6 percent lower than was considered "normal" before that. With the earlier average as a base, annual yields were still improved by 12 percent, but the crop-ha. improvement was negative. See Table 5-23.

[81]Had the rise in income occurred over an extended period of time it would more likely have been dissipated in a concomitant rise in the standard of living (consumption) and would have had less effect on investment.

Table 5-23

Rice Production and Disposition in Phu Thu Village

Average	15 Present Tenants	16 Title recipients	14 Owner culti-vators[4]	All 45 Farmers
Paddy land holding (ha.)	1.22	1.24	1.00	1.16
Ha. received under LTTT Program	.09	1.21	.04	
Gross Paddy Production per Farm, 1971-2 (gia)[1]	96	127	98	108
Annual yield/ha.,1971-2 (gia)	84	106	98	96
Annual yield/ha.,1969-70(gia)	80	80	85	81
Annual yield/ha.,before 1969(gia)	95	86	74	86
(% increase 1969 to 71)	(5)	(32)	(15)	(18)
Portion of Riceland double-cropped, 71-2	.13	.26	.18	.19
Portion of riceland double-cropped, 69-70	.03	.03	.11	.05
(% increase 1969-71)	(352)	(781)	(58)	(270)
Yield/crop ha., 1971-2 (gia)	74	84	83	80
Yield/crop ha., 1969-70(gia)	77	78	77	77
(% increase 1969-71)	(-4)	(8)	(8)	(4)
Stipulated Rent/ha. before LTTT(gia)	10.7[5]	12.3		11.5
Stipulated Rent/1969-70 annual yield	.13	.15		.14
Percentage increase or decrease in last 2 years of (rice paddy use):				
Gross Paddy production	5	31	14	18
Rent	-25	-87	-100	-59
In-kind labor payments	6	- 4	60	16
Home consumption and feed	5	12	3	7
Paddy sales & debt repayment	36	512	77	178
Disposable paddy[2]	8	46	12	23
(MPC disposable paddy[3])	(.57)	(.25)	(.23)	(.28)

---

[1]See Note 1, Table 5-8.

[2]Gross paddy production minus both rent and in-kind labor payments.

[3]See Note 3, Table 5-8.

[4]Due to military clashes on his land one owner-cultivator of 3.14 ha. produced nothing in 1969-70. For purposes of the comparisons made on this table his average production of previous years was substituted for 1969-70.

[5]One tenant is omitted from rent figures since his rent was stipulated in cash, VN$3500 for 1.43 ha.

landlords to change agricultural techniques or to try crops other than rice on rented land. A few gave examples of how they had asked permission to build better irrigation dikes or ditches, or to plant fruit trees on the dikes, and had been denied. Most indicated they never even bothered to ask because they knew the answer would be no. One farmer said his landlord gave him permission to plant two crops a few years ago, but incredibly denied permission at the same time to build the necessary dikes and ditches, fearing the land would be ruined. This was despite the fact that rents could be legally raised in the future, as old rental agreements expired, if the 5-year average yield rose in the meantime. This attitude on the part of some landlords was confirmed in our landlord interviews in Can Tho.

Another former tenant expressed the fear that if he had worked harder, invested his money and successfully raised his production, and then spent his higher income on better housing, better clothing, better equipment, and consumer durables, so that he began to look like a prosperous farmer, his landlord would hate him for getting out of his place and trying to be richer than his landlord; and he would start quarrels and make demands with an eye toward eventual eviction in favor of a tenant who would know his proper place in society. The sumptuary consumption standards in the region (they appear to be otherwise along with Central Coast) say that since a tenant is socially inferior to a landlord, he must not only act like an inferior in the presence of his landlord, but he must live on an obviously inferior standard of living, as well. It would never do for a tenant to appear better off than his landlord.

Through the effects of agricultural and economic ignorance and feudal concepts of status, the old landlord–tenant system imposed a low incentive to invest in higher production, in addition to the natural hesitance on the part of the tenant to make permanent improvements on land not belonging to him, for fear of losing his cultivation rights before the investments had paid for themselves, and the similar hesitancy on the part of the landlord to permit such improvements, for fear they might make it harder to evict the tenant who had made them.

This appears to fly in the face of classical economic theory, which would insist that, given a competitive market in agricultural land (based primarily on its productive potential) and perfect knowledge, both landlord and tenant would be interested in making productive investments to increase output. What we found in Phu Thu and elsewhere was that the "givens" did not exist. Knowledge was very imperfect and there was a highly distorted market for land, which was desired by the wealthy more for its prestige value and as a store of wealth, as a secure form of savings, than for its economic productivity. The sumptuary standards of class consumption denied the tenant the consumption side of his production incentives, as well, rendering the classical economic model of the West irrelevant to the old system, except as a more efficient model toward which to build.

Aside from the negative aspects of tenancy, however, land ownership has a deeper dimension in Vietnam than in the West, as has been mentioned elsewhere in this volume. There are positive incentives to invest and increase production that are ignored by classical economic analysis, which discusses the long-run returns from farm improvements, the higher share of the income increment going to the decision-maker, and the other economic returns to investment. In Vietnam, land ownership among cultivators, in addition to freeing a tenant from the sumptuary and operational restrictions mentioned above, carries with a social **responsibility** to invest more and try harder, because a higher standard of living is **expected** of an owner-cultivator than of a lowly tenant.

If you don't own land, you are expected to be poor; no extra stigma is attached to being poor if you are already in the tenant class. But if you own your land the reverse is true; you are expected to have a nicer house, better clothes and furniture, and most of your children should be in school. If you own your own land and are still dirt poor, it is a reflection on your ability as a farmer, since you can no longer blame your impoverished condition on your landlessness. This "responsibility" is not thought of as a burden by the new owners, but rather as a welcome opportunity to share the higher social status, personal dignity, and standard of living their new ownership classification makes possible. The enthusiasm with which they greet their new economic independence, social freedom, and private opportunities permeates the air they breathe. It has a radiance unmistakable to anyone who visits their homes. We found that enthusiasm in all four villages; but it seemed brightest here in Phu Thu, the poorest and most isolated village of all.

The percentage of gross paddy production sold (or used to repay in-kind debts) remained far lower here than in the other three villages, but it was climbing fast, rising from 8 percent in 1969-70 to 20 percent two years later, while the amount consumed at home dropped from 80 percent to 73 percent.[82] This trend was also led

---

[82]Home consumption of paddy actually rose in Phu Thu by 7 percent during this period, but gross production increased by 18 percent while paddy rents fell by 59 percent for the sample, providing an increase in disposable paddy (the amount remaining after in-kind rents and labor payments) of 23 percent. The amount sold, starting

Table 5-24

Production and Disposition of Rice Paddy, 1969-70 and 1971-72 Crops

Location, Number, & Tenure Status of Farms Averaged	Rice Area Cultivated Annually per farm (ha)	Paddy Production per ha (kgs)[1]	% in-kind rent	% in-kind Labor Payments	% Seed[2]	% Home Use & Feed	% Sold
44 Khanh Hau, 1969	2.27	3,614	7.4	11.7		30.9	50.1
1971	2.27	5,596	2.7	11.7		21.6	64.0
15 tenants, 1969	1.19	3,802	15.9	9.9		31.7	42.5
1971	1.19	5,692	10.3	10.0		21.9	57.8
14 new owners,1969	1.61	3,130	17.1	11.4		43.6	27.8
1971	1.61	4,888	0.6	12.0		30.6	56.8
15 owner-cult.,1969	3.96	3,740	1.7	12.3		26.6	59.5
1971	3.96	5,838	1.1	12.1		18.6	68.2
44 LBD Village, 1969	1.55	2,942	9.5	12.5		30.1	48.0
1971	1.53	2,656	4.9	12.1		35.1	47.9
14 tenants, 1969	1.35	3,132	13.9	12.0		24.1	49.9
1971	1.35	2,714	15.1	11.4		26.7	46.8
15 new owners, 1969	1.28	2,758	18.2	12.7		39.3	29.8
1971	1.28	2,602	0	12.0		49.9	38.0
15 owner-cult., 1969	2.00	2,938	1.2	12.7		28.6	57.5
1971	1.95	2,654	1.4	12.6		31.1	54.9
97 Dinh Tuong farmers[3] Sansom's sample, 66-67	1.52	2,588	11	13	1	43	32
45 Phu Thu, 1969	1.05	1,672	6.7	5.5		79.7	8.1
1971	1.12	1,922	2.3	5.2		73.0	19.6
15 tenants, 1969	1.14	1,594	8.9	5.3		77.5	8.3
1971	1.14	1,674	6.4	5.3		77.6	10.8
16 new owners, 1969	1.21	1,602	8.9	5.7		79.6	5.8
1971	1.20	2,122	0.9	4.2		68.1	26.9
14 owner-cult., 1969	0.78	1,918	0.5	5.5		82.8	11.3
1971	1.00	1,952	0	6.7		75.4	17.9

(cont.)
from such a low base, increased by 178 percent. See Tables 5-23 and 5-24.

Table 5-24

(continued)

Location, Number & Tenure Status of Farms Averaged		Rice Area Cultivated Annually per farm(ha)	Paddy Production per ha. (kgs.)[1]	% in-kind rent	% in-kind Labor Payments	% Seed[2]	% Home Use & Feed	% Sold
46 HBT Village,	1969	5.99	1,540	11.1	20.0	6.7	22.6	39.6
15 tenants,	1971	5.25	1,736	4.2	19.4	8.9	25.5	42.0
	1969	3.17	1,916	14.2	20.1	6.1	26.0	33.6
15 new owners,	1971	3.12	2,993	10.6	16.0	5.6	23.9	43.9
	1969	6.13	1,240	20.4	24.6	9.2	25.0	20.8
16 owner-cult.,	1971	5.19	1,301	1.8	25.3	11.9	33.7	27.4
	1969	8.50	1,610	4.9	17.6	5.7	19.9	51.9
	1971	7.32	1,524	0.4	18.6	9.9	22.2	48.9

[1] Production averages have been converted from gia to kilograms by assuming each gia weighed an average of 20 kg.

[2] Seed paddy is included in "home use and feed" in the first 3 villages, where it comprised a small (1-2%) and stable fraction of total production. Single-transplant cultivation is practiced in Khanh Hau and LBD, double-transplanting in Phu Thu, and broadcast cultivation (both floating and non-floating) in HBT. Only in the latter area does seed paddy require a significant and variable proportion of each year's crop.

[3] Robert Sansom interviewed 97 rice farmers in two villages of Dinh Tuong Province, LBD and Than Cuu Nghia. The paddy disposition results were similar in both villages and only the aggregate averages were reported. --Sansom, op. cit., pp. 74 and 100.

NOTE: The table following this one (5-25) is provided for comparison with an earlier study of the 1968-9 crop by an agricultural specialist. Khanh Hau and LBD are both in single-transplant areas, Phu Thu in the double-transplant and HBT in the broadcast rice areas.

Table 5-25

Production and Disposition of Rice Paddy, 1968-69 Crop

(From USDA-AID Study by Ray S. Fox)

Number and Tenure Status of Farms Averaged	Rice Area Planted per Farm (ha.)	Paddy Production per ha. (kg.)	% in-kind Rent	% in-kind Labor Payments	% Seed	% Feed	% Consumed at Home	% Sold
113 Single Transplant[1]	2.00	1,900	9.2	5.5	2.0	10.9	36.1	36.2
33 owned only	1.87	1,973	0	7.9	2.2	10.8	36.5	42.5
69 rented only	1.84	1,895	13.1	4.3	1.9	12.6	37.3	30.9
11 owned & rented	3.45	1,791	11.3	6.0	2.4	4.6	30.3	45.5
18 Double Transplant	1.60	2,021	8.8	14.1	1.3	5.3	54.9	15.6
2 owned only	0.85	2,471	0	4.8	2.4	7.1	57.1	28.6
16 rented only	1.69	1,993	9.5	14.9	1.2	5.1	54.7	14.6
35 Broadcast (non-floating)	1.66	2,045	7.9	5.1	5.8	3.8	44.4	33.0
14 owned only	1.23	2,385	0	2.7	4.6	5.9	54.8	31.9
17 rented only	1.36	1,919	13.0	4.1	5.8	2.0	49.4	25.7
4 owned & rented	4.48	1,877	11.0	9.5	7.1	3.6	25.0	43.8
87 Broadcast (floating)	3.81	1,480	13.0	22.1	7.9	4.8	25.1	27.2
35 owned only	3.93	1,400	0	19.0	9.1	5.2	29.3	37.5
44 rented only	2.89	1,527	22.4	21.3	7.4	4.8	26.8	17.4
8 owned & rented	8.32	1,556	19.4	29.5	6.7	4.0	14.1	26.4

[1] Of the total area planted, 5.5% was double-cropped. Fox has apparently double-counted this area, as agricultural economists are wont to do.

SOURCE: Ray S. Fox, Rice Cost of Production in Vietnam—1968/69 Rice Crop and Preliminary Estimates for 1970, (Saigon, Vietnam: U. S. Agency for International Development, March 1970), Tables 1 and 2, pp. 19-20. Farmers were interviewed in 7 provinces of the Southern Region: An Giang, Ba Xuyen, Dinh Tuong, Gia Dinh, Long An, Phong Dinh, and SaDec (plus two in the Coastal Lowlands, not reported here). The percentage calculations are mine.

by the title-recipient group, whose percentage of paddy sold rose from 6 to 27 percent, while that consumed dropped from 80 to 68 percent.[83]

Our Phu Thu sample used only 5.2 to 5.5 percent of their crop for in-kind labor payments, compared with 12 percent in the upper Delta villages and 20 percent in HBT, and compared with 14 percent in the double-transplant portion of the Ray Fox study[84] In 1968-69 (see Tables 5-24 and 5-25). This reflects the larger number of our Phu Thu sample who harvested their grain with family labor or who engaged in the practice of "**doi cong**," forming labor pools and trading labor days with their neighbors (without payment).

Hoa Binh Thanh, An Giang Province

Hoa Binh Thanh Village (HBT) also stretches back from the southwest bank of the Hau Giang River, but it begins some 68 kilometers (42 miles) upstream from Phu Thu village, and about 9 kilometers upstream from Long Xuyen, the capital of An Giang Province. It is in the middle of the broadcast, floating-rice cultivation area, where the waters of the Hau Giang rise each year in September and October several feet above most of the ground. Houses must be built either on high ground, which is scarce, or on stilts or pilings. Though An Giang is considered the most prosperous province in the Mekong Delta, it has very few paved, all-weather roads, and water transportation remains a way of life with most people, especially during the rainy season (June-October). The traditional variety[85] of rice is one that, if given a sufficient head start, will grow above the rising waters, its stem lengthening 8 or 9 feet if necessary, and will then lie back down and re-root closer to its head as the water recedes—thus the popular name, "floating rice." Its yields are low, averaging only 1.5 MT of paddy per

---

[83]The disposable paddy of the title-recipient group increased by 46 percent. Their home consumption rose by only 12 percent, however, while the amount sold increased by more than 5-fold. (Tables 5-23 and 5-24.)

[84]Ray S. Fox, **Rice Cost of Production in Vietnam—1968/69 Rice Crop and Preliminary Estimates for 1970**, U.S. Agency for International Development (Saigon: March 1970). Mr. Fox was detached to USAID from the Foreign Economic Development Service, U.S. Dept. of Agriculture.

[85]The variety called **nang tay** was used by two-thirds of our respondents.

**MAP OF HOA BINH THANH VILLAGE
CHAU THANH DISTRICT, AN GIANG PROVINCE**

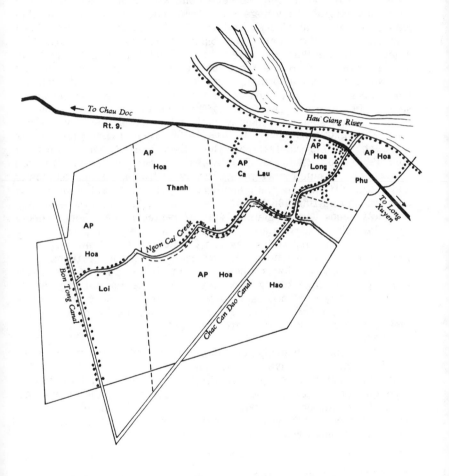

△ Village Office

hectare, but it requires very little attention or labor between a successful sowing and the harvest.[86]

Interprovincial Route 9, a paved, all-weather highway constructed above the high-water level, cuts through the eastern corner of HBT on its way between Long Xuyen and Chau Doc. The seven hamlets of the village are inter-connected by the Chac Can Dao and Ngon Cai Creeks and the Chac Can Dao and Bon Tong Canals, and the Hau Giang River bank. A dirt road wide enough for a jeep, with one-lane concrete bridges, stretches from the highway 13 kilometers out to the most distant hamlet, Hoa Loi, following the banks of the two principal creeks; and a similar road connects Hoa Hao and Hoa Phu hamlets to the highway on the southeastern side of the Chac Can Dao Creek. The local teen-aged boys provided a fast though somewhat bumpy motorbike taxi service over these roads during dry weather. It took 45-50 minutes riding piggy-back to reach Hoa Loi hamlet from the village market, and it cost (in July 1972) $100 VN (about 25§ U.S.) per passenger. A fast **tac ran** motorboat is a much more pleasant way to travel, but it was slower and more difficult to find, making the trip to Hoa Loi in 1 hour or more and costing 300 to 500 piasters (U.S. $.75-$1.25), depending on one's needs and bargaining skill, if rented alone. Some people ran a **tac ran** bus service along the principal water route, terminating at the market; but, while they ran frequently in the morning, they were rare in the afternoon. If you could catch one of them, their rates were slightly lower than the motorbikes. These dirt roads were built up high enough to stay above the normal high-water mark; but they are impassable during and for several hours after a rain, especially for the motorbikes. At the height of the rainy season all traffic is forced into the boats.

The village itself is accessible by either highway or water traffic from Long Xuyen. The trip takes about 30 minutes and costs (in 1972) 30 piasters (7.5§ U.S.) per passenger in the little 3-wheeled Lambrettas or their 4-wheeled Japanese-made equivalent. Route 9 was in bad shape but was being widened and repaved while we were there, with young Vietnamese women at the controls of the heavy machinery.

---

[86]Sometimes the seed must be sowed 2 or 3 times, if the farmer misjudges the beginning of the regular rainfall. In July 1977 some farmers had already sowed a third time. The rains had been very irregular that year and their earlier seedlings had died for lack of water. They feared a total crop failure, especially if the third sowing failed, since there was barely enough time left to give the seedlings a sufficient head start on the high water due in September.

Table 5-26

Population Data — Hoa Binh Thanh Village, 1972

Hamlet	Population	Percentage of total Village Population	Number of Farmers Interviewed	Percentage of total Interviewed
Hoa Long	4,541	34.5	16	34.8
Hoa Phu	3,351	25.5	12	26.1
Hoa Hao	1,626	12.4	6	13.0
Ca Lau	483	3.7	3	6.5
Hoa Thanh	1,796	13.6	6	13.0
Hoa Loi	1,366	10.4	3	6.5
Village Totals	13,163	100.1	46	99.9
Male	6,305	47.9		
Female	6,858	52.1		

Number of Households: 2,144
Average Household Size: 6.14

SOURCE: Village Office, July 1972

Table 5-27

Interviewee Data from Hoa Binh Thanh Village, An Giang Province

Total		15 Present Tenants	15 Title Recipients	16 owner Cultivators	All 46 Farmers
Interviewees:	Male	13	14	15	42
	Female	2	1	1	4
Average:					
Age of Interviewee:	Male	46.2	44.6	47.2	46.0
	Female	36.0	58.0	56.0	46.5
Education (years):	Male	3.3	3.0	3.6	3.3
	Female	1.5	0	0	0.8
No. of household residents		9.1	8.1	7.9	8.2

Demographic Data

HBT was the largest village we visited, having a population of 13,613, more than double the population of any of the other three, and encompassing a total of 5,438 hectares in area, or 3.4 to 4.5 times the area of the others. Hamlet rosters listed a total of 2,144 households, so that the average household size works out to be 6.14 people. The village population was listed as 47.9 percent male, 52.1 percent female, not nearly as uneven as the 59 percent female figures reported for Khanh Hau and Long Binh Dien villages, no doubt reflecting the higher level of security and peace experienced in HBT in recent years—**and** the relatively greater success the young men of HBT had in avoiding the draft of one side or the other. (See Tables 5-3, 5-9 and 5-26).

Village statistics show 91 percent of the population as belonging to the Hoa Hao Buddhist sect, with the remainder (8.6 percent) Catholic and (0.2 percent) Cao Dai. This is surely an example of ethnocentricity on the part of the village officials, since the same set of charts listed 4.3 percent of the population as Cambodian. The Cambodians have their own brand of Buddhism—and are certainly not Hoa Hao. We also interviewed one Vietnamese farmer who claimed to be traditional Buddhist, and not Hoa Hao, while the Village Office listed none of these.

In addition to the Cambodians, 0.3 percent were listed as Chinese by ancestry, with all the rest Vietnamese. Forty-two percent of the population were reported as 17 years old or under, 20 percent between the ages of 18 and 38 (inclusive), 21 percent between 39 and 50, and 17 percent were above the half-century mark.[87]

The village office had estimated the basic occupational structure of its population as being 80 percent farmers, 10 percent landless laborers, 5 percent merchants, and 5 percent other trades.

Political and social activity seemed to involve a larger proportion of people in HBT than elsewhere. The village office reported the following totals of political party membership:

---

[87]Village Office, August 1972.

Party	Membership
Vietnam Social Democratic Party (**VN Dan Chu Xa Hoi Dang**)	550
The Liberal Democratic Force (**Luc Luong Tu Do Dan Chu**)	275
The Progressive Nationalist Movement (**Phong Trao Quoc Gia Cap Tien**)	176
Nguyen Trung Truc Veterans Association (**Hoi Cuu Chien Si Nguyen Trung Truc**)	475

In addition, the Parent-Teachers' Association boasted a membership of 576, the Hoa Hao Buddhist Relief Committee membership stood at 900, and a Service Society (**Hoi Ai Nghia**) listed 16 members.[88]

Sample Selection

Hoa Binh Thanh was the only village studied in which we were free to go unescorted to all of its hamlets. The sample was accordingly drawn on a proportionate basis, the 15 sets of farmers divided among hamlets in direct proportion to each hamlet's share of the village population (see Table 5-26). The village was so large, however, that the 46 farmers interviewed comprised a smaller percentage (2.1 percent) of the total number of households in the village than in the other three cases. The selection, introduction, and interviewing procedures used were the same as before.

A higher percentage of interviewees turned out to be male, 91 percent in HBT as opposed to only 57 percent in the other three villages, and they tended to be about 6.5 years younger than elsewhere, as well. This is no doubt due to the smaller impact of the war in An Giang Province. (See Table 5-27.)

Land Tenure

The Land-to-the-Tiller Program got off to a slower start in An Giang Province than other parts of the Delta, due mostly to powerful local landlord opposition and resultant feet-dragging by local officials from province on down to village levels. By the summer of 1972, the time of our research visit, the program was in full swing and had pretty well caught up with our other villages in terms of applicant approvals, although they were still trailing in

---

[88]Village Office, August 1972.

terms of the percentage of new titles already distributed (see Table 5-2).

New land registers had not yet been compiled, however, at either village or province level, so we could not obtain sufficient data for before-and-after Lorenz curves of land ownership redistribution. What preliminary data we did obtain, moreover, was rather confusing and incomplete, with ostensibly the same information showing up with different figures on different documents within the same office. The total hectarage of riceland cultivated within the village was reported as 5,078.36 hectares by one source, for example, while another document gave it as 5,290 ha., though the 60 ha. figure for orchard land was the same on each.[89]

One breakdown by tenure status accounted for 99.6 percent of the higher figure reported for riceland area, as follows:[90]

Land tenure status	ha.	% of total
Owner-cultivated	2,192	41.4
Subject to LTTT redistribution	2,419	45.7
Church land (Catholic)	473	8.9
Huong Hoa ancestor worship land	106	2.0
Rented land owned by relatives, for which tenants refused to apply for title	80	1.5
Unaccounted for	20	0.4
TOTAL	5,290	100.0

Thus, of the total riceland area, between 56-58 percent was farmed by tenants before the LTTT Program, depending on how much of the Huong Hoa Land was rented out. The LTTT Program was expected to reduce this range of rented land to between 10.5-12.5 percent by distributing 45.7 percent of all riceland in the village. By the time of our visit 40.8 percent of all riceland had been approved for distribution, or 89 percent of the expected LTTT total, and by March 1973 applications had been approved for 42.4 percent

---

[89]Village Office, July 1972.
[90]Village Office, July 1972.

of all riceland, or 93 percent of the anticipated total. Actual title distributions were lagging at about 72-74 percent of approvals.[91]

The percentage of all farmers who were tenants is a more difficult figure to calculate, since so many in this village are of mixed tenure status or rent more than one plot of land. Statistics obtained from the computer print-out progress report of the LTTT Program for March 26, 1973, show that 39 percent of the land recipients in HBT Village were receiving more than one LTTT title. Since we were seeking relatively "pure" land tenure categories we avoided several interviews in which the farmer would have had mixed tenure status, but we still interviewed 13 of them (28 percent of the sample) where we could clearly count them as predominantly in one category or another, since it seemed almost impossible in some neighborhoods to find enough "pure" choices.

A total of 1,197 individual tenants had been approved for title distribution by March 1973, however (as opposed to 1,666 **applications** approved), and this group represented 55.8 percent of all households. They were to receive 2,241 hectares of land, or an average of 1.87 ha. each.[92] Projecting this average holding of land to the total 2,419 hectares identified for redistribution would give us 1,292 expected title-recipients, or 60.3 percent of all households, expected to receive 45.7 percent of all village riceland—a significant redistribution of landownership no matter how you look at it.

If we compare these figures just with the estimated 80 percent of all households who are farmers, we see that 70 percent of all farmers had had title applications approved by March 1973, and that the final goal would reach some 76 percent of all farmers. On the other hand, 622 landowners were reported to have submitted form "A" to retain land as either directly cultivated or as Huong Hoa worship land, and they comprise 29 percent of all households or 36 percent of all farmers. In addition, between 330 and 386 tenants will reportedly remain renters on church land, Huong Hoa

---

[91]Village Office, July 1972, and computer print-out for March 26, 1973.

[92]Computer print-out reporting LTTT Progress, March 26, 1973. Again, actual title distribution had reached 73 percent of those approved. Our own title-recipient sample averaged 4.18 hectares each received under the program; but this was because several of them discussed land received by their children as well as by themselves, even though in order to qualify for the program the children had to be either married or over 21 and had to move out of their father's home to establish a formal "household" of their own.

land, and land belonging to relatives,[93] so that tenancy will remain somewhere between 15.4-18.0 percent of all households, 19.2-22.5 percent of all farmers.[94]

In summary, by March 1973 the LTTT Program had reduced the tenanted riceland ratio from around 57 percent to 16 percent and was expected to knock it down to 11 or 12 percent; and it had approved ownership redistribution to some 56 percent of all households, or 70 percent of all farmers, reducing tenancy to 15-18 percent of all households, 19-23 percent of all farmers.

By comparison, the Ordinance 57 land reform program distributed a total of 644 hectares (12.2 percent of all riceland) to 195 tenants between 1960 and 1966, expropriating the land from 5 landlords.   By July 1972, some 115 landlords of HBT land had submitted form B requesting compensation for 1,786 hectares expropriated in the LTTT Program, representing 74 percent of the total hectarage expected to be expropriated.

Of the 44 landlords discussed by our farmer sample, 18 percent were relatives, 52 percent not relatives (but private individuals), and 30 percent were institutions (25 percent Catholic Church, 5 percent Village). If we leave the institutional owners to one side[95] and compare the tenure categories, however, we find the LTTT recipients reported that only 7 percent of their private landlords were relatives, while those who were still paying rents listed 44 percent as relatives.   No significant differences among tenure categories were noted, however, in the proportions of private landlords residing in the village itself as opposed to elsewhere: 37 percent of the private landlords resided in the village, 37 percent elsewhere in the district (which includes the province capital, Long Xuyen), 10 percent in Saigon-Cholon, 13 percent in other provinces, and 3 percent in France.

---

[93]Legally the latter **must** be distributed, but how much of it ever will be is open to question if the tenant lets the landlord claim it as directly cultivated, and if the village officials go along.

[94]The extent of overlap due to mixed tenure status is obvious, as we have categorized 104.7 to 107.3 percent of all households as farmers (whereas only 80 percent are supposed to be) and we have listed 131.2 to 134.5 percent of all farmers in the three tenure groups.

[95]The village-owned land was being redistributed under the LTTT Program, while the church-owned land was exempt.   The priest responsible for administering the church-owned land was a resident of the village, since the village had its own Catholic Church.

A slight majority (55 percent) of all those renting riceland from private owners before 1970 held written contracts, while the rest had only verbal agreements. A somewhat larger majority (69 percent) of those who were receiving title under the LTTT Program had held written contracts, however, while most (55 percent) of the remaining tenants had only verbal agreements. The importance of the written contract as opposed to the verbal agreement becomes clear when we compare the amounts of rent paid by the two groups. The four tenants who held written contracts with private landlords had agreed to rents averaging 21 **gia** per hectare, while the five with verbal agreements had accepted rents averaging 55 **gia** per hectare and ranging from 20 to 88 **gia**.

Most of the high-rent verbal agreements had been recently negotiated and were based on the higher productivity of small plots of land near enough to reliable sources of water to be double-cropped in Miracle Rice. This is a clear indication that the landlords do not hesitate to raise their rents as productivity increases. We did not find the same divergence in stipulated rents between the written and verbal contracts reported by the LTTT-recipient group, probably because all those agreements were terminated in 1970, before Miracle Rice had made its impact.

All church land is rented out with written contracts, and rent levels in this village are at very reasonable levels, between 10 and 22 **gia** per hectare, depending on whether the land could be double-cropped or not. There were several instances, however, in which the original leaseholder verbally sublet the land to a third party, and the rental rate tended to rise in the process, so that the actual tiller of the land was sometimes paying 2 or 3 times as much per hectare as was stipulated in the original contract. Of the 11 farmers in our sample who were renting church-owned land, 5 of them were subleasing it verbally from the original lessees.

In all, 24 parcels of land were still being rented by our HBT sample. Eleven of these belonged to the church, 11 had been declared Huong Hoa worship land (though some of these cases were of questionable legality), and one was categorized as orchard land—all exempt from the LTTT Program. The remaining parcel was rented by a relative of the owner, and the farmer did not want to apply for fear of damaging the family relationship.

Stipulated rents averaged 21 **gia** per hectare for the tenants,[96]

---

[96]The high rental rates noted above on verbal agreements were for very small parcels of high-yielding land. Since this average rent figure is weighted by hectarage these small-farm rents are

20 **gia** per hectare for the LTTT recipients.   (See Table 5-32.) These rents represented 30 percent of the normal pre-1969 crop reported by the title-recipients, 25 percent of that claimed by the tenants.   Four tenants and ten title-recipients reported pre-1969 rents in excess of the legal 25 percent rate.   Four other tenants reported new rental agreements of 77 and 88 **gia** per hectare on double-cropped land, a fantastic jump, but representing only around 20 percent of the annual harvest of successfully double-cropped Miracle Rice.

The title-recipient group actually paid only 23 percent of their 1969 harvest in rents, the lower amount reflecting tolerance given by some landlords for bad crops, since stipulated rents would have taken 32 percent.   The tenants paid only 18 percent in rent that year, however, and the drop can be attributed only partly to tolerance, since full stipulated rents would have taken only 22 percent (as opposed to the stipulated 25 percent of a "normal" crop). Some members of the tenant group were already beginning to plant Miracle Rice, discussed more below, and their total harvest was larger than before.   In fact, between 1969 and 1971, the percentage of annual paddy production actually paid in rents by this group dropped from 18 percent to 12 percent, despite a 16 percent **rise** in total rents paid, since gross paddy **production** rose by a whopping 55 percent.   (See Table 5-28.)

Regarding form of payment, all of the tenant respondents said they paid rents in kind, although 2 of them also paid cash rent on part of their holding.   The title-recipient group was split about half-and-half, however, between those who paid rents in paddy and those who paid in cash.

Living Standards

The quality of housing among HBT farmers follows the same pattern found elsewhere, with the most attractive and durable houses belonging to the owner-cultivator group and most of the thatch houses belong to the tenants, while the LTTT-title recipient group had already constructed a position in between and were rapidly gaining on the owner-cultivators: 73 percent of the title recipients were repairing, remodelling or reconstructing their houses in 1971-

---

(cont.)
swamped into insignificance by the much larger low-yielding, low-rent farms. If weighted by the number of farmers only, the average rent figure for tenants equals 33 **gia** per hectare while for title-recipients it is still only 20 **gia.**

Table 5-28

Proportion of Annual Paddy Harvest Paid in Rents in 1969 and 1971, by Village and Land Tenure Status[1]

Village	Present Tenants 1969	Present Tenants 1971	LTTT-title Recipients 1969	LTTT-title Recipients 1971	1969 Total
Khanh Hau	.159	.103	.184	.006	.171
Long Binh Dien	.163	.153	.190	.000	.178
Phu Thu	.142	.100	.104	.010	.119
3-Village Total	.158	.116	.171	.006	.165
Hoa Binh Thanh	.178	.122	.228	.021	.207

[1]Calculated only from those farmers specifying paddy rents, eliminating those reporting cash rents and adjusting for land owned in mixed cases.

Table 5-29

Type of Housing in Hoa Binh Thanh Village, 1972

(Percentage of Farmer Sample)

Roofing	15 Present Tenants	15 Title Recipients[1]	16 Owner-Cultivators	All 46 Farmers
Tile	13	40	50	35
Pressed cement fiber	0	20	0	7
Corrugated metal	7	0	31	13
Thatch	80	40	19	46
Walls				
Brick or cement block	0	7	6	4
Wood	40	53	88	61
Metal sheets	13	0	0	4
Thatch	47	40	6	30
Floors				
Tile	0	7	0	2
Cement	0	0	6	2
Wood	93	87	94	91
Earth	7	7	0	7
Percentages repairing, remodelling, or reconstructing in 1971-2	53	73	50	59

[1]Included in this column is one house presently under construction (tile roof, tile floors, cement block walls). The interviewee had already torn down his old house made of thatch and was temporarily residing with his brother.

72, compared with only about half of the tenants and owners-cultivators (see Table 5-29).

The pattern is most marked with respect to roofing material, since the percentage of houses with the preferred tile roofs varies 50 to 40 to 13 percent among the three tenure categories: owner-cultivator, title-recipient, present tenant, in that order. An even greater spread is found in the percentages having the thatch roofs, and in reverse order, 19 to 40 to 80 percent (for owner-cultivators, title-recipients, present tenants), with the impoverished tenants clearly in the bottom stratum either way you look at it.

The same trend is apparent in comparing wall material, since 88 percent of the owner-cultivators had wooden walls while only 40 percent of the tenants did, with the new owners again stretching up in between at 53 percent. Forty-seven percent of the tenants constructed their walls from thatch, while 40 percent of the new owners and only 6 percent of the owner-cultivators did so. Only 2 houses in the whole HBT sample were constructed with cement block walls, in contrast to the preferred use of this material in the other provinces. Houses in HBT must be built either on high ground, which is rare, or on stilts, due to the annual rise in the water level to several feet above ground. Most houses in HBT are constructed on stilts, or pilings, and wood is used rather than the heavier cement.

These same factors dictate the use of wooden floors rather than bare earth, cement, or tile, and we found 91 percent of our whole sample with wooden floors, without a noticeable difference among the tenure groupings.

The skew of wealth by land tenure status is equally evident in the ownership distribution of vehicles and consumer durables, and appeared to be even more pronounced in HBT than elsewhere, because HBT was both secure and relatively wealthy. As a look at Table 5-30 will show, a higher proportion of owner-cultivators owned every type of vehicle and consumer durable on the list; and new owners led the tenants on owning most of the items. In fact, the small proportion of present tenants and title-recipients owning most of the items bespeaks the intense poverty still found in this supposedly "wealthy" community, and the disparity between them and the owner-cultivators demonstrates a substantial degree of economic inequality in this supposedly unified, tightly-knit, and peaceful area of the Mekong Delta. The LTTT Program may help some of its title-recipients, and Miracle Rice may help some of the tenants (if they can keep rents from going too high); but substantial inequalities are likely to remain.

Table 5-30

Ownership of Selected Consumer Durables
and Vehicles Among Hoa Binh Thanh Sample Farmers,
1972

| Item | Percentage owning at least one: | | | |
	15 Present Tenants	15 Title Recipients	16 Owner-Cultivators	All 46 Farmers
Wardrobe cabinet	60	73	88	74
Glass-Front cabinet	27	27	81	46
Chinese-character fresco	20	20	25	22
Brass altar fixtures	27	47	75	50
Table and chair sets	47	67	100	72
Worship table or cabinet	80	73	100	85
Wood plank bed (bo van)	53	60	94	70
Wall clock	13	13	44	24
Pressure or electric lamp	40	67	100	70
Sewing machine	27	40	81	50
Radio	53	67	81	67
Television	0	0	19	7
Bicycle	33	40	75	50
Motorbike or scooter	0	13	25	13
Sampan or tac ran (motor or hand)	87	100	100	96
Sampan, or tac ran, motor	60	73	94	76
Sampan, hand	40	33	50	41
Percentage of sample purchasing consumer durables in 1971 or planning to in 1972	20	53	50	41

In fact, while the percentage of owner-cultivators in HBT owning the 11 consumer durable items on our list averaged 30 percent **higher** than owner-cultivators in the other 3 villages, the percentage of tenants owning the same items averaged 24 percent **lower** than tenants elsewhere. Especially noticeable were the lack of sewing machines, tables and chairs, and the favored wood-plank beds (**bo van**) in HBT tenant households—the proportions of HBT tenants owning these items were .27, .47, and .53, respectively, while the HBT owner-cultivators reported .81, 1.00, and .94. The proportions of tenants in the other three villages owning these same items were, in the same order, .51, 1.00, 1.00 (see Table 5-30).

A much higher proportion of our entire HBT sample owned 2-wheeled vehicles and sampans than in the other villages, no doubt because of the greater distances involved in HBT between house and field or house and market, and also due to the impossibility of travelling anywhere during the high-water season without a boat. Whereas land-tenure differences elsewhere show strong positive correlations only with the ownership of motorbikes, however, in HBT the owner-cultivators lead in the ownership of all four items listed—bicycles, motorbikes, hand sampans, and motor sampans or other motorized boats.   Every one of the owner-cultivators and title-recipients in HBT owned either a hand-operated or a motorized sampan or **tac ran** motorboat, but only 87 percent of the tenants did.   Seventy-five percent of the owner-cultivator households had a bicycle, while only a third of the tenants did; and although 25 percent of the owner-cultivators owned motorbikes, not one tenant did.

With respect to the ownership of consumer durables, as with housing, the LTTT title-recipients in HBT were already pulling themselves above the remaining tenants and were staking out a position midway between the tenants and the owner-cultivators. Their percentage ownership of vehicles and consumer durables averaged 21-24 percent higher than that of the tenants, but they still had a long way to go to catch up with the owner-cultivator group, who were 50-60 percent above them.   The proportion of title-recipient households reporting consumer durable or vehicular purchases in 1971 or plans to make such purchases in 1972 was .53, compared with only .20 of the tenants and .50 of the owner-cultivators, which, together with their high investment figures in house construction and repair (see above) and their lack of apparent investment in agriculture (discussed below), helps to show what title-recipients in HBT were doing with the additional income they were realizing from remitted rents.

Indebtedness

The proportion of our HBT farmer sample in debt increased from 63 percent in 1969-70 to 80 percent in 1971-72, the highest incidence of debt in our four villages. Half of the whole sample borrowed more cash in 1971-72 than they did 2 years before, although the addition of several small debtors to the lists lowered the size of the **average** debt reported by 20 percent, from 59,146 $VN to 47,267 $VN.

The sources of cash credit followed the same pattern reported in Phu Thu, downstream along the same river, with government loans making up a much smaller proportion of the total (9 percent of the number of loans, 11 percent of the amount of funds borrowed) than was the case in the two upper-Delta villages. Relatives and friends and neighbors provided all the rest of the credit in HBT, with **no** funds reported borrowed from landlords, moneylenders, pawn shops, or stores. (See Table 5-14.)

The LTTT Program seems to have had an interesting effect on title-recipient farmers in HBT, encouraging or forcing more of that group to borrow than before, but mostly for consumption purposes rather than for agricultural investment. The number of title-recipients borrowing increased from 5 in 1969-70 to 10 in 1971-72, but 50 percent of the latter had borrowed money for consumption purposes **only**, as opposed to 9 percent of the tenant and 38 percent of the owner-cultivator debtors. Only 20 percent of the title-recipient debtors had borrowed solely for farm expenses or investments, compared with 43 percent of the tenant and 31 percent of the owner-cultivator debtors. The HBT title-recipients and owner-cultivators were the only two land tenure groups out of the 12 we interviewed (3 in each of 4 villages) that reported more loans for consumption rather than for farm expenses.[97]

Agricultural Production

A higher proportion of HBT farmers owned most of the farm implements on our list than in the other three villages. An exception was the threshing sledge, owned by only 4 percent of the HBT sample compared with 58 percent of all farmers interviewed elsewhere. In An Giang Province, the more labor-saving method of

---

[97]Two other groups, the owner-cultivators of Khanh Hau and the tenants of Long Binh Dien, reported an equal number of loans for both purposes, but all 8 of other groups borrowed mostly to meet farm expenses and to make agricultural investments. (See Callison, **Land-to-the-Tiller**, Tables 5-12, 5-24, 5-36, 5-41, and 6-10.)

threshing by cow or by tractor is practiced. Paddy stalks are spread out on dry ground and cows are led around to tread on them or a tractor is driven over them, knocking the grains of rice off.

Only 4 percent of the HBT sample (2 owner-cultivators) owned mechanical rototillers, but a total of 72 percent of them had at least part of their holdings plowed by machine, the majority hiring someone else to do it. One third still did all or part of their plowing with animal power, and all but one of these farmers owned their own draft animals. There is a surprising absence of water buffalo in this area. Only one of our 46 farmers owned a pair of water buffalo and used them for plowing, compared with 26 who owned cattle. Cows were used for plowing by 15 members of the sample, or 33 percent.

The owner-cultivators owned more farm implements than the other two groups, as expected, 63 percent owning a motor pump and 69-75 percent owning the hand plow, harrow and roller, compared with 47 percent of the tenants who owned these four items. It was **not** expected, however, to find a much lower proportion of LTTT-title-recipients than tenants owning these implements (see Table 5-31); and still less expected was the low percentage (13 percent) of title-recipients purchasing or planning to purchase new farm implements in 1971-72, compared with 33 percent of the tenants and 44 percent of the owner-cultivators in HBT, and compared with 27 percent of the title-recipients in the other three villages.

Of the entire HBT farmer sample, 41 percent used the Miracle Rice varieties in 1971-72 and 57 percent planned to use it in 1972-73. An interesting picture of progressiveness among the tenant group, as compared with the LTTT-title-recipients and owner-cultivators, begins to emerge as we break these proportions down. The proportion of tenants using Miracle Rice seed in 1971-72 was .60, and this was expected to rise to .80 in the following year. For title-recipients, however, this proportion was only .20 rising to .33; and for owner-cultivators it was .47 rising to .63.

Although several farmers in HBT used Miracle Rice seed for only one crop per year, for most its attraction was two-fold, as elsewhere. Not only did it improve yields per crop, but its fast-growing characteristic with proper irrigation permitted 2 crops per year instead of only one. Total hectarage double-cropped in HBT remained very low, only 7 percent in 1971-72 (of the total land area farmed by our sample), because of the lack of sufficient irrigation canals, but 41 percent of the farmers double-cropped at least part of their land that year and 46 percent of them planned to do so the next year, compared with only 17 percent in 1969-70.

Table 5-31

Ownership of Farm Implements in Hoa Binh Thanh Village, 1972

And Percentage Who Hire Labor

Implement	Percentages owning of:			
	15 Present Tenant	15 Title Recipients	16 Owner Cultivators	All 46 Farmer Sample
Hand Plow	47	33	75	52
Harrow	47	20	69	46
Roller	47	20	69	43
Threshing sledge	0	0	13	4
Paddy cart	0	0	6	2
Motor pump	47	40	63	50
Rototiller	0	0	13	4
Threshing machine	0	0	6	2
Percentage purchasing new implements in 1971-2	33	13	44	30
Percentage who hire labor:	100	93	100	98

Surprisingly, however, it was again the tenants who were leading the way, with 73 percent of them double-cropping in 1971-72, compared with 38 percent of the owner-cultivators and only 13 percent of the title-recipients. The tenants were double-cropping 24 percent of their total holdings, while the owner-cultivators were experimenting with this method on only 4 percent of their land and the title-recipients on only 0.8 percent of theirs. (See Tables 5-22 and 5-32.)

The introduction of Miracle Rice seed and the double-crop method of production was causing average yields to rise in HBT as elsewhere, but mostly for the tenants, who improved their annual per hectare yields by 56 percent in just two years, while crop-hectare yields rose 35 percent. LTTT-title-recipients registered a mere 5 percent increase in annual yields and obtained only 43 percent as much per annual hectare as did the tenants, only 53 percent as much per crop-hectare, in 1971-72. The owner-cultivators had a bad year in 1971-72, experiencing a 7 percent decline in productivity per crop-hectare, compared with 2 years before (see Table 5-32).

Our HBT sample sold 42 percent of its gross paddy production in 1971-72, up slightly from 40 percent two years before. The largest increases in amount and percentage sold came from the tenants, who sold and used as debt repayments 102 percent more than two years before, raising their proportion of gross paddy production sold from 34 to 44 percent, and this despite a 16 percent rise in in-kind labor payments. Although the tenants kept 42 percent more paddy for home consumption and livestock feed, the proportion of the total harvest retained for these purposes fell from .26 to .24, thanks to the enormous rise in production. (See Table 5-24.)

The 34 percent rise in disposable paddy retained by the LTTT-recipients, mostly from the remission of rents, permitted them to increase both consumption and sales, by 25 and 47 percent, respectively. The owner-cultivators had to reduce both sales and consumption, since their disposable paddy dropped by 7 percent.

Out of the whole sample of 46 HBT farmers, only one said he and his family did all their own work, without hiring any outside help. Ninety-eight percent of the sample did hire labor, at least at harvest time, exceeding the already high proportion (95 percent) who did so in the other three villages.

Table 5-32

Rice Production and Disposition in Hoa Binh Thanh Village

Average	15 Present Tenants	15 title Recip- ients	16 owner- Culti- vators	All 46 Farmers
Paddy land holding (ha.)	3.4	5.3	7.6	5.5
Ha. received under LTTT	.2	4.2	0	
Gross paddy production per farm, 1971-2 (gia)[1]	466	338	558	456
Annual yield/ha. 1971-2 (gia)	150	65	76	87
Annual yield/ha. 1969-70 (gia)	96	62	81	77
Annual yield/ha. before '69 (gia)	83	66	77	74
(% increase last 2 years)	(56)	(5)	(-5)	(13)
Portion of riceland double-cropped, 1971	.24	.008	.04	.07
Portion of riceland double-cropped, 1969	.07	.003	.02	.02
(% increase 1969-71)	(236)	(200)	(53)	(151)
Yield/crop ha., 1971-2 (gia)	121	65	74	82
Yield/crop ha., 1969-70 (gia)	90	62	79	75
(% increase in 2 years)	(35)	(4)	(-7)	(9)
Stipulated rent/ha. before LTTT(gia)	21	20[2]		
Stipulated rent/1969-70 yield	.22	.32		
Percentage increase or decrease in last two years of (rice paddy use):[3]				
Gross paddy production	55	3	-3	14
Rent	16	-90	0	-44
In-kind labor payments	23	4	4	9
Home consumption and feed	42	25	-10	14
Paddy sales and debt repayment	102	47	- 6	26
Disposable paddy[4]	78	34	- 7	21
(MPC disposable paddy[5])	(.25)	(.44)	(.44)	(.27)

[1]See Note 1, Table 5-8.

[2]Average for 14 title recipients: one paid cash rents.

[3]Based on figures adjusted to a constant hectarage level.

[4]Gross production minus rent, in-kind labor payments and seed.

[5]See Note 3, Table 5-8.

Chapter VI

ON THE FARM

Introduction

In this chapter the farmer interviews have been divided by land tenure status for comparisons more relevant to our particular investigation. As discussed in Chapter I, several theoretical considerations indicate that, under land tenure conditions previously existing in South Vietnam, a land reform program such as Land-to-the-Tiller should not only generate greater political support for the responsible government, but should also release forces and funds which would help to increase agricultural investment and production, and thus should contribute significantly to the overall development of the national economy. Some observers would disagree, maintaining that the labor supply curve of peasant farmers is essentially backward-bending, and that an increase in their incomes would result in less, not more, effort applied to farm production, with a resultant drop in total output. Another concern is that, with the remission of rents and in the absence of tenant payments to purchase the land distributed, the marketable surplus of agricultural goods would drop even if total production does not because the marginal propensity to consume their own produce among poor rural families is very high. Other analysts have expressed concern about the size of the farm operating unit, fearing that land reform would either cause further fragmentation into inefficiently small farms or, by freezing an existing small farm system, prevent consolidation into larger, more efficient operating units.

The latter argument is based on the notions that small farms cannot profitably mechanize and therefore are inherently less progressive than larger farms, since, so it is said, only through mechanization can output per man be significantly improved; and efficient mechanization requires large operating units. One man and his machines would be able to farm, say, 100 hectares, replacing 50 to 100 men each operating only 1 or 2 hectares as at present. Some Vietnamese writers believed that, without consolidation and mechanization, which in their view was made much more difficult by the Land-to-the-Tiller Program, the Vietnamese farmer would be forever doomed to apply back-breaking muscle and animal power to small plots of land for near-subsistence yields per man.

This argument can sound persuasive to Asians anxious for rapid progress into the modern economic world and to Americans used to large, highly mechanized farms and **abundant employment opportunities elsewhere.** This last factor is the unstated assumption and the chief flaw in this line of reasoning, however, since alternative employment opportunities (in significant numbers) did not exist in Vietnam at this point in time, except in the unproductive military service. Rational discussion of agricultural developmental policies based on output per man must take into account not only those workers left in agriculture after implementation of the policy and their production, but also those workers whose agricultural jobs have been eliminated and their production, as well.

Mechanized farming by itself does not normally result in significant (if any) improvements in yields per hectare, at least not in rice farming. So, if one farmer with machines replaces 100 farmers without machines, but does not achieve an increase in yield per hectare (in fact it may drop, since the one farmer will have so much land he will not worry so much about every little corner of it), production per man likewise does not increase unless the other 99 men can be productively employed elsewhere—and their combined productivity must be sufficiently high to cover the costs of imported machines, petroleum and parts, and of their own relocation, social adjustment, and retraining for new occupations. In a country where the growth in industrial employment is as yet absorbing only a tiny fraction of the annual increase in the labor force resulting from natural population growth, those 99 men would remain effectively unemployed, their productivity would be reduced to near zero, and the expensive imported machinery purchased with scarce foreign exchange would represent a wasteful use of economic resources. In addition, the social and political strains caused by rising unemployment and by the urban migration of those looking for jobs enter the balance sheet of such an investment policy as negative returns.

Until the non-agricultural sectors have progressed to the point where they can productively absorb more than the natural increment of labor each year, the rural sector will not only have to maintain existing employment levels, but it must absorb that part of the labor force increment left over by the other sectors as well. At the same time agriculture must provide for the increasing food and fiber demands of the growing population and the industrial sector. Rather than superficially increasing farm output per farmer by ignoring those thrown off the land, the most urgent requirement is to increase production per hectare on a static land area while providing useful employment and livelihoods for growing numbers of people. This can best be done by labor-intensive farming, using scientific technology on small family farms, with the government providing essential large-scale services such as agricultural research, extension, and credit and assuring the satisfactory development of marketing, transportation, input supply, and water control systems. Rather than wasted on premature farm mechanization, foreign exchange and investment capital should be directed toward more rapid industrialization, the ultimate answer to long-run employment and per-captia productivity problems.

This is not to say that any and all farm mechanization should be avoided, but rather that government measures to encourage indiscriminate mechanization of the type associated with land consolidation schemes are often premature in early stages of development under conditions of capital scarcity and abundant labor. Obviously, if the use of rototillers and motorized water pumps, for example, permits a more intensive use of both land and labor (through double-cropping) than otherwise, then their use makes good economic sense and would be consistent with the labor-intensive technological development of small farms, aimed primarily at increasing output per hectare.

Our research was designed primarily to explore the other questions mentioned above. Will land-ownership redistribution from landlords to the cultivators create new incentives to invest money, time, and labor into higher farm production, while also providing more investment capital for the decision-maker, or will it impinge on effective backward-bending supply curves of labor and/or high marginal propensities to consume farm output on the part of farmers themselves, thus resulting in lower total production and in a lower marketable surplus?

There is no doubt that the LTTT Program resulted in a significant redistribution of real income toward former tenant farmers. Paddy rents averaging 17 percent of the gross annual harvest in 1969-70, as paid by the LTTT-title recipients in our first three villages (23 percent in the fourth one), were completely rescinded, while no payments at all were required to offset landlord compensation, the latter financed from general tax levies (which fell mostly on urban residents), foreign aid (from American taxpayers), and deficit financing (the inflationary impact of which reduces the real income of the urban salaried workers, soldiers, and civil servants and reduces the real value of landlord compensation more than it affects the farmer, who produces real goods for sale). (See Table 5-28 for rent levels by village.)

The amount of immediate income redistribution was of course less in those areas of the Delta where no or only token rents had been collected in recent years, except where increased security had also managed to eliminate tax collections by the Viet Cong, which were comparable or greater in amounts.

The question is how much of this increased income was being used for consumption versus investment purposes and whether the farmer traded some of it for more leisure, allowing total production to fall. These are matters of individual preferences and incentives determining investment and consumption decisions, very elusive topics to investigate and difficult ones to quantify. The present analysis relies mostly on factual information elicited about farm production and investment decisions over a period of three years, although we also asked some straightforward and possibly leading questions to probe farmer perceptions of the process and their preferences.

The evidence indicates that the incentive and income factors of Land-to-the-Tiller were helping to improve agricultural production and to increase paddy sales in the first three villages we visited, but not in the last village. Except in the remarks of a very few old-timers, who said they were too old to change their ways or to work as hard as before (and whose sons were away in the army), we found no evidence of a preference for more leisure over a higher material standard of living—indeed it was quite the contrary, and a major complaint was the scarcity of family and village labor (again due to the war) to use or to hire for higher production.

The paddy production and disposition figures derived from our survey must be used with caution. There was a natural tendency on the part of some farmers to understate their yields—a few of them admitted to it and revised their figures upward before the termination of the interview. This tendency was especially true of the new title recipients, who expected soon to be hit with high taxes on their new land. This bias is probably not too serious, however, as we learned to save questions on production until nearly the end of the interview, after better rapport and trust had been established with the interviewees. Our primary interest is in **changes** in production and disposition, which information was after all obtained, albeit in slightly dampened proportions.

A second problem results from the fact that we were relying on memories, which were generally pretty clear about last year's harvest, but which often faded into uncertain estimates about the crop three years ago. Minor variances were often lost, but whenever there had been a crop failure or a significant increase in production, due to the introduction of double-cropping and/or Miracle Rice, for example, memories were much more vivid.

We were fortunate, in fact, in conducting this study in the midst of the so-called "Green Revolution," since we were able to observe how this package of technological innovations was being accepted under different conditions, and to consider the effects of land reform on its adoption.

The first three villages have been taken together and the last one, Hoa Binh Thanh in An Giang Province, set in contrast. The immediate effects of the LTTT Program seemed to be different in the latter for both socio-political and economic reasons. HBT is in the high-water, floating-rice region where low yields and low labor requirements per hectare have traditionally been combined with larger farm holdings than in the rest of the Delta, averaging well over the 3-hectare limit imposed by the LTTT Program. One result of the LTTT Program in HBT was to speed the fragmentation process, producing smaller farms and leaving some farmers with less, not more, disposable income. Such effects were insignificant in the first three villages, where a holding larger than 3 hectares was rare, especially among tenant farmers.

In addition, HBT is in the middle of Hoa Hao Buddhist country, with its tightly-knit social and political fabric and its many years of relative peace and security, as compared with the rest of the Delta. If the LTTT Program can be said to have introduced an element of greater security into the lives of the farmers in the other three villages, in HBT it introduced elements of uncertainty and disruption, at least in the initial phases of the program. Indeed, whereas elsewhere we generally met warm enthusiasm for the LTTT Program and its goals, in HBT the public attitude was commonly one of reservation, diffidence, disapproval, and even scorn for those who would "break their promises (rental agreements) and take another person's land away from him." Title recipients often made excuses for themselves by explaining that village officials told them they **had** to apply for title or the land would be given to someone else.

Agricultural Investment and Production: The First Three Villages

We interviewed 140 rice farmers in the first three villages of Khanh Hau, Long Binh Dien, and Phu Thu: 46 present tenants, 48 LTTT-title recipients, and 46 owner-cultivators. Seven of them have been omitted from some or all of the calculations because they had been farming for less than 3 years or for some other reason. For the most part, those with mixed land tenure status have been included in the category of their predominant status by hectare, although a couple were omitted because their land was equally divided between two or more categories. A few averages dealing with investment and consumption decisions have been developed from "purified" categories, however, with eight mixed tenant cases[1] and one title-recipient still part tenant removed, and the five Ordinance 57 recipients taken out of the owner-cultivator group and placed in a separate group of their own.

Investment

Sample farmers were asked about changes made recently or planned soon in several agricultural activities, and eight of these have been tabulated as representing pre-planned decisions to invest more in farm production. A few types of change were omitted as not necessarily indicative of this. A change in rice seed variety, for example, was found to be a routine practice of traditional farming, and not a risky or expensive innovation. The new Miracle Rice seeds, for example, were seldom tried until the farmer had witnessed a successful crop from them elsewhere, and then they were often tried on a small piece of land first, to be expanded the following year only if successful. An increase in fertilizer and a switch from single to double-cropping represent the risky investments associated with the new Miracle Rice technology, and separate responses about changes in rice seed itself were found unnecessary. Another example is the use of insecticides, which was found to be normally a response to observed infestation and not a pre-planned preventive investment. It was not, therefore, indicative of a pre-planned productive investment decision and has likewise been omitted from the list.

Table 6-1 records the number of farmers in each land tenure category who invested more or for the first time in eight productive investment activities within the last two years, or who planned to do so during the coming year. The averages at the bottom of the table demonstrate that the LTTT-title-recipients were making 46 percent more of these investments per farm than the present tenants and 17 percent more than the wealthier and better-educated owner-cultivators. A recalculation of only the "pure" cases, eliminating farmers of mixed land tenure status and placing the earlier Ordinance 57 land reform recipients in a separate category raises these percentages to 80 and 22, respectively, and reveals that the five Ordinance 57 title-recipients were making the same higher number of investments per farm as the LTTT-title-recipients. The investment average of the eight mixed-tenant cases was 3.63, or 115 percent more than the average of the 36 "pure" tenants. Eliminating this group, as probably influenced in investment matters

----

[1]Four of these tenants had received title to small amounts of land and four were part owner-cultivators, although they all still rented most of their holdings.

Table 6-1

Agricultural Investment by Land Tenure Status

Khanh Hau, Long Binh Dien, Phu Thu

TYPE OF INVESTMENT	NUMBER MAKING INVESTMENT			
	Present Tenants (n=44)	Title-Recipients (n= 45)	Owner-Cultivators (n=44)	All Farmers (n=133)
Single to Double-cropping				
Within last 2 years	11	16	10	37
Planned this year	4	7	8	19
Increased Fertilizer per ha.				
Within last 2 years	22	27	21	70
Planned this year	7	12	15	34
New Irrigation Canal or Dike				
Within last 2 years	3	6	3	12
Planned this year	3	5	2	10
Planting Secondary crops				
Within last 2 years	3	5	0	8
Planned this year	3	2	2	7
Raising Fish				
Within last 2 years	6	10	2	18
Planned this year	0	1	2	3
Increased Animal Husbandry				
Within last 2 years	8	20	11	39
Planned this year	9	10	15	34
New Breed of Livestock				
Within last 2 years	1	2	3	6
Planned this year	2	0	5	7
New Farm Implements				
Within last year	5	5	7	17
Planned this year	3	7	7	17
TOTAL NEW INVESTMENTS	90	135	113	338
AVERAGE NEW INVESTMENTS PER FARMER	2.05	3.00	2.57	2.54
PURIFIED GROUP AVERAGES[1]	1.69	3.05	2.51	

[1] Eight mixed cases have been withdrawn from the tenant category, leaving 36; one title-recipient was withdrawn since he still rented part of his rice-land; and five Ordinance 57 land-recipients were withdrawn from the owner-cultivator category, leaving 39. The five Ord. 57 farmers alone averaged 3.00 investments, the eight mixed tenants averaged 3.63. Of the latter 8, 4 are part LTTT title-recipients and 4 are part owners.

An analysis of variance computation performed on the "purified group averages" reported above for the first three villages indicates the differences among them are significant at the 99% level of confidence ($\alpha = .01$). Below are the results of that computation:

	Sum of Squares	Degrees of Freedom	Mean Square	F Ratio
Category means	36.29	2	18.15	$F = \dfrac{18.15}{3.61} = 5.03$
Within groups	419.29	116	3.61	$F_{.99}(2,116) = 4.80$
Total	455.58	118		

by their partial non-tenant status, leaves the rest of the tenants with even fewer investments per farmer. (See Figure 6-1.)

The LTTT-title-recipients lead both the other groups in switching from single to double-cropping, increasing the use of fertilizer, constructing irrigation canals and dikes, starting to raise fish, and increasing animal husbandry. In addition, they lead owner-cultivators in planting new secondary crops and are ahead of the tenants in purchasing new farm implements. The only category in which they did not do as much is switching to new breeds of livestock—not a very important activity in view of the limited success new breeds have had in the Delta.

In Phu Thu, where the income effect of LTTT and the availability of agricultural credit were both very low, the difference in investment activities among the three land tenure groups is the most pronounced. The Phu Thu title-recipients averaged 135 percent more investments than their (pure) tenant neighbors, 52 percent more than the (pure) owner-cultivators. These percentages are 62 and 16 and Long Binh Dien, 42 and -7 in Khanh Hau, respectively. This is another indication that the LTTT Program produced a strong incentive effect on productive investment in Phu Thu simply by giving the cultivator ownership and the right to make operational decisions on his own.[2]

Evidence from other research supports the conclusion that both the incentive and the ability to invest improved among LTTT title-recipients. In randomly selected, unstructured interviews of 985 farmers conducted in 23 villages of 6 provinces, the Control Data Corporation reports that 35 percent of the 483 new owners attributed recent changes in their villages at least in part to improved farming methods, whereas only 5 percent of the 148 present tenants in the sample did so.[3] Some 18 percent of the title-recipients remarked on their own use of new techniques or additional crops or more animal husbandry, while only 2 percent of the tenants did.[4]

---

[2]See Tables 6-2, 6-3 and Chapter V, "Phu Thu, Phong Dinh Province," above.

[3]Henry C. Bush, Gordon H. Messegee and Roger V. Russell, **The Impact of the Land to the Tiller Program in the Mekong Delta,** (Vietnam: Control Data Corp., October 1972), pp. 42-11 (available in both Vietnamese and English).

[4]**Ibid.,** p. 50.

Table 6-2

Agricultural Investment Averages by Tenure Status and Village, Basic Tenure Categories

Village and province	Present Tenants	LTTT-title Recipients	Owner Culti- vators	Total Sample
Khanh Hau, Long An	1.87	2.43	2.80	2.36
Long Binh Dien, Dinh Tuong	1.79	2.73	2.40	2.32
Phu Thu, Phong Dinh	2.47	3.75	2.50	2.93
Hoa Binh Thanh, An Giang	3.00	1.73	2.69	2.48
First Three Villages	2.05	3.00	2.57	2.54
All Four Villages	2.29	2.68	2.60	2.53

Table 6-3

Agricultural Investment Averages by Tenure Status and Village, "Purified" Tenure Categories

Village and province	Present Tenants	LTTT-title Recipients	Ord.57 Owners	Remaining Owners
Khanh Hau, Long An	1.71	2.43	4.00	2.62
Long Binh Dien, Dinh Tuong	1.69	2.73	3.00	2.36
Phu Thu, Phong Dinh	1.67	3.93	2.00	2.58
Hoa Binh Thanh, An Giang	3.30	1.50	3.50	2.42
First Three Villages	1.69	3.05	3.00	2.51
All Four Villages	2.04	2.67	3.22	2.49

Figure 6-1

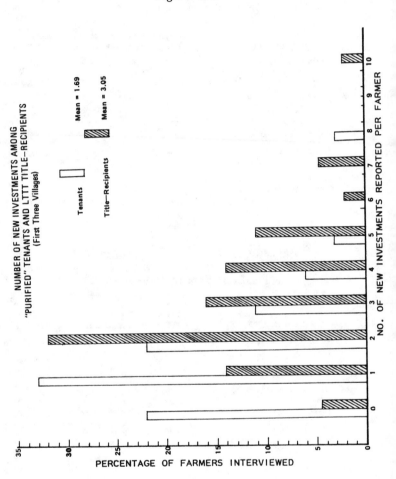

Production

Increased investment should result in higher output, and indeed, our 3-village sample reported an overall rise of 30 percent in gross paddy production between 1969-70 and 1971-72, despite the 1971-72 crop failure reported in Long Binh Dien. The improvement was due mostly to more double-cropping, the hectarage of which grew by 58 percent during these two years, but also to a 14 percent improvement in yields per crop-hectare achieved by the partial shift to Miracle Rice seeds, more liberal use of fertilizer and better water control. Annual yields per hectare rose from 147 **gia** (2.94 metric tons) to 192 **gia** (3.85 M.T.), while yields per crop-hectare rose from 111 to 127 **gia** (2.22 to 2.54 M.T.).[5]   (See Table 6-4)

The owner-cultivator group reported the largest increase in paddy production, 36 percent over the 2 years, while the title-recipients scored 30 percent and the tenants only 18 percent. These aggregates can be slightly misleading, however, in that the apparent superior performance of the owner-cultivator group is due to the weight of the Khanh Hau sample, where the owner-cultivators operated 2.5 times as much land per farm as the title-recipient group, but where the gross paddy production growth rate was an identical 56 percent for the two groups. The LTTT-title recipients out-performed the owner-cultivators in Phu Thu (31 percent growth to 14 percent) and suffered smaller losses in Long Binh Dien (-5 percent to -11 percent), where the average holdings were more equal among the three tenure groups. Averaging all three villages by land tenure status, however, causes the owner-cultivator group to look better because of the greater hectarage weight of its Khanh Hau member, while in fact it did no better in Khanh Hau than the LTTT-title recipients and actually did worse in the other two villages. (See Table 6-5.)

The important comparison is between the title-recipients and the remaining tenants, however, since without the LTTT Program the former would still be tenants themselves. The two-year growth rate in paddy production was 72 percent higher for the new owners than for the remaining tenants, and the former led in all three villages. Their highest lead was in Phu Thu, where they increased production more than 6 times faster than the tenants did, 31 percent to 5 percent. In Long Binh Dien it was again a matter of holding crop losses to a smaller proportion than the tenants, -5 percent to -13 percent.

---

[5]Conversions assume one **gia** averages 20 kilograms in weight, or 50 **gia** = 1 metric ton.

Table 6-4

Rice Production and Disposition in the
First Three Villages

(Khanh Hau, Long Binh Dien, and Phu Thu)

Average	44 Present Tenants	45 title Recipients	44 owner-Cultivators	All 133 Farmers
Paddy land holding (ha.)	1.3	1.4	2.4	1.7
Ha. received under LTTT	.03	1.3	.01	
Gross paddy production per farm, 1971-2 (gia)[1]	207	223	514	314
Annual yield/ha. 1971-2 (gia)	169	165	220	192
Annual yield/ha. 1969-70 (gia)	144	126	162	147
Annual yield/ha. before '69 (gia)	147	126	168	151
(% increase last 2 years)	(17)	(31)	(36)	(31)
Portion of riceland double-cropped, 1971	.42	.53	.55	.51
Portion of riceland double-cropped, 1969	.26	.24	.40	.32
(% increase 1969-71)	(59)	(120)	(35)	(58)
Yield/crop ha., 1971-2 (gia)	119	108	141	127
Yield/crop ha., 1969-70 (gia)	114	102	115	111
(% increase in two years)	(4)	(6)	(23)	(14)
Stipulated rent/ha. before LTTT(gia)	27	23		
Stipulated rent/1969-70 yield	.19	.18		
Percentage increase or decrease in last two years of (rice paddy use):				
Gross paddy production	18	30	36	30
Rent	- 7	-96	- 2	-49
In-kind labor payments	15	27	37	29
Home consumption and feed	2	14	4	7
Paddy sales and debt repayment	41	150	55	65
Disposable paddy[2]	22	58	37	38
(MPC disposable paddy[3])	(.05)	(.16)	(.04)	(.08)

[1] A gia is a unit of dry measure equal to 40 liters. One gia of paddy can range from 16 to 24 kilograms in weight, depending on the variety of rice, its quality and its moisture content. Taking 20 kilos per gia as a good average, 50 gia will equal one metric ton.

[2] Gross paddy production minus both rent and in-kind labor payments.

[3] Marginal Propensity to Consume (and use as feed) disposable paddy equals the change in home consumption and feed divided by the change in disposable paddy, and it is calculated from the absolute amounts of change, not from the percentage change figures shown in this table.

Table 6-5

Percentage Growth in Paddy Production by Tenure Status and Village, 1969-70 to 1971-72

Village, province	Present Tenants	Title recipients	Owner Cultivators	Total Sample
Khanh Hau, Long An	50	56	56	54
Long Binh Dien, Dinh Tuong	-13	- 5	-11	-10
Phu Thu, Phong Dinh	_5_	_31_	_14_	_18_
First Three Villages	18	30	36	30
Hoa Binh Thanh, An Giang	55	3	- 3	14

The superior production performance of the LTTT-title-recipient group was due almost entirely to a more rapid switch from single to double-cropping. The area double-cropped by our new owners increased by 120 percent between 1969-70 and 1971-72, compared with 59 percent for the tenants and 35 percent for the owner-cultivators. The fact that the owner-cultivator group already had 40 percent of its riceland area double-cropped in 1969-70, before the LTTT Program, compared with only 26 and 24 percent for the tenant and title-recipient groups, itself says something for the incentive and income-investment effects of landownership as compared with tenancy.[6]

A significant portion of the production gains achieved by the owner-cultivator group was due to higher yields per crop-hectare, which it was able to increase by 23 percent, compared with only 6 and 4 percent for the other two groups, thanks to skillful handling of Miracle Rice (mostly in Khanh Hau). It must be remembered, however, that some understatement of current rice yields is likely, especially among title-recipients, and crop-hectare yield levels would be particularly affected by it.

Marketable Surplus

The important question of the "marketable surplus"--whether the amount of rice and other farm products available to the cities will rise or fall due to the LTTT Program—is complex, as it involves a number of interrelated factors: the propensity of the title-recipient to consume his incremental farm income (from abolished rents) in kind or in trade for something else, his incentive and ability to invest in increased farm production, which in turn depend on the availability of localized technical information and other modern inputs (such as new seeds, fertilizers, insecticides, irrigation, and sufficient agricultural credit), the marketability of his produce at profitable prices, and even on the market availability of consumer goods he desires to purchase. The proportion of rental income previously consumed in kind by the landlords is also relevant, and the landlord side will be discussed in the following chapter.

The marginal propensity of the LTTT-title-recipients in the first three villages to consume their disposable paddy production

---

[6]The heavier weight of Khanh Hau owner-cultivators in the averages is again operative here, but in fact the owner-cultivators did lead the others in double-cropped hectarage in both Long Binh Dien and Phu Thu, but not in Khanh Hau, where the three tenure groups were about even in the proportion of land double-cropped before the LTTT Program. See Table 5-8.

was apparently low—only .16 over the last two years.[7]   This is higher than the same ratio for present tenants and owner-cultivators, .05 and .04, respectively, but it is so low as to allay any fears of a significant drop in paddy sales so long as total production is rising.

The 30 percent growth of total paddy production among title-recipients combined with the decline of rents from 15.9 to 0.5 percent of gross output to raise their disposable paddy by 58 percent. Paddy sales jumped by 150 percent, while home consumption rose by only 14 percent. Sales as a proportion of gross paddy production increased by 22 points, from .24 to .46, during the same two years, while home consumption decreased by 6 points, .49 to .43. (See Table 6-4.)

This effect depends on a substantial increase in disposable paddy, however. In a comparison of the figures by village it becomes apparent that at lower rates of disposable paddy growth the marginal propensity to consume (MPC) rather than sell is significantly higher, as is illustrated by Figure 6-2. In Long Binh Dien, where title-recipients suffered a 5 percent drop in total production despite an increase in hectarage double-cropped (the average yield per crop-hectare fell by 16 percent), the 21 percent rise in disposable paddy came solely from the remission of rents, and .56 of that increment was retained for use on the farm. In Phu Thu, where a 31 percent growth in production combined with rent remission to raise disposable paddy by 46 percent, the MPC disposable paddy was .25. But in Khanh Hau, where disposable paddy rose by 91 percent, the MPC was only .06. The Hoa Binh Thanh title-recipients, to be discussed

_____

[7]The marginal propensity to consume (MPC) disposable paddy equals the increase in home consumption over the increase in disposable paddy.   Home consumption includes paddy used as livestock feed, and disposable paddy is here taken to be total production minus in-kind labor payments and rents, leaving the amount sold plus the amount kept for home use. These figures are only rough approximations, since the disposal categories have hazy edges. For example, cash labor costs are taken out of "paddy sold" by some farmers and "home consumption" by others, and many housewives habitually keep more at home than they need to feed their families each year, dipping into this reserve to sell for petty cash needs or to feed livestock. In fact, much of the increase in the "home consumption" category has been due to an increased need for livestock feed by farmers who are raising more animals for the market. Only a small number were able to give separate estimates of how much paddy was actually used for feed each year, but many of those who did indicated an increase.

Figure 6-2

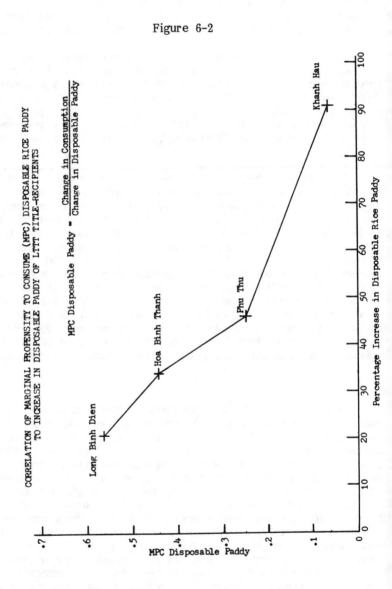

CORRELATION OF MARGINAL PROPENSITY TO CONSUME (MPC) DISPOSABLE RICE PADDY
TO INCREASE IN DISPOSABLE PADDY OF LTT TITLE-RECIPIENTS

$$\text{MPC Disposable Paddy} = \frac{\text{Change in Consumption}}{\text{Change in Disposable Paddy}}$$

in the next section, fit smoothly into this simple correlation curve, consuming .44 of a 34 percent increment in disposable paddy.

The remission of rents alone, without the concomitant new ownership incentive to increase investment and production, or without a favorable service and market environment to encourage higher production, could have resulted in a smaller marketable surplus than before, if landlords consumed a smaller proportion of their rent receipts than their tenants did later. The high MPC small increments of disposable paddy makes this a likely possibility, but we do not have sufficient data on the landlord side of the question. It is clear, however, that the landlord families must continue to eat; and if they ate, say, 25 percent of their rent receipts as rice paddy before losing their land, instead of collecting cash rents or selling paddy rents, they must now buy that much rice on the market, thus raising market demand for rice by the amount of lost rents previously consumed. This means that any proportion of the cancelled rents consumed on the farm reduces the market supply in relation to the (now increased) demand, and that the previous ratio can only be maintained or improved by a growth in total production sufficient to offset the farmers' MPC disposable paddy. Of course, the landlords are now required to purchase their rice out of other income and compensation payments, reducing their effective demands in other areas and forcing some of them to become more productive themselves; but their rice consumption will probably not decline to an appreciable degree.

These considerations stress the importance of achieving a substantial overall growth in paddy production in order to avoid a decline in paddy sales relative to market demand as a direct result of the LTTT Program. The incentive and investment effects of the Program in our first three villages appear to be strong enough to achieve this, but rely on a relatively favorable economic environment. Where the environment is not so favorable, as perhaps in less accessible or less secure areas, or in broadcast rice areas as in Hoa Binh Thanh Village, where the Program is causing considerable economic disruption, the outcome is likely to be less satisfactory in this regard.

It is also true, however, that in many of those areas where the economic environment is not so favorable landlords have not been able to collect rents for years anyway, and wherever this is the case, there is no way the LTTT Program itself can **reduce** the marketable surplus. Since there were no rents to cancel in the first place, any increase in disposable paddy would have to come from higher production; and no matter how small a portion of the increment is sold, it would still represent an increase in market supply. There is no reason to suspect the incentives of legal ownership are not operative at least to some extent in these areas as well as elsewhere, although the LTTT income effect on investment will be nil.

Agricultural Investment and Production: Hoa Binh Thanh Village

A sample of 45 farmers, split three ways, is too small to be very reliable, especially in a village as large and diverse as Hoa Binh Thanh, which is more than twice as large as our other three villages in population and 3 or 4 times their size in area. The indications we obtained, however, tend to verify the observations of many government officials and other commentators that the LTTT Program was not well-tailored to suit the special economic and social conditions in the Hoa Hao, floating-rice area, and that its problems of implementation and its initial effects are at variance with experience in other parts of the Mekong Delta.

Of the 15 title-recipients interviewed, two lost cultivation rights on land formerly rented but which, due to the 3-hectare LTTT Program limit, was distributed to others; another lady had to let two sisters claim title to most of her land and now rents it back from them; three farmers hold usufruct rights to "excess" land uncertain about its ultimate distribution; two of the above and four others had to split the family holding among sons and brothers, requiring in some cases the premature establishment of separate households and resulting in a more fragmented management of the land; at least three title recipients had to pay bribes (10,000 $VN per title) to village officials for their deeds of ownership; and one family that had refused suggestions of squeeze had yet to receive two of its titles.[8] Only four out of the sample of 15 had experienced a simple, uncomplicated transfer of ownership, and they were the smallest farmers, averaging only 1.8 hectares each.

In addition, 9 of the 15 present tenants in this sample rent or sublet land belonging to the Catholic Church, which, in this village, was supervised by a progressive priest who was encouraging his tenants to make the heavy investments required to double-crop Miracle Rice, and who was himself seeking a sizeable loan to extend his existing irrigation canals to that end. Eight of the 15 tenants rent plots declared Huong Hoa worship land, thus exempt from expropriation, and there is evidence here as elsewhere that landlords have understandably contrived to keep the more productive parts

----

[8]For the record, none of the land involved in these four reported cases of corruption lies in Hoa Binh Thanh Village, but rather in the more distant reaches of An Giang Province.

of their former holdings, notably land which can be more readily irrigated and double-cropped.

The present tenants are the **most** progressive group of farmers in this village and the LTTT-title-recipients are the **least** progressive—just the opposite of the other three villages. Our agricultural investment averages stand at 3.00 per tenant, 2.69 per owner-cultivator, but drop down to only 1.73 per title-recipient. "Purifying" these categories, by omitting five mixed tenants and one mixed title-recipient and separating four Ordinance 57 beneficiaries into a fourth group, accentuates the observed differences. (See Tables 6-2, 6-3 and 6-6.) The tenant average goes up and the title-recipient and owner-cultivator averages go down. The pure tenants were making 120 percent more investments than the title-recipients, the owner-cultivators were making 61 percent more.

The Ordinance 57 owners topped everyone else with a 3.50 investment average, providing a strong suggestion that the Diem land reform, by distributing to each farmer his entire holding[9] instead of imposing a disruptive 3-hectare limit, has created incentive effects here similar to those released by the LTTT Program elsewhere. All four of the Ordinance 57 land recipients in this village sample had still been making annual payments to the government for their land when the LTTT Program cancelled the remainder. The government only recently gave them permanent title to the land, making them legal owners; so it should not be surprising they are behaving more like one would expect "new owners" to behave, rather than like "old owners." With the Ordinance 57 title-recipients averaging 133 percent more productive investments than the LTTT title-recipients, perhaps there is a lesson to be learned here about how **not** to conduct a land reform in the broadcast rice areas.

Gross paddy production was up over the last two years by 55 percent on rented farms, compared with only 3 percent growth on transferred lands and a 3 percent decline on owner-operated land.[10]

---

[9]The holdings distributed to our sample under Ordinance 57 were 6, 7, 8 and 12.7 hectares in size.
[10]Since hectarage farmed by our sample decreased over the last 2 years in this village, production calculations are based on figures adjusted to a constant hectarage.

Table 6-6

Agricultural Investment by Land Tenure Status

Hoa Binh Thanh

TYPE OF INVESTMENT	NUMBER MAKING INVESTMENT			
	Present Tenants (n=44)	Title-Recipients (n=45)	Owner-Cultivators (n=44)	All Farmers (n=133)
Single to Double-cropping				
Within last 2 years	7	2	4	13
Planned this year	4	3	4	11
Increased Fertilizer per ha.				
Within last 2 years	9	5	6	20
Planned this year	5	6	5	16
New Irrigation Canal or Dike				
Within last 2 years	4	4	4	12
Planned this year	1	1	3	5
Planting Secondary Crops				
Within last 2 years	5	1	1	7
Planned this year	0	0	0	0
Raising Fish				
Within last 2 years	2	0	6	8
Planned this year	0	1	0	1
Increased Animal Husbandry				
Within last year	2	1	0	3
Planned this year	1	0	3	4
New Breed of Livestock				
Within last 2 years	0	0	0	0
Planned this year	0	0	0	0
New Farm Implements				
Within last year	2	1	4	7
Planned this year	3	1	3	7
TOTAL NEW INVESTMENTS	45	26	43	114
AVERAGE NEW INVESTMENTS PER FARMER	3.00	1.73	2.69	2.48
PURIFIED GROUP AVERAGES[1]	3.30	1.50	2.42	

[1]Five mixed cases have been withdrawn from the tenant category, leaving 10, one was withdrawn from the title-recipients, leaving 14, and four Ord. 57 land recipients were withdrawn from the owner-cultivators, leaving 12. The four Ord. 57 farmers averaged 3.50 investments, the five mixed tenants averaged 2.40. Of the latter, 3 were part LTTT title-recipients and 3 were part owners (one was both). The one mixed title-recipient was part owner-cultivator and had made or planned 5 new investments.

An analysis of variance computation performed on the "purified group averages" reported above for Hoa Binh Thanh Village indicates the differences among them are significant at the 90% level of confidence ($\alpha = .10$). Below are the results of that computation:

	Sum of Squares	Degrees of Freedom	Mean Square	F Ratio
Category means	19.12	2	9.56	$F = \frac{9.56}{3.71} = 2.58$
Within groups	122.52	33	3.71	$F = {}_{.90}(2,33) = 2.48$
Total	141.64	35		

Disposable paddy[11] rose by 34 percent for the title-recipients, thanks to rent abolition, but their marginal propensity to consume that increment (and to use it as feed) proved to be fairly high at .44. Combined with the apparent low incentive to invest in higher production (at least so far), this might indicate a reduction in the marketable surplus of rice here, depending on the proportion of rents consumed previously by expropriated landlords. If the market flow was maintained in Hoa Binh Thanh it was by the remaining tenants and their double-cropped Miracle Rice,[12] which increased their disposable production by 76 percent, despite higher labor, rent and seed requirements. Their MPC disposable paddy was only .24. (See Table 5-32.)

Service Institutions

If the LTTT Program is creating new ownership incentives to invest and raise production and is simultaneously providing the new owners with higher incomes out of which to make such investments, as seems evident in 3 out of 4 villages of this study, these factors can result in higher production only if the economic environment is favorable enough to encourage productive investments and to bring satisfactory rewards to the farmer who makes them. This section will discuss the current effectiveness of various service institutions in rural Vietnam—agricultural credit, research and extension, farmer cooperatives, marketing, input supply, and transportation systems—from the point of view of the farmers.

Rural Indebtedness and Agricultural Credit

Fifty-six percent of our total sample in the first three villages and 80 percent in Hoa Binh Thanh had borrowed money during the

---

[11]Same as above (see note 7) except that seed grain stored each year is also subtracted from gross production, since it amounts to a significant and variable proportion of gross (6-12 percent) in this region, where seeds are sown directly in the paddies (sometimes 2 or 3 times if the rains are unfavorable) and seedlings are not transplanted as elsewhere. In the first 3 villages seed paddy was included in home consumption, but was a very small, constant percentage, averaging between 1.3 and 2.0 percent of gross production.

[12]The tenants increased their double-cropped hectarage by 236 percent, up from 7 to 24 percent of their holdings, while the other groups increased it hardly at all. The tenants also improved yields per crop-hectare by 35 percent, compared with only 4 percent by the title-recipients and a decline of 7 percent by the owner cultivators.

year preceding our visit.   This was up slightly from 50 and 63
percent, respectively, who had borrowed two years before, due
mostly to larger numbers of LTTT-title-recipients borrowing in Phu
Thu and Hoa Binh Thanh.   In Phu Thu more were borrowing in order
to make productive investments, while in Hoa Binh Thanh more
were borrowing for consumption purposes.

The availability of credit was apparently much less in Phu
Thu than elsewhere.   Although 22 percent of all 105 debtors
interviewed were in that village, their combined cash indebtedness
amounted to only 9 percent of the total amount borrowed.   The
average debt in Phu Thu was only 34-38 percent of those in the
other three villages. Average debts increased by 39 and 36 percent
in the two upper-Delta villages, by only 1 percent in Phu Thu, and
declined by 20 percent in Hoa Binh Thanh.   The latter two averages
were pushed downward by the increase in number of farmers (mostly
title-recipients) borrowing,[13] since the new ones borrowed less than
the others.

If we compare all 134 farmer interviews in the first three
villages by land tenure status, we find a 37 percent increase in the
number of LTTT-title-recipients borrowing over two years before,
compared with zero to 4 percent of the owner-cultivators and
tenants.   The average debt of the former declined by 15 percent,
however, while it rose by 28 percent for the tenants and 75 percent
for the owner-cultivators.[14]   The remission of rents apparently
enabled some of the habitual borrowers to reduce their indebtedness
(especially in Khanh Hau), but it encouraged others to borrow for
the first time in order to make productive investments (especially
in Phu Thu).

In Hoa Binh Thanh, on the other hand, while the number of
title-recipients borrowing doubled, the total value of their debts
decreased 41 percent and 80 percent of the loans were made in
whole or in part for consumption.

Although the three major sources of credit (the government,
relatives, and friends and neighbors) were about equally divided in

---

[13]The number of farmers borrowing increased over 2 years
before by 35 percent in Phu Thu and 28 percent in Hoa Binh Thanh,
compared with only 4 percent in the other two villages.
[14]If we look only at those 67 farmers who were debtors 2
years before, we find that 42 percent of the title-recipients have
reduced their debt status, while a 52 percent majority of the owner-
cultivators increased theirs and 40 percent of the tenants reported
no change.   See Callison, **Land to the Tiller**, Table 6-9.

the number of loans granted, the government agricultural credit program was providing 45 percent of the total amount borrowed in the first three villages. Of the total amount of government loans held by our respondents, 47 percent were in owner-cultivator hands, 31 percent had gone to title-recipients and only 22 percent to tenants.[15] This confirms verbal reports that bank officials are reluctant to loan to tenants and prefer applicants with land ownership deeds and fine houses of brick and tile. It is evidence, however, that at least some of the government credit is going to tenants (but only in the two upper-Delta villages—no tenants in Phu Thu and only one in Hoa Binh Thanh, 2 years before, had been able to borrow from this source of credit, though many wanted to).

The benefits of cheap (subsidized) government credit are also unevenly spread among villages. Our farmer samples in each village vary in number by only 2 to 5 percent, but 60 percent of all government funds reported borrowed were in Long Binh Dien, only 3 percent in Phu Thu and 10 percent in Hoa Binh Thanh, with 27 percent in Khanh Hau. Fully 79 percent of all cash borrowed in Long Binh Dien came from the Agricultural Development Bank, but only 10 percent did in Phu Thu, besides which the LBD sample borrowed altogether 178 percent more than the Phu Thu sample. Government loans to our LBD respondents totalled 22.6 times as much as in Phu Thu, 6 times more than in HBT, and more than twice as much as in Khanh Hau.

Agricultural Research and Extension

Although some progress had been achieved in recent years, there was still a great need for localized agricultural research and improved extension efforts. Plant and animal diseases and pests took a heavy toll, and the farmers not only lost much of their crops and livestock but also wasted considerable sums in futile efforts to save them. Swine and poultry losses especially were high in **every** village, and this was one of the main reasons given why the farmers would not try to raise more livestock for the market. Several farmers explained that, because of the high loss rate, raising livestock for the market was not profitable but merely served as a form of real savings (not diminished by inflation), for which they were willing to take occasional losses.

Since the landlords, as a general rule, provided no inputs into the production process after World War II, least of all technical expertise, the LTTT Program could not have diminished these inputs.

---

[15]Even though the owner-cultivator sample numbered only 44, one less than the other two groups.

Any improvement in research and extension is therefore to be considered pure gain, not a replacement for lost landlord services. It is pertinent to our current research, however, to note some evidence which indicates the different impact of extension services on the three land tenure groups.

While overall village differences are often more pronounced, with the two upper-Delta villages (nearer Saigon) reporting more favorable attitudes toward and experiences with government extension efforts and modern technical information than the two lower-Delta villages, it is also clear that owner-cultivators have been more favorably affected than the tenants.

Seventy-two percent of all farmers interviewed in the first three villages thought the distribution of technical information had improved in recent years, but more owner-cultivators and LTTT title-recipients expressed this sentiment than tenants. More tenants than owner-cultivators said their main source of information about new agricultural techniques was by word of mouth from friends, neighbors, and relatives, and more owner-cultivators than tenants received such information at village meetings and from the local agricultural extension agent or the agricultural extension office. More owner-cultivators than tenants had ever met the local agricultural extension agent, and 57 percent of the former thought the extension agent had information which could help them increase production, while only 40 percent of the tenants thought so.

Village differences are striking throughout this data. The agricultural extension agent had a more limited impact in Phu Thu, where only 33 percent of the farmers had ever even met him, compared with 62 percent in LBD and 86 percent in Khanh Hau, and where only 24 percent thought he had useful information, compared with 51 percent in LBD and 75 percent in Khanh Hau.

If, as these data seem to indicate, owner-cultivators are more likely to attend village meetings, talk with agricultural extension agents and generally be more receptive to technical information and advice from outside their immediate circle of friends and relatives, then the LTTT Program, by making 800,000 more owner-cultivators out of tenants, might well deserve credit for improving the **effectiveness** of agricultural extension services, even though further improvement in the services themselves depends on other programs. The LTTT Program does seem to have stimulated former tenants' interest in new ideas and change. Fewer title-recipients than either tenants or owner-cultivators said they were **not** interested in learning new agricultural techniques (in response to an admittedly leading question), and more title-recipients and owner-cultivators than tenants said they had only recently become interested.

Farmers' Cooperatives

There was a Farmers' Union office in Tan An, 4 kilometers from Khanh Hau Village, where 20 percent of our sample said they were members of either the union or a local buyers cooperative. The Farmers' Association had an office in LBD Village, and 24 percent of our LBD sample were members. Organizational efforts were just underway for a new chapter of the Farmers' Association in Phu Thu, and only 3 of our respondents (7 percent) had joined so far (only 18 percent even knew about it); and the nearest one to HBT Village was 9 kilometers away in Long Xuyen (only one HBT farmer, 2 percent, said he was a member).

Again, differences among villages were more pronounced due to the variety of circumstances and experience found among them; but somewhat fewer tenants were convinced of the value of farmers organizations than were owner-cultivators or LTTT-title-recipients.

Although it is a sample of only one village, local farmer criticisms of the Farmers' Association in LBD (where 98 percent of our sample knew about the Association but only 24 percent were members and only 40 percent thought it could help its members) are instructive as to the problems inherent in government-sponsored organizations of this type. Of the 11 members in our sample, only 6 thought the Association had done them any good.

Favorable comments included an explanation that Association members pool their resources to obtain new seeds, fertilizer, insecticides and other supplies and can sometimes obtain them when they are scarce on the market. Some said the Association sold fertilizer and insecticides cheaper than elsewhere, though most said only **slightly** cheaper; and a few said it would loan farmers money or let them buy on credit.

It was also noted that information about new crops and other technical information was disseminated by the Association. Farmers near the Association office cited the convenience of having such a source of needed supplies close at hand.

Unfavorable reactions were more numerous, including some direct contradictions to the above with many farmers claiming Association prices were higher or at least no lower than prices elsewhere, that it would **not** sell on credit, and that it only sold fertilizer and insecticides, nothing else, and that even these items were sometimes not on hand when needed. Several complaints were registered about time-consuming paperwork and poor organization, so that farmers had to wait around a long time to make a purchase and often had to make several trips in to catch the right official for approval. One member complained they seldom told him what was going on, so that he often missed meetings he might have liked to attend. One tenant in an outlying hamlet said he was told they had a maximum limit on membership and that by the time he heard about the Association its membership rolls were already filled with farmers from the central hamlets. Several gripes were made about the "requirement" that you let Association workers deliver your purchases to your home or field, at a cost of 10 piasters per bag, whether you wanted to carry it yourself or not. One (paraphrased) response deserves quoting in full:

> "The Farmers' Association is run by the government. Its officials are government employees and act like petty bureaucrats. They keep bankers' hours, keep customers waiting while they finish a leisurely chat and require them to fill out forms for every purchase and show their identification cards. They cannot sell on credit, not even to old customers, neighbors or friends. Farmers liked the Association at first, but later became disillusioned about its benefits—its prices are not much better than outside anyway. A young lady nearby does a good business at a small, roadside stand selling fertilizer, insecticides and some other items because she keeps more convenient hours (including evenings and Sundays), she can sell on credit, she doesn't require any paperwork or ID cards, and she is polite and responsive to customers."

The problem is an old one: how to make a large government-sponsored organization responsive to the farmers' needs, wishes, and sensitivities at the local level.

Marketing and Transport Services

Attempts to learn about marketing and transport systems from the farmers proved futile. Very few farmers had to bother with specific arrangements to take their goods to the nearest large town to sell.

For the most part, buyers went from house to house throughout the year, but especially at harvest time, and will purchase as much or as little as the farmer wishes to sell on the spot, paying for it in cash. Rice paddy, hogs, and poultry are all marketed through house to house buyers, except for very small amounts sold from time to time during the off-season, usually by the farmer's wife, for petty cash needs. In the latter case the wife will merely carry a bushel or two of paddy or a couple of chickens to the mill or to the market herself.

The marketing system works well for the farmer in the sense that he does not have to worry about finding a buyer—they seek him out—or about transporting his goods to the market—the buyers take care of that in their own vehicles or boats. Most farmers expressed satisfaction with the fairness of the prices they received on the farm, compared with the going wholesale prices in the local markets. If the buyer offers too low a price the farmer can always wait for another buyer or take his crop to the market himself, but few of them consider it worthwhile to do this for the small price differences that comprise the buyers' margin.

Much concern has been expressed in the literature about monopolistic control of rice markets by large merchants and millers based in Saigon, with different views expressed as to whether the farmer was getting his fair share of the (Saigon) market price of rice. Our study was not designed to throw any light on this controversy.[16]

Housing and Consumer Durable Expenditure

Housing construction and consumer durable purchases represent both volatile elements of aggregate demand and significant forms of investment in the economy. Residential construction typically accounts for about 30 percent of gross private domestic investment in the United States, as measured by the Department of Commerce in calculating the annual Gross National Product (GNP). Consumer durable purchases are counted as part of consumption demand in the GNP accounts; but, conceptually, they too represent an investment providing a stream of future real income. The U.S. Department of Commerce calculates the annual returns on previous housing investment as the "rental" portion of National Income, imputing the market rental values of all owner-occupied homes. Conceptually, annual real income from other consumer durable investment should be calculated in the same manner, but obvious difficulties make it impractical to do so.

---

[16]For a more in-depth analysis of the marketing and transportation systems in the Mekong Delta see Robert L. Sansom, **Economics of Insurgency**, pp. 94-103. Sansom found that "In 1966-67 not only was the Delta paddy price as high as or higher than the Saigon price but Delta farmers were, with the exception of the transport and labor handling costs, taking home most of that price."

The quantity and value of houses and consumer durables owned are also important indicators of the comparative wealth of households and of their comparative real incomes, providing useful information on the skew of income distribution among land tenure groups.

The quality of housing is clearly correlated with land tenure status, with owner-cultivators having a much higher proportion of the nicer and more durably constructed homes than the tenant and former tenant groups, and with the LTTT-title-recipients slowly beginning to push their way up from tenant levels. The "ideal" house in the first three villages has a tile roof, tile floors, and walls of brick or cement block. This is the house every successful and self-respecting farmer aspires someday to build. The "cheapest" house has a roof of thatch or corrugated metal,[17] walls of thatch or bamboo, and floors of packed earth. Table 6-7 presents a breakdown of housing types owned by our sample. It is clear many more of the owner-cultivators have "made it" than of the other two groups; and, conversely, many more tenants and former tenants live under thatch or corrugated metal roofs and on packed earth floors.

Many of the farmers interviewed were in the process of repairing, remodelling, or rebuilding their homes, and a sizeable number either had or were planning to upgrade the type of their houses. While the more enthusiastic plans for future reconstruction were recounted by the title-recipient group, such an investment typically called for more funds than could be saved from remitted rents for several years and usually involved expected returns from successful double-cropping with Miracle Rice, as well. The figures show, nevertheless, that 71 percent of the title-recipients had either spent money for house repairs, remodelling, or reconstruction in the year preceding our interview or planned to do so during the coming year, compared with 64 percent of the owner-cultivator group and only 49 percent of the tenants. In addition, the average amount of money being invested in such house improvements by the title-recipients, while only about 2/3 the average spent by owner-cultivators, was well over double the average amount spent by the remaining tenants.

A similar story is evident in the consumer durable statistics. A higher proportion of owner-cultivators owned at least one of all but two of the 16 items on the list than the tenants did, while the title-recipients were already purchasing their way up to a position

---

[17]See discussion of roofing material in Chapter V, Khanh Hau, Long An Province; "Living Standards," pp. 102-4.

Table 6-7

Type of Housing by Land Tenure Status, First Three Villages

| Type of Housing | Percentages of: | | | |
	45 Present Tenants	45 title Recipients	44 owner-Cultivators	All 134 Farmers
Roof:				
Thatch	47	53	32	44
Corrugated metal	42	24	20	29
Sub-total	89	77	52	73
Cement Fiber	2	4	7	4
Tile or Concrete	9	18	41	22
Sub-total	11	22	48	27
Walls:				
Thatch or bamboo	47	42	20	37
Wooden	36	38	34	36
Brick or Cement Block	18	20	39	25
Earth	0	0	2	0.7
Metal	0	0	5	1.5
Floor:				
Packed Earth	76	78	57	70
Cement	13	13	7	11
Tile	11	9	36	19
Percentage Repairing, Remodelling, or Re-constructing in 1971-2	49	71	64	61
Average Amount Spent ($VN)	80,375	191,043	294,462	197,300
Number Repairing, etc.	20	30	26	76

in between. Land-tenure correlations were especially marked in the proportions owning such modern utilities as the radio, the pressure lamp, the wall clock, and the motorbike, as well as such traditional prestige items as brass altar fixtures, Chinese character frescos, and the glass-front cabinet. In addition, the owner-cultivators owned more of the four most commonly found items on the list than did the tenants—wardrobe cabinets, worship tables or cabinets, wood plank beds (**bo van**), and table and chair sets—with title-recipients again emerging between the other two groups in owning the first two items and slightly surpassing the owner-cultivators in the last two. The last four named items were not only the most commonly found in farm households, with many owning more than one of each item, they were also the items most often reported as recently purchased or planned for purchase soon—items of basic household furniture. (See Table 6-8.)

Thirty-one percent of the LTTT-title-recipients said they had made one or more consumer-durable purchases during the year preceding the interview or planned to do so in the following year, about equal to the 30 percent of the owner-cultivators who made similar claims, but half again as many as the 20 percent of the tenants who said so. The title-recipients (who represented roughly one-half of all farm families in the Delta) were buying twice as many consumer durables per household as were the tenants and more than half again as many as were the owner-cultivators.

The LTTT Program was clearly stimulating rural investment in both house improvements and consumer durables and thereby increasing market demand for these domestic industries.

Education

Slightly more tenants and former tenants had school-age children or grandchildren (6-11 years old) **not** in school than did the owner-cultivators, but the difference was hardly significant. Village differences were much more pronounced, with 37 percent of the farmers in Phu Thu and 27 percent in HBT having young truants in their households, compared with none in Khanh Hau and only 2 percent in LBD. Several reasons were given for this parentally approved truancy: that the nearest school was too far from home, especially where the children would have to cross one or more "monkey bridges" enroute, that it cost too much to send them, that they were needed at home to help their mother look after the younger children and the livestock, and that they were afraid to go. Many of these children will be sent to school when they are a little older. It is common practice among many families in more isolated areas not to start their children in first grade until they are 8 or 9 years old and are better able to negotiate the long walk

Table 6-8

Ownership of Selected Consumer Durables by Land Tenure Status, First Three Villages, 1971-72

Item	45 Present Tenants	45 title Recipients	44 owner Cultivators	All 134 Farmers
A. Percentage Owning at least One:				
Table & chairs	100	100	100	100
Wood plank bed (bo van)	100	96	95	97
Wardrobe cabinet	73	82	84	80
Worship table or cabinet	84	87	95	89
Glass-front cabinet	24	29	32	28
Brass altar fixtures	24	29	39	31
Chinese character frescos	27	36	45	36
Wall clock	22	31	32	28
Pressure lamp	31	49	52	44
Sewing machine	51	64	57	57
Radio	51	69	89	77
Television	0	0	7	2
Bicycle	38	42	39	40
Motorscooter or motorbike	9	7	25	13
Sampan, hand-operated	7	16	16	13
Sampan, motorized	29	27	25	27
Percentage of households purchasing consumer durables in 1971 or planning to in 1972	20	31	30	27
B. Average Number Owned per Household in Sample:				
Table & chair sets	1.78	2.11	2.05	1.98
Wood plank bed (bo van)	1.84	1.96	1.91	1.90
Wardrobe cabinet	.98	1.18	1.52	1.22
Worship table or cabinet	1.27	1.64	1.82	1.57
C. Average Number of Items per Household:				
Purchased last year	.24	.49	.25	.33
Planned for purchase this year	.16	.31	.27	.25
Purchased last year or planned for purchase this year	.40	.80	.52	.57

and monkey bridges involved. Then the boys, at least, will be sent to school a few years until they learn to read and write and handle basic arithmetic. Some of the girls will not be sent at all.

More pertinent to the present inquiry were the answers to the question, asked of those with children or grandchildren currently attending school, as to how far they wanted their offspring to study before quitting. Most of the answers were vague and indefinite: "As far as they are able," "As far as they want to go." "As long as we can support them," or "It doesn't matter." The first answer quoted was by far the most frequent, and it must be understood as expressing an honest desire to keep the children in school for as long as they can keep passing to higher grades and for as long as the parents can keep supporting them. It could mean up to the 5th grade for some, the 9th for others and the 12th grade for still others.

Of more interest, however, is the much higher proportion of owner-cultivators who named specific grade levels as goals for their children's education, and the fact that most of these goals were 10th grade or above. Tenants and former tenants had fewer specific educational goals and those who were specific tended to cite lower grade levels, especially for their daughters. There is no evidence here that the LTTT Program has as yet had any noticeable impact on the educational goals of former tenants for their children, except that, by placing so many of them in an owner-cultivator social status and raising the level of their incomes, we can legitimately expect them gradually to adopt the values and lifestyles of their owner-cultivator neighbors, who clearly do have higher educational goals than the tenants.[18]

Village differences were again significant, with higher specific educational goals expressed in the two upper-Delta villages of Khanh Hau and LBD than in the two lower-Delta villages. The highest grade-level goal given in Phu Thu was the 6th grade.

Social and Political Change

So much time was spent inquiring about purely economic matters that very little serious probing could be done into questions

---

[18]In this regard it should be noted that the owner-cultivator men averaged 3.9 years of formal education in the first three villages, while the tenant and former tenant men averaged 2.3. The averages for women were not significantly different at an overall average of 1.5. (See Table 5-1 and Callison, **Land to the Tiller**, Table 6-18.)

of political and social interest. An attempt was made to elicit some general observations about the local scene and about the reception of the LTTT Program. In most cases little relevant information was obtained; the most common answers, especially from the women, were "I don't know about that" and "nothing much has changed." When a respondent was inclined to talk, however, as the older men more often were, we kept the discussion going without taking notes, later summarizing the key points made from memory. Since this was the most sensitive part of the interview, from the standpoint of the interviewees' willingness to be candid and truthful, it was always reserved for last and a minimum of notes were taken on the spot.

With a few exceptions, there is no attempt in the summary below to quantify the answers or to state exact proportions favoring one view or the other, but rather to present the composite picture as described by the informants interviewed. The views of one perceptive and observant individual in a village may be more accurate and offer better insights than all the other comments taken together anyway, so not much can be gained by trying to weight them equally. Research results reported in this section represent the opinions of those farmers interviewed who cared to express them, and not a definitive study of social and political change.

The following topics were discussed :

1) What changes have occurred in:

    a. Relationships between landlords and tenants?

    b. Villagers' attitudes toward title-recipients?

    c. Farmer participation in village and hamlet meetings?

    d. Leadership positions, political power and influence of different groups?

2. Political leadership selection process--village and national elections:

    a. What are the ideal qualities of a hamlet or village chief?

    b. How do villagers decide to vote in elections?

3. Opinions about the LTTT Program:

    a. Why did the government undertake the LTTT Program?

    b. What do villagers think of it?

    c. What does the NLF say about it?

4. What problems still need to be solved to help villagers improve their lives?

Relationships between Landlord and Tenant

Under the landlord–tenant system of the 1930's landlords wielded almost total authority over the lives and fortunes of their tenants. Since they controlled not only the land, the only secure source of wealth and food in the Delta, but also the political machinery at village, district, and province levels, their power was described as nearly absolute from the tenants' point of view. This concentration of power led to frequent social, economic, and political abuses, against which the tenants had no recourse but the extra-legal rebellion so many of them supported in the 1950's and 60's.

The old landlord–tenant system was described vividly and in similar terms in all four villages and by all three land tenure groups interviewed. It was especially interesting to hear the comments of so many owner-cultivators, who themselves had no axe to grind and can presumably be considered more objective in making their observations. That a great change had occurred over the previous 30 years is beyond question, the only differences of opinion being about the date of the beginning of the end of the old system and who or what events were responsible for its demise.

A broad consensus would agree that before 1945 the position of the tenant was like that of a servant or slave to his landlord (both words were used, with "slave" the more frequent), who had to work from dawn to dusk to satisfy the conditions of his tenancy while earning enough food to keep his family from starving, and who lived in mortal fear of losing his cultivation rights to the land and thus falling into an even worse condition. There were always landless workers around who would try to offer the landlord a little higher rent or a little more "key money" for the same land.

Landlords could take back their land, if rents or debts weren't paid on time, and rent it to another tenant for a higher return. Population pressure on the land continued to force rent levels up, moreover, so that this system became permanently stacked against the tenant. With rent levels at 50 or 60 percent of a good harvest, a crop failure, which could be counted on periodically, would leave a tenant no way to meet his stipulated rents; and, until the Diem reforms of 1955, landlords were under no obligation whatsoever to grant tolerance for a bad harvest. In many cases tolerance was not granted and the tenant was considered to have "borrowed" the amount he could not pay until the following year, at 100 percent real interest. Even if he did pay all his rent the tenant then had to borrow rice before the next harvest anyway, usually from his landlord, in order to feed his family, also at 100 percent real interest.   Either way, by simply not granting tolerance in a bad year, the landlord was able to place the tenant in a debtor position and erase all legal claim the tenant had to continued cultivation rights on the land. From then on, the tenant remained completely at the mercy of the landlord.

Tenants were expected to provide, in addition to the rents, free labor in the landlord's unrented fields (in one case 15 days per hectare rented) and ceremonial labor by both the tenant and his wife in the landlord's house—cleaning, sweeping, repairing, cooking, even cleaning the toilet area—before days of ceremonial feasts; and they had to bring gifts of poultry, pigs, fruit, vegetables, and rice for these ceremonial feasts. Landlords were often very restrictive about what could be grown or done on their land, fearing, often through sheer ignorance about farming, that some damage would be done to their land. They often would not permit the construction of satisfactory bunds, irrigation or drainage ditches or the planting of fruit trees or vegetable crops. One tenant reported his landlord refused him permission to keep livestock, fearing damage to the land.

The landlord class was protected by the administrative system operated by the French colonial regime, in which local administrative positions were appointed by higher authorities and could therefore be purchased by the highest bidder. Most of our respondents placed the beginning of the end at 1945, when the Viet Minh rose up and forced the landlords to flee their country villas to seek the safety of the cites, though many noticed little change until after the French were officially forced out in 1954, or until the government of Ngo Dinh Diem initiated rent and tenure control legislation in 1955 and some land redistribution in 1956. A few placed the date as late as 1967 and 1969, when more recent rent and occupancy freezes were decreed.

Most agreed that the erosion of landlord power had been a gradual process over the preceding two or three decades, with the LTTT Program delivering the final blow, the **coup de grace.** The Viet Minh were instrumental in initiating the process, by expelling most of the landlords to the cities, eliminating the worst abuses of the system, and eradicating the foolhardy souls who resisted. The presence of the NLF after the early 1960's, preventing any landlord attempt to regain their lost position, caused a further erosion of their power. The Diem rent controls and contract requirements were given a considerable amount of credit, however. Even though rents often exceeded legal levels, the landlords seldom tried to push as hard as before and rents rarely approached the old 50 percent levels, while most of the extra requirements were dropped. It became much harder to evict a tenant or to maneuver him into an exposed legal position where he could be easily evicted.

As far as the LTTT Program was concerned, very few farmers in our sample seemed inclined to give the NLF much credit for "forcing" the Thieu government into it, as a more sophisticated view might well do. The NLF was given its due in keeping the landlords out and in redistributing some land in its own manner;[19] but the LTTT Program was conceived in 1969 and launched in 1970, a period when NLF power and influence in the Mekong Delta was at low ebb,[20] due to the decimation their ranks and prestige suffered after the Tet Offensive of 1968, and a period when government prestige and influence was on the rise. That the government was trying to "buy the hearts of the farmers" and win greater rural support was unquestioned, but this was perceived as a good thing for the government to do **and** an excellent way to do it. Its motives were clear and acceptable (even to many of the landlords); but the timing of the move seemed to disassociate it from the NLF threat, except in a rather vague and distant way.

There is no denying that a very real social, political and economic revolution was underway in the Mekong Delta. Its importance and human interest value warrant a little space to record the voices of some of those involved:

> "The landlords once had an awful lot of power. Tenants were merely their slaves and had to work from dawn to dusk . . . For every ceremonial feast the tenants had to come work and to bring rice or poultry to put on the altar . . . They were afraid if they did not do so the landlord would be angry and might take back his land . . . Now they are no longer afraid."
> —owner-cultivator in Khanh Hau Village.

---

[19]See Chapter III, "Viet Cong Reforms."
[20]And it remained at low ebb until the Spring Offensive of 1972.

"Before 1945 landlords were all the bad things you hear about, demanding high rents, ceremonial labor and livestock, etc. But it was partly due to the population pressure on the land. Farmers would insist a landlord let them rent the land at a higher rent than the present tenant, and if the landlord was reluctant they would work on his wife. Pressure and organization from the Viet Minh changed the system after 1945. In recent years landlords have had to plead with their tenants and treat them nicely to get any rent at all, and whatever the tenants wanted to pay the landlords had to accept."
—owner-cultivator in LBD Village.

Some of the worst abuses in the old system were reported by farmers in Phu Thu Village, Phong Dinh Province:

"In the old days tenants had to perform ceremonial labor (around the landlord's house) and free labor (in his fields), and still the landlord kept demanding higher rents. He would not give his tenants permission to build bunds, plant fruit trees or vegetables—there were so many restrictions[This was true until 1969, when rents and land occupancy were frozen and the new LTTT law was proposed."
—owner-cultivator in Phu Thu Village.

"Before, rents were 70 **gia** per hectare. If the crop failed the tenant had to pay the following year. Landlords controlled the village government. They refused to give tenants permission to build dikes or to dig irrigation or drainage ditches, and if the tenant tried to do anything against his landlord's will he would be arrested and put in jail."
—owner-cultivator in Phu Thu Village.

"Before 1945 tenants remained in heavy debt to their landlords the year around, often having to give him their entire crop in payment for rent and repayment of loans plus interest, and then they had to borrow again immediately in order to have enough to eat. If anyone reneged on payments, the landlord simply reclaimed the land and rented it to someone else. Tenants also had to provide ceremonial labor. That system started to change under Viet Minh influence after 1945 and it no longer exists."
—tenant in Phu Thu Village.

"Landlords would charge high rents, 35 to 56 **gia** per hectare, and force tenants on poor land to borrow and get deep in debt, then they would make a tenant on good land who was not in debt trade places with the one on poor land. After a few years the debtor had paid back his loans with interest and the other tenant would be heavily in debt, so the landlord would make them switch land again. This old system of landlord oppression changed rapidly after 1956."
—LTTT-title-recipient in Phu Thu Village.

" . . . if the harvest was too little to cover the rents the landlord would send his men around to confiscate furniture and other valuables to make up the difference. If you borrowed rice from the landlord to eat, you had to repay twice as much at harvest time. The landlords controlled everything, tenants were nothing. Whenever a landlord came to call, a tenant had to bow and scrape and kill a chicken for dinner, doing everything to make him feel at home, but even so the landlord seldom reduced rents."
—LTTT-title-recipient in Phu Thu Village.

" . . . landlords often forced their tenants to make their young daughters provide sexual favors. All this changed rather suddenly after 1945, thanks to Viet Minh influence. Landlords fled for their lives. One of the meanest land managers was killed not far from here by a tenant getting revenge for what had been done to his daughter."
—owner-cultivator in Phu Thu Village.

"Landlords wanted to cut their tenants' throats and peel their skin off. Since 1965 things have changed for the better."
—tenant in Phu Thu Village.

"Landlords were very oppressive to their tenants before 1945, . . . All that started to change about 1945 with Viet Minh influence scaring landlords into the cities; and landlord power gradually faded until the LTTT Program struck the final blow."
—owner-cultivator in Phu Thu Village.

The farmers in the Hoa Hao village of Hoa Binh Thanh (HBT), An Giang Province, painted a picture very similar to the one above, though their memories were not nearly so bitter as those in Phu Thu, contrary to a belief commonly held among Americans that the old landlord-tenant system did not undergo the same early changes in the Hoa Hao area as elsewhere, but rather remained fairly intact until the Diem and LTTT reforms, simply because the Viet Minh had little influence there. To quote Robert Samsom, after a discussion of Viet Minh reforms elsewhere:

"However, in An Giang and other areas of the lower Delta over which the Viet Minh had never exerted control, the tenancy system was not modified, and pre-1946 Delta-wide conditions prevailed throughout the 1950's and 1960's."[21]

This view is erroneous and fails to appreciate the fact that the Hoa Hao movement itself, which had its own beginnings in the 1940's, "was designed to appeal primarily to the oppressed and poor,"[22] and had a strong anti-landlord bias.[23] Armed Hoa Hao bands rose up against local administrative leaders and chased many rich landlords out of the villages and into the cities in 1945, like the Viet Minh did elsewhere, and they put an end to some of the worst abuses of the old landlord-tenant system in Hoa Hao areas.

Some rich landlords were "converted" to the new sect, making financial contributions in an effort to buy protection and even assuming leadership positions in it,[24] but most were not. Of the ten landlords interviewed with landholdings in HBT Village, only one was Hoa Hao; and out of 110 form B applications for compensation payments for land expropriated in HBT under the LTTT Program,[25] only 9, or 8 percent, were village residents. Some of the large landlords interviewed spoke of the flight from their village home in 1945, of still being afraid to spend the night in the village where they owned land, and of a 3-year period (1945-48) when "all men of wealth were in danger." Although landlords remained, after a brief interlude, in a much stronger position than elsewhere, the old tenancy system had been irreversibly modified by the Hoa Hao movement.

"Before 1945, some landlords required free labor and gifts of poultry for ceremonial feasts and they loaned money at 100 percent interest, but then the Hoa Hao

---

[21]Sansom, **Economics of Insurgency,** p. 56.
[22]Buttinger, **Vietnam: A Dragon Embattled,** p. 256.
[23]Ibid., p. 260.
[24]Ibid., p. 261
[25]On file in the An Giang Province Land Affairs Office in August 1972, and representing 1,836 ha., or 86 percent of all HBT land expropriated by March 1973.

sect reduced landlord power and eliminated the worst aspects of their oppression of tenants."
—LTTT-title-recipient in HBT Village.

"Landlords were very difficult before 1945. They allowed no tolerance for bad harvests, rice-rents had to be very clean, they demanded ceremonial (free) labor, and they could evict tenants.
—three different owner-cultivators in HBT Village.

"During the French period landlords had close ties with the French. Tenants were afraid they would be evicted and were more afraid of their landlords than they are of the district chief today."
—owner-cultivator in HBT Village.

"Landlords haven't lived in the village since 1945."
—owner-cultivator in HBT Village.

Villagers' Attitudes toward Title-Recipients

Most respondents had not noticed any change in the attitudes of other villagers toward LTTT-title-recipients. A few said everyone was happy for them and a few tenants and owner-cultivators said people disliked the new boastfulness or haughtiness they saw in some title-recipients. Some of the farmers, however, felt that significant changes were occurring:

"Before the LTTT Program the title-recipients had to hire themselves out to other people; but now that they are owners, they only help other people when their own work is done. Because of this their morale is higher and village residents show them more respect."
—title-recipient in Khanh Hau Village.

"Before the rich people in the village treated the poor workers and tenants very badly, making them work long hours for one day's pay without providing good food to eat.[26] Now most farmers around here are owners and because of it they are in better shape, they do not have to hire themselves out to others. The rich people must plead with them to work and let them return home at 5PM instead of 6PM, with better food to eat. Everyone

---

[26]The noon meal is provided by the farmer who hires wage labor, and labor is typically paid for by the day, not by the hour.

treats the LTTT-title-recipients with more respect now than before."
—title-recipient in LBD Village.

"Village officials used to act pompously, expecting tenants to bow and scrape and stand in their presence. Now they act like equals and try to help farmers improve their crops."
—owner-cultivator in Phu Thu Village.

"Title-recipients have more rights now than before."
—owner-cultivator in HBT Village.

"Title-recipients are happier now, they don't meet so many obstacles as before."
—title-recipient in HBT Village.

"Village officials are more polite with title-recipients than they used to be."
—tenant in HBT Village.

Farmer Participation in Village Meetings

With respect to farmer participation in village meetings, two changes had been perceived: a long-run change since the 1940's wherein landlord and rich owner-cultivator domination of village affairs, to the total exclusion of the tenants, had gradually given way to more participation and control by middle-income groups, including at first smaller owner-cultivators and tenants and then many LTTT-title-recipients, to the virtual exclusion of the landlords; and a more recent change due mostly to the LTTT Program itself, wherein frequent meetings were called and were attended by mostly tenants and new title-recipients, in connection with fast-breaking developments in and paperwork required by land redistribution procedures, and in which owner-cultivators had no part to play.

The long-run change toward wider participation in village affairs occurred mostly before the LTTT Program was initiated and was due to the evolution of village-level politics that began with the expulsion of the big landlords from the village. It was continuing, at the time of this research, with each new election of village council members by popular vote.

The more recent change was directly due to the LTTT Program itself and to the organizational and informative meetings called during its implementation. Since they reinforced the historical process already underway, the closer relationship between the former tenants and their village leaders and the broader farmer participation in village affairs stimulated by the LTTT Program would probably have had a lasting impact.

These village-level changes occurred in part due to policy changes from above—the election of village leaders instead of their appointment and the LTTT Program—and in part due to pressures from below—the expulsion of landlords, the favorable results of the elections, the overall pressure of the NLF insurgency, which made land reform both feasible and imperative, and the overwhelmingly favorable response to the LTTT Program. Several farmers remarked that, although they went to village meetings only when invited, in recent years there had been a significant change in **who** was invited to attend and participate in these meetings.

"Before, the landlords controlled the village administration, when the government wanted to call a meeting they **made** the villagers go. Now the tenants have the power to choose the village leaders, and therefore the village leadership must be more polite with the tenants."
—owner-cultivator in Khanh Hau Village.

"Before the LTTT Program tenants seldom attended meetings. Since LTTT, everyone goes to meetings of the village and Farmer's Association to learn about new changes and new cultivation techniques. Before, landlords met very frequently. Now most of them are angry and stay at home. Owner-cultivators still attend meetings like they always did."
—owner-cultivator in LBD Village.

"Nowadays everyone is invited to village meetings. In the old days tenants couldn't even go into the village office unless they were called. They had to stand around outside and wait. Everything was decided by others inside and whenever a tenant was finally approached or called in he had to bow and scrape before the officials."
—title-recipient in Phu Thu Village.

"Before the tenants didn't dare to voice their opinions, but now (as new owners) they are speaking up at village meetings and are at least listened to."
—owner-cultivator in Phu Thu Village.

"In the old days landlords attended many meetings, but tenants did not go. Now everyone goes together."
—owner-cultivator in HBT Village.

Leadership Positions, Political Power and Influence of the Different Land Tenure Groups

Political control over village affairs and the selection of village officials had undergone three decades of change parallel to the economic and social changes described above. Farmers in Khanh Hau, LBD and Phu Thu described a 3-stage process very similar in each village, while in the Hoa Hao-controlled HBT the course of change and its outcome had so far been somewhat different.

One former tenant in Phu Thu Village put it simply, "Under the French, village officials were picked (for appointment) by the landlords. Under Diem, village officials bought their positions. At present, they are elected freely by the people." This theme was repeated in various forms by a large number of the farmers interviewed in the first three villages. The change had been significant and noticeable. Along with it came a tendency for younger men to assume positions of leadership and for the jobs to become more arduous, while the total remuneration from the jobs, from both legal and illegal sources, had declined.

The LTTT Program cannot, of course, take credit for changes occurring before it was initiated. It can be viewed as complementing and enhancing the historical trend, however, by reducing the economic power and social prestige of the landlord class still further and adding to that of the former tenants, thereby encouraging still broader political participation by the latter.

The causal factors of the political "revolution" were first the removal of the landlords from fairly direct local control in the mid-1940's, before which they had been able to obtain the appointment of either their own relatives or of "trusted" friends and tenants, leading to a period of waning landlord influence during which wealthy village residents (rich owner-cultivators and small landlords) would "buy" village positions for their younger sons or nephews from district or province authorities, and then use these positions to further enrich themselves.

The opportunity to purchase village appointments from higher authorities (who themselves were appointed by still higher levels of the government) lasted in most areas until village elections were instituted in 1967. In more secure villages elections were held earlier, and one respondent marked the beginning of change as a 1963 election in Khanh Hau. Another in LBD Village reported that the village chief has been selected by the Village Council from among its members since 1961, and that the situation began to improve after that, even though the Village Council members themselves were appointed until the 1967 elections.

Farmers in the first three villages agreed, however, that the most important event was the 1967 election of village council members, who thereafter selected the village chief from among themselves and had general supervision over village affairs. A second election was held in 1970, and although many of the old regimes survived the 1967 contest, more new faces were reported in village offices after 1970.

There were a few in every village who felt otherwise, but most respondents thought their village officials had recently become much more responsive to their needs and wishes than before and were no longer able to purchase their positions or to become rich by virtue of their public service. Even though resident landlords and the wealthier owner-cultivators were acknowledged to have retained considerable influence (especially in Khanh Hau), that influence was seen to have been significantly weakened by the election process.

"In earlier times the wealthy farmers and landlords picked old men to be village officials. Now the villagers elect the men they like and most of them are young men."
—LTTT-title-recipient in Khanh Hau Village.

"Before, the village leadership came from wealthy families. Now, there is no particular group in control. The change began about 1963, because the villagers started to elect the leaders they like. Before then, village officials were appointed by higher authorities."
—owner-cultivator in Khanh Hau Village.

"Before about 1961, the wealthy farmers and landlords bought tax collection rights and other village offices for their children, who used these positions to make themselves rich. This was because those positions were appointed at district or province level. After 1961 the Village Council appointed village officials and the situation began to change. The council itself has been elected by popular vote for the last 6 years."
—owner-cultivator in LBD Village (in 1972).

"Landlords held village offices before 1945, but since then village leaders have been ordinary farmers, both rich and poor."
—owner-cultivator in Phu Thu Village.

"Before 1945 landlords bought all the public offices for themselves and their children, but now whoever has enough ability holds them."

—LTTT-title-recipient in Phu Thu Village.

"Even up until 3 years ago, village officials had to respect a landlord's wishes very highly, usually deferring to him and letting him have his way. But since the LTTT Program they treat landlords more equally, more like they do everyone else, opposing their wishes or refusing their requests if they think they are out of line."
—LTTT-title-recipient in Phu Thu Village.

In Hoa Binh Thanh (HBT) Village political power had shifted from the landlords to the leaders of the Hoa Hao religious sect, and a new stratification of power and influence had developed, with the wealthier and better educated families still having the upper edge and many landlords still able to bring strong pressure to bear at province and district levels. More allegations of current corruption were heard in HBT than in the first three villages, especially with respect to the military draft. Nevertheless, local elections and the new official emphasis on helping the farmers emanating from Saigon—**via** such vehicles as the Rural Development Program, agricultural extension efforts, and the LTTT Program—had a noticeable impact on the type of individual in village and hamlet leadership positions and on the manner in which they deal with ordinary farmers.

"In the old days landlords were close with the French. Village officials were very fearful of them. When the village chief went to collect taxes, if a landlord did not pay that was that; no one dared to ask him again for fear his wealth and influence might be used against you. This is no longer true. Former tenants are receiving much more help now than before."
—owner-cultivator in HBT Village.

"Village and hamlet chiefs used to be friends and relatives of the landlords. Then in 1967 we had our first elections and things began to change. Before, village officers were appointed. Now, they are ordinary citizens."
—owner-cultivator in HBT Village.

"Rich families used to control the village. Anyone who wanted to work in the village office had to have 10 hectares of land or two rich people recommend him. This is no longer the case and now the villagers elect whomever they like. In the old days, if a farmer was called to the village office he got so scared his face turned blue. Nowadays he thinks nothing of it."

—owner-cultivator in HBT Village.

"Nowdays village officials are both rich and poor, but all of them are chosen by leaders of the Hoa Hao sect. No other candidate has a chance even if he is a very good, talented, and dedicated leader. There is a lot of corruption here. In order to get into the Popular Defense Force and to stay there a young man's parents must pay off village officials. Those who don't pay (or who cannot) see their sons sent far away with the regular army. Draft dodgers are caught, but if one pays the price the boy is allowed to escape, if not he is drafted."
—owner-cultivator in HBT Village.

"The same clique keeps running the village office; and they must pay for their positions. People don't dare challenge village and hamlet leaders because they control the Popular Defense Force, which has guns. And the Popular Defense Force members don't dare challenge them because the village officials have the power to send them (the PDF soldiers) to the regular army."
—owner-cultivator in HBT Village.

"Village leadership positions were dominated by the rich before 1945, but the Hoa Hao influence changed that so now rich, middle, and poor alike hold village offices. However, in the more distant and less secure villages people are afraid to cross village officials for fear the officials will claim they are Viet Cong and have them arrested and jailed."
—LTTT-title-recipient in HBT Village (with land elsewhere).

"Before, the rich, landlord, and well-educated families were appointed to village leadership positions by higher authorities, from whom the former often bought their appointments which they would then use to make corrupt profits. They were interested in lining their own pockets and cared nothing about the welfare of the ordinary citizens. Since elections were first held 6 years ago, everything has changed. Thanks to the elections the villagers can put ordinary citizens into these positions. We still have the problem of corruption, now the candidates pay Hoa Hao leaders for their endorsement (in the election) instead of higher authorities (for appointment); but it's less of a problem than before . . . . The Hoa Hao organization endorses certain candidates for office, and they are sure to win. The

Hoa Hao leaders themselves are chosen by democratically elected representatives at each level, but if the higher levels don't approve they have the power of veto."
—LTTT-title-recipient in HBT Village.

"The attitude of village officials has changed. They are more helpful now than before.
—tenant in HBT Village.

Village and National Elections

Farmer opinions about election procedures were similar in all four villages. There seemed to be a general consensus that elections of village council members (who in turn elected key village officials from among their own numbers) were fairly run and that the voters' choices were truly validated in the outcome. Respondents noted that since most voters knew something about the various village candidates they had a meaningful choice to make, and that if they later became disappointed with the winners they could vote for someone else the next time. Most felt that the present village officials were people the villagers themselves had picked, in contrast to those in office before 1967.

The most frequent response to a question about the personal qualities desired in a village or hamlet chief was that a village leader should be an individual who was concerned with the welfare of the ordinary villager or that he not give the villagers a hard time about things (63 percent). Secondly, leaders were desired who were "good" people by nature and who were courteous and considerate in their dealings with village residents (38 percent). Following these were comments that a village official should be fair and treat everyone equally, performing his duties impartially and expeditiously for all (29 percent), and that he should be free of corruption, straightforward and honest (21 percent).

National elections were a different story. With respect to representatives and senators elected to the National Assembly, many farmers said that, since they did not know much or anything about any of the candidates, they merely followed the suggestions or instructions of their village and hamlet officials in casting their ballots. Several asserted the village and hamlet chiefs received instructions from the district chief, who in turn had been instructed by the province chief, as to which candidates should be assured of victory. Officials or PDF guards were stationed around the polling booths to remind everyone which candidates to choose, and the favored candidates' ballots were placed on top of the stack before they were handed to each voter. (In Vietnam, the names and photographs of each candidate or each slate of candidates were printed on separate ballots, and voters had to place one ballot in an envelope for deposit in the ballot box, discarding the rest in a trash can). Some respondents remarked that, despite this pressure, the voting booths were private and no one outside really knew which ballot a voter placed in his envelope. Others feared the contrary, while many went along out of respect for their village leaders or simply because they did not have a clear choice of their own anyway.

In the 1971 presidential election, since there was only one candidate and only one ballot, true freedom of choice was reportedly even less apparent. A voter received the ballot for the incumbent President Thieu along with the envelope, and in many cases respondents said the polling officials had already obligingly placed the ballot in the envelope, so that all the voter had to do was to place it in the ballot box. (One or two farmers said that even this was done for them.) In order to register a "no confidence" vote against the President, a voter had to tear or mark across the ballot before placing it in the envelope or throw the ballot away, leaving the envelope blank. This made it much easier for a guard or official standing near the voting booth to tell how a voter cast his ballot, especially when the ballot had already been placed in the envelope, since a "for" vote made no sound and no fuss while an "against" vote did. Many farmers said they were afraid of subsequent harassment if they cast "no confidence" votes, and a few recounted actual stories of such harassment after the 1971 election.

It was unheard of to miss an election in any of our four villages. Every person "had" to go vote in every election, unless he had urgent medical or family excuses acceptable to his hamlet chief. Many respondents said it was a citizen's duty to go vote and it was the village and hamlet chiefs' duty to see that everyone performed his duty. Village and hamlet officials and their men would make the rounds on election day to make sure no one forgot, and staying at home brought a good scolding from your chief. In addition, each registered voter carried a voter registration card along with his government identification card, and the former was punched with a special punch at each election. Both cards were routinely checked on the highways by government soldiers and in village offices when completing the paperwork required for various activities. A large number of respondents feared they would be detained, questioned, harassed, and beset with delays and difficulties later if they failed to have their voter registration card properly punched on election day. A few said such harassment didn't really happen anymore, but that memories of it under the Ngo Dinh Diem regime, when it was common practice, were enough to keep most villagers voting. Others, however, said their cards were checked frequently enough to keep them worried about it.

Opinions about the LTTT Program

Asked why they thought the government launched the LTTT Program, slightly over half of the farmers sampled (52 percent) said the government was trying to help poor farmers raise their standard of living. Many of them cited the government slogan **"Dan giau, nuoc moi manh,"** which means "only if the people prosper will the country be strong," as the basic rationale behind this and other agricultural development programs. More than a fourth (28 percent) of the farmers said the government wanted to end the oppression of the rich over the poor by reducing the unequal distribution of wealth and income, by "levelling" social inequalities, or words to that effect. Smaller numbers gave as government motives the desire for more rural support in order to shorten the war (13 percent) and the desire to use the incentive effects of cultivator ownership to increase production (5 percent).

> "The government decided it should consider its citizens like the building blocks of the nation; if the blocks are strong and rich the country is strong. Under the old system only a few landlords were wealthy, while the vast majority of farmers were very poor. Now that almost all farmers have their own piece of land and the freedom to cultivate it as they wish, they have enough to eat and sufficient left over to buy a few things and to fix up their houses, there is much less crime (petty larceny) in the village, and fewer people will go over to the enemy."
> —owner-cultivator in Phu Thu Village.

While opinions about official motives were fairly uniformly spread throughout the sample, those about popular reaction to the LTTT Program showed some noticeable differences by village. In general, great enthusiasm was reported for the Program everywhere but in HBT Village, although several respondents pointed out some inequities in the program and gave examples such as the old couple who had rented out their 1 or 2 hectares because both sons had been drafted into the army and who now were losing their land to the new tenants, or the small owners who had fled an insecure area to side with the government only to have the government give their land away to the NLF sympathizers who remained behind. Many also pointed out that none of the small landlords who were losing their land shared the general enthusiasm for the program, though they thought most of the big landlords were probably happy to receive cash payment for land on which they could no longer collect much rent anyway. Several comments were made to the effect, however, that while maybe 10 percent of the villagers had lost land and were unhappy about it, 90 percent had either gained land or were happy for friends, relatives, or neighbors who had received land, thereby generating the general atmosphere of enthusiasm.

The enthusiasm was especially apparent in Phu Thu, the poorest village studied and the one where pre-LTTT landlord restrictions and demands had apparently been the most oppressive. Much notice was taken of the new freedom felt by title-recipients to make their own decisions.

> "(Popular reaction to the LTTT Program is) very favorable. Nowdays when the new owners meet together they talk about how to increase their crops, new techniques and farm equipment, and how to improve their land. When they farmed someone else's land they were not interested in these things."
> —owner-cultivator in Phu Thu Village.

> "They like (the LTTT Program) because they no longer have to pay rent and because, as owners, they are free to do as they please with the land. Furthermore, if a man owns his own land he will work harder to take care of it. For example, if the surface of the field is uneven with high spots here and low spots there, he will work to make it level and will not fear being evicted by the landlord later and wasting his labor."
> —tenant in Phu Thu Village.

Popular reaction to the program was subdued in HBT, and respondents interlaced their comments with more qualifications and criticisms. More concern was expressed about the unfairness of expropriating land from small holders. The 3-hectare limit drew criticism for causing some tenants to lose cultivation rights on some of the land they had originally cleared (and had been tilling for years) and for discouraging other tenants from applying for title at all, preferring instead to let their landlord claim the land was directly cultivated and then staying on the whole farm in an illegal tenant status. Four respondents voiced the complaint that since the program had closed the rental market (by making tenancy illegal except on Huong Hoa ancestral-worship-land), much good land was being under-utilized by owners who lacked the family labor or managerial skills to farm all of it effectively, while many poor, landless farm workers were unable to find land to rent. The owners knew that if they rented out a portion of their land the tenant could claim title to it. About 30 percent of the HBT sample (including more than a third of the title-recipients) qualified their responses about how well the villagers liked the LTTT Program with specific criticisms, 23 percent noted the unhappiness of (especially the small) landlords, and only 36 percent said villagers like the program without qualification (most of the latter were title-recipients).

Only four responses were recorded to the question, "Have you heard what members of the NLF are saying about the LTTT Program?" Everyone else answered either "I don't know," "I haven't heard," or "none of them have been around here lately."

> "The (NLF) is taking the opportunity to play on the sympathies of small landlords who are losing land, saying that the NLF never took their land away from them but merely divided up cultivation rights more equally and reduced rents. They point to the slowness of government compensation and call it too little."
> —one owner-cultivator and one tenant in LBD Village.

> "The Viet Cong at first claimed the government LTTT title was worthless and they tried to prohibit and prevent tenants from applying for title. Later, they dropped this line, since almost all the tenants around here were applying anyway; and now they are claiming the LTTT Program is a victory for the NLF, confirming the land redistribution they had already performed. Farmers know the differences, however, between the NLF distribution, followed by high taxes and other demands for labor, soldiers and support, and the government LTTT Program, which is distributing land for free and is coupled with agricultural development policies."
> —tenant in LBD Village.

> "I heard a rumor the Viet Cong would kill anyone who accepted a land title, but I have yet to see them around here."
> —tenant in Phu Thu Village.

Current Village Problems

The farmers in our sample voiced a strong desire for local public works—infrastructure investment—of various kinds, with 44 percent of them listing one or more such needs in response to the open-ended question, "Aside from the LTTT Program and the land issue, what other problems need to be solved in this village in order to improve the life and well-being of its residents?" Other needs expressed were far behind public works projects, with agricultural assistance (mostly in obtaining machinery) listed by only 16 percent and improved agricultural credit programs named by only 10 percent. (See Table 6-9.)

Table 6-9

Priority Village Needs Expressed by Farmer Sample, By Village and Compared with 1967 Hamlet Resident Survey of SRI

Priority Need	Number of responses from samples of:					Percentages of:	
	46 in Khanh Hau	46 in Long Binh Dien	48 in Phu Thu	47 in Hoa Binh Thanh	All 187	Our survey of 187 Farmers	SRI survey of 554 Farmers (1967)
Land problems resolved	0	1	1	0	2	1	37
Credit	5	3	1	9	18	10	36
Agricultural assistance							
Equipment	5	5	10	10	30	16	27
Livestock	1	1	1	2	5	3	15
Other agriculture	1	1	2	4	8	4	9
Public Works							6
Roads	33	13	11	26	83	44	
Bridges	20	0	10	6	36	19	
Canals & water control	13	4	1	16	32	17	
Schools	7	3	3	5	24	13	
Health facilities	4	2	0	8	19	10	
Electrification	4	4	0	1	10	5	
Other public works	4	1	1	1	16	9	
Better administration	0	1	0	1	2	1	3
Other Government help	2	0	0	0	2	1	4
Security	1	3	0	0	4	2	10
Peace	2	3	5	2	12	6	3
End to defoliation	0	0	0	0	0	0	5
Lower cost of living	0	0	1	0	1	0.5	2
Help landless poor	2	1	2	0	5	3	
Other	0	1	1	1	3	2	3
No Needs	3	10	10	0	23	12	6
Do not know	5	11	10	9	35	19	1

SOURCE: The SRI percentages are calculated from Wm. Bredo, Summary Volume, Table 17, p. 175. The Hamlet Resident survey conducted by the Stanford Research Institute included 554 farmers, 93 of whom were landless farm workers, from whom these responses have been tabulated.

Comparison with a similar question posed by the SRI in its Hamlet Resident Survey (HRS) to 554 farmers[27] indicates that, once the land question is solved, farmers of the Mekong Delta will turn their attention toward local infrastructure investment projects. This should provide considerable political support for public works projects that will not only benefit the local communities but will also further the long-run national goal of economic development. This has important implications for national policy decisions and developmental planning.

The SRI showed 37 percent of its farmer sample listed resolution of the land issue as a priority need, 36 percent cited the need for more agricultural credit, 27 percent listed agricultural needs of various kinds (again, mostly machinery), and only 6 percent listed public works projects. In our sample, with the land issue assumed away as (mostly) resolved by the LTTT Program, the farmers placed these last three items in reverse order, as noted above, with public works given emphatic priority while agricultural assistance and credit needs appear much less important than before.

Some of the credit for the reduced importance of agricultural needs must be given to the relative success of more recent agricultural development programs implemented by the government, especially the introduction of Miracle Rice and its modern input requirements. The demand for agricultural credit has probably diminished for two reasons, the first being the greater availability of government credit than before, though it is still considered insufficient by most farmers, and the second being the higher net farm income due to increased production and the remission of rents under the LTTT Program.

Local needs vary. More farmers in Khanh Hau and Phu Thu Villages desired better roads and bridges. In HBT the chief demand was for more, deeper, and improved canals and irrigation facilities, while in LBD the existing network of roads and canals was deemed sufficient by those we interviewed (in the more accessible hamlets). In the richer and more secure villages that had already seen more

---

[27]Bredo, **Summary Volume**, Table 17 on p. 174. The HRS Survey selected a truly random sample of village residents, including 554 farmers (of whom 41 percent were owner-cultivators, 34 percent were tenants, 8 percent were part-owner, part-tenants, and 17 percent were landless farm workers) from whom the responses discussed below were obtained. The results of our stratified sample are not, strictly speaking, comparable with those of the random HRS sample; but the two samples are similar enough to give a rough comparison some value.

successful public works projects completed, more farmers saw a need for still more of them, apparently responding to a demonstration effect; while in Phu Thu, the least secure, poorest, and least developed village, which clearly had the greatest objective need for better and more roads, bridges, health facilities, schools, etc., the farmers demonstrated the least interest in them. (See Table 6-9.)

Chapter VII

THE LANDLORD SIDE

The Landlord Sample

Sample Selection

Expropriated landlords were interviewed mainly to find out how compensation funds were going to be used—whether they were able and planning to reinvest their family savings, now involuntarily liquidated, into productive enterprise, thus maintaining their capital intact and, in effect, purchasing a new stream-of-income source to replace the old, or whether they were reduced to consuming the principal itself, thereby eroding their economic position. The question was obviously of national importance, as well as personal, in view both of the large capital sums involved and of the considerable amount of human capital represented by the higher levels of education and experience of the landlord families—scarce and valuable resources in a country notably short of private capital investment and of entrepreneurial and managerial skills.

The ideal land reform program, of course, is one that would cause the transfer of landlord skills and energies, as well as their investment funds, to more productive activities in the industrial and commercial sectors, enabling those families not only to purchase, but indeed to **create** new income streams for themselves, thus contributing to the general economic development of their society.

This being our basic interest, we stratified the landlord universe in each village according to the number of hectares lost, and therefore roughly according to the amounts of compensation received, choosing the ten to be interviewed randomly from each stratum in rough proportion to the percentage of all expropriated land that stratum lost. For example, in January 1972 the files of the Dinh Tuong Province Land Affairs Service (PLAS) held requests for compensation (on Form "B") from 88 landlords who had lost 527 hectares in Long Binh Dien Village, 654 ha. total (including 127 ha. elsewhere). The distribution of land expropriated and the number interviewed from each stratum is shown in Table 7-1.

The file numbers were separated by stratum and those to be interviewed were drawn randomly from each group. The selection process was the same for each village, and a total of 40 expropriated landlords were chosen for interview, ten from each village. This procedure allowed us to concentrate on the large landlords who

Table 7-1

Ownership Distribution of Land Expropriated from LBD Landlords, and Number of Interviewees Chosen

Ha. lost	Number of Landlords	% of Landlords	Total Ha.	% of Total Ha.	Number chosen for Interview
0.1-5.0	59	67	136	21	2
5.1-10.0	16	18	115	18	2
10.1-25.0	8	9	135	21	2
25.1-100.0	4	5	164	25	3
100.1+	1	1	104	16	1
TOTALS	88	100	654	101	10

Source: LTTT Form "B" files, Dinh Tuong PLAS, My Tho, as of January 14, 1972.

were receiving most of the compensation money and thereby to focus on macro-economic issues, while retaining a measure of randomness in the sample. It would be inappropriate for a study mainly concerned with sociopolitical matters, where the numerical, instead of the economic, strength of each stratum should be proportionately represented.

The landlords selected for interview gave us an apparently well-represented sample of those losing more than 5 hectares (34 out of 134, or 25 percent) in our four villages, but a much smaller sample of those losing 5 hectares or less (6 out of 158, or only 4 percent). (See Table 7-2.) Our landlord sample size is very small, due to pressing time constraints, and it should be clear that the tiny proportion of small landlords interviewed prevents us from making reliable generalizations of their particular situation as a separate group, despite their numerical importance and the logical expectation that their problems and attitudes would be different.

One major surprise developed during the course of the interviews. More landlords than expected turned out to own more land than indicated on the papers we saw at PLAS. They owned land in other villages declared on other forms, which were not in the village file we were using. They owned land in other provinces, for which they had to file in those provinces and not where we were. It was common for different members of a family to own different plots of land and for some plots to be still registered in the names of deceased parents, spouses or other relatives. In the usual case, however, all the land belonging to the different members of an extended family was administered as a single unit by the acting family head, and one member of the family handled all the paperwork necessary for compensation, obtaining signatures from the others as required. When asking to meet the legal landlord drawn by lot, we were often referred to another individual who "knew about those matters," and who would discuss the whole family estate as a single unit, the smaller pieces having no meaning alone.

As a result, many of the landlords jumped out of the original ownership stratum in which they had been classified, and the total amount of land actually expropriated from our 40 interviewees alone exceeded the total land area for which compensation was requested on all 292 application forms we reviewed in four provinces. Our attempt to stratify the landlord universe by the number of hectares expropriated was thus based on too little information and, indeed, there was no way to obtain this information without interviewing all the landlord families first. To the extent that the other landlords in each stratum would jump to higher levels like those we interviewed, our sample would still be representative, however; and some confidence can be placed in the fact that, except for the lowest level (from which jumping did not occur), more than 19 percent of each original stratum had been chosen for interview. (See Table 7-2.)

We were very successful in locating the landlords drawn. Only one had to be replaced as inaccessible—an owner of 5 hectares residing in Kien Hoa Province—and only one on our original list of 40 was never found—an owner of 7 hectares who was unknown at the Saigon address listed (a Chinese restaurant). One drawn residing in Paris and one in Ban Me Thuot turned out to be brothers of another drawn and interviewed who administered the whole family estate. In such cases it was our practice not to interview more than one member of the extended family anyway, and if more were drawn we would draw replacements once we identified them as close relatives.

We interviewed one "extra" landlord not on our original list, part of a father-son combination originally lumped together as members of an extended family, but later counted separately since their estate decisions were clearly not being made jointly. The elderly, retired father, interviewed first, suggested we also talk to his son about certain matters. We did, and found that the two respondents discussed different pieces of land and had different plans for compensation use. This brought the total from 39 back up to 40 interviewees. The information provided by the additional interview is probably worth more than any further bias it might introduce.

Another source of bias should be mentioned. Our study came too early to obtain a good landlord survey. Only about half of our sample had received any compensation at all, and most of them had received only part of it. In addition, especially in the case of our first village, some landlords had not yet accepted defeat in their attempts to retain their land, even where it had already been distributed, and they had not yet applied for compensation. They were thus left out of our "universe." For all these reasons it seemed hardly worth the effort to obtain a larger sample than we did, and the results of our landlord survey must be recognized as only tentative, preliminary indications at best.

Basic Interviewee Data

Of the 40 landlords interviewed, 16, or 40 percent, could be classified as rural residents, and the rest, 60 percent, were urbanites. Only 7.5 percent were resident landlords living in the villages under study, while 92.5 percent were absentees; but 7 of the 11 "absentee" rural landlords also rented out land in their own villages and another

Table 7-2

Hectarage and Number of Landlords
by Amount Expropriated,
All Four Villages

A. Hectares on file	Hectare Stratum					Totals	% of Total
	0.1-5.0	5.1-10.0	10.1-25.0	25.1-50.0	50.1+		
Khanh Hau	17	52	36	0	85	190	6
LBD	136	115	135	54	214	654	21
Phu Thu	103	121	216	58	0	498	16
HBT	149	136	411	297	843	1836	58
TOTALS	405	424	798	409	1142	3178	101
% of Total	13	13	25	13	36	100	

B. Number of applications on file							
Khanh Hau	10	8	2	0	1	21	7
LBD	59	16	8	2	3	88	30
Phu Thu	39	17	15	2	0	73	25
HBT	50	16	25	9	10	110	38
TOTALS	158	57	50	13	14	292	100
% of Total	54	20	17	4	5	100	

C. Number of landlords							
Drawn	6	11	11	3	9	40	
Interviewed	6	3	8	9	14	40	
Drawn as % of those on file	4	19	22	23	64	14	

Source: Compensation applications (Form "B") on file in the Province
Land Affairs Service as of 23 Nov 71 (Khanh Hau), 14 Jan 72
(LBD), 29 Apr 72 (Phu Thu), and 24 Jul 72 (HBT). Not all
landlords expropriated had yet applied for compensation as of
these dates.

lived so near as to be almost a resident of the village under study.[1] (See Table 7-3.)

The average amount of land expropriated was 99 hectares per interviewee family (usually the extended family), but the amounts ranged from 0.5 to 1,200 hectares, and the median was 35.5. The average for Hoa Binh Thanh Village alone was 283 hectares, while for the other three villages it was 38. (See Table 7-4.) The three largest landlords interviewed were drawn from the HBT Village files.

The largest landlord discussed total holdings of an extended family numbering some 20 households, who retained 200 hectares of land, 100 directly cultivated and 100 rented to tenants as Huong Hoa worship land. The other 39 families retained an average of 5.2 hectares, 1.7 directly cultivated and 3.4 rented out; and of the land rented out, 2.8 ha. was Huong Hoa worship land and 0.7 was rented to relatives. Most of the land owned before the LTTT Program, 87.8 percent, had been acquired through inheritance, and another 2.6 percent as gifts from living relatives. The remaining 9.6 percent had been purchased by the present, or expropriated,

---

[1]Previous surveys have concentrated on particular groups of landlords, as did ours, and there have been no random samples of the whole landlord universe in South Vietnam. It is, therefore, impossible to say what percentage of the landlord universe was absentee or resident, rural or urban. The SRI Hamlet Resident Survey found that 57 percent of all **tenants** had landlords residing in the same village or district and 43 percent had landlords residing elsewhere or in unknown locations. This is interesting in itself but it is clearly **not** the same as saying 57 percent of all **landlords** are rural residents and 43 percent urban absentees, as both SRI and Dr. Bush did. Dr. Bush used an SRI table which left out most of the unknown cases and thereby came up with a 30 percent figure for absentee landlords—but equating tenants to landlords was illegitimate, anyway. The large landlords are almost all urban absentees, and each one had numerous tenants. Forty-three percent of the tenants, therefore, could very well have been renting from only 10 percent of the landlords, and the percentage of rural resident landlords is probably much higher that 57. See Bredo, **et. al.**, **Summary Volume**, pp. 175 and 205, **Working Papers**, vol. 4-1, Table 18, p. 59, and vol. 4-2, Table 252, p. C-145, and Henry C. Bush, **Small Landlords Dependence on Rent Income in Vietnam**, Control Data Corp., ADLR, USAID, (Vietnam: October 1970), pp. 6-7.

Table 7-3

Location of Landlord Sample

	Number	Percentage
Villages studied	3	7.5%
Other rural villages	11	27.5
District seat	2	5
Total Rural	16	40
Province Capital	10	25
Other provinces	3	7.5
Saigon-Cholon	11	27.5
Total Urban	24	60

Table 7-4

Average Hectares Expropriated per Landlord

Village	On File	Drawn	Interviewed
Khanh Hau	9.0	15.8	39.1
LBD	7.4	31.4	37.5
Phu Thu	6.8	11.5	36.9
HBT	16.7	62.2	282.9
All Four	10.9	30.2	99.1
First Three (excluding HBT)	7.4	19.6	37.8

Source: Same as Table 7-2.

Table 7-5

Religious Orientation of Landlords

	ALS (N=128)	Our Sample (N=40)
Buddhist	63%	62.5%
Confucian	18	17.5
Christian	15	12.5
Cao Dai	1	7.5
Hindu	1	0
Other	2	0
	100%	100%

Source: Bredo, Working Papers, Vol. 4-2, p. B-60.

owner.[2]

Eight of the interviewees were women. They averaged 55.1 years old, and seven of them reported an average 4.6 years of education. The 32 men averaged 57.2 years of age, and 31 of them had received an average of 8.0 years of schooling.[3] Thirty-seven reported an average of 7.0 residents per household (the other 3 discussed extended families totalling 36 households).

Only one respondent was Chinese, the rest were all of Vietnamese descent. Religious orientations were listed as 22 Buddhist, 1 Hoa Hao Buddhist, 2 Buddhist-Confucian, 3 Cao Dai, 7 Confucian (ancestor worship), 4 Catholic and 1 Protestant. This is very similar to the proportions of religious preferences reported in the SRI Absentee Landlord Survey (see Table 7-5).

Rental Income

Rental Income and Its Use

The interviewees reported stipulated annual rents on expropriated land averaging 28.6 **gia** per hectare (N=35). Two had

---

[2]Contrast this with the results of the SRI Hamlet Resident Survey (N=36 landlords), which reported 65 percent of the land inherited, 3 percent gifts and 32 percent purchased. Their Absentee Landlord Survey (N=187) of Ordinance 57 landlords (meaning only those families who once had more than 100 ha.) revealed 54 percent of the **holdings** (not hectarage, as above) were all or partly inherited, 5 percent gifts and 36 percent purchased. Bredo, **Working Papers**, vol. 4-1, pp. 79-80.

[3]One man and one woman avoided the education question. Compare these education averages with those of the farmers we interviewed: 119 men averaged 3.1 years of schooling, 63 women averaged 1.5. Our male education average for landlords compares favorably with that of the SRI ALS (N=180), which reported the following education levels for landlord household heads (and a median age of 59):

None	2%	6-10 Years.	33%
1 yr. or less	6	11-15 yrs.	11
1-5 yrs.	28	more than 15 yrs.	21
			101%

—**Ibid.** Vol. 4-2, p. B-60

25 percent sharecropping agreements with their tenants,[4] and 3 had no rental agreements. The average annual rent collected on this land in 1968-69, however, was only 9.8 **gia** per hectare, or about a third of the amount due and only 10.4 percent of the average yield.[5] In 1968-69 the average landlord family in our sample received about 970 **gia** each year on land now expropriated, 1,034 **gia** on all rented land.[6]   Excluding Hoa Binh Thanh, the average rent received on expropriated land was roughly 370 **gia** per family.

Averages hide the fact that 11 landlords (27.5 percent) had received no rents for the period in question (1968-71). Of these, 6 reported no rents since the mid-1940's, and one each claimed none since 1957, 1961 and 1965.[7]

The 17 landlords who retained tenanted riceland have agreements stipulating an average annual rent of 21.5 **gia** per hectare, somewhat less than on expropriated land. They actually collected

---

[4]SRI found 16 percent of a Delta tenant sample (N=122) had sharecropping agreements, 82 percent fixed-rent. **Ibid.,** Vol. 4-2, Table 131, and vol. 4-1, p. 75.

[5]Average paddy yields by province for 1967-78 and 1968-69 can be calculated from tables on pp. 32-3 in **Nien Giam Thong Ke Nong Nghiep, Nam 1969** (Agricultural Statistics Yearbook 1969) (Saigon: 1970),   Ministry   of   Land   Reform   and   Agricultural Development. These were weighted by the number of hectares lost by each of our village landlord samples to find the 2-year average annual yield for the whole sample—94 **gia**/ha. (using 50 **gia** = 1 M.T).   The resulting 10.4 percent rent figure is close to Robert Sansom's estimate for the Mekong Delta in 1966-7, which was 5-10 percent, except that we are weighted much more heavily in the secure An Giang area (which included 71 percent of our sample's hectarage), where Sansom reported rental averages of 25-40 percent. The 1968 Tet Offensive reduced rent collections of several landlords in our sample, but did not affect those from An Giang. See Sansom, **Economics of Insurgency,** pp. 60-1.

[6]At roughly 50 **gia** = 1 Metric Ton, 1,000 **gia** = 20 M.T.

[7]The SRI ALS reported 60 percent of their absentee, Ordinance 57 landlords (N=187) seldom or never collected rents, and only 15 percent collected rents regularly. On the other hand, only 8 percent of their HRS rural landlords (N=36) were unable to collect rents. —Bredo, **Working Papers,** vol. 4-1, p. 62, and vol. 4-2, Table 112. Our sample included only 9 Ordinance 57 landlord families (22.5 percent), however, and 7 of these had land in An Giang. Only 2 of them had been unable to collect rent—one who had land in An Giang, the other in Dinh Tuong.

slightly more on retained land, however, than on expropriated land, averaging 10.8 **gia** per hectare over the last four years.

About 42 percent of the 33 landlords who discussed rents normally receive rents in-kind, 33 percent in cash, and 24 percent said some of each.

In answer to the question, "What did you do with your rental income before the LTTT Program?", only 16 percent of 32 respondents cited productive investments outside the family, 22 percent named household investments such as education of children and house construction, and 78 percent listed consumption or religious feasting. Of 19 who answered a similar question about current rental income from retained land, 11 percent spoke of non-family investments, 16 percent of household investments, and 84 percent of general consumption and religious celebrations[8] (See Table 7-6). The vast majority of landlords in our sample have apparently used their rental incomes simply for consumption expenditure, and not for productive re-investment.

Household investment was evidently a more important item in landlord budgets than indicated above. Only 10 percent of our landlords resided under a thatched roof, only 12.5 percent had floors of packed earth; but rather 77.5 percent had tile or concrete over their heads, 87.5 percent walked on floors of tile or cement, and 77.5 percent lived in houses walled with bricks or cement[9] (See Table 7-7). Most of the landlord houses we visited were very comfortably, or even luxuriously furnished, especially by Vietnamese standards.

Of 37 landlords who discussed the educational attainments and occupations of their children, 51 percent had children who had already reached college level studies or had definite plans to get them there, and 7 of these families (19 percent) had children at the graduate level. Another 30 percent had children at least to the 11th grade level or set that as their minimum goal. Only 19 percent neither had children who had reached the 11th grade nor expressed an interest in seeing them achieve that level.[10] It seems clear that investments in comfortable, well-built housing and in the

---

[8]Multiple answers were frequent, so the percentages exceed 100.

[9]Compare this with the farmer sample, Table 6-7.

[10]This can be compared with the farmer group, Chapter VI, "Education," pp. 218-20 above, and Callison, **Land to the Tiller**, Table 6-18.

Table 7-6

Use of Rental Income by Landlords

Expenditure	Lost Rents (N=32) Number	Percentage	Current Rents (N=19) Number	Percentage
Consumption	24		15	
Religious feasts	1		1	
	25	78%	16	84%
Savings	2			
Land purchase	1			
	3	9%		
Taxes	2	6%	2	11%
Education	6		3	
House Construction	1			
	7	22%	3	16%
Agricultural Investments	3		1	
Non-agricultural Investments	2		1	
	5	16%	2	11%

Note: Multiple answers were common, so percentages add to more than 100.
Agricultural investments consisted of, for lost rents: farm improve-
ments--2, livestock--2, and farm machinery--1; for current rents:
livestock--1. Non-agricultural investments consisted of, for lost
rents: nuoc mam sauce plant--1, commercial trading and moneylending--
1; and for current rents: book store--1.

The total landlord sample = 40. Eight landlords had not been
receiving rents in recent years.

Table 7-7

Type of House—Landlord Sample
(N=40)

	Number	Percentage
Roof:		
Thatched	4	10%
Corrugated metal or pressed cement	5	12.5
Tile	26	65
Flat-top concrete	5	12.5
Walls:		
Thatched	1	2.5
Wooden, board	8	20
Brick or cement	31	77.5
Floor:		
Packed earth	5	12.5
Cement	1	2.5
Tile	34	85

education of children have been major expenditures of landlord families.

Former Dependence on Rental Income

Asked to estimate what proportion of their family income had been provided by land rents before the LTTT Program, answers ranged from 100 percent (5 landlords) down to zero (11 landlords). The average for 37 responses was 29 percent (3 did not know), and many said it had been much more in earlier years. Of the 5 families totally dependent on rental income, 2 were aged, retired gentlemen, one of whom had been forced to borrow heavily during the last 2 years while waiting for his compensation payments to begin, and the other had turned to his grown children for support. The other 3 families had been forced to go to work, one raising vegetables, one raising livestock and planting fruit trees, and one opening a restaurant and a soft drink wholesaling business.[11]

Altogether six families, including the 3 just mentioned, said they had to change their economic activities because of the LTTT Program. One had intensified work on secondary crops and another had begun commercial trading activities. The loss of his rice paddy rents had forced the sixth landlord to give up a thriving livestock business, in which he had been raising 15 to 20 hogs for market

---

[11]In a 1967-8 survey of 187 large, absentee landlords (ALS), SRI found 21 percent were dependent on their children for support and 17 percent were entirely dependent on whatever rents they could collect from their tenants. None of this 38 percent was wealthy, and a few were impoverished. In a 1970 sample of 694 small, rural landlords, Dr. Bush found only 1.7 percent entirely dependent on rental incomes. He estimated his farmer landlords to be, on average, 34.2 percent dependent on rental incomes, assuming they collected rents equal to 30 percent of the annual crop. This rental assumption is probably too high, as he later pointed out; but farmer landlords certainly collected higher average rents than the absentee group, and therefore higher rents than the Delta-wide average (60 percent of the ALS landlords seldom or never collected rents, while only 8 percent of the HRS rural landlords could not collect. See footnote 7, above; —Bredo, **Working Papers,** vol. 4-1, p. 62; Bush, **Small Landlords,** pp. iv, 5, and 14-18; Henry C. Bush, "Small Landlords Dependence of Rent Income Survey," Memorandum from USAID, ADLR/P&R/CDC, dated 28 May 1971, pp. 5 and 8; and Henry C. Bush, "Further Data on Rent Income, Farm Income Other than Main Crop, and Main Crop Gross Net Income," Memorandum from USAID, ADLR/P&R/CDC, dated 25 June 1971, p. 1.

annually, because he no longer had a source of feed or investment funds with which to buy it. He wanted to use his compensation to help purchase a mechanical rototiller, so he could earn some income by plowing for others; but since he only had 3.4 hectares to lose, the compensation would not be nearly enough. Loss of rents in previous years (due to refusal of tenants to pay) had already forced five other landlords to change occupations, seeking military or civil service employment, opening a book store, or working up from laborer to a successful manufacturer's agent.

Slightly more than half of our sample claimed that the sudden loss of rents had created serious financial problems for their families. Fifteen blamed the LTTT Program for this, since they had been forbidden to collect rents for 2 years or more before receiving any compensation. Six were speaking of earlier times. Those with children in college were hard-pressed to continue their support, several had to borrow money, and one said he had to sell 2 houses and some jewelry in order to get by.

Landlord Contribution to Agricultural Production

In return for their rental incomes, the landlords provided very few productive services for their tenants. Only 10 percent claimed to have recently helped their tenants obtain fertilizer or seed or to have shared irrigation and drainage costs. Seven of them (18 percent) said they had financed the excavation of drainage and irrigation ditches or canals, but only 2 of these were recent, the rest dating back to the 1930's—and six of these seven were An Giang landlords, including both of the recent cases.[12]

Nine landlords said they had at one time or another loaned money to tenants, but again at least 2 of these were speaking of the pre-1945 period. Fifteen percent claimed to have offered technical advice to their tenants on how to improve their crops, but most landlords admitted their tenants knew far more than they about agricultural production.

---

[12]None claimed to have made any other capital improvements, such as buildings, sheds, roads, ponds or livestock shelters. These findings agree with those of the SRI study, which found both resident and absentee landlord groups providing almost no help or services to their tenants. Sansom reported that landlords often opposed canal construction on grounds that "it took portions of their land and led tenants to seek lower rents." Bredo, **Working Papers**, vol. 4-1, pp. 77-9, and Sansom, **Economics of Insurgency**, p. 156.

Only six landlords said their tenants had to receive their permission before trying a new technique or method of production or a new crop variety, but many who answered this question in the negative indicated they were describing a **de facto** situation, and not necessarily one that met their approval. Many of our landlords had fled to the cities in the late 1940's and were reduced to receiving no or only partial rents at the pleasure of their tenants. About half of them said they were still afraid to spend the night in the village where they owned land.   They had long ago lost control over what their tenants did.

One such landlord living in Can Tho expressed bitterness toward his tenants, whom he felt had "completely ruined his riceland with dikes and fruit trees." He recalled that in former times landlords could and did prohibit tenants from building dikes or canals and from planting fruit trees or secondary crops in order to protect the land. Another landlord in the same city confirmed that this attitude was held by many landlords in former times, and is still held by some. One respondent in Long Xuyen had recently refused a tenant request for permission to plant fruit trees. Landlord attitudes along the Lower Mekong seemed somewhat less liberal in this regard than in the two upper-Delta provinces we visited.

LTTT Compensation

LTTT Compensation and Its Uses

Our landlord interviews were conducted too early to obtain definitive answers on the use of compensation funds. Only 21 of the 40 families had received any compensation at all, and many of these payments were for only part of the land expropriated. In all, a total of 41,000,087$VN (about US$97,042) had been received from the initial cash payments plus some of the first year bonds, including the accumulated annual interest of 10 percent from March 26, 1970. The 21 recipients averaged 1,952,385$VN, or an equivalent of US$4,621, per (extended) family.[13]

One individual had not yet cashed his check, but of the 20 families who had, only 6 had invested the money in productive economic pursuits, while 11 cited consumption, debt repayment, or religious celebrations. Three listed household investments, and 8 had put at

---

[13]U.S. dollar equivalents are calculated with the average legal exchange rate for the period, 422.5$VN = US$1. The legal rate was 410$VN = US$1 in November 1971 and rose to 435$VN = US$1 by September 1972, and was kept fairly close to the free market rate in Hong Kong.

least part of the money into interest-earning bank deposits, treasury savings bonds, or private loans. (See Table 7-8.)

Thirty-eight discussed plans for using future compensation payments (2 expected no money and had no plans). Of this group, those planning productive investments and those listing consumption and debt repayment were almost evenly divided at 14 and 15, respectively, or 37 percent and 39 percent. Four, or 11 percent, were planning to use it for house repairs or education expenses, while 24 percent spoke of savings institutions or private moneylending.

In discussing consumption expenditure plans, 18 landlords (45 percent) indicated they had invested in house repairs, remodelling, or reconstruction last year and/or plan to do so in the coming year. Two-thirds of these specified LTTT compensation as the source of funds. Only 22 percent reported making or planning consumer durable purchases last year or this year, 8 percent using compensation funds (most indicating they already had almost everything they needed in the way of consumer durables).

Consumption of rental income from land ownership is one thing, but consumption of compensation payments represents a loss of capital savings to the family—an irreparable worsening of its economic position, in addition to real losses suffered due to inflation (which had been running at a rate more than double the 10 percent interest paid on compensation funds). All landlords interviewed were aware of this and expressed deep regret at the loss of their family estate, knowing this meant less future income for themselves and their heirs. For those who had been able to collect rents, savings bonds or bank deposits were a less attractive alternative, since interest rates were hardly keeping up with inflation, let alone providing any income. Those who had been unable to collect rents were happy to recover some of their investment, but few had any better idea of what to do with their money.

Many of their comments centered around the lack of good investment opportunities, especially for the small amounts of cash received each year, and around the high rate of inflation that was rapidly diminishing the original value of the compensation. Compensation was conceded by most to be fair enough in 1970, but reduced by half its real value by 1972.[14] Inflation was also blamed

---

[14]Compensation was calculated as 2.5 times average annual yields per hectare, but fixed in terms of piasters at a 1970 average price for paddy of 480$VN/**gia**. By the summer of 1972 that price was fast approaching 1,000$VN/**gia**.

Table 7-8

Use of LTTT Compensation Funds

	Uses of Funds already received (N=20)		Planned uses of expected funds (N=38)	
	Number	Percentage	Number	Percentage
Productive investment	6	30%	14	37%
Agriculture	2		5	
Industry & Commerce	5		10	
Household Investment	3	15	4	11
House repairs	3		3	
Education of children	1		1	
Savings	8	40	9	24
Treasury bonds	4		4	
Bank deposits	6		4	
Private loans	1		1	
Consumption	11	55	15	39
Household consumption	6		14	
Debt repayment	6		2	
Religious celebrations	1		0	
Undecided	NA		5	13

Note: Multiple answers cause percentages to exceed 100.
The total landlord sample = 40. Two landlords did not think they
would receive any compensation funds and therefore did not answer
this question.

by many for a tight squeeze on their household budgets, forcing them to dip into their capital savings. Rents, where collected, had represented a real annual income unaffected by inflation, since they were fixed in paddy terms, and this income had been completely wiped out by the liquidation of land assets into fixed piaster amounts, carrying interest rates lower than the rate of inflation. Under conditions of zero inflation the 10 percent interest paid on compensation funds would have equalled 25 percent of the average annual crop, the legal limit for land rent, in addition to which capital values would have suffered no deterioration—but not so under the actual conditions of more than 20 percent inflation.[15]

Article 10 of the Land-to-the-Tiller Law guarantees the negotiability of the bonds received as part of landlord compensation. Only 9 of our 40 landlords thought they could use their bonds as collateral for a bank loan, however, (though none had yet done so) while 9 others, including 3 who had already inquired at some banks, said no one would accept them. Another said that banks would consider such a deal only if the amount of money represented by the bonds was very large. The other 21 landlords did not know. One of these who had already inquired said the government banks had no authority from higher echelons to accept the bonds as collateral or for purchase at a discount, and the private banks did not dare to do so. One who said the banks would accept them noted that they would still require the signature of a third party as guarantor.[16]

Sixteen members (40 percent) of our sample expressed an interest in obtaining such loans. One of these wanted to make needed house repairs, but the other 15 wanted to invest larger sums than they presently had at their disposal into productive enterprises.

---

[15]The Consumer Price Index for middle-income families in Saigon rose 29 percent between March 1970 and March 1971, 18 percent between March 1971 and March 1972, and 31 percent between March 1972 and March 1973. **Nien Giam Thong Ke Vietnam** (Vietnam Statistical Yearbook), 1971, and **Thong Ke Nguyet San** (Monthly Bulletin of Statistics), (Saigon: National Institute of Statistics, 1972 and 1973).

[16]It was later reported by officials in USAID/Saigon that the GVN granted its banks authority to accept LTTT land bonds as collateral for loans in April 1973 and that it was at that time planning to sell government-owned shares in a number of manufacturing companies to ex-landlords in return for LTTT land bonds. USAID/Saigon, April 1973.

Complaints and Criticisms

The two major complaints about LTTT compensation procedures were the slowness with which initial payments were being dispersed, mentioned by 25 respondents, and the high level of corruption found at all levels of government in the process, remarked by 20, or 50 percent of our sample. The two complaints were often linked; the latter was felt to be a prime cause of the first, with much unnecessary delay caused by petty officials who were waiting for an offer of money before completing their part of the paperwork.

Our landlord interviews were conducted very early in the LTTT Program before many landlords had actually received their initial compensation checks, and thus before many of them had been forced to put up a bribe. Our responses show that of the 14 landlords interviewed between 25 November 1971 and 22 March 1972, only 21 percent spoke of corruption, whereas of the 26 interviewed between May and 12 September 1972, 65 percent did. Broken down another way, of the 19 who had not yet received any money by the time of the interview, only 37 percent complained of corruption, but of those who had received at least some of their money, 62 percent complained of it.

Corruption was the complaint most irritating to the landlord group, and it sparked the most vehement responses during our interviews.

Only 10 percent of the respondents admitted paying bribes themselves, but this was a question we seldom asked directly.[17] Most of them spoke of friends or relatives who had been forced to pay, saying they themselves had not yet done so due to personal contacts, influence, or to a preference to wait for their money rather than pay. They usually spoke with such outrage and detailed knowledge of how the squeeze was applied, however, that it was obviously a topic close to home.

At village level, officials could delay distribution of a particular landlord's holding, which the law required be completed before compensation, until palms were greased; or they could classify the land in a higher or lower productive category, thus affecting the rate of compensation per hectare. Province officials could easily keep someone's paperwork at the bottom of the stack until

---

[17]Those giving bribes had been considered equally as guilty as those receiving them, under the law, until September 1972. A new decree then absolved the victim of corruption and guaranteed the return of his loss if reported, but its actual impact is unknown.

it was brought to their immediate attention with an appropriate consideration—the most common figure mentioned was 25 percent of the initial check (or 5 percent of total compensation). (An extra two years' delay would cost about that much just through inflation—some alternative!)

Many landlords received their checks in Saigon, some against their will (having specified an address in the Delta), and met further delaying tactics there, even after having received official notification the check was ready, until a deal was made to help expedite their "special" case. Provincial courts and district offices took their cuts from inheritance cases, which were numerous since the Vietnamese had been slow to update land titles over the last decade or so. Much land was still registered in the names of deceased ancestors, and legal documentation proving inheritance rights, such as birth certificates, was often non-existent. The complex and rigid Treasury procedures required of the heirs provided opportunities for corruption in many offices left out of normal Land-to-the-Tiller processing.[18]

Such "deals" were seldom suggested or made in the government offices involved. Contacts were made on the outside, usually by low-level officials or clerks. Higher officials could claim innocence and ignorance of graft, and in some cases such claims could have been valid. It would be incorrect to leave the impression that **all** government officials were corrupt. Many of the landlords specifically exempted certain villages or certain officials from their allegations. All four of the villages we visited rated fairly high marks from our landlord sample for honesty in compensation matters, and most of the allegations concerned officials in more distant, less-secure, and less-accessible areas. In one of our provinces the PLAS seemed to have a very good overall reputation, although allegations were levelled at other offices there; and in the other three provinces it was not clear how much the PLAS chief himself was involved (although he was suspect—otherwise some landlords would have gone to him with their complaints). Fear of reprisals kept most landlords from making specific allegations public; and suspicion that higher authorities were in on the take prevented them from reporting corruption to them or to police.

The third major complaint about compensation, mentioned by 13 landlords, was that the 20 percent cash formula—followed by 10 percent bonds for 8 years—resulted in such small dribbles of money,

---

[18]Later information indicated that (by 1973) many of these requirements were being simplified and relaxed. USAID/Saigon, April 1973.

especially when reduced by intervening inflation, that productive investments could not be undertaken.[19]   A typical comment was:

> "The money comes out in such small dribbles and so
> late that nothing can be done with it.   Inflation is
> destroying most of its value.   Landlords don't even have
> enough land left to build a house on.   Paperwork is so
> complex that opportunities are created everywhere for
> corruption.   The asking price at province level is 25
> percent of the check."

Part of the complaint about dribbles concerns the practice of handling each small plot of land separately, each plot requiring separate documentation and many follow-up trips.   The landlord holding 15 or 20 plots scattered over several villages was common.

One landlord had inherited 17 hectares of Huong Hoa worship land from his maternal grandmother that had been in the family for 5 generations.   He had collected rents from all his tenants for more than 25 years, and local officials all recognized him as the rightful heir and owner.   Under the LTTT Program he was allowed to retain 4 hectares of orchard land, which he cultivates directly, and 5 hectares of tenanted riceland; but he could not obtain compensation for the 8 hectares expropriated because he lacked legal proof of inheritance rights (his mother and grandmother never had birth certificates), even though he still possessed land titles issued before the French came, as well as those reissued in French later, made out to his grandmother's ancestors.   His complaint, naturally enough, was that if tenants could have their cultivation and new ownership rights confirmed by village officials, it seemed unfair that long-standing ownership and inheritance rights of landlords for compensation purposes could not be confirmed in a similar manner, at least in cases where records were lost or non-existent and where there were no competing claims.[20]

Only 11 landlords (28 percent) thought the amount of compensation per hectare was a fair price for their land, while 55

---

[19]This echoes the complaint of 66 percent of the large ALS landlords interviewed by SRI, who said they would have invested their Ordinance 57 compensation in commerce, industry or real estate if they had received it all in a lump-sum cash payment.   As it was, they said, the amounts received were not large enough to make significant investments.   Bredo, **Summary Volume**, p. 187.

[20]As the compensation program progressed, many cases like this one were in fact handled routinely based on village and province certification of inheritance rights.   USAID/Saigon, April 1973.

percent considered it too low. Six of the latter specified the effects of inflation as the reason for their answer. Twenty-seven respondents said they were receiving an average of 124,000$VN per hectare while 17 of those who thought compensation was too low claimed that a fair price would be an average 398,000$VN per hectare.

One other complaint deserves mention. Two landlords in Can Tho claimed that the law expropriated their riceland, but left them as owners of record of fragmented residential plots in areas planted in trees and classified as "orchard land" (where their former tenants built their houses). Their tenants would not pay rent on this land nor would they purchase it, since the LTTT Program gave them the adjacent riceland and they considered the residential plots theirs too, while in fact the landlords still retained title and believed they were legally subject to taxes on it. The landlords would rather have seen these plots expropriated with the rest.

Socio-Political Effects of LTTT: Landlord Views

Land Tenure Security

Landlord comments on pre-LTTT land tenure arrangements confirm what we know from previous studies. About 73 percent claimed to have written contracts with their tenants, 38 percent verbal (10 percent had some of both). Only 30 percent had contracts which had not yet expired or had been formally renewed, however; and tacit renewal understandings were more common.[21]

De facto tenure security under prevailing political conditions was greater than this would appear to indicate, though. Only 18 percent of our landlords thought they could have evicted their tenants to take back their land, and most of these said they could do so only for cause (such as nonpayment of rent). Two-thirds (68 percent) of them admitted that, as a matter of practice, their tenants could have retained cultivation rights for as long as they wished.

---

[21]SRI found that only about 37 percent of their absentee landlord sample (N=155) had written contracts with their tenants, and 63 percent verbal agreements. This could refer only to those still in force or formally renewed, in which case it would be close to our results. Their HRS turned up 34 percent of the rural landlords (N=35) with written contracts, 66 percent with verbal agreements (only half of the former were registered). Bredo, **Working Papers,** Vol 4-2, p. B-35 and Table 115.

Landlord-Tenant Relations

More than half of the landlords (58 percent) said their tenants had shown respect toward them and their relatives before the LTTT Program, 8 percent said some had and some had not, and 30 percent said none had.   More than one-third (35 percent) of the sample reported a change for the worse in tenant attitudes since the land was redistributed under LTTT.   Several reported that tenants did not act very friendly toward them anymore, often not speaking to them at chance meetings in the market.   One surmised they were embarrassed at taking away someone else's land.   Another maintained friendly relationships with his older tenants, but reported that some of the younger men, who did not know how good his family had been toward tenants in former times, often became disrespectful. Several others reported that such attitudinal changes had already occurred in the more distant past.   Some felt it was for the better, others would disagree.   Typical comments were:

> "Before the 1940's, tenants had to show great respect for their landlord.   They had to bring clean paddy to his front door and to provide ceremonial labor and poultry, and so on.   But all this changed after World War II, and relations have become much more egalitarian and more friendly."

> "I don't see them anymore, but they talk straight to people like my nephew, who is also a landlord and whom they do meet.   They don't act fearful or subservient to anyone anymore."

> "They used to be polite and respectful, and they would bring the paddy rent to my house nicely cleaned and perform other small favors for me.   In the last few years, however, they ceased all that.   If I wanted my rent I had to go to them and insist on it, and I got no more special favors."

> "In the old days tenants were the little brothers of their landlords, but after 1945 they became the fathers of their landlords."

Relations with Village Leaders

Twelve landlords (30 percent) observed changes in the behavior of village officials toward them since the LTTT Program began. One said relationships had become more friendly than before, but the rest felt they had deteriorated.   Paperwork delays and difficulties were cited, often in connection with allegations of corruption. according to one large landlord with land in several villages:

>"Before 1945 village officials were small landlords and tenants of large landlords. They had to respect the wishes of landlords. Now they treat former landlords like dirt and try to squeeze as much money out of them as possible—money to have your land declared type A or B, money to complete routine LTTT paperwork so you can receive compensation, money to arrange the formal (but illegal) redistribution of abandoned land so you can get compensated for it."

National Issues Related to LTTT

Asked for their understanding about why the government undertook the LTTT Program, 31 landlords responded. Of these, 61 percent stressed political motives, to give the poor farmers a stake in society so they would stop supporting the Viet Cong insurgency. A common expression was "to buy the hearts of the people." Two of these thought the Americans were primarily responsible, pressuring Saigon into the programs and promising to pay for it, for political reasons. A fourth of them emphasized macro-economic purposes, mostly that of encouraging an increase in production through the incentive effect of broader land ownership among the cultivators, though one saw an enhanced ability to tax as a government motive and another thought the government was trying to push landlords into investing in more productive activities to stimulate economic development. Some 13 percent cited social welfare objectives, to "help poor farmers" and to redistribute incomes more equally (these last two points were frequently mentioned by the other respondents, as well, as a means to achieve political or macro-economic goals).

Fully 85 percent of the landlord sample thought the LTTT Program was in fact helping the farmers, and 5 percent more agreed in part. Most responses were similar, "Of course, they no longer have to pay rents nor worry about a landlord taking back his land." One was more explicit:

>"Yes, it really helps them, not only by raising their living standards and their spirits, but also by enabling them to support their children through more schooling, especially in the new agricultural schools, in order to develop the agricultural sector."

Two respondents were concerned about unfair losses to small landlords, especially those who lost their land because their sons were in the military and they were too old to farm it alone. Three who owned land in An Giang Province noted that many tenants were hurt by the 3-hectare limit on land distribution, since many of them in the floating-rice areas had been farming 5 to 10 hectares before, but lacked adult children to claim all of it. One asserted that instead of holding this land until the tenant's children reached maturity or distributing it to landless workers, village officials were in effect selling it to the rich and influential, thus creating a new wealthy class in the rural areas. Another problem cited in An Giang was that many small landowners who could not effectively farm all their land (because someone was ill or their sons were in the military) were afraid to rent any of it out for fear of losing it. So good land was being poorly used while poor families with labor to spare could not rent it.[22]

On the macro-economic question of how the LTTT Program would affect agricultural production, 50 percent of the landlords thought it would directly stimulate greater production efforts by the new owners, primarily through the incentive effect, though two of them noted that the reduction of rents and the greater availability of agricultural credit to owners would place more investment capital in the hands of farmers, as well. A new freedom to make desirable changes and a loss of the fear that if productive improvements were made, the landlord would take back his land, were cited. Two of the more complete responses are instructive, both quoted from small, resident landlords who were quite unhappy with the loss of their land, rental incomes, and financial security, but who were also in close contact with their former tenants and other farmers:

> "As long as tenants were working my land, they were not interested in repairing dikes, canals, or drainage ditches, or in getting the utmost from the land, because they had to share the increased output with me. It wasn't their land, so why should they worry about improvements? But now that it is theirs they work very hard to take care of it and to try new seeds, fertilizers, and crops to get more income."

> "Production is increasing because the farmers are now working harder taking care of their land and trying to get more out of it—just like you would take care of your own house better than a rented one. They never

---

[22]While it was illegal to rent out the land, a landowner could cultivate it with hired labor, though the latter technically required more personal supervision and management by the owner than renting to a tenant did.

acted like that as tenants. As owners, they seem to be more aggressive farmers, trying better ways to do things."

Another 20 percent thought the effect of LTTT on production was inconsequential in either direction. Three of these respondents remarked that production is increasing, but for other reasons, such as the introduction of Miracle Rice seeds, government price policies allowing higher prices for rice, good weather and plenty of fertilizer. One felt that a significant rise in production would come only after other government programs became more effective, notably the agricultural extension program to teach farmers better methods. Another said farmers were not trying to increase production for fear of heavier taxes.

Only 7.5 percent thought the LTTT Program would tend to reduce agricultural production (3 absentee landlords: 2 in Long Xuyen, An Giang Province, and one in Saigon).[23]   One cited the disruptive effects of the 3-hectare limit in An Giang; and the other two expounded the backward-bending supply curve of labor theory—that the farmers are essentially lazy and will only work hard enough to provide a sufficient amount of food for their families, and so now that they no longer have to pay rents they will work less, invest less, and grow less than before. One of the latter, however, admitted this was merely a personal opinion and not based on any hard facts or personal verification. The other one, in An Giang, also noted that since large landlords are being eliminated, no one will take care of the canals, which will soon fall into disrepair with detrimental effects on production.   This argument seemed to have more substance,[24] and, given the lack of voluntary cooperation frequently observed among Vietnamese farmers, it should have become a matter of concern for appropriate government agencies.

While the remaining 22.5 percent said they did not know what production effect the LTTT Program would have, two of them observed that farm output was definitely rising, but that this may be attributable to other government programs encouraging agricultural development and to the increased availability in rural

---

[23]Only 3 of the 10 An Giang landlords saw beneficial effects of LTTT on production, or 30 percent compared with 57 percent of the other 30 landlords.

[24]But see the section of this chapter on "Rental Income," pp. 250-6, above, for evidence that very few landlords had made much investment in this direction, either, and in fact often opposed the construction of irrigation canals.

areas of consumer goods desired by farmers. They saw all farmers working harder than before, not just the new owners.

A majority of landlords (57.5 percent) thought that farmers supported the Saigon government more strongly because of the LTTT Program.[25] Only 15 percent disagreed, while 27.5 percent offered no opinion. Most positive comments centered around the idea the government was then helping farmers more than the Viet Cong were, so they were more willing to help the government in return. Another point made was that those farmers who were new owners of a piece of land had a much stronger desire for peace than before. They wanted to be left alone by both sides so they could cultivate and improve their land; and since in the areas under study it was normally the Viet Cong who intruded from elsewhere to stir up trouble, this desire for peace worked against them and for the government.

Opposing views expressed were that the LTTT Program would have no effect, since the farmers would follow whichever side seemed stronger, or that everyone had already chosen sides and the LTTT Program would not change their minds. One man feared the LTTT program would look like a concession to previous Viet Cong land reform efforts, and would actually cause farmers to support the VC more strongly for having forced the government into it. Other landlords disputed this suggestion by saying the current GVN program went much farther than the VC land reform, since the latter never attempted to eliminate all tenancy, and that the GVN program was recognized by most people as more fair, with provisions for landlord compensation the Viet Cong did not have. One landlord illustrated the existing polarization of political loyalties as he saw them:

> "One of my tenants, a widow, sent her daughter to study in My Tho and to obtain a government job there. The mother was captured by the VC, held for a few days and threatened with her life unless she made her daughter spy for them. The mother went to My Tho to see her daughter and just stayed there, leaving everything she owned behind. The Viet Cong gave her land to one of their members to farm, and the latter now receives full title to it under the LTTT Program. The original tenant came to me to seek help in obtaining title and recovering her cultivation rights, but the law is quite clear—the

---

[25]SRI found that 53 percent of their ALS landlords thought a new land reform program would help win rural support for the government. Bredo, **Summary Volume**, p. 186.

Viet Cong tiller gets it. As to political effects, the mother will stay with the government side, but the Viet Cong LTTT-title-holder will no doubt remain loyal to his original benefactors on the other side."

Asked about what other factors, besides the land question, had the most important influence on villager political support for the government, or on the lack of it, 11 of the 24 responding[26] emphasized the various agricultural and rural development programs as being very popular among farmers. Said one resident landlord in Long Binh Dien Village, a former village chief:

"There have been many development programs recently that the farmers like, which taken together have brought visible progress to the village, and these programs are perhaps even more important than LTTT—such as the community self-help program to build schools, canals and roads, the agricultural extension and credit programs, the new bridge (over Cho Gao Canal). The farmers around here are tired of fighting. They want to be left alone now to run their farms and build up their community."

Seven others emphasized the negative effects of official corruption and abuse of power. A couple of them singled out the Phoenix Program as especially unpopular, alleging that

"Its cadres often arrest innocent people and hold them illegally, beating them in the process, until they or their relatives pay money for their release. Higher authorities cannot control their agents in the field, and ordinary people dare not denounce them."

The last six said the most important desire of the people was for peace and security. If the government could guarantee these in the rural areas, they felt, the villagers would support the government.

Regarding their knowledge of general landlord reaction to the LTTT Program, only 6 responses were wholly favorable, most of them citing previous difficulties in collecting rents as a reason. One small landlord was candid:

---

[26]Fifteen responses were "don't know," and another said, "only the LTTT Program is having much effect" in this regard.

"Most landlords have, because of their greater wealth in the past, been able to give their children fairly high levels of education already, and their children now occupy high positions and are doing well independently of land income.   So the landlords are not really hurting very much."

The largest group of answers, 50 percent of the sample, were partly favorable, partly unfavorable.[27]   Most of these indicated general acceptance of the main goals of the program as written, but unhappiness with the way compensation was being handled, especially the complex paperwork, long delays, loss of value due to inflation, piecemeal payments and bureaucratic corruption.   Said one large landowner:

"Most landlords are unhappy about losing title to their land; but they see how the program will help the cultivators and the whole country, so they are willing to accept some personal sacrifice for the good of the many. The way the program is actually being administered, however, as opposed to the way it was designed, fills them with disgust at all levels of the government."

Others of this group explained that landlords themselves were divided between those with generally favorable reactions and those strongly opposed to the LTTT Program—the favorable group described as large, absentee landlords who had been unable to collect rents for some time, or as "progressive" landlords willing to sacrifice for the national good, and the opposition described as small, resident landlords who had been able to collect rents, or as "conservative" individuals who scheme and plot to keep their land.   One man split those opposed and unopposed between those whose land was in secure areas, and who thus could collect rents, and those whose land was in less secure areas, where they could not collect rents.

Finally, 12 responses (30 percent) were wholly unfavorable.[28] The complaints mentioned have all been covered above.   A few examples are quoted in summary:

---

[27]SRI found that 83 percent of their ALS landlords approved of the Ordinance 57 land reform in principle (and in retrospect), compared with 56 percent approval here of the LTTT Program in whole or in part.   Bredo, **Summary Volume**, p. 186.

[28]SRI reported 22 percent of their ALS sample were strongly opposed to the idea of a new land reform program.   **Ibid.**, p. 186.

"We have lost our secure property—money is insecure because inflation destroys its value."

"Landlords are very unhappy about the time-consuming and costly red-tape requirements for compensation on every little piece of land and the multiple opportunities for corruption along the way. They are also unhappy over the fact that, once they do get paid, they only get a small amount each year, not enough to use as capital in productive investment, and they apparently cannot even borrow on the bonds."

"Landlords have been hurt a lot—at least those who have been able to collect rents in recent years. Inflation, high interest rates on bank loans, delay in compensation payments and government corruption at all levels have combined to destroy many families."

" . . . Landlords have lost their land, lost the rent income from their savings, waited more than two years without compensation and then are eaten to death by petty bureaucrats taking their cuts at each level of government."

Chapter VIII

LOCAL LEADERSHIP OPINION

Village Leaders

Sample Selection

In an attempt to gain additional insight into the processes of change occurring in the villages and what part of them might be attributable to the LTTT Program, we interviewed 35 village leaders, 10 in each village except Phu Thu, where we settled for only 5.[1] The interviewees included 2 village council chairmen, 3 village chiefs and one deputy village chief, 17 hamlet chiefs and one deputy hamlet chief, one agricultural commissioner, one elementary school principal, 4 school teachers, one medical dispensary chief, a Catholic priest, one rice mill owner and 2 storekeepers, all of whom had been both residents of and working in their villages for at least several years (and in most cases, for most or all of their lives).

These interviews were in the nature of an opinion poll, similar to the latter portions of the farmer and landlord interviews, except that no effort was made to be random in the selection of the interviewees. Village officials and other "leaders" were sought who had had long experience in the village and whose occupation put them in frequent contact with a large cross-section of village residents, enabling them to observe the progress of village affairs and to comment on villagers' attitudes and opinions.

Village leader respondents included 32 men and 3 women, who reported an average age of 44.1 years and an average level of education of 5.5 years. One was of Cambodian descent, but all the other 34 were ethnic Vietnamese. Twenty-seven regarded themselves as followers of a Buddhist faith, which included 9 members of the **Hoa Hao** sect, 3 **Cu Si**, and 1 Cambodian Buddhist. Seven followed the practices of Confucian ancestor worship with the Buddhist overlay, while the Catholic priest was the only interviewee professing the Christian religion.

---

[1]Phu Thu was not only the smallest village in our survey, but also the most isolated. All of its school teachers and the principal, for example, resided in Can Tho and commuted to Phu Thu daily on the water bus, and so they knew very little about life and politics in the village. Whereas we averaged 5 hamlet chiefs in each of the other villages, only 2 were accessible to us in Phu Thu.

Progress and Problems of the LTTT Program

The village leaders confirmed the statistical reports that most of the tenants in each village had applied for and were receiving, generally with no serious delay, ownership titles to the land they had been tilling. The exceptions noted were those tenants on Huong Hoa ancestral worship land, church land, village land, Ordinance 57 land, those claiming tenancy rights to abandoned land, and those so sympathetic with their landlords (often a relative) they refused to apply for title. In addition, land reform officials in HBT Village were still processing applications and had not yet been able to deal with all eligible tenants.

Huong Hoa land, church land, and abandoned land are legally exempt from redistribution. The order went out to redistribute village land toward the end of our field research; and the redistribution to new tenants of land which had already been redistributed once under the earlier Ordinance 57 land reform was also delayed, but finally approved. It was illegal for landlords to retain tenanted land as directly cultivated even if their tenants refused to apply for title out of sympathy or fear or in consideration for a financial bargain with the landlord (all three reasons were reported), and technically the village was supposed to go ahead and expropriate the land in such cases for redistribution to a third party. This requirement of the law was successfully used in most cases to persuade the reluctant tenants to apply and to convince his landlord he had no choice; but many such cases remained to be resolved at the time of our interviews, especially in HBT Village, where landlords were reportedly putting up much more resistance to the program than elsewhere and were fighting, brow-beating, buying off, and pleading with their tenants not to apply for title, and where the 3-hectare redistribution limit per recipient often worked in the landlord's favor. Several cases had reportedly been carried to the land courts, usually involving newly declared Huong Hoa land for questionable legality, especially in the two more secure villages under study, Khanh Hau and HBT.[2]

The village chief in Phu Thu said one of his hamlet chiefs was demanding a duck or 500 $VN (about one dollar, U.S.) for each title he delivered, so he and his men could share a celebration feast with the title-recipient. This form of corruption may seem harmless enough compared with stories heard elsewhere, but when the Phu Thu Village chief found out about it he had the offending hamlet chief removed from office. Corruption was suspected (but unproven) in the "last-minute" declaration of some parcels as Huong Hoa land

---

[2]See the section on "Grievances" in Chapter IX, below.

in Khanh Hau, and stories of petty corruption in An Giang Province (10-20,000 $VN per title, or $20-$40 U.S., for land worth 15 to 30 times that much) were repeated; but on the whole the title redistribution part of the program was considered to be remarkably free of corruption.[3]   As one respondent put it, "petty corruption (of the magnitude found in An Giang Province) does not really hurt farmers who are receiving free land worth 100,000 $VN per hectare, but it irritates them."

Only a small minority of the resident landlords had received compensation checks for land expropriated.   Village officials did not know about the absentee landlords, since their compensation requests were processed at province level.   The village commissioner for agriculture in LBD reported that of 133 LBD landlords who had requested compensation, only 18 had received checks by March 1972, two years after their land had been declared legally expropriated and rents remitted.   The situation was the same elsewhere, though exact figures were not available.   The delay was thought to be in Saigon, since most of the paperwork was known to have cleared the province level.

Less than half of the respondents thought the rate of compensation per hectare was fair and about one third of them thought it was too low, the rest saying they did not know.   One gentleman pointed out that while the rate of compensation was considered fair in 1970, when it was calculated and converted to a fixed piaster amount, inflation had already severely reduced its real value by 1972, two years later, with no relief from continued inflation expected in the near future.

Very few other implementation problems were mentioned in the first three villages. One respondent in Khanh Hau was concerned about the dissension created in the village between landlords and tenants, and one in Phu Thu was concerned by reports that many of the titles contained errors of land measurement and he wondered if they would ever be properly corrected.   For the most part, however, the redistribution process was seen as going smoothly with few real problems.   The Phu Thu Village chief credited this success to increased security and the use of aerial photography.   He did not think the LTTT Program could have been implemented in his village before 1969.

---

[3]Naturally the village leader sample can hardly be expected to speak freely of alleged corruption among their own numbers. It was surprising so many spoke as frankly as they did.   The results of this survey tend to corroborate other information obtained on this subject, however.

More village leaders sounded off about "other problems" in HBT Village than in all three of the other villages put together. Landlord-tenant conflicts were reportedly at a higher level in HBT, with one respondent saying "many people have been killed because of this program," and several reporting the local name for the program as **"Nguoi Cay Do Ruot"** (Spill the Tiller's Guts) instead of the official **"Ngoui Cay Co Ruong"** (Land-to-the-Tiller). The 3-hectare maximum limit was seen as too low to provide a satisfactory level of family income. The court system was considered stacked against the poor tenants, who were forced to battle ownership rights out with their landlords in court even, in some cases, after they received LTTT titles to the land. Other HBT respondents sympathized with the problems created for landlords, especially the small landlords who lost their rental income 2 or 3 years before receiving any compensation and then met difficulty in trying to cash their compensation checks unless they shared some of it with clerks and officials in provincial offices. One man complained because a policy giving landlords until September 15, 1970, to declare Huong Hoa land was not publicized until after the deadline, and many landlords were unaware of it until too late.[4] He thought there should have been a small retention limit for all landowners, regardless of whether the land was tenanted or directly cultivated.

All 35 of the village leaders interviewed agreed that the LTTT-title-recipients were favorably impressed by the program, although 3 of them in HBT qualified this with the remark that some tenants had wound up losing cultivation rights to some of their land because of the 3-hectare limit, and more feared they would lose land in the future. The response was completely favorable in the first three villages, however. The village chief in Phu Thu thought the response was especially important in his village:

> "About 50 percent of the tenants in this village were Viet Cong or VC sympathizers before the LTTT Program; but now, due in large part to this program, they are beginning to believe the government is trying to help

---

[4]This "policy" was the result of an unauthorized decision by the chief of the An Giang Province Land Affairs Service, since the LTTT Law stated that tenanted Huong Hoa land could be retained (up to the 5 ha. limit) only if it had been legally registered as Huong Hoa land by the day the law was promulgated, March 26, 1970. The An Giang PLAS chief was subsequently replaced because of this decision and his replacement was directed to go to court on behalf of the tenants to have the illegal Huong Hoa registrations stricken from the official land register.

them and they are much more cooperative and responsive than before."

Regarding landlord response, the general consensus seemed to be that the larger landlords did not really mind too much, since they had been unable to collect much rent for several years anyway and would receive enough compensation to invest productively elsewhere, but that the more numerous smaller landlords were very unhappy and felt unfairly treated.

Only about half of the interviewees thought the response of other village residents (aside from title-recipients and landlords) to the LTTT Program was completely favorable. Several cited concern among villagers for the poor families of landless farm workers who did not benefit from the LTTT Program, and they wondered how the government could help them.[5]

Three-fourths of the interviewees thought villagers could see positive benefits from the program for the village as a whole, however, as opposed to its benefiting only the title-recipient group. The following composite answer illustrates their reasons:

> "New owners can pay more taxes, can hire more labor to work for them and can contribute more (labor and money) to public works projects, so the whole village is richer than before. They work harder on and invest more in their own land to increase production. Since the distribution of wealth is more equal, village society is more egalitarian; the new owners are more enthusiastic about things and take a more active part in community affairs. Everyone is happier because their friends, neighbors and relatives have received title to their land and are better off than before."

None of the village leaders in Khanh Hau admitted knowing what the NLF was saying about the LTTT Program. One respondent in HBT Village said he had heard the NLF cadre were trying to claim credit for the program, saying they had conducted a land reform first. This theme was repeated by a respondent in Phu Thu, who said the NLF was also telling people in insecure areas that

---

[5]Others noted concern about soldiers and their families who lost land because they were away fighting for the government and about the unfairness to small landlords, especially aged village residents; and some concern was expressed about the dissension created by the program among villagers and even among relatives (landlords vs. tenants).

the government LTTT Program was a fraud. The Phu Thu Village chief said the Viet Cong at first tried to divide tenants and landlords with propaganda about the LTTT Program, but they have since dropped that line and have not interfered with its implementation.

Four interviewees in LBD Village discussed NLF reaction. In the early days of the program (1970) the local Viet Cong cadre told people in the more distant hamlets of LBD not to apply for title, since only the NLF distribution of land was valid and the government was giving ownership titles to tenants so that it could raise land taxes to levels higher than the previous rents. They claimed the LTTT Program was unfair (to small landlords and landless workers). In areas of Dinh Tuong Province still firmly under their control they still forbade tenants to apply for title and hated the program so much they assassinated a land affairs cadre two weeks before our interview (in March 1972). One respondent pointed out that in LBD Village this propaganda effort did not accomplish much, and that since the VC had already redistributed large areas of land to their own sympathizers, who themselves did not hesitate to apply for LTTT titles, the VC themselves were major beneficiaries of the program.

One interviewee in Phu Thu had heard that some tenants in the more isolated (and "less secure") areas believed the NLF line and were reluctant to apply for title, but none of the rest of the sample thought so. Respondents in each of the first three villages pointed out that no one taxed more heavily than the NLF itself did in areas within its reach, and that farmers were pretty tired of it.

Economic Effects

All but two of the village leaders said the former tenants had certainly benefitted from receiving ownership rights to their land. One dissident in Phu Thu said most of the title-recipients he knew were still paying rent to their landlords, despite the transfer of ownership, and the other one in HBT complained that since a number of title-recipients had lost cultivation rights to some of their land due to the 3-hectare limit, they were worse off than before. To all the rest, however, the remission of rents and the freedom to manage one's farm as one pleased were obvious gains.

In response to an open-ended question, "To your knowledge, on what are most of the former tenants spending their additional income (from the remission of rents)?" The most frequently mentioned responses were domestic consumption expenditures (57 percent), agricultural investments (49 percent) and house construction and repair (37 percent). Also mentioned were education for children (9 percent), transportation (6 percent), public works (3 percent), and more leisure (3 percent).[6]

Regarding the disposition of the tenants' farm produce, now that they no longer have to use part of it for rental payments, most village leaders said the former tenants were both eating more and better food than before and also selling more on the market than before—a response which is in complete agreement with the statistical results of our own farmer interviews (see Tables 6-4 and 5-32).

About 90 percent of the respondents agreed that the farmers in their villages had adopted a number of significant innovations in agricultural methods and techniques of production during the last two years (such as the use of new seed varieties, machinery, more fertilizer and insecticides, the planting of two rice crops instead of one, the planting of secondary crops and fruit orchards, the raising of more livestock, and the construction and use of more irrigation facilities); and about half of them said it appeared to them that the LTTT-title-recipient farmers were adopting these innovations at a faster pace than the other farmers. Asked why this latter observation should be true, the explanations given were that (1) the title-recipients now have more money (from rent remissions) to invest, (2) they can keep all their additional output, (3) they no longer have to ask permission from an often reluctant landlord to plant additional trees and crops or to dig irrigation ditches, (4) they no longer have to fear possible eviction and the resultant loss of their investments, and (5) farmers simply take better care of something they own than they do of something someone else owns.

Half of the village leaders affirmed that some landlords, especially the smaller ones, were in a financial bind because of the LTTT Program, primarily because their rent receipts were cut off 2 or 3 years before they received any compensation for their land. More than a third of the respondents knew of resident landlords who had been forced to change occupations or to look for work elsewhere because they had lost their rental income. These former landlords were engaging in a wide variety of new economic activities, including the retail trades, bus driving, house construction, animal husbandry, rice milling, working as a wage-earner in Saigon and on other peoples' farms, tenant farming, operating a sawmill, planting

---

[6]Percentage figures represent proportions of sample making each response, and multiple responses cause them to total more than 100. (N=35).

a new orchard, performing tractor services for hire, and working as an office clerk or secretary.

As to their knowledge of what landlords were doing or planning to do with their compensation money, the list was equally as varied: invest in commerce, orchards, buses, sawmill equipment, rice mill equipment, brick factories, small boat factories, furniture, house reconstruction (usually their own house), government savings bonds, bank savings accounts, and industry.

Social Effects

Villagers occasionally meet together to perform some task of public value, such as to repair or build bridges, roads, schools, dispensaries, canals, and village offices or temples, or to hear speakers discuss new farming techniques, seeds, credit, land reform, or other programs. Most (77 percent) of the village leader sample agreed that all farmers were attending and participating in such meetings and work projects more than they were a few years before, and that such participation was not limited to or dominated by any particular group. Only a few (17 percent) thought they could discern a significantly greater increase in participation by LTTT-title-recipients as compared with other farmers; but most or them (71 percent) did perceive a general change in the way title-recipient farmers conducted themselves in the community. Title-recipients were seen to be more self-confident and proud, happier and more satisfied with life; they have more money and are more willing to participate in and contribute to village projects; they see themselves as equal to others, not inferior as before; they are nicer to each other and more willing to help authorities than before, but more aggressive in dealing with officials, merchants, and landlords; and they have a greater sense of freedom, independence, and dignity than before.

All but two of the village leader sample said farmers were sending their children to school more regularly than they were a few years before, and most of them thought the farmers themselves were visiting with teachers and taking a more active part in school affairs than before, as well. About half the respondents reported that title-recipients had changed in this regard more than the others. Asked to explain why, most of the comments centered around the fact that because the title-recipients had higher incomes they could better afford to keep their children in school than before. Proper clothes and supplies are costly, and parents are also expected to contribute time and money to the repair and maintenance of the school. In addition, in many tenant families the mother had to hire her own labor out to others whenever she could, keeping older children at home to watch after younger children and livestock.

One village chief pointed out that their new land-owner status has increased the family pride of title-recipients, and that they now feel more of a social obligation to give their children a better education and to participate in community projects such as maintaining the schools.

An elementary school principal, who was critical of several aspects of the LTTT Program, had this to say about its effects on education:

"Before the LTTT Program only landowners sent their children to school (in the province capital) above the 5th grade, while tenants wanted only for their children to learn how to read and write and gave no thought to schooling above the 5-year level; indeed, many never made it that far. Now many of the new landowners (former tenants) are supporting their children to secondary school in (the province capital), because they have more money and feel more like they can and should do so. They worry about whether their children will pass the 5th grade exams and thus be eligible to go on in the public schools, whereas before, they did not care. Supporting a child through school is expensive for farmers, and having to purchase clothes, school supplies, transportation (for some), and losing the children's help on the farm and around the house is too much for many families. The elimination of rents has helped in many cases . . .. Before the LTTT Program only landowners took much interest in meeting with teachers or in helping to maintain the school. Now many (former tenants) come to Parent-Teachers' Association meetings and contribute money and labor to repair and maintain old schools or to build new ones."

About half of the village leaders thought the title-recipient farmers were more willing to accept social responsibilities in the community than before the LTTT Program, but the other half could not yet discern any change. The first half said the former tenants were more concerned about village security than before and were more willing participants in the Popular Defense Force, "because they now have a stake in society to protect," and they were also more active in the PTA, contributed more to schools and other public and social welfare projects, accepted more official positions in the hamlet and village governments, and more actively supported rural development projects than before.

Very few leaders thought other village residents were treating the title-recipients any differently than before, nor did they think other village residents were treating former landlords and their families much differently socially because of the LTTT Program.

More than three-fourths of the respondents said landlords formerly participated heavily in village affairs and activities, but only about one-half said they still did so. Eighty-nine percent agreed that tenants used to be fearful of their landlords, but only 6 percent thought they still were. Several interviewees gave the Viet Minh much of the credit for this change, but most agreed that a lingering fear of eviction remained until the LTTT Program ended the landlord's legal claim to the land.

In a striking assertion of the decline of landlord influence over village affairs, 77 percent of the sample said village leaders used to come from wealthy and landlord family groups, whereas only one respondent (3 percent) listed these groups as the social origin of present village leaders, who were instead reported to be mostly middle and poor farmers or from no specific group.

Political Effects

Almost all of the sample denied that any one particular group of people presently controlled the village, but stated rather that all village residents had equal influence because of the election procedure now used in choosing village leaders. Eighty percent said this represented a change over former times when landlord and wealthy families could purchase official appointments from higher authorities. The change was mostly attributed to the village elections held in the last 5 or 6 years; but a few went back farther to give some credit to the Viet Minh influence in chasing landlords out of the village, to independence and the dismantling of the French colonial administration, to a gradual improvement in the political awareness of village residents, and to changes at the higher levels of government which made village positions much harder work and more hazardous than before while the real remuneration from them declined.

The chiefs in all four villages in our sample were from middle-level farming families; three were lifetime residents of their villages, the other had lived in his for 17 years. All had fairly recently been elected village chief, two serving for only 2 years so far, one for 3 years, and one for 5 years; though all had held other positions in the village office previously. For the most part they were expected to be re-elected for another term in the next election, except for some concern as to whether they would care to run again because of the hard work and low pay.

The qualities most often named by village leaders as desirable in a village leader were much the same as those listed by the farmer sample. "Caring for and helping ordinary citizens and not giving them a hard time" headed both lists, mentioned by 60 percent of the village leaders and 63 percent of the farmers. The leaders placed "equal and fair treatment for all" in the number two spot with 54 percent (only 29 percent of the farmers had listed it) while "good hearted, kind, polite and courteous" was given a 37 percent rating (farmers gave it 38 percent). Somewhat more village leaders (34 percent) listed "honesty, straightforwardness, incorruptibility" than farmers, but it remained in 4th place.

More than half of the village leaders (60 percent) thought that the LTTT-title recipients as a group had more influence over village affairs than before, and the reasons why are revealing: because they had more money; because ownership made them independent of fear; because they held more leadership positions, were more active and expressed their opinions more often; because they had been given guns (as members of the PDF); and because they had more money to pay off officials to get things done.

Most of the village leaders assured us that the villagers were free to vote in elections for whomever they chose, and that no one from the village office would give them a hard time later if they did not vote at all. Several of the comments were more revealing, however:

> "In village elections they know the candidates and can choose more wisely. These are fair. But in national elections villagers do not know the candidates, and the latter usually arrange with province and district chiefs to assure their victory (for appropriate sums). Village and hamlet chiefs are told to make sure certain candidates get the most votes. Ballot stuffing, block voting, and placing favored ballots on top of the stack for illiterate voters are common practices."

> "No one forces anyone to vote for certain candidates, so voters can vote for whomever they please; but very few polling places are watched closely during the counting and reporting phase."

> "Some votes are bought with money, and some voters are threatened with guns and the draft."

> "Everyone must vote. If someone does not show up the hamlet chief must go roust him out. It is the

citizen's duty to vote and the village officials' duty to
see that he does it."

"Village officials will criticize a person later, if he
did not vote, when he comes to the village office for
some document or permission to do something.   They
will say that since he did not help them or execute his
responsibility as a citizen during the election, why should
the official help him now?   But generally it is just vocal
criticism and nothing is done against the person.   The
officials finally go ahead and help him anyway, after
voicing their displeasure."

"No one in the village will cause him trouble (if he
does not vote), but outside the village he can have
problems if his voter registration card is not properly
clipped or punched."

The reasons given by village leaders as to why the government
launched the LTTT Program were similar to those given by farmers,
except that the leaders were more inclined to give more than one
reason and only one (3 percent, as opposed to 29 percent of the
farmers) said he did not know.   The reason most often mentioned
(by 63 percent) was the government's desire to help the poor farmers
improve their economic condition, followed by the desire for social
reform to remove excessive inequalities and to end the landlord
oppression of tenants (40 percent), and by the desire to obtain
greater rural support in the war against the NLF and in the next
presidential elections (40 percent).   A few (11 percent) mentioned
the need for agricultural development to increase the production of
foodstuffs as the reason, with land reform seen as a step in that
direction.

All but two of the respondents (94 percent) agreed that the
LTTT Program was in fact helping farmers, and was therefore
accomplishing one of its major goals as they understood them.

Only a few (20 percent) said people credit the NLF with
forcing the government into the LTTT Program, in whole or in part,
which is not surprising, since all the village leaders interviewed
were openly anti-communist themselves.   Since many, if not most,
outside observers do credit NLF pressure and appeals on the land
issue with precipitating government action on this front, it is of
interest to see how local officials explained this connection away.
Below are some of their comments.

"No one in this village thinks the Viet Cong land
reform program forced the Saigon government into the

LTTT Program. The LTTT Program is much better than the Viet Cong program, since the latter was designed to allow maximum taxation and did not really help the poor farmer. Until 1968 farmers in this hamlet, including myself, had to pay 25 percent of each rice harvest and 10 percent of all other produce to the Viet Cong, as well as the normal rent to the landlord."
—Village leader in Khanh Hau Village.

"(No one credits the NLF) because the reform actually started under President Ngo Dinh Diem in 1957, before there was any trouble from the Viet Cong. The LTTT Program is merely a continuation of that effort, so it was not forced by the Viet Cong."
—Village leader in LBD Village.

"The government has gone farther than the Viet Cong, who distributed small parcels (.5 hectare) of land to many, but then demanded high taxes and took many chickens, ducks, etc. Also, they only gave land to those who followed them; and if a Viet Cong landowner was killed, they did not leave the land for his surviving family to farm, but instead they took it back to give to another Viet Cong soldier. The people got very tired of them, because they were not fair."
—Village leader in LBD Village.

"A small number have said (that the NLF deserves credit), but they are wrong because the government program goes farther and is far better than the Viet Cong land reform, and it was undertaken at a time when the government was strong and the Viet Cong weak (after the 1968 Tet Offensive had failed)."
—Village leader in Phu Thu Village.

"The Viet Cong were very arbitrary in distributing land, often taking it back and giving it to someone else, and they taxed heavily and arbitrarily, demanding more if the farmer had more, leaving him only enough to live on and little incentive to increase production—very poor economic policy."
—Village leader in Phu Thu Village.

"About 50 percent of the people understand enough to give credit to the NLF; but the government program is different in that it is more peaceful, it does not

denounce the landlords but rather gives them fair compensation."
—Village leader in HBT Village.

The village leaders were asked whether they could give any examples of other problems, programs, or issues, aside from the LTTT Program, which affect the popularity of the government among village residents. A high percentage (46 percent) said they did not know; but 31 percent listed various agricultural development projects and public works, or cited economic development efforts in general as having a favorable impact among villagers; 23 percent complained that corruption, high taxes, inflation, the military draft and crime were having a negative impact; 9 percent said villagers merely wanted peace and security, and if the government could provide that they would support it; and 6 percent said villagers supported the government because of its strong anti-communist stand.[7]

At the end of each interview the same open-minded question was asked of village leaders as of the farmers, "In your opinion, what other problems, aside from the LTTT Program, need to be solved or improved in this village or district in order to make your life better and more satisfying?" The responses were again very similar to those of the farmers, and the same general rankings were obtained. Public works of various kinds were the most frequently listed need, cited by 31 percent of the respondents, agricultural development efforts were a close second with 26 percent, and improved credit facilities placed third with 11 percent.

Provincial Officials

Interviews were obtained with the director of the government-sponsored Agricultural Development Bank (ADB) and with the chief of the Province Agricultural Affairs Service in each of the four province capitals, in which the respondents were asked to give their assessment of the effects of the LTTT Program in their province, particularly with respect to agricultural development.

One of the bank directors had only recently assumed his post in that province and said he had not yet had time to make many observations of the type requested. All seven of the other interviewees remarked on the importance of the incentive effect of ownership, which they often termed the psychological factor, in increasing production. LTTT-title-recipients were reportedly working harder on their own land, investing more in its care and

---

[7]A few multiple answers cause these percentages to total more than 100 (See Callison, **Land to the Tiller,** Tables 8-1 to 8-4).

improvement, and investing more in new crops, machinery and other inputs just because the land was theirs and no longer belonged to someone else, and because they no longer feared possible eviction and the resulting loss of invested capital.

In addition, six of the respondents noted that, along with the increased incentive to invest, these new owners now had an increased availability of investment funds due to rent remissions and to the increased availability of agricultural credit to title-recipients. All four of the ADB chiefs confirmed that they were loaning much more money to the LTTT-title-recipients now than before they had received ownership titles, simply because land ownership places them in a much lower risk category than they occupied as tenants. One bank director remarked, "Even if the farmer suffers a bad crop and has to repay a loan late, the bank still does not fear default if it holds a land title as collateral."

One respondent in Long An Province said the LTTT Program was causing an increase in the land area under cultivation, since large landowners were being forced to put previously idle land under the plow for fear of losing it to squatters or to the government for second-phase redistribution, and former tenants and squatters are bringing abandoned land back under cultivation so they can apply for ownership titles as tillers.

The two officials interviewed in Long Xuyen noted that some fragmentation of holdings was occurring in An Giang Province because of the 3-hectare limit on distribution, but they differed as to its effects on agricultural development. One of them thought such fragmentation not only reduces the farmer's income and his savings potential for investment purposes, but would also make mechanization and the use of large-scale technology, which he saw as essential to agricultural development, more difficult. Even apart from fragmentation, he saw the 15-year ban on land transfers as perpetuating a pattern of small farm holdings and preventing the consolidation and large-scale mechanization he considered necessary for successful agricultural development, and in this latter concern he was joined by one of the officials interviewed in Long An Province.

The other An Giang official acknowledged some fragmentation, but denied that it was necessarily harmful to developmental goals. He saw it as a positive influence forcing many farmers (on reduced holdings) to put forth the additional effort and capital investment required to switch to double-cropping Miracle Rice, in which the returns per hectare are far above single-cropping with the traditional floating-rice variety.[8] He noted that those farm families who are still farming 10 hectares of land are rarely interested in making this switch, since with little effort they can maintain a satisfactory standard of living by producing an annual 650 **gia** (about 13 metric tons) of traditional paddy; and they are afraid to rent or sublet their land out in smaller plots to tenants who could apply the greater effort required for double-cropping. If the farm is reduced to 3 hectares, however, it can no longer produce enough floating rice paddy (195 **gia**, or about 4 M. T.) to feed a family, so the farmer must try to apply the new double-cropping techniques with Miracle Rice. If he is successful, his 3 hectares can produce up to 1,800 **gia** (36 M. T.) of Miracle Rice paddy per year, or almost 3 times as much each year as 10 hectares of the traditional floating rice. Small plots of land, he noted, have not prevented the use of the machines (tractors for plowing, motor pumps for irrigation) necessary for more efficient farming: tractors have been used extensively in An Giang Province for 20 or 30 years, since the land is too hard for cows or buffalo to plow.

---

[8]This view was also held by one of the larger landlords interviewed in Long Xuyen, An Giang Province.

Chapter IX

EVIDENCE FROM OTHER RESEARCH

In Rural Villages

A major research effort was conducted in 1972 for the U.S. Agency for International Development and the Republic of Vietnam Ministry of Land Reform, Agriculture, Fisheries and Animal Husbandry Development by the Control Data Corporation (CDC), under the direction of Dr. Henry C. Bush, to determine the political effects of the LTTT program.[1] The study included behavioral observations in 44 rural villages of 9 Delta provinces and 985 randomly selected, unstructured interviews with rural families in 23 of these villages in 6 provinces.[2] The field work was completed between January and June 1972.

The CDC effort was complementary to our own in several respects, especially since it was undertaken during the same time period. Its primary focus was on political effects, rather than economic. It developed random samples of all village residents, rather than the stratified sample of farmers by land tenure groups that we sought. Its interviews were "unstructured," developed only around the general questions of how the village had changed in the preceding few years and what were the causes of that change, whereas our interviews were "structured" and more "in depth," asking for specific details about particular economic activities. The CDC sample was not only much larger than ours, including 985 interviews, compared to our total of 270, but it also included a much larger number of villages (23 compared to our 4) and can thereby claim to be more representative of the whole Delta. Although still biased toward somewhat more secure villages, it is less so biased than our sample.

---

[1]Henry C. Bush, Gordon H. Messegee and Roger V. Russel, **The Impact of the Land to the Tiller Program in the Mekong Delta,** (Vietnam: Control Data Corp., December 1972), (Sponsored by ADLR, USAID, Vietnam, under Contract No. AID-730-3449).

[2]Observations were made between January and March 1972 in the provinces of Chuong Thien, Dinh Tuong, Go Cong, Long An, Vinh Binh, Vinh Long, Kien Hoa, Kien Tuong, and Phong Dinh; but the interviews were conducted between April and June 1972, after the beginning of the "Spring Offensive" by the North Vietnamese and the NLF, only in the first six, since many of the less secure villages originally selected became inaccessible to the research team.

The composition of the sample was reported as follows:[3]

"Of the 985 farm families interviewed:

49%   are farm owners who own the land they farm because of LTTT.

8%   are tenants who have applied for title to the land they farm, under LTTT.

15%   are tenant farmers. Of these:

> 56% farm worship land exempt from LTTT.
> 27% farm village communal land, then exempt from LTTT but no longer so. (Word that communal land might be distributed had got around, and 30+ percent of these had already applied to their villages for title.)
> 9% farm privately owned land subject to LTTT, not yet distributed.
> 3% farm relatives' land and presumably will not apply for title.
> 3% farm church land, exempt from LTTT.
> 1% farm garden land, exempt from LTTT.
> 1% farm land subject to LTTT but prefer tenancy.
>
> 100%

17%   are farmers who owned and farmed their land before LTTT. Of these:

> 21% purchased their land under RVN's earlier land distribution program (Ordinance 57, 1956).
> 4% are beneficiaries under LTTT in that they had never been able to pay for land applied for under Ordinance 57, and LTTT eliminated their unpaid debt and gave them clear title.

7%   are landless farm laborers.

2%   are landlords or ex-landlords whose land has been transferred to ex-tenants under LTTT.

1%   are landless skilled persons such as carpenters or shopkeepers.

1%   are villagers or hamlet officials or local military who do not farm.

100%

---

[3]**Ibid.**, p. 13.

Of the total number of farm operators in this sample, 81 percent were tenants before the LTTT Program and only 19 percent cultivated their own land. This tenancy ratio is significantly higher than the 67 percent "best estimate" for the Southern Region discussed above,[4] and indicates a bias in the selection of villages toward those with higher pre-LTTT ratios of tenants,[5] but it does not affect the general validity of the results summarized below. The 23 villages in which interviews were conducted were part of 29 picked, as noted above, because LTTT Program implementation seemed to be proceeding more rapidly than elsewhere; and it was found that these villages had also experienced a considerable amount of political and economic progress between January 1970 and January 1972.[6] Interviewers were asked to call the respondents' attention to some of the positive changes that had taken place in the village, to ask them what they thought about these changes, and then to ask them why and how they thought these changes had occurred, without suggesting any answers. The LTTT Program was not mentioned by the interviewers unless the respondents brought it up.[7]

---

[4]See Chapter III, "Land Tenure in the 1960's, Extent of Tenancy," p. 55-60, above.

[5]The villages in which these interviews were conducted were initially chosen to represent those in which LTTT implementation had progressed most rapidly, as opposed to another group in which little or no implementation of the LTTT Program had occurred. They were therefore the villages which showed up statistically as having relatively high numbers of approved LTTT applicants in proportion to an "assumed" tenant population, the latter estimated as a straight 60 percent of the total village population in each village. The 60 percent ratio was taken as an average for the Delta as a whole, and naturally some villages would have higher tenant ratios and some lower than the overall average. A village with, say, an actual 80 percent ratio of tenants will more easily develop a higher percentage of approved applicants over an assumed tenant population figure of 60 percent; and, in fact, several of the sample villages had already exceeded 100 percent of the assumed tenant population. While CDC used the 60 percent tenancy ratio of total village population as a Delta-wide average in their selection process, 72 percent of their sample families were tenants before the LTTT Program, according to the breakdown reported above. See Bush, **et. al., Impact of Land to the Tiller Program,** p. 5.

[6]**Ibid.,** p. 10. According to historical data generated by the Hamlet Evaluation System (HES) of the Civil Operations and Rural Development Support, Research and Analysis Directorate, Military Assistance Command Vietnam (CORDS/RAD, MACV).

[7]**Ibid.,** p. 106-7.

292   LAND-TO-THE-TILLER IN THE MEKONG DELTA

The mere correlation of more rapid LTTT implementation and improved economic and political conditions offers no evidence about possible causal relationships involved.[8]   The tabulated responses, however, form a clear picture of what the villagers themselves, out of their own observations and experiences, consider to be the major causes of the changes affecting their own lives and communities. (See Table 9-1.)

Two-thirds of all villagers attributed the improved conditions at least in part to LTTT land redistribution, and an equal number attributed them to improved security conditions (with many listing both together as causal factors).   About one-third listed general economic causes and a fifth thought improved farming techniques were important factors. It is also significant that, proportionately, 7 times more LTTT-title-recipients named new agricultural techniques and investments as causal factors than did tenants, and 6 times more title-recipients than tenants listed general economic improvements.   CDC also tabulated the number of title-recipients and tenants who mentioned that they or their fellow-villagers were using new agricultural techniques.   They found that a much higher proportion of title-recipients showed an awareness of new technology than of tenants, and that proportionately 9 times more new owners (18 percent) mentioned that they themselves were using these new techniques than did the tenants (2 percent). (See Table 9-2.)

According to CDC, these results "suggest strongly either that the quicker and more enterprising farmers apply for their land under LTTT earlier and the backward and unalert ones hang back, or that LTTT itself stimulates them to greater awareness of agricultural possibilities available to them."[9]   CDC was being overly cautious in stating these two possible implications on an equal footing, since by their own data only 13 percent of the remaining tenants were farming land then subject to LTTT redistribution.   The other 87 percent were stuck on land legally exempt from redistribution, and their continued tenancy status can in no way be attributed to their personal characteristics. [10]   The CDC results are a valid confirmation of our own evidence of the important incentive effects of the LTTT Program.

---

[8]Fifteen villages selected for observation as examples of little or no LTTT implementation had also experienced improved conditions, but they were far behind and improving much more slowly than the 29 "dynamic" villages. **Ibid.**, p. 11.
[9]**Ibid.**, p. 43.
[10]See Table 9-1.

Table 9-1

MAJOR CAUSES OF CHANGES:
What New Owners and Tenants Say Did It
(Many name more than one cause,
so percentages total more than 1000)

Things changed in the village and the hamlet because of:	New Owners (N=483)	Tenants (N=148)[1]	All Villagers (N=985)
Security (military help, village security no more VC terrorism, no more VC "tax"squeeze)	74%	68%	67%
LTTT land distribution (which ends tenancy and ends rent)	70	40	68
Roads (also bridges, waterway development or repair, and transportation linkage to towns)	2	2	3
Changes in farming methods (miracle rice, 2 rice crops, increased secondary crops, more use of fertilizer and insecticides, mechanization, improved irrigation, improved animal husbandry	35	5	20
Economic causes (less poverty everywhere in SVN, increased trade, more jobs, agricultural credit, good prices for rice)	30	6	32
Natural causes (good crops, high yields, good weather, no natural disasters, or God)	10	8	10
Villagers' initiative (much hard work, careful spending, increased unity and community and self-help)	6	4	10
Village governments' responses to village needs (self-development projects, good village and hamlet government, more schools, instruction in farming methods, training in village self-protection)	5	7	7
TOTAL	232%	140%	217%

[1] The reader is reminded that 79 other tenants had somehow already got word that most communal land would also be distributed under LTTT and had already applied to their villages for title. Also, it is clear from other research that tenant farmers think of themselves as tenants until they receive title to their land. It is possible that some of these tenants had already applied for title under LTTT but did not mention that they have done so, simply identifying themselves as tenants. In cases where they did so mention, or if they remarked that they till privately owned land (in which case the interviewer would ask), we classify them as "applicants." Persons known to have applied for title are not included as tenants.

Reprinted from Henry C. Bush, Gordon H. Messegee, Roger V. Russell, The Impact of the Land to the Tiller Program in the Mekong Delta (Saigon: Control Data Corp., December 1972), p. 41.

Table 9-2

AWARENESS OF AGRICULTURAL TECHNIQUES: New Owners and Tenants Compared
(Many mentioned more than one technique so percentages total more than 100)

Agricultural techniques attributed to farmers in their hamlet or village	% of New Owners Who Spoke of It	% of Tenant Farmers Who Spoke of It
Use of fertilizer or insecticide or both	83%	56%
Use of farm machines such as tractors or rototillers	72	49
Increases in rice yields, use of miracle rice seed, or conversion of rice land to 2-crops	35	17
Increase in secondary crops or in fruit or vegetable production	18	17
Increases in poultry and animal husbandry	10	4
Percentage who mentioned that they themselves use one or several of the above	18	2
TOTAL	236%	145%

Reprinted from Bush, et. al., Impact of Land-to-the-Tiller Program, December 1972, p. 42.

Once a respondent mentioned the LTTT Program or any other cause of the observed changes in the village, CDC interviewers were then to probe more deeply for details and to ask what changes specifically are attributable to it. Most of those discussing the LTTT Program attested to its effective redistribution of income, providing them with the increased means to raise their standard of living. About half of them said the program resulted in more social equality, more freedom, less fear of and exploitation by landlords, and more unity and friendliness in the village; and almost as many said the LTTT Program was generating more political support for the government, counteracting Viet Cong propaganda and reducing their influence in the village.[11]

When these responses were broken down by land tenure status, it was found that 16 percent of all new owners said they were now working harder, farming more (formerly abandoned) land, adopting new techniques, and were now able to buy more fertilizer, insecticides, machinery or livestock than before **because of the LTTT Program.** This represents 23 percent of the new owners who discussed the LTTT program, and is further evidence of a positive incentive effect.[12]

A greater availability of investment funds was due partly to higher levels of retained income and partly to the greater availability of official agricultural credit. In reviewing Agricultural Development Bank (ADB) reports for 1971, CDC found a 983 percent increase over the preceding year in small loans, 50,000 $VN or less, and a 132 percent increase in larger loans to individual farmers, compared with an increase of only 62 percent for **all** loans in Delta provinces.[13] They found, as did we, that ADB officials considered farm owners better credit risks than tenant farmers.[14] The 1971 ADB loans to farmers were repaid on time by more than 90 percent of the borrowers, and the other 10 percent merely had to be extended,

---

[11]Bush, **et. al., Impact of Land to the Tiller Program,** Table 13, pp. 46-48. CDC percentages in the table referenced are based on the total sample, whereas I am discussing them here as proportions only of the 68 percent who mentioned the LTTT Program, since the others were not asked.

[12]**Ibid.,** Table 14, p. 49.

[13]**Ibid.,** p. 27. The inflationary rise in prices during the same period, which must be discounted to obtain the rise in **real** credit availability, was around 17 percent in Saigon. "General consumer price index excluding rent for middle class families in Saigon," Table 274, p. 314, **Nien Giam Thong Ke Vietnam, 1971** (Vietnam Statistical Yearbook 1971), (Saigon: National Institute of Statistics, RVN, 1972).

[14]Bush, **et. al., Impact of Land to the Tiller Program,** p. 27.

due to crop failures or other emergencies, and were not written off. This compares with less than 20 percent of such loans that were repaid to ADB's predecessor agency between 1963 and 1966.[15]

Commenting of the fact that "31 percent of all farmers, and 40 percent of all new owners, spoke of freedom from the landlord and from the indignities of his demands, because of LTTT," CDC concluded, "It is evident that LTTT had decreased inequality," and had this to say about its political significance:[16]

"It is also good for prospects of rural democracy and decreased insurrection. **Political scientists** conclude that equality is one of the things that most revolutions and insurrection are about and for. **Sociologists** conclude that those down at the bottom of the social strata in any community are suspicious of authority (of police, clergymen, teachers, public officials), that they believe politics is to exploit the poor and that they lack self confidence. **Psychologists** conclude that when persons feel powerless with respect to public affairs they are cynical about political democracy and that, conversely, 'feelings of efficacy and sense of gaining relative power with respect to public affairs produce idealism about political democracy.'[39]

"**Economists** increasingly conclude that if a nation or region somehow reduces inequality between strata or classes, then it has created a major condition necessary for self-sustaining economic development. Regression analyses of **statistics of 75 series of political and social indicators, from 133 countries**, show that inequality of land distribution among farmers correlated with lack of economic development.[40]
. . .

" . . . (the same regression analyses) indicate that an increase in land distribution which reduces inequality of holdings of farm land 'appears . . . to be a potent pacifier . . . a one-point (out of 100) decrement in the land Gini index has the effect of decreasing domestic violence by 3 percent . . . There would appear to be much truth in the common beliefs about land inequality and democratic instability. The **distribution** of wealth

---

[15]Ibid., p. 28.

[16]The following quotations and their footnotes are from **Ibid.,** pp. 55-6.

may be more relevant politically and theoretically than its **level.**[50]

"39 See for example Bernard Berelson and Gary A. Steiner, **Human Behavior: An Inventory of Scientific Findings,** (Harcourt, Brace and World, 1964) pp. 489-90, and Charles C. Moskos and W. Bell, 'Attitudes towards Democracy', in **Attitudes** (Penguin Modern Psychology Series, Penguin Books, 1966), p. 69.

"40 Bruce M. Russett, Hayward R. Alker, Jr., Karl W. Deutsch, and Harold D. Lasswell, **World Handbook of Political and Social Indicators** (Yale University Press, 1964), pp. 1-12 on the great extent of the data, p. 292 for the conclusion cited above.

. . .

"50 Russett and others (cited in note 40). See pages 237-8 for an explanation of the Gini index (the higher the index the greater the inequality of farm land); and pp. 320-1 for the above quotation. The 'common beliefs about land inequality and instability' — the hypothesis tested—are 'that above-average inequality (of distribution of agricultural land) promotes above-average social and political discord or, conversely, that substantial equality means the existence of a large and relatively prosperous middle class which will support the existing political system.' (p. 320.)"

CDC found that the LTTT Program is causing a stronger identification among Delta farmers with the national government. There is also evidence of "increased identification, by local officials, with the villagers, because of LTTT," and "Relations between local officials and local military and the villagers are less authoritarian, more personal and democratic in dynamic villages (where the LTTT Program was progressing rapidly)."[17]   Their data also showed that "Village and hamlet government officials are more representative of the people they govern because of LTTT (in terms of land tenure)."[18]   Table 9-3 illustrates this latter point. In 1970, some 60-70 percent of village residents were tenants, while only 27 percent of the village and hamlet officials were. In 1972, after the LTTT Program was underway and after a second round of village and hamlet elections in late 1970 and 1971, 75 percent of the villagers were owner-operators or LTTT-applicants as were 67 percent of the local officials. The proportion of tenants, non-farmers and landlords

---

[17]Ibid., pp. 57-9.
[18]Ibid., pp. 61-2.

Table 9-3

Land Ownership and Tenancy Among Village and Hamlet Officials and Their Constituents, in the Delta, Before and After LTTT.[1]

Land Tenure	Offi- cials in 1970	Villa- gers in 1970	Officials in 23 dynamic Villages in 1972	Villagers in 23 dynamic Villages in 1972
Farm owners (owners before LTTT, owners, because of LTTT, and applicants for title under LTTT)	23%	16%	67%	75%
Tenant Farmers	27	60-70	7	15
Landless; not farming	40	-	26	1
Landless; laborers	-	10-20	-	7
Landlords or ex-landlords	10	4- 5	0	2
TOTAL	100%	100%	100%	100%

[1] "Officials in 1970" is taken from Land Ownership and Tenancy Among Village and Hamlet Officials in the Delta (Control Data Corporation to ADLR, USAID, March 1970, p. 28), N-679 from Long An and 4 delta provinces.

"Villagers in 1970" is derived from Land Reform in Vietnam (Stanford Research Institute to USAID, 1968, 4 volumes).

"Officials in 1972" consists of 54 village and hamlet officials, 50 of whom were interviewed in our random sample of 985 village families in 6 provinces and 4 of whom happened to mention their land tenure or that they do not own land or farm, in our behavioral observations in 44 villages in 9 provinces.

"Villagers in 1972" is our random sample of 985 farm families minus 50 whose family heads are village or hamlet officials.

Reprinted from Bush, et. al., Impact of Land-to-the-Tiller Program, December 1972, p. 62.

holding official positions all dropped significantly. CDC notes that Ministry of Interior election statistics "show a high percentage of turnover (defeat of incumbents) in village and hamlet elections in late 1970 and 1971."[19]

In analyzing their interview notes, the CDC researchers identified certain social values expressed by the respondents. They found that 90 percent of the values identified emphasize self-discipline, individual achievement, austerity, hard work and thrift and the acquisition and use of more knowledge (especially important was the education of children), quite contrary to the traditional, Confucian, Vietnamese values emphasizing status and harmony and suppressing individual initiative and social and technological changes.[20] The values expressed are middle-class values. CDC thinks that, at least in the Mekong Delta, the LTTT Program, by creating a large, new middle class, probably accelerated the shift from the traditional to the modern value orientation among farmers, thus improving prospects for social and economic development and for more peaceful political change.[21]

> "In sum, the Land to the Tiller Program is a splendid means to pacification. It creates equality among farmers and abolishes lifelong tendencies of tenant farmers to think of their lives as static, hopeless, poverty-ridden and of themselves as inferiors. It stimulates them to greater production and more investments in farming. It is helping change their values to those of the middle-class. It is helping turn a once-disaffected, politically neutral mass of potential and sometimes actual revolutionaries (formerly providing rice, information, labor and military manpower to the enemy) into middle-class farmers in support of the regime."[22]

Landlords

Information on landlord's use of compensation funds is scarce. Two surveys were conducted in the spring of 1973 that shed some additional light on the subject. The first one consisted of 100 questionnaires answered anonymously by landlords affected by the LTTT Program for the Landlord's and Ex-Landlord's Association.

---

[19]Ibid., p. 62.
[20]Ibid., pp. 73-4.
[21]Ibid., p.76.
[22]Ibid., p. 88.

The questionnaires were given to Dr. Henry C. Bush, CDC, for analysis on April 4, 1973.[23]

Of the 100 landlords responding, 57 had received part of their compensation and 22 were in the process of applying for it. Of these 79 landlords, 57 percent said they were using or intended to use all or part of their compensation money for consumption purposes (household expenses, to repay debts and to buy things), 41 percent said they were dividing at least some of it among their children or other relatives, and 38 percent said they were or would put some or all of it into savings or investments.

Regarding corruption in the compensation process, 10 percent said they were asked to pay someone a bribe, 24 percent said they were not asked, and 66 percent did not answer the question.

Another survey of landlords was carried out in April 1973 in 14 provinces of the Mekong Delta by Pacification Studies Branch teams and reported by Richard H. Eney.[24] This report tabulates responses from 307 landlords (out of 350 interviewed) who indicated they had already applied for compensation for land expropriated under the LTTT Program. Of these 307 responses, 223 had already received a first payment; 179 were willing to answer the question about what they were doing or intended to do with the money they had received or expected to receive; and 128 declined to answer.[25]

Of the 179 who were willing to answer, 52 percent indicated they intended to divide their compensation among relatives. They were then asked how they expected their relatives to use the money. A total of 65 percent intended to use at least some of the money, or expected their relatives to, for trade, business, or money lending, 45 percent intended or expected relatives to "keep it," presumably for consumption expenses, 30 percent said at least some of it would

---

[23]Memorandum from Henry C. Bush, CDC, P&P/ADLR, to Mr. William Fuller, ADTS/ADLR, USAID, Saigon, "Findings of Survey of 100 Ex-landlords, on Payments to be Compensated, and on Uses and Intended Uses of Compensation Money," dated April 16, 1973.

[24]"Anticipated Use of Landlord Compensation Payments, MR 4," memorandum from Richard H. Eney, Chief, Land Reform Division, CG4/RRO, dated May 7, 1973.

[25]This information was passed to me personally by Mr. Eney, based on other documents in his possession. It was omitted from **Ibid.**

go toward the repayment of debts, and 15 percent indicated at least some of it would be deposited in banks.[26]

The Eney data indicate that those landlords receiving the larger sums of money more often expected to use at least some of it (or to see their relatives use it) for trade, business or lending or to put at least some of it in a bank and they less often expected to have some of it kept for consumption or used to pay off debts.[27]

Grievances

The U.S. Agency for International Development and the GVN Directorate General for Land Affairs collaborated in a joint study on "Grievances and Land-to-the-Tiller" in August and September, 1972.[28] The investigation was limited geographically to the Mekong Delta and the area around Saigon (MR 3 and MR 4). The general conclusions of this review were:[29]

"The magnitude of complaints and grievances resulting from Land-to-the-Tiller appears inexorably low. Serious grievances or disputes involve one to three percent of farmers and landlords participating in the program. Lighter grievances classified as complaints, inquiries, demands, or requests encompass five to fifteen percent of the rural population. Neither the level of serious grievances nor that of lighter grievances appear to be severely detrimental to the overall impact of the program. There are, however, specific provinces (An Giang and Chau Doc) and particular villages where grievances and abuses may be impairing social objectives of the land reform.

---

[26]Another 4 percent of the responses were listed as "other," with a note indicating "build house" (4), and "build shop," "lease riceland," and "buy treasury bonds" (1 each). A final 1 percent indicated they thought their relatives would in turn divide their share up among their relatives. (These percentages total 159 percent due to multiple responses. —See Table 9-4.)

[27]Ibid., Table I, II, and III. Responses are tabulated for those landlords receiving 500,000 $VN and up and for those receiving 2,000,000 $VN and up. The actual number of landlords in each category, however, was not recorded. See Table 9-4.

[28]Keith W. Sherper and Phi Ngoc Huyen, "Grievances and Land-to-the-Tiller," February 15, 1973, mimeographed.

[29]Ibid., pp. 46-7.

Table 9-4

Anticipated Use of Landlord Compensation Payments, MR 4

(From the Eney Memorandum)

Anticipated Use by Landlord or his Relatives	Of all 179 Landlords Answering:		Of those Receiving:		
	% of 179 Landlords	% of 285 uses listed	Less than $VN500,000 (% of 150 uses listed)	More than $VN500,000 (% of 135 uses listed)	More than $VN2,000,000 (% of 42 uses listed)
1. Trade, business, and/or lending	64.8	40.7	34.0	48.1	47.6
2. Deposit in banks	14.5	9.1	5.3	13.3	21.4
3. "Kept," presumably for Consumption Expenses	44.7	28.1	33.3	22.2	16.7
4. Repayment of Debts	30.2	18.9	24.7	12.6	9.5
5. Divide among other Relatives	1.1	0.7	--	1.5	--
6. Other	3.9	2.5	2.7	2.2	4.8
TOTALS	159.2	100.0	100.0	99.9	100.0

NOTE: Column 1 adds to more than 100% due to multiple uses listed by some landlords.

SOURCE: Calculated from Richard H. Eney, "Anticipated Use of Landlord Compensation Payments, MR 4," Report from Chief, Land Reform Division, CO4/RRO, dated May 7, 1973.

" . . . The grievance system has tended to be a slow process for completing actions, but there are signs it is now speeding up. Disputes channeled through the judicial process are biased toward landlords, but are subsequently given balance by the Central Agency for Land Courts and the National Land Reform Council. Courts do not appear fully cognizant of either the letter or the spirit of the Land-to-the-Tiller Law . . . Generally, the system is fairly open for an individual to the village level. The major exception is when village officials are a party to the grievance; in this situation there are some options available to the aggrieved, depending on his knowledge and motivation. However, most recourses beyond the village are inclined to be long and drawn out, possibly dissuading some aggrieved from pursuing them . . . "

A formal grievance system was established after the promulgation of the LTTT Law to handle grievances and complaints about it received through administrative channels, and a Special Land Court System was established outside the normal civil court system to handle the more serious disputes that might arise. In November 1971, local responsibility to conciliate land distribution disputes was placed in the hands of the Village Land Distribution Committee (VLDC), which is composed of the village chief as chairman, a village council representative, the village commissioner for land reform and agriculture, the chief of the hamlet involved, and the village land registrar.[30] In many villages, however, the older Village Agricultural Committee, established under the Diem Ordinance 57 land reform and composed of two landlords, two tenants, and the village chief, was still hearing disputes, and in many other cases the village chief alone attempted to mediate disputes in the traditional manner without referral to any committee.

Solutions or compromises obtained through the latter two methods may not have been legally binding, but they were often accepted by both parties and the matter was dropped. In any case, neither disputant was obliged to accept a village level decision, not even from the VLDC, and the aggrieved party retained the right to pursue the matter in court.

"The kinds of cases handled by the village mainly . . . concern who is the proper land owner, who is the proper tiller and boundary disputes . . . (and are) often very complex, encompassing inheritance, family

---

[30]Decree 138-LS/CCDD/PTNNN, November 8, 1971. See Appendix A of **Ibid.**

relationships, verbal and written contracts sub-leasing, exemption of land and new occupants tilling the land. Village level officials mediate the bulk of these disputes, seldom informing (province authorities) of the problem or the outcome."[31]

The village was supposed to report grievances and their disposition to the Province Land Affairs Service (PLAS), which in turn submitted a consolidated monthly report to the Directorate General of Land Affairs (DGLA) in Saigon; but in fact only 15 or 20 percent of the villages made any reports at all, and these were sporadic and concerned mostly the more serious disputes.

Within the Inspectorate of DGLA was a Grievance Office, which received all complaints and grievances about the LTTT Program, including newspaper articles, letters sent directly to the DGLA and letters forwarded from assemblymen and other government agencies or officials, as well as the monthly reports from subordinate PLAS offices. Complaints and inquiries arose mainly from misunder-standing or ignorance of some detail of law, and they usually required no more than a return letter of explanation. Those categorized as grievances were the more serious disputes which required an investigation and some action be taken.

From the beginning of the LTTT Program until the end of August 1972, a period covering the first 2 years and 5 months of the program, 7,150 grievances, complaints and inquiries of all kinds had been received by the DGLA, which, as a proportion of the number of titles issued and landlords compensated by the latter date, represents only 1.5 percent of those already affected by program. Most of these were placed in the complaints and inquiries category, which totalled 6,395, and most of them were received in the early months of the program, reflecting uncertainties and a quest for more information. Only 755 were listed as serious grievances requiring more than a simple explanatory letter, 10.6 percent of the 7,150 total and only 0.2 percent of those affected by the program.[32]

Table 9-5 summarizes the complaints and inquiries received by the DGLA. Landlord complaints and inquiries account for almost two-thirds of the first list. About one-third of the landlords were

---

[31]Ibid., p. 7.

[32]By August 31, 1972, DGLA and USAID official statistics listed 585,856 LTTT titles issued to 451,356 former tenants and compensation payments already made to 40,783 landlords. **Ibid.**, pp. 10 and 24.

Table 9-5

Complaints or Inquiries[1]

Category	Number of Cases	Percentage
Organizations (e.g. TFU)	91	1.4
Agencies (primarily letters received by other government agencies)	321	5.0
Newspapers (letters and articles)	260	4.1
By landlords	4,223	66.0
-Request retention of land for self-cultivation	441	10.4
-Request exemption from expropriation	1,021	24.2
-Offers for voluntary expropriation	52	1.2
-Ask about compensation regulations	1,260	29.8
-Ask about declaration regulations	53	1.3
-Matters related to worship land	301	7.1
-Disputes with tenants	203	4.8
-Miscellaneous problems	892	21.1
	4,223	99.9
By Tenants	1,500	23.5
-Request to continue cultivation	57	3.8
-Request land distribution	558	37.2
-Disputes with landlords	492	32.8
-Miscellaneous problems	382	25.5
-Request direct purchase from landlord	11	0.7
	1,500	100.0
TOTAL:	6,395	100.0

[1] Report on Settlement of Disputes from LTTT, August 1972, DGLA.

Source: Keith W. Sherper and Phi Ngoc Huyen, Grievances and Land-to-the-Tiller in Vietnam, (Washington, D.C.: A.I.D., Dept. of State); (Saigon: DGLA, Ministry for Land Reform and Agriculture and Forestry Development, February 15, 1973), p. 11.

requesting exemption from expropriation or asking about the worship land exemption, another third were asking about compensation regulations or volunteering land for expropriation, and 10 percent were requesting retention of land for self-cultivation (not permitted under the law if tenants were currently tilling it). Tenant complaints and inquiries comprise less than a fourth of the list, with about a third of the tenants reporting disputes with landlords and 37 percent requesting land distribution. The small number of tenants initiating complaints and inquiries as compared with landlords, especially as a proportion of those affected by the program (.003 of the tenants affected compared with .104 of the landlords), no doubt reflects in part the higher education levels, greater savvy, experience, and aggressiveness in dealing with the government of the landlords; but it surely also reflects the greater emphasis and speed of the government in implementing the distribution side of the program and in providing for local, village-level responsibility in dealing with disputes concerning the distribution process. There was no local mechanism to mediate landlord disputes and grievances arising from the compensation process.

Of the 755 serious grievances received, 50 percent alleged improper implementation of the LTTT Law by village and province officials, 9 percent claimed landlords or military personnel had hindered proper implementation of the law, 17 percent were about direct disputes between landlords and tenants, 13 percent were miscellaneous LTTT matters, and 10 percent were personnel grievances indirectly related to the LTTT Program.

A further analysis of 449 dossiers (out of the 755 grievances cases on file at the DGLA) revealed a total of 684 grievances, with some individuals reporting more than one. Of these 684, about one-fourth alleged false registry of worship land, one-fifth alleged landlord coercion of tenants, and about one-third contained charges against local officials of corruption, error, delay, refusal to implement the law, or connivance with landlords to prevent land transfer. (See Table 9-6.) The notorious An Giang Province case of 373 illegal declarations of worship land, accepted and registered after the LTTT Law was promulgated by the An Giang PLAS chief, is not included in this table.[33] If it were, the false registry of

---

[33] An investigation of these complaints was conducted, the An Giang PLAS chief was removed from office, and his replacement was instructed to initiate court proceedings on behalf of the aggrieved tenants to have the illegal entries stricken from the land register. During the first half of 1973, the An Giang prosecutor was notifying the 288 landlords involved that they had 15 days to "voluntarily" renounce worship land status. If they failed to do so

Table 9-6

Grievances and Disputes from DGLA Records[1]

Category of Grievance	Number	Percentage
False registry as worship land, by landlords	162	23%
Coercion of tenants, by landlords Evictions: 46 Threats or violence: 58 Collecting back rent: 23 Annulling or preventing transfer: 8	135	19
Refusal to implement LTTT, or connivance with landlords, by village officials, to prevent or annul transfer Refusal to implement LTTT: 48 Connivance with landlords: 41	89	13
Error, by local officials Distributed exempt land: 31 Distributed land to other than present tillers: 21 Title issued for only part of plot: 12 Paid compensation twice: 1	65	10
Corruption for money or land, by officials Demand money to process compensation: 14 Demand money to process title applications: 13 Distributed land to friends, relatives who are not tillers: 9 Unspecified corruption: 10 Demand payment for title distribution: 1	47[2]	7
Demand for exemption of their land, by landlords Allege it was or was intended to be worship land: 9 Allege special hardships: 33 Claim they are owner-cultivators: 5	47	7
Delay, hindrance in compensation, by GVN officials alleged by landlords	38	5
Demand for LTTT implementation or for title, by tenants or applicants	41	6
Tenants or applicants ineligible for title	36	5

(cont.)
they would then be taken to court. In neighboring Chau Doc a province committee examined 134 cases of allegedly false worship land and found 99 cases illegal. Those 99 landlords were also being asked to "voluntarily" renounce worship land status. Cables Can Tho 0033 and 0061 from AM CONSUL/CAN THO to USAID/ADLR/FSLB, Saigon, Subject: "Highlights of Visit to An Giang 4-6 April 73," and "Highlights of Trip to Chau Doc 10-11 April 73," Ed Rose sends, dated 9 April 73 and 14 April 73, respectively.

Table 9-6

(Continued)

Category of Grievances	Number	Percentage
Alleged to be hired laborers: 9		
Not actual tillers: 16		
Not "real" long-time tenants, but "new" recent or "subtenants": 7		
Unspecified reasons: 4		
Delay in distribution titles by GVN Officals, alleged by applicants	4	1
New Owners afraid; want to return titles	5	1
Malfeasance by local officials against landlords	4	1
Threat to transfer or expropriate land if owners do not pay back taxes: 2		
Falsifying landlord's declarations to obtain land: 1		
Urging tenants to apply for exempt land: 1		
Land-grabbing by hoodlums, mainly military	11[3]	2
Rent shakedown by non-owners: 2		
Use of force to impede application for title: 2		
Eviction and land-grabbing: 7	—	—
TOTAL:	684	100%

[1] A universe of 449 dossiers involving 684 grievances, with the noted exceptions. If an individual had multiple grievances, each grievance is tabulated. In cases of unspecified numbers of tenants, they were considered as four complaints (an assumption of 2 1/2 ha./tenant and 10 ha/landlord.)

[2] Not included is one village listing 80 tenants (counted as 1).

[3] Excluded are one case of 137 and one case of 595 farmers displaced by ARVN squatters; they are not necessarily tenants and it may be outside LTTT.

Reprinted from: Sherper and Huyen, Grievances and Land-to-the-Tiller, pp. 27-8.

worship land category would comprise 51 percent of the total.

The Sherper-Huyen study provides a cross-check of this data by analyzing grievances and complaints logged in files maintained separately by the Land Reform Division of USAID, CORDS, and Dr. Bush of the Control Data Corporation. After eliminating the duplication and excluding specific large-scale violations in nine villages, they were left with 1,128 complaints and disputes, listed by category in Tables 9-7 and 9-8. False registry of worship land again appeared as the largest proportion of grievances reported in the Delta (MR 4) with 44 percent, almost all of them emanating from the Hoa Hao, floating-rice area of An Giang and Chau Doc Provinces. Landlord coercion of tenants comprised 74 percent of the grievances in the region around Saigon (MR 3) and the second largest category in the Delta (18 percent).

A tabulation of grievances reported in 49 newspaper articles collected by the USAID Land Reform Office in Can Tho, also revealed the principle categories of grievances as: 1) landlord repossession effort, 2) worship land claim, and 3) landlord retention claim (see Table 9-9). Again, a large share (41 percent) of these grievances came from An Giang and Chau Doc Provinces, but another 38 percent were reported from Ba Xuyen Province, apparently as the result of an incident involving one or two villages.[34]

A large portion of the more serious reported grievances were being taken to court. The Special Land Courts were established under the Diem Ordinance 57 Land Reform of 1956. So far only four Special Land Courts had been set up—in Saigon, Long An, Dinh Tuong and An Giang—but by 1970 there were 36 Courts of First Instance, which assumed the responsibilities of Special Land Courts where the latter did not exist separately. No fee was charged for land court suits. The PLAS Chief served as a public prosecutor and presented the required documentation to the court regarding each case. Judgments handed down by Special Land Courts were not final or binding until confirmed by the National Land Reform Council (NLRC), which was an organ of the executive branch of government, composed of representatives of the Prime Minister, six ministries and the Directorate General of Planning. NLRC decisions were final and could not be appealed. The Special Land Court System was only quasi-judicial, leaving the final decisions to the executive, in recognition of the essential revolutionary or extra-

---

[34]The 49 newspaper articles reported grievances involving a total of 229 individuals. The percentages used above are of the 229 figure, not the number of articles.

Table 9-7

Grievance and Disputes in MR 4

Category of Grievance	No.	Percent	Distribution and Exception:
False registry as worship land, by landlords	459	44	343 (75%) in An Giang. 102 (22%) in Chau Doc.
Coercion of tenants, by landlords Evictions: 45 Threats or violence: 50 Annulling or preventing land transfer: 33 Collection of or claims for back rents: 55	183	18	28 evictions (62%) in Chau Doc. 25 threats or violence (50%) in Bac Lieu. 14 preventions or annulments of title (42%) Bac Lieu. All back rent claims occurred in Phong Dinh. All were TFU mediations. In 1 of 36 villages of Sadec, all applicants were forced to pay back rents.***
Refusal to implement LTTT, or connivance with landlords to annul or prevent land transfer, by village officials Refusal to implement LTTT: 24 Connivance with landlords: 66	90	9	In 1 of Kien Giang's 34 villages there are 25 "general disputes"[1] In 1 of Kien Phong's 45 villages there are "numerous disputes"[1] In 1 of Vinh Long's 64 villages, officials refuse to act on "the majority" of applications[1]
Error, by local officials Distributed exempt land: 14 Distributed land to other than present tiller: 0 Title issued for only part of plot: 16	30	3	
Corruption for land or money, by officials Demand money to process compensation: 13 Demand money to process title applications: 18	84	8	11 (85%) in Phong Dinh. 10 (55%) in Kien Phong.

[1] Not included in tabulation.

Table 9-7

(continued)

Category of Grievance	No.	Percent	Distribution and Exception
Distributed land to friends, relatives who are not tillers: 12 Demand payment for title distribution: 41			In 1 of Kien Phong's 45 villages. VLDC distributed an entire island to nontillers, 595 are excluded from LTTT title.[1] 15 (37%) in Sadec, 13 (32%) in Chuong Thien. In 2 of Kien Phong's villages, about 200 have paid bribes for titles. In 1 village of Kien Phong, 28 have paid bribes for titles.[1]
Demand for exemption of their land, by landlords Allege it was or was intended to be worship land: 38 Allege special hardships: 15 Claim they are owner-operators: 10	63	6	28 (58%) in An Giang. 10 (26%) in Kien Phong.
Delay, hindrance in compensation by GVN officials, alleged by landlords	43	4	20 (47%) in Dinh Tuong.
Demand for LTTT implementation or for title, by tenants or applicants	0	0	
Tenants or applicants ineligible for title Alleged to be hired laborers: 3 Not actual tillers: 13 Not "real" long-time tenants, but "new", recent or "subtenants": 32	48	5	11 (85%) in Kien Hoa. 20 (63%) are in 1 of Kien Tuong's 13 villages.
Delay in distributing titles by GVN officials, alleged by applicants:	15	2	13 (87%) in Kien Hoa.
New owners afraid: want to return titles	0	0	
Malfeasance by local officials against landlords	0	0	

[1] Not included in tabulation.

Table 9-7

(continued)

Category of Grievance	No.	Percent	Distribution and Exceptions
Land-grabbing by hoodlums, mainly military Rent shakedown by non-owners: 4 Use of force to impede applications for title: 0 Evictions and land-grabbing: 6	10	1	1 case of 137 evicted by military, in Chau Doc***
TOTAL:	1,025	100%	8 villages, of 733 having LTTT goals in MR 4, violating LTTT in major ways, and 1 flagrant case of land-grabbing by military persons.

[1] Not included in tabulation.

Sources: USAID/ADLR and CORDS/MR 4 records.

Reprinted from: Sherper and Huyen, *Grievance and Land-to-the-Tiller*, pp. 30-1.

Table 9-8

Grievance and Disputes in MR 3

Category of Grievance	Number	Percent
False registry as worship land, by landlords	5[a]	5

Coercion of tenants, by landlords
  Evictions: 58
  Threats of violence: 5[a]
  Collecting back rent: 12[a]
  Annulling or preventing transfer: 1
	76	74

Coercion of officials, by landlords: Violence	1	1
Coercion of landlords, by tenants: Violence	1	1

Refusal to implement LTTT, or connivance with landlords, by village officials to prevent or annul transfer
  Refusal to implement LTTT: 10
  Connivance with landlords: 5
	15	14[b]

Error, by local officials Distributed exempt land: 2	2	2
Demand for exemption of their land, by landlords Allege it was or was intended to be worship land: 2	2	2
Delay, hindrance in compensation, by GVN officials, alleged by landlords	1	1
	—	—
TOTAL:	103	100%

[a]All cases in Long An Province

[b]47% in Long An Province; 33% in Bien Hoa Province

Sources: USAID/ADLR and CORDS/MR3 records, reprinted from Sherper and Huyen, Grievances and Land-to-the-Tiller, p. 29.

Table 9-91

Complaints and Grievances from Vietnamese Newspapers

	1971		Jan.-June 1972		Total		% of 229
	Cases	Individuals	Cases	Individuals	Cases	Individuals	
Worship land claim	0	27	4	25	10	52	22.7
Unjust distribution	4	5	3	5	7	10	4.4
Compensation squeeze	1	1	3	3	4	4	1.7
Landlord retention claim	11	45	1	1	12	46	20.1
Labor contract fraud	1	14	0	0	1	14	6.1
Landlord repossession effort	4	25	1	60	5	85	37.1
Compensation request	2	2	2	3	4	5	2.2
Miscellaneous	2	2	4	11	6	13	5.7
Total	31	121	18	108	49	229	100.0

1 "Summary of Newspaper and Directly-Reported Complaints," Memorandum by Richard Eney, Director of Land Reform, CORDS/MRIV, Can Tho, to files, August 24, 1972.

Source: Sherper and Huyen, Grievances and Land-to-the-Tiller, p. 32.

legal nature of a land reform program as far-reaching as the LTTT Law.[35]

All provincial Land Court cases were first reviewed by the Central Agency for Land Courts in the Ministry of Land Reform and Agriculture. The commissioner general of this agency presented his recommendations on each case to the NLRC, which then either approved or disapproved the recommendations. Between March 1970 and August 1972, only 659 cases had been received from provincial Land Courts by the Central Agency, 385 had already been reviewed by the NLRC and 274 were being prepared for a January 1973 session.[36]

An analysis of the 212 cases reviewed by the NLRC in June and October, 1972, revealed the breakdown by category presented in Table 9-10. Disputes between landlords and tenants arising out of the LTTT Law comprised 69 percent of the total, the 105 cases reviewed plus 42 of the cases rejected. Of the 105 landlord-tenant cases reviewed, 71 percent involved landlord attempts to retain ownership of their land, and another 3 percent represented landlord efforts to collect back rent only. The other 26 percent of the cases were brought to court by tenants claiming tilling rights.

The high proportion of cases brought to court by landlords, as opposed to those in which a tenant is plaintiff, demonstrates the effect of the higher levels of education, experience with government procedures, wealth, and mobility of the landlords.

The Land Courts ruled in favor of the tenants in 64 percent of this 105-case sample, and all of these decisions were upheld by the NLRC. Of the other 36 percent, however, originally decided in favor of the landlords, more than three-fourths were overturned by the NLRC in favor of the tenants, leaving only 9 percent of the final decisions favoring landlords. Sherper and Huyen concluded

---

[35]Sherper and Huyen, "Grievances and Land-to-the-Tiller", pp. 15-18.
[36]Ibid., p. 17.

Table 9-10

Categories of Cases Reviewed by the National Land Reform Council (NLRC)

	June	October	Total	Proportion
LTTT disputes between landlord and tenants or ex-tenants	52	53	105	.495
LTTT disputes between tillers and former tillers	14	6	20	.094
Disputes between middlemen and tenants	4	1	5	.024
Disputes between tenants and village officials	0	1	1	.005
Cases rejected (of which 42 were land-lord-tenant disputes)	21	25	46	.217
Cases postponed	7	17	24	.113
Cases which the NLRC declared the Courts incompetent to judge	7	2	9	.043
Cases not involving LTTT	0	2	2	.009
	105	107	212	1.000

[1] Records of the Commissioner General of Land Courts, DGLA.

Source: Sherper and Huyen, Grievances and Land-to-the-Tiller, p. 19.

that "The large percentage of Land Court cases reversed by the National Council indicate unfamiliarity of land law by the courts, strict interpretation of the letter and spirit of Land-to-the-Tiller by the NLRC, or a combination of these factors."[37]

In addition, 42 of the 46 cases rejected by the NLRC were landlord-tenant disputes, and in all 42 cases the lower court decisions had favored the landlords. By rejecting these decisions out-of-hand, therefore, the NLRC in effect ruled for the tenants in all of these cases.

Considering the total of 147 landlord-tenant disputes included in this sample, the NLRC reversed or rejected 48 percent of the Land Court decisions. Whereas the Land Courts had held in favor of the tenant in 46 percent of the cases, the NLRC judgments favored the tenant in 94 percent.[38]

A large proportion of the Land Court cases were located in the provinces of Long An and An Giang, which together accounted for 36 percent of all Land Court cases involving LTTT. One problem noted with the Special Land Court System was the long delay and numerous hearings a typical case had to undergo before a judgment was reached. A tenant farmer often had to travel long distances to the province capital for monthly hearings, only to have his case postponed again for lack of some document or deposition, and many farmers became discouraged from pursuing the matter further.[39]

To determine the nature and extent of unreported grievances and complaints related to the LTTT Program, the Sherper-Huyen team obtained the cooperation of Vietnamese employees of provincial CORDS offices, who interviewed village officials in 72 villages, at least 3 villages per province in 17 provinces of the Southern Region (MR 3 and MR 4). The officials reported a total of 194 disputes and grievances during the preceding 6 months, of which 43 percent had been settled by the village, 35 percent had gone to the courts and 22 percent remained unsettled. Less than two-thirds of the villages kept records of disputes, and only 8 percent sent copies of them to the district office for information.[40]

Almost half of the disputes (45 percent) involved tenants against tenants (multiple applicants) over "who should get title," or tenants against landlords over the tenants' status as the bona fide

[37]Ibid., p. 20.
[38]Ibid., p. 21-22.
[39]Ibid., p. 18.
[40]Ibid., pp. 37-9.

tiller, or whether the land was exempt from redistribution (mostly worship land challenges). Another 30 percent involved mostly landlords in conflict over "who owns the land" in the first place and other disputes about compensation.

As to lesser "requests, demands, complaints concerning LTTT or land for farming," the village officials reported a total of 559 in the survey, more than three-fourths of the requests for land from landless laborers and military personnel (87 percent if veterans and their families are included).

The results of this survey indicate that about 2.5 percent of all landlords and pre-LTTT tenants had brought serious grievances to village authorities during the 2.5 years of the program, and that about 5 percent of the entire rural population had voiced lesser complaints and requests.[41]

Sherper and Huyen also reviewed field reports from official (U.S. advisory) visits to villages and Pacification Attitude and Analysis Surveys (PAAS), the latter consisting of actual surveys with rural people on the land reform and other matters. Reports of petty corruption in the distribution process were frequently made through these channels, though not elsewhere. This "squeeze" consisted of small payments to local officials for each title distributed—small in relation to the value of the title or the value of the annual rent formerly paid. It appeared to be specific to particular villages or hamlets, and other villages could be identified where this form of corruption did not exist.[42]

The major Control Data Corporation study cited earlier also analyzed the "complaints, needs, problems and grievances" mentioned by the villagers in their unstructured interviews. Most of these concerned economic or agricultural problems, but 21 percent of the sample voiced technical or administrative complaints against the government about the LTTT Program or its other agricultural policies, and most of these were complaints that the LTTT Program does not help landless laborers or the tenants on ancestral worship land. Most resident ex-landlords (95 percent of them) complained about the delay in the compensation procedure, but they comprised only 2 percent of all farmers. Some title applicants complained of delay and a few noted errors in the title received. Some 2.5 percent of the LTTT title-recipients complained that they still had to pay token rent or that ex-landlords demanded back taxes. About 1 percent complained of landlord coercion or of abuse of authority

<hr>

[41]Ibid., pp. 38 and 40.
[42]Ibid., pp. 42-45.

by local officials.[43]   (See Table 9-11 for a summary of this part of the CDC analysis.)

Corruption

USAID Officials were concerned about reports of corruption connected with the LTTT Program. Informed sources explained that, as far as they could tell, corruption in the title application and distribution process was fairly widespread, though many villages seemed to be completely free of it, but that the level of payments required from tenant farmers was so low[44] as to be little more than a minor irritant to them, and that it was by no means a matter serious enough to damage the political or economic impact of the program.

Reports of much higher levels of corruption in the landlord compensation process were common, and USAID officials were more worried about it than about the "tea money" sometimes required from farmers. Bribes to province and central government officials, in order to expedite the paperwork, were frequently reported to be as much as 20 to 40 percent of the value of the initial compensation check (which itself, however, was only 20 percent of the total amount of compensation, plus accumulated interest).[45]   Hard evidence was difficult to acquire, however, and what few surveys were made, such as the survey of 100 ex-landlords reported above, indicated that only about 10 percent of the ex-landlords would admit to personally having paid or being asked to pay a bribe (although 66 percent did not answer the question).[46]

The primary cause of corruption was considered to be delay or the opportunities for delay in the administrative process, along

---

[43]Bush, **et. al., Impact of Land to the Tiller Program,** pp. 67-72.

[44]Typical reports indicated payoffs of VN$ 200 to VN$ 500, though in some villages it went as high as VN$ 5,000 to VN$ 10,000, for each application or title processed. An average title, however, was worth between VN$ 150,000 and VN$ 200,000 by official reckoning in 1970, and more than that on the free market. Even the higher levels of squeeze reported did not approach one year's legal rent level, which was 10 percent of the official value of the land.

[45]It should be noted that even the highest levels of payoff reported in the landlord compensation process amounted to only 8 percent of the total value of compensation, since there were no reports of squeeze extended to the cashing of land bonds (.40x.20 = .08).

[46]Bush to Fuller Memo, April 16, 1973, p. 1.

Table 9-11

Complaints, Needs, Problems, Grievances

(Some had more than one problem, so percentages sometimes total more than 100.)

Complaints, needs, problems, grievances, by type (see text for details)	Long An N=148 who had 152 problems	Go Cong N=307 who had 131 problems	Dinh Tuong N=150 who had 112 problems	Vinh Long N=181 who had 160 problems	Vinh Binh N=112 who had 176 problems	Chuong Thien N=87 who had 137 problems	All 6 Provinces N=985 who had 868 problems
Economic problems	35%	11%	26%	35%	69%	72%	33%
Basic agricultural handicaps	10%	5%	17%	18%	23%	22%	14%
Technical problems	14%	8%	5%	4%	6%	17%	9%
Insecurity hazards	16%	.3%	1%	16%	0%	31%	8%
Technical or administrative complaints against GVN re LTTT or agriculture	20%	14%	23%	13%	59%	15%	21%
Complaints of abuse of authority by officials	2%	2%	2%	1%	0%	0%	1%
Worries that the ex-landlord might return and take back the land, complaints that the ex-landlords still hounds them for token rents or back taxes, or fear of what might happen if they had the courage to apply for title	6%	1.7%	1%	1%	0%	0%	2%
Total	103%	42%	75%	88%	157%	157%	88%

Table 9-11

(continued)

Notes:

Economic problems are complaints about prices. The overwhelmingly preponderant one is that the prices of fertilizer and insecticide are so high
they cannot afford enough of them.

Basic agricultural handicaps are mainly that their village or hamlet does
not have enough land. Others are that they need help to clear more land,
need help to fix the irrigation dam, have poor soil, or salt water
intrusion, etc.

Technical problems are that they do not know how to use insecticide, that
their livestock die for want of vaccines, and such.

Insecurity hazards complain of occasional mines or booby traps in some
fields, or of VC instrusion and VC "tax" squeeze.

Technical or administrative complaints against GVN re LTTT or agriculture,
which particularly interest us, are regrets that the program does nothing
for the landless, grievances about the administration of LTTT (e.g. by an
applicant that he applied long ago but had not received title; e.g. by ex-
landlords that they have not been compensated yet) or about agricultural
policies other than LTTT (e.g. that ADB loans are slow or inadequate).

A note on each province's grievances re LTTT:

1. In Long An 13% of those 20% are complaints about the "bad fit" of LTTT,
   that it leaves some out (e.g. by tenants on worship land who do not
   see why they should pay rent forever, exlandlords who say they lost
   by LTTT, landless laborers who say they got nothing.) 7+% are
   administrative grievances (e.g. by exlandlords that they have not
   been compensated yet and by tenants who applied long ago and have not
   yet received titles).

2. In Go Cong 9% of those 14% are complaints by those left out of LTTT
   (the landless and tenants on land, particularly worship land, exempt
   from LTTT). 4% are administrative grievances (by exlandlords that
   they have not yet been compensated, by applicants that their title
   has not yet been received or that their title has an error in it.)
   1% complain that ADB loans are too hard to get and too small when one
   does get them.

3. In Dinh Tuong 17% of those 23% are about the "bad fit" of LTTT to the
   landless and those farming land in tenancy which is exempt from the
   program, and some from relocated refugees that although they have
   received title where they now farm they eventually want to return
   and receive title to land in their native villages. 4% are
   administrative grievances (that compensation is slow.) 2% complain
   that ADB loans are slow or inadequate, that more miracle rice seed
   should be available, or that insecticides are not of good quality.

Table 9-11

(continued)

<u>Notes</u>:

4. In <u>Vinh Long</u> 3% of those 13% are complaints that LTTT excludes the landless and those farming worship land in tenancy. 8% are <u>administrative</u> grievances and most are complaints that they applied long ago but have not yet received title. 2% are that ADB loans are slow or inadequate.

5. In <u>Vinh Binh</u> 58% complain that LTTT does nothing for the many landless! Vinh Binh is 60+% Cambodian, and our sample there was 73% Cambodian. They are poor. 69% complain of high prices. When, as in LTTT, they do receive help from the GVN, more seem grateful than seems true of ethnic Vietnamese, as Table 13 shows. And when, as in our interviews, somebody is listening, they tell you of their poverty and of the many landless. Vietnamese Cambodians tend to be more community-minded and less individualistic than ethnic Vietnamese.

   That LTTT does nothing for many landless is their only complaint about LTTT. There is only one <u>administrative</u> grievance, about failure of the Land Court to act.

6. In <u>Chuong Thien</u> 14% are complaints that LTTT leaves out many (the landless, families of war dead, disabled veterans, and tenants paying rent on worship land). A few object that the law extends to Viet Cong and ex-Viet Cong families. <u>One</u> is an <u>administrative</u> grievance, by a farmer who applied years ago but still has not received his title.

<u>Re complaints about LTTT in all provinces</u>:

1. Complaints that LTTT does nothing for some (the landless, and those who are tenants on worship land) are the only quantitatively significant grumble. 15% of all farm families interviewed murmur that somehow some land should be found for the landless. 27% of such complaints are made by tenants and the landless (N=148 and 79, respectively); 40% of all landless laborers so complain.

2. <u>Complaints about how LTTT functions</u>:

   a. 18 of 19 exlandlords want their compensation money and have not yet received it. This is 95% of all in-village exlandlords, but only 2% of all farmers.

   b. 12 of 79 applicants for title applied long ago but complain that they still have not yet received title. This is 15% of all applicants but only 1% of all farmers.

   c. 7 complain of title issued by mistake, then recalled; or of errors in their title, usually in the size of the plot. This is only .7%

Table 9-11

(continued)

Notes:

  of all farmers. Two complain of landlord coercion (crop seized, eviction). This is nil.

3. <u>Miscellaneous worries pre-or post-LTTT</u>, 19 in all---2% of all respondents:

 a. 12 new owners still pay rent or token rent to exlandlords or complain that exlandlords hound them to pay back taxes. This is 2.5% of all new owners.

 b. Tenants who are unwilling to apply for title, for sentimental reasons or because they are afraid of what might happen, are only 2 of 148.

4. <u>Complaints of abuse of authority by somebody in some offices</u>, 8 in all---8% of all farmers. Each is unique. Two <u>allege</u> corruption. One expressed <u>doubt</u> that the land he farms in really worship land and therefore exempt from LTTT. Net assertions of injustice are only 5. Examples:

"Brother died and funeral expenses too much. Borrowed from neighbor, couldn't pay back, so had to let him farm the land. Then LTTT, damn, so neighbor declared he had farmed that land for 30 years, so officials gave him title. Chief of village got money. Now he is in jail since last month."

            (in Long An)

"One landowner falsely back-dated his land as worship land and so registered it with connivance of PLAS, so his land may not be expropriated and distributed. No way from village records to disprove it. It is back-dated to 1958 and in 1958 there was no village government here. The village was under Viet Cong control until 1970."

            (in Dinh Tuong)

Reprinted from: Bush, et. al., <u>Impact of Land-to-the-Tiller Program</u>, pp. 67-70.

with uncertainty or ignorance on the part of private individuals as to their rights or the procedural requirements involved. Where these were reduced to a minimum, as in the title distribution process, the level of corruption was low. Where, however, documentary requirements were complex and strict, and where there was no administrative emphasis on speed of execution, as in the landlord compensation procedure, corruption rose to higher and more irritating levels.

Legislation by Executive Decree—Worship Land Retention

Our own research and some investigative probing in Long An Province and Saigon turned up one clear example of legislation by executive decree in the Land-to-the-Tiller Program, in which the executive branch changed the wording and violated the intent of the basic legislation when it issued its implementing decree, producing a compromise favoring the landlords.

Several cases illustrating abuse of the Huong-Hoa worship land retention provision were on file in the Long-An Province Special Land Court. One man in Khanh Hau, his wife and eight children were on record as owning a total of 50 hectares of Huong-Hoa land (this may not have been all of it, since tenants claimed the family had declared 80 hectares of Huong Hoa land and even had a young grandson listed as an owner). The family head, who bought and registered most of this land just days before the LTTT Law was promulgated, brought a large number of his tenants to court for refusing to pay rent. The tenants claimed rights to title under paragraph 5.2 of the LTTT Law, which limits the amount of Huong Hoa land each **gia-toc** can retain to 5 hectares. The Province Land Affairs Service Chief recommended a court decision in favor of the landlord, based on the wording not of the law, but of paragraph 7 of the implementing decree.[47]

The word **gia-toc** confused many American advisors, because it was commonly translated merely as "family," as was the word **gia-dinh**. But the word **gia-toc** is quite different from the word **gia-dinh**, as every Vietnamese knows, and the two are not at all confusing even to the most illiterate tenant farmer. The implementing decree promulgated by the executive branch changed the wording of that provision from **gia-toc** to **moi so-huu-chu sang-lap**

---

[47]It was reported to me later that although the Long An Land Court found in favor of the landlord in these cases, at least some of those decisions were overturned by the NLRC in Saigon (see the section on "Grievances" of this chapter), but my information was incomplete and not specific.

(any property owner who established it), and thereby simply rewrote the law. This is evidence not only of landlord influence at the highest levels, but of their cleverness as well. A more correct translation of **gia-toc** would be "a five-generation family," while **gia-dinh** is "a nuclear family."

The establishment of Huong Hoa land is an ancient Vietnamese tradition. The net income from its operation must be used for five generations to worship the family ancestors in whose honor it was established. During this time it passes into the custody of the eldest male descendant of each succeeding generation; it cannot be sold (except under certain stringent conditions), nor can it be claimed by another in payment of an overdue debt. It does not belong to the inheritor as personal property, but to the whole **gia-toc,** for which the inheritor acts as custodian and must perform certain costly religious duties, such as the annual feasts on death anniversaries, connected with the worship of deceased ancestors. Any important decisions about Huong Hoa land must be approved by the **Hoi-Dong Gia-Toc,** the extended family council, including all relatives bearing the same surname. This is well-established law.[48]

Records of floor debates in the Vietnamese House of Representatives show that the assemblymen made clear distinctions among a **gia-toc,** a **gia-dinh,** and an individual owner. When answering a suggestion to lower the Huong-Hoa retention limit from the Lower House Provision of 15 hectares, the chairman of the Committee on Agriculture, who was presenting the bill paragraph by paragraph for floor debate and vote, said that since they had already decided (in the 1956 Ordinance 57) that a number of individual landlords may retain 15 hectares, he could think of no reason why a whole **gia-toc** should not have right to retain the same amount.[49]

Another representative objected to the **gia-toc** limitation as too restrictive, precisely because several individuals within the same **gia-toc** are often the recipients of separate parcels of Huong Hoa land. He recommended the word **gia-toc** to be amended to read **moi nguoi duoc thu-huong** (each recipient).[50] Still another repre-

---

[48]See Vu-Van-Hien, **Che-Do Tai-San trong Gia-Dinh Viet-Nam. Tap I** (Property Regimes in the Vietnamese Family, Vol. I), (Saigon: Bo Quoc-Gia Giao-Duc, (Ministry of Education, 1960), pp. 145-210.

[49]Ha-Nghi-Vien (House of Representatives), **Bien-ban Phien hop cua Ha-Nghi-Vien** (Session Minutes of the House of Representatives), Number 68/69/H/BB/BT, 3 September 1969, Republic of Vietnam, pp. 81-2.

[50]Ibid., p. 92.

sentative objected for similar reasons and wanted the word **gia-toc** changed to read **gia-dinh** (nuclear family.)[51]   Neither of these proposals was approved, and the **gia-toc** limitation became law (with the Senate reducing the amount from 15 to 5 hectares).

There are other references in the debate to the fact that a **gia-toc** includes "very many older brothers, younger brothers (**anh em** can also include cousins), younger and older paternal uncles related to each other,"[52] but enough has been said to illustrate the point.   The executive interpretation of **gia-toc** as "any property owner" cannot be legally justified, nor can the failure of the courts to declare that interpretation invalid.

---

[51]Ibid., p. 94.
[52]Ibid., p. 95.

Chapter X

CONCLUSIONS AND SPECULATIONS

This chapter will seek to summarize the major economic and socio-political effects of the LTTT Program, following the format presented in Table 1-1. The first nine chapters of this monograph were written before the precipitous fall of the Republic of Vietnam. As this chapter is being drafted, however, it is clear that the LTTT Program will not finalize the history of social, political and economic reform in the Mekong Delta. Already there are reports that the new government of South Vietnam has declared the LTTT Program abolished and is preparing to place the stamp of its own ideological formulations on the socio-political and economic institutions of rural Vietnam.[1] The remainder of this discussion has therefore become rather more academic than anticipated, and will deal more with "what might have been" than the author is normally inclined to do, recognizing the large amount of present uncertainty as to what the future holds for the Delta farmer.

Enough evidence is reported above, however, to credit the LTTT Program with significantly favorable effects, in both the economic and political spheres, in three of the four Mekong Delta villages we studied. The other surveys reported in Chapter IX indicate that our own results were not unique and were more or less indicative of what was going on throughout the larger part of the Delta.

The LTTT Program had been almost completed before the demise of the Republic. By February 1975, title applications had been approved for 1,297,132 hectares, and titles had actually been distributed for 1,136,705 hectares throughout Vietnam.[2] The approved hectarage represented 45.8 percentage of the estimated national total of riceland crop-hectarage in 1973-74, and a larger

---

[1]"New Land Reforms for South Vietnam," **The New York Times,** October 19, 1975.

[2]"**Terminal Project Appraisal Report**" for Land Reform in Vietnam, (Washington, D.C.: Agency for International Development, Department of State, October 7, 1975).

proportion of the actual hectarage cultivated annually.[3]

The Program had established an institutional foundation of small, family-owned farms run by an energetic and experienced class of farmers. It had re-oriented the rural incentive structure in ways which held high promise for rapid economic development in the future. It had redistributed wealth and income in ways which had profound implications for the more equitable distribution of social status and political power in the future, as well as for greater social justice itself. The formerly small middle-class of owner-cultivators had been enlarged to a position of both numerical and economic dominance in the rural areas, and the ramifications of that development would have taken years, perhaps generations, to work themselves out on the social and political fabric of Vietnam.

Economic Effects

The purely economic effects of the LTTT Program were predominantly favorable, given the overall objectives of agricultural development and a more equitable distribution of income. The only significantly unfavorable economic effect was the inflationary impact of the program's landlord compensation payments, which were neither balanced by increased tax revenue nor paid for by the former tenants, and which were only partially offset by increased budgetary support from declining foreign aid receipts.

Agricultural Production

There is considerable evidence, as presented in the chapters above, that, by giving ownership titles to farm operators, the LTTT Program vastly improved farmer incentives to invest more capital, labor and managerial resources into improving their farms and increasing production, and that it also gave many of them an important new **freedom** to make investment decisions and to

---

[3]No recent data are available on the amount of land double-cropped, and it has grown considerably in the last 5 years. Official agricultural statistics include estimates of total crop-hectarage per year only, which double-counts areas double-cropped. A total of 2,830,100 hectares was reportedly planted to rice in the 1973-74 growing season, 890,400 hectares of which were in high-yield varieties. If half of the high yield hectarage represented a second crop, the hectarage approved for LTTT title distribution would have represented 54.4% of the total land area under rice cultivation. **Dac San Kinh te Nong Nghiep, 1974** (Bulletin of Agricultural Economics, Special Issue) (Saigon: Ministry of Agriculture, 1974), p. 26.

implement them.   In the cultural and economic context of the Mekong Delta in the early 1970's, such incentives on the part of new owner-cultivators were apparently much stronger than the combined landlord-tenant incentives of the former system.

In addition, a major effect of the LTTT Program was to increase the amount of funds available to the new owner-cultivators, who numbered about one-half of all the farmers in the Delta. The complete remission of rents, coupled with only minor increases in rural taxes and no attempt to have title-recipients pay for their land, increased the disposable incomes of former tenants by the amount of their previous rent levels, still significant in many areas. The ownership title was also the key to qualifying for the much larger amounts of Agricultural Development Bank credit being made available in some areas.

Improved incentives and the greater availability of investment funds resulted in the larger average number of new investments per title-recipient farmer and the more rapid growth in their production as compared with tenant farmers, in the first three villages of this study. Official production estimates for the entire Southern Region indicate that favorable production trends were the rule and that the production declines reported among title-recipients in the broadcast-rice area of Hoa Binh Thanh Village represented a minor exception.   Rice production increased by 41 percent between the 1969-70 crop and 1973-74 in the Southern Region, from 4,307,400 metric tons of paddy to 6,073,500 M.T., and total agricultural production for the nation as a whole increased by 36 percent during the same 4-year period.[4]

Since by the 1960's Delta landlords were not generally performing any service to enhance the productive efforts of their own tenants, no productive agricultural services were lost by severing the landlord-tenant connection. The same can generally be said about socially-productive services—nothing of social importance was being performed for the tenants by their landlords. On the other hand, the government was engaged in a many-faceted and rather successful program to upgrade agricultural services available to all farmers—credit, extension, rural education, transportation and communication, marketing, water control, and the provision of modern agricultural inputs such as high-yielding seeds, fertilizers, and insecticides.

---

[4]Ibid., p. 23 and 27, and **Nien Giam Thong Ke Nong Nghiep, 1970 (Agricultural Statistics Yearbook),** (Saigon: Ministry of Agriculture, 1970), p. 33.

The LTTT Law did restrict the right of new owners to sell their land for 15 years, and as such would have tended to perpetuate the existing small-farm sizes. In a country with plenty of labor, however, (the underemployment and unemployment rate in 1973 was estimated as between 15 and 20 percent of a total labor force of about 8 million)[5] this was not a bad thing at Vietnam's stage of development (with a tiny and very slowly growing industrial sector). The average size of existing Delta farms was not sub-optimal, especially with the potential offered by the Miracle Rice varieties of seed.

Some additional fragmentation of farm operating units was occurring in Hoa Binh Thanh, and reportedly elsewhere in the floating rice areas, resulting in some plots too small to support an average family under traditional techniques of floating rice (low yield) cultivation. Where this was in fact forcing farmers more rapidly into irrigated double-cropping of Miracle Rice, however, as reported by some, it could be listed as a long-run favorable effect for developmental purposes. Our own research indicated the immediate effects of the fragmentation and disruption forced on HBT farmers by the LTTT Program were demoralizing and productively adverse, but that in fact those farmers still tenants on small plots of land were showing the way to a more productive future in this area. Floating rice areas occupy a minor (although by no means insignificant) portion of the Delta, however, and fragmentation of farm operating units could not be attributed to the LTTT Program elsewhere.

With respect to the land area under cultivation, there were perhaps some minor losses due to landowners' reported refusal to rent out land previously but no longer intensively cultivated by themselves (renting it out was in fact illegal), for fear of seeing it expropriated, preferring instead to cultivate it by themselves less intensively than would been possible by renting it out in small plots to able-bodied tenants. This was no doubt a short-run phenomenon, however, as the law permitted such landowners to use all the **hired** labor they wished to farm such land, which could certainly include hiring supervisory labor. The prohibition was only against rental agreements, with a tenant paying the landlord so much per year for the use of his land. There was nothing said against a landowner paying a worker so much a day for the use of his labor. It surely would have been only a matter of time before landowners fully appreciated the distinction.

---

[5]"Economic Background Data" (Saigon: Joint Economic Office, USAID, July 26, 1974), p. 2.

Probably more than offsetting this minor loss in land area intensively cultivated was the reported increase in land area cultivated due (1) to the fear by abandoned or fallow land owners of losing it if they did not bring it back into cultivation and (2) to the expectation of gaining title to such land if it were brought back under cultivation by former tenants, squatters and others who knew of its whereabouts.

Marketable Surplus

The chief contribution of the land reform to increased marketing of rice paddy was through its stimulating effect on production. Without the substantial rise in production, it is probable that paddy sales would have dropped relative to demand as a result of the LTTT Program.

The evidence presented in Chapter VI regarding the LTTT-title-recipient "marginal propensity to consume (MPC) disposable paddy" makes it pretty clear the former tenant's income-elasticity of demand for food is positive, and that they tended to consume (or use as feed) a higher proportion of any incremental rice paddy at their disposal the smaller the increment itself.   With rents abolished, with no payment for the land received exacted from former tenants, and with land taxes on redistributed land remitted completely for one year and then remaining at very low levels (total rural property taxes amounted to less than 1.0 percent of the value of the total rice harvest in 1973-4),[6] the amount of paddy remaining in the hands of former tenants increased by about the amount of their former rents, and their on-farm consumption would have increased by a portion of that amount.

Many landlords had formerly received rental payments in-kind (in rice), out of which they retained at least a portion for their own household consumption. The LTTT Program, by abolishing this source of rice, forced these landlord families onto the market to purchase their consumption needs, thus increasing the total **market** demand for rice. If the level of production had remained unchanged, there is no question but that increased farm consumption by former tenants and higher market demand by ex-landlord families would have reduced the marketable surplus **relative** to market demand, assuming the landlords did not substantially reduce their daily rice consumption habits.

---

[6]"**GVN Tax Performance**," attached to Enclosure 3 of a letter from Robert S. Ingersoll, Acting Secretary of State, to the Hon. John Sparkman, Chairman, Committee on Foreign Relations, U.S. Senate, March 18, 1975.

As it turned out, the land reform program, by enhancing investment incentives and simultaneously making a larger aggregate pool of investment funds available (through abolished rents and more accessible credit) to up to 50 percent of the Delta farmers, at a time when the vastly more profitable Miracle Rice seeds were being introduced and made readily available (along with all the required technical knowledge and modern inputs) through other government programs, no doubt contributed in large measure to the rapid growth in total rice production, and therefore to the resulting increase in the marketable surplus. The point is that a net positive effect on the marketable surplus can only be attributed to the LTTT program as a result of its stimulating effects on total production, and that due credit must also be given to the favorable timing and progressive economic environment surrounding the program. This favorable environment includes, moreover, the ready availability of non-agricultural consumer goods, durable goods, housing materials, and capital equipment which the farmers desired to purchase with the money earned from selling rice. It is these items which provide the real and basic incentive to produce more rice for the market in the first place—the possibility of an actual rise in the farmer's **real** standard of living, his **real** income.

Distribution of Income

There is no question that the LTTT Program effected a major redistribution of wealth and income from the landlord to the tenants. Whether as the percentage reduction in cultivated land area tenanted, in the number of farmers renting or in the Gini index of land ownership distribution by size, it is clear that the LTTT Program, as the capstone of two decades of reform, had a major effect on the distribution of land-based wealth.[7] Close to half of the total riceland area in South Vietnam was redistributed under the program from landlords to about half of all farm operators. If, as estimated, some 65 percent of all farmers were tenants before LTTT and 15 percent remained tenants afterwards, 77 percent of the tenants became owners under the program.

The degree of income redistribution resulting from the transfer of productive land resources was diminished neither by purchase payments from the former tenants to the landlords or the government, nor by higher taxes. The new owners received the full amount of remitted rents in real, inflation-proof rice paddy, while government compensation payments to the landlords rapidly lost their real value due to high levels of inflation and a lack of

---

[7]See Chapter V for a discussion of these measures of land ownership distribution among farmers in the villages under study.

productive investment mechanisms and opportunities. Where production costs equalled approximately 25 percent of the annual harvest and rents another 25 percent, the remission of rents raised the proportion of the rice harvest left for the farmers' use by around 50 percent.

In addition, there is the more important question of incremental income distribution as agricultural development proceeded and average farm productivity increased. The LTTT Program eliminated the non-cultivating landlord's claim on any future increases in production (on all but about 15 percent of the riceland) and assured that the farmers themselves would share such benefits with only hired labor and their local governments (since local taxes were bound to increase eventually).

Employment

The LTTT Program was apparently having a positive effect on the rural demand for labor, with enhanced investment incentives and increased investment funds coming at a time when extremely profitable, labor-intensive, modern technology was available in the form of the high-yield, Miracle Rice varieties, permitting, in large areas of the Delta, a switch from single-cropping to irrigated double-cropping patterns of cultivation.

In addition, farmers were spending a significant portion of their higher incomes on such things as housing materials, construction labor, basic household furniture, local education and other services, in effect replacing at least a portion of their former landlord's demand for more luxurious and more often imported items and for education abroad with a greater demand for goods and services produced locally. This effect was also increasing aggregate demand for domestic labor.

There was some increase in investment in domestic industry and commerce by landlords, using their compensation payments, as indicated in the discussions of Chapters VII and IX, above. The government was slow to encourage or facilitate this use of funds, however, and its total impact was probably minor, especially with inflation so rapidly eroding the real value of these funds and corruption in the compensation process eating away at their nominal value, as well. Other government programs provided subsidized credit for productive investments of many kinds, and the principal positive effect of the LTTT Program on industrial employment was to help redirect aggregate demand away from imports and toward the more basic, domestically produced goods and services desired by poor farmers, and thus to increase profitability of investment in these areas.

Industrial Development

The income transfer and production effects of the LTTT Program increased the disposable income of lower-income farmers, resulting in a greater effective demand for the kinds of manufactured goods, construction materials and services desired by that economic stratum. The positive agricultural production effects alone meant that more food and industrial crops would be available to support the domestic industrial sector, to reduce import requirements, and perhaps to eventually provide some surplus for export, thus conserving and earning foreign exchange needed for industrial investment. Part of the landlord compensation funds were being invested in domestic industry and commerce, but for the reasons noted above this probably had a very minor impact. More important was the rapid growth of the private rural banking system. Many of these banks were capitalized in part with landlord funds, building a more efficient financial capability to attract savings from not only the ex-landlords, but eventually from the masses of farmers themselves, and to serve as a mechanism to transfer rural savings to productive non-agricultural investments as rural development progressed and rural incomes increased. The production and income effects of the LTTT Program and the stronger institutional foundation the program was helping to build in rural areas greatly enhanced the future prospects of enterprises like the rural banks, and this had profound implications for the success of the economic development process for the nation as a whole.

Infrastructure Development

The pages above report an increasing farmer interest in local projects to build and maintain schools, roads, bridges, health facilities, irrigation canals, and the like, and a special interest in the education of their children. Many interviewees spoke of landownership status as a stimulus to farmer participation and initiative in local projects and activities, although hard, convincing evidence of the LTTT Program's effects **per se** in this regard was not obtained.

With rents abolished and farm productivity rising, due to new technology, the local land tax potential was rising, and that can be attributed in large part to the LTTT Program. Influential and predominantly (in terms of power) urban-based landlords had managed to keep both land taxes and rural infrastructure investment low, until for reasons of political strategy the central government undertook to raise rural development expenditures in more recent years (but without raising rural taxes significantly). There seemed to be little resistance among the new owners to at least a moderate increase in land taxes, and certainly there was an expectation that such an increase **would** occur "to help pay for the land." Combined with the farmer's interest in improving his own local facilities, it would no doubt have been even more acceptable to most farmers to raise his "developmental taxes" to cover desirable local public works. This was already being done on a very modest scale in conjunction with some of the "self-help" rural development programs, with the central government contributing materials, and such programs seemed to be enthusiastically received.

The contribution of the LTTT Program to the potential infrastructure development of the rural areas can only be listed as positive.

Inflation

Since the apparently detrimental effect of the LTTT Program on the marketable surplus of rice was more than offset by concurrent increases in production, the only significantly negative macroeconomic effect of this land redistribution was its inflationary impact on prices. Landlord compensation payments were supported by neither an increase in tax receipts nor payments from former tenants, and they were only partially offset, along with the rest of the government deficit, by U.S. budgetary support (from the sale of U.S.-financed imports) and government borrowing from the private sector. The U.S. provided US$ 40 million in direct support of the estimated US$ 400 million LTTT Program. It is not clear that the rest of the economic aid actually provided was at all higher because of the LTTT Program than it would have been without it, since the decisions on annual aid magnitudes were the result of political realities and compromises in the U.S. Congress and bore little relation, in the early 1970's, to the amounts requested by the President.

Had the landlords saved all of their compensation funds they would have prevented the inflationary effects. In fact, however, they were spending a large portion of them for consumption purposes and investing in consumer durables, house repair and reconstruction, and business activities of various kinds, all of which increase aggregate domestic demand insofar as they purchase domestic goods and services.

Nor were the farmers counteracting these pressures by selling the rice representing remitted rents and saving the cash proceeds. They were consuming more rice at home, reducing the amount marketed out of normal yields relative to an aggregate demand made higher by new ex-landlord market requirements, and they were selling the rest, not in order to save cash, but in order to purchase other consumer and investment goods and services, increasing aggregate demand relative to supply.

Insofar as increased investment and work incentives raised the former tenants' productivity per hectare and per unit of capital expended and caused him to substitute more work and output for formerly leisure time, a counter-inflationary force was created in the form of higher production. The evidence indicates this counter-force of productivity growth was probably of some significance, but it was probably not large and rapid enough to balance the short-term inflationary impact of the unsupported compensation payments.

Socio-Political Effects

The LTTT Program, like most land reforms, was undertaken primarily for reasons of political strategy, in this case in the struggle against the Viet Cong insurgents. The general success of this and other elements of the Republic of Vietnam's "counter-insurgency" effort in the Mekong Delta reduced the insurgent forces to very low levels of potency in the early 1970's. One of the ironies of the tragic conflict in Vietnam is that by 1975 the RVN had apparently won the war of insurgency, considered the more intractable threat by their American ally, and then lost the conflict to a conventional invading army due to reduced logistical support and a classic battlefield blunder.

The focus of the research reported in this volume, however, was not related to the more immediate, tactical objectives of the LTTT Program so much as to its long-run impact on the Vietnamese society and polity and how it might help or hinder long-run goals of economic development. Our evidence on political and social matters is more scanty than on the economic effects, and therefore our conclusions are more speculative. What clues and opinions we did find, as discussed in the chapters above, tended to confirm rather than contradict normal theoretical expectations, given the nature of the reforms and the context in which they were undertaken.

It seems to the writer that the LTTT Program can be credited with significant contributions toward conditions 1) more conducive to political stability than had existed before, 2) leading toward a more equitable distribution of social status and political power, as well as of wealth and income, 3) establishing the basis for greater institutional flexibility in the future, 4) broadening the base of the national talent search to include a much larger proportion of farm families, and 5) stimulating more favorable social attitudes toward change and innovation. These conditions would have provided a more favorable institutional framework for the processes of modernization and economic development.

Political Stability

Many of the more vivid descriptions by our interviewees were of the inequities and injustices of the old landlord-tenant system. Most of the farmers in our sample viewed the elimination of that system as a positive contribution toward greater equity and social justice.

With few exceptions, landlords were no longer in a position to exercise excessive influence in community affairs, to demand menial services and excessively high rents from tenants, and to put themselves above the law in their dealings with tenants and village officials. Much of this had occurred before the LTTT Program, and considerable credit must be given to the influence of the Viet Minh, Viet Cong, Hoa Hao and other peasant-based movements; but the LTTT Program severed the last legal link with the old tenure system and formally established a new one, with no small psychological impact on former tenants, even in areas where **de facto** landlord influence had almost been eliminated already.

With ownership, former tenants received a **security** of income probably as important to most of them as the increase in income levels provided by the remission of rents. New title-recipient farmers no longer had to fear that the return of peace and political stability would bring landlords home to demand higher rents, to threaten them even implicitly with eviction, and to exercise such pervasive social and political control as in the prewar era.

It was to be expected that a government implementing such reforms and providing such important benefits should enjoy greater active and passive political support, and less active opposition, from its beneficiaries, and we found contrary evidence in neither our own research nor in the relevant research of others. The exact degree of the greater political support creditable to the LTTT Program alone cannot be identified, but it was clear that support for the insurgents in the Delta was waning in the early 1970's as the whole package of the government's rural development programs was being favorably received.

Nor was political stability reduced by any discernable "leadership gap" created by the further reduction in landlord influence and power. Landlord control over local public affairs had seldom been exercised through their direct involvement as village officials, but rather through the appointment of "trusted" tenants or relatives to key positions. Some of these officials retained some positions in local affairs, but were now catering to a new political power base and, in the case of former tenants, were operating with a new sense of personal status and independence as new landowners themselves. In other cases the more recent village elections were disposing of the old slate of officers and installing a new one more in tune with the new political realities of the village. The LTTT Program deserves credit for only a complimentary role in this process. Many farmers interviewed described it as an historical process beginning many years ago, with two recent village elections seen as the most significant recent steps in a chain of events that had transferred village political control from the exclusive domain of wealthy, landlord families to a popularly-elected group of middle-class and even poor farmers. Some former landlords questioned the **quality** of the new village leaders, but most farmers seemed to feel much more satisfied with them as representative of and working for their own interests. In any case, although the official village positions were seen as much more work for much less actual remuneration than before, the four villages we visited had filled them with capable and respected men.

An increased level of conflict between landlords and tenants could have been damaging to political stability, but disputes leading to physical harassment or violence were surprisingly few and isolated and, as discussed in Chapter IX, the level of non-violent landlord-tenant disputes settled within the village framework or in the Special Land Courts was extremely low. Since in most cases the aggrieved party was the landlord losing his land, and since the landlord had to depend on the government for security against the insurgents, the anger of a landlord seldom led him into a direct challenge against the government. Many of the former tenants, on the other hand, did have the option of providing more help to the insurgent forces; but since they saw the government siding with them against the landlords in the LTTT Program they were more willing to let the legal processes take place peacefully, including long, drawn-out court proceedings where necessary.

Another threat to political stability during a land reform program can stem from irregularities in the implementation of the law by local authorities or from extensive corruption in the process, whether irregular or not. Again, as discussed in the preceding chapter, the LTTT Program seemed to be remarkably free of either irregularities or corruption in its implementation, particularly in the distribution of land titles to the former tenants. Where bribery was reported in connection with title distribution it was, with rare exceptions, for such small amounts—"tea" money or a duck for a celebration feast—as to be no more than a minor irritant to farmers receiving the cherished gift of landownership.

Corruption was reportedly much more serious in the landlord compensation process, and a large number of landlords were livid with rage over the situation. Again, however, the landlords were trapped. Their numbers were small, they did not dare do anything which could seriously damage political stability and weaken the government side, and they could find no solace in going over to or strengthening the hand of the communists. They needed the government more than it needed them.

This is not to say that the LTTT Program completely solved the problems of political instability facing the Republic of Vietnam, for obviously it did not. It is to say, however, that, at least in large parts of the Mekong Delta, it would appear the land reform had a stabilizing effect and that there was no evidence of any significantly destabilizing effects. The relative stability of the early 1970's allowed the government to implement several rural developmental projects in the Delta that were producing some very positive economic results.

Distribution of Social Status and Political Power

A tremendous amount of prestige and social status accompanies the ownership of a piece of land in Vietnamese society, as opposed to being a landless tenant. Even without an increase in real wealth and income, the redistribution of land effected a greater redistribution of social status and, with it, political influence within the local community than most Americans unfamiliar with Vietnamese cultural characteristics would realize. In addition, the actual redistribution of income that did accompany the land was significantly large and further enhanced the social position and political influence of the former tenants, as it would in most societies. The simple fact that the title-recipients were better able to pay the small, "tea-money" bribes required for timely official service on routine matters enhanced their ability to use the system to their own advantage.

Operating from much reduced circumstances and without their former landownership base, landlord families saw their economic and social positions seriously eroded, and with those positions also went much of their former political power and influence, especially within the local communities where they lost their land. Many landlord sons retained influential military or governmental positions due to their education and family connections, but they would not be able to rely on the same "wealthy landlord" base to secure the future of **their** sons.

With the rise of a landed, small-farmer class into numerical and (at least potentially) social and political dominance in rural areas, and with the prospective fall of most of the landlord class back onto more of a dependence on their own intelligent efforts for future success, a more egalitarian social polity was being established with brighter prospects for modern economic development.

Institutional Flexibility

The LTTT Program provided a major input into the creation of a larger "middle-class" of small owner-cultivators in the rural areas of the Delta, and there was some evidence it was helping to encourage and stimulate broader participation by farmers in local political and social affairs. The Program was responsible for a further sizeable reduction in the economic and political power of the landlords and many of the traditionally elite families of the village, and it was simultaneously raising the economic and political power potential of lower and middle income groups of farmers. This had profound implications for the future development of local institutions—their character, their power structure, their chief concerns, activities and operating procedures, and their flexibility to meet the changing needs of a modernizing agricultural sector.

A military-dominated elite had actually taken the political reins of power from the landlords, but it was a modernizing elite that sought the active support of the rural population and that saw itself as building the institutional base for more rapid economic progress and broader political participation in the future. So even though institutional flexibility based on broader participation became for the moment more of a potential and an ideal than an actuality, it was nevertheless a real potential that was closer to achievement than before, with positive implications for future economic progress.

National Talent Search

With the reduction in rural class distinctions, formerly polarized between the wealthy landlord elite and the broad mass of poor and landless tenants and farm workers, with a relatively small middle-class of owner-cultivators in between, it could be expected that vertical social mobility would be enhanced and would improve as the years went by. So many old attitudes and social rigidities were no longer relevant and could no longer be sustained.

In addition, it seemed that a latent interest and support among farmers for various aspects of rural development, such as the improvement of educational facilities and opportunities, was being mobilized, and that ownership status and the social possibilities **and responsibilities** it conferred deserved some of the credit. Government-sponsored programs to develop rural infrastructure (and hopefully to gain more political support thereby) were indeed being met with considerable enthusiasm by Delta farmers, with a resultant expansion of educational and economic opportunities for rural youth, providing the promise of a fuller and more efficient future utilization of the nation's resource pool of human talent.

Social Attitudes Toward Change and Innovation

The LTTT Program represented a major change in the institutional structure of land ownership and tenure in Vietnam. Its obvious benefits won it a welcome reception among most Delta farmers. In a context where the traditional land tenure institution was distasteful, but where previous attempts to alter it extralegally had brought conflict and danger, the experience of a legal and relatively peaceful reform of such magnitude was enlightening. Many of the farmers in our sample discussed other new ideas and innovations they would like to see tried or, in the case of new production techniques, intended to try themselves (or were already doing so). The possibilities for improvement through change and innovation were frequently recognized, and there was no hankering (except among a few landlords) for a return to the "good old days," nor even for a continuation of the current status quo. The Mekong Delta seemed to be poised for a period of significant and rapid economic and social change toward a more equitable and efficient society.

The LTTT Program in Perspective

As discussed in Chapter I, a reformation of landownership institutions is only one step in the process of modernization—the process of rationalizing social, economic, and political activities and relationships to take advantage of the productive potential offered by modern scientific and technological knowledge. That step was a difficult one, taking three decades in South Vietnam; but it had been successfully completed before the fall of the Republic of Vietnam in 1975. Except for the achievement of political and military peace a favorable institutional framework had apparently been established for rapid agricultural development.

The long-hoped-for conclusion of the war and the achievement of peace in 1975 left political control in the hands of a communist government that lost little time in announcing the abolition of the Land-to-the-Tiller Reforms and its own intentions to re-distribute landownership. The ultimate nature of landownership institutions in South Vietnam is therefore yet to be determined, and whether the communist institutions will be as successful in stimulating and sustaining higher agricultural productivity as the small-farmer ownership pattern established by the LTTT Program will no doubt be an intriguing topic for future analysis and debate.

Post Script

As this manuscript is being edited in late 1979 for publication, it appears the agricultural potential of the Mekong Delta has so far eluded the authorities of the new Socialist Republic of Vietnam (SRV). After reaching 11.0 million metric tons in 1973 and 1974 and rising to 12.1 million M.T. in the exceptionally good year of 1976, rice paddy production dropped to 10.9 million M.T. in 1977 and 9.9 million in 1978, below the total for 1969.[8] At the minimum per capita requirement of 240 kilograms of paddy annually, total domestic production fell 0.8 million M.T. short of national self-sufficiency in 1977, 2.1 million M.T. short in 1978.[9] After averaging above 240 kg. per person from 1970 through 1976, despite a population growth rate of 2.2 percent, annual paddy production dropped to 223 kg. per capita in 1977 and 198 kg. in 1978.

An official Hanoi estimate prepared in early 1979 projected a 1979 food deficit equivalent to 3.8 million tons of paddy, but subsequent floods in Central Vietnam and the loss of production in war zones could push this year's deficit even higher. An August 1979 Radio Hanoi broadcast indicated the spring 1979 rice harvest in the North was much lower than in previous seasons, due to late planting and fertilizer shortages.[10]

Bad weather and lack of foreign exchange to purchase fertilizer have certainly contributed to the recent decline in rice production, but institutional and economic incentive factors seem to be plaguing the South. "In a sort of passive resistance to the socialization policy, peasants in the rich Mekong Delta often do not grow more than the amount required for their own consumption and they would rather feed surplus grain to cattle or make alcohol rather than sell to the government."[11]

This observation is supported by other research and commentary, including that from within the SRV itself. According to Professor Duiker, the 1975 rural situation in the South was considered by the communist leadership to be ready for a fairly

---

[8]**Key Indicators,** Asian Development Bank (ADB), October 1979, p. 14, citing FAO as source.

[9]See footnote 25, Chapter III, on page 39. The population of Vietnam was estimated to be 48.73 million in 1977, 49.89 million in 1978. **Key Indicators,** p. 1, citing as its source the United Nations **Monthly Bulletin of Statistics,** August 1979.

[10]Nayan Chanda, "Vietnam's Battle of the Home Front," **Far Eastern Economic Review,** November 2, 1979, p. 45.

[11]Ibid., p. 48.

rapid advance toward socialism. The Land-to-the-Tiller Law had reduced the power of feudal forces and the "nearly completed" land reform had almost eliminated landlords and created a large base of private land-owning peasants. Therefore, another land reform program similar to that conducted in the North in the 1950's prior to collectivization was apparently not considered necessary. Le Duan, the Secretary General of the Vietnamese Workers' Party (VWP), told the Fourth Party Congress in January 1977 that the socialist transformation of the rural South must be completed by 1980.[12]

Discussing the drop in grain production in 1977, Douglas Pike lists "confusion over the program to collectivize agriculture in the South" as a contributing factor. Although a Communist Party plenum in June 1977 resolved to complete the collectivization process in 1978 and 1979, later reports became vague about the exact timetable. Pike describes the collectivization process as apparently inevitable ("It is not a question of **whether,** but of when . . . "), to be "accomplished in stages, moving progressively from market-ing/production co-ops (much like those elsewhere) to true collectives, communes, and state farms, and then finally to the ulti-mate—creation of some 500 giant agro-farms each employing 100,000 or more farm workers." The early stages are "designed to condition farmers to the essential changes brought about by collectivization, chiefly loss of ownership of land, a new system of allocating the fruits of the harvest, and the replacement of individual incentive with communal spirit."[13]

Citing the "general opposition to the collectivist regime" in the South, "combined with bad management, sloth and corruption and finally inclement weather," the **Far Eastern Economic Review** concluded that the sharp decline in agricultural production in 1977 and 78 "was affected by a more fundamental factor" than the problems of floods and pests—"the peasant's unwillingness to produce more than he needed when the surplus did not fetch much money or consumer goods." **Nhan Dan,** the Communist Party daily, carried an article in May 1978 lamenting the poor agricultural performance in the South and expressing resentment that the peasants did not seem to understand "their obligations to the state and expected consumer goods in exchange for rice." Another **Nhan Dan** article in September 1978 "complained that peasants left paddy fields

---

[12]William J. Duiker, "Ideology and Nation-Building in the Democratic Republic of Vietnam," **Asian Survey,** University of California Press, May 1977, pp. 421-2 and 426.

[13]Douglas Pike, "Vietnam in 1977: More of the Same," **Asian Survey,** University of California Press, January 1978, pp. 68-70.

uncultivated and wasted rice by using it to distill alcohol or to feed pigs and ducks, while rice is in short supply in a number of cities."[14]

Some reports indicated that, in the Fourth Plenum of the Party Central Committee, meeting in July 1978, a majority group of hardliners led by Defense Minister Vo Nguyen Giap upheld the orthodox Marxist view that peasants were backward and needed the guidance of the working class. "The plenum is believed to have decided to accelerate collectivisation of southern agriculture . . . "[15]

How soon this approach can enable the SRV to realize the enormous productive potential of the Mekong Delta remains to be seen.

[14]"Vietnam," **Far Eastern Economic Review**, **Asia 1979 Yearbook**, pp. 317 and 321-22.
[15]Ibid., p. 317.

APPENDICES

APPENDIX A

LAND-TO-THE-TILLER POLICY
IN THE
REPUBLIC OF VIET-NAM

Following is an unofficial translation of the complete text of Law No. 003/70 of March 26, 1970 governing the Land-to-the-Tiller Policy in the Republic of Viet-Nam.

Chapter I

OBJECTIVE-MEASURES TO BE APPLIED

Article I

Land-to-the-Tiller Policy set forth by this law is aimed at:
— Providing ownership to farmers by making those people actually cultivating landowners and allowing them to receive all of the benefits from their labor.
— Equal opportunity for advancement among all farmers.

Article II

In order to achieve the above-mentioned objectives, the following measures shall be applied:
1. Expropriate with fair compensation lands which are not directly cultivated by landowners for distribution free of charge to farmers.
2. Eliminate tenancy, and land speculation by middlemen.
3. Distribution of communal riceland.

Chapter II

SCOPE OF APPLICATION

Article 3

This law applies to riceland and secondary cropland belonging to private persons or legal entities, under public or private jurisdiction.

Article 4

Lands recorded in the Land Register under the name of one owner will be considered as a single property unit. Any transfer not registered prior to the promulgation date of this law is null and void. Lands registered separately under the names of a man and his wife shall be considered as a single private property unit, except in case of marriage under the separate property system.

Article 5

This law does not apply to the following categories of land:
1. Land presently directly cultivated by landowners or their spouses or parents or children or legal heirs not exceeding fifteen hectares. Landowners directly cultivating their land have the right to hire laborers to farm.
2. Ancestral worship land (Huong Hoa, Hau Dien, and Ky Dien) and cemetery land not exceeding five hectares for each family.
3. Land presently owned by religious organizations.
4. Industrial cropland and orchard land (excluding crops having a life of less than one year).
5. Industrial building sites.
6. Salt fields, lakes and ponds, and pasture land on livestock farms.
7. Land designated on maps for urban planning, residential areas, and gravesites.
8. Land in experimental centers and agricultural demonstration projects.
9. Land specifically reserved in Montagnard **buons** and hamlets in accordance with Decree-Laws 003/67 and 034/67 dated August 29, 1967.
10. Land for public interest.
11. Land that has never been planted in rice and is cleared after promulgation of this law.

Article 6

Categories of land indicated in items 2, 3, 4, 5, 6, 8, 10 and 11 of Article 5 shall be governed by separate supplemental laws.

Any change in land use aimed at avoiding application of this law shall be considered null and void.

Chapter III

LANDLORD COMPENSATION

Article 7

Landlords having land expropriated will be compensated quickly and fairly.

The rate of compensation will be determined by a Special Committee. This Committee shall be established by a Decree.

Article 8

The rate of compensation shall be equivalent to two and one-half times the annual paddy yield of the land. Annual yield means the average yield during the past five years.

Article 9

Landlords shall be compensated according to the following standards:
— 20 percent of the value of the expropriated land shall be paid immediately in cash.
— The remainder shall be paid in bonds guaranteed by the Government over eight years and bearing 10 percent interest.
In case land ownership and usufruct right belong to two different persons, the compensation to each should be determined by the Special Committee mentioned above.

Article 10

Bonds may be pledged, transferred, used as payment of hypothecs and payment of land tax, or to buy shares in private or national enterprises.

Article 11

Rights of privileged creditors, pledgers, hypothecators or heirs will become the creditors' right with respect to the amount of compensation to landlords based on the legal status of the land in the Land Register.

Chapter IV

BENEFICIARIES

Article 12

Land for distribution will be distributed free of charge to each farm family with a maximum area of:
— Three hectares in Southern Viet-Nam
— One hectare in Central Viet-Nam.
A farm family is comprised of parents, spouses and children living together in a house and listed on the family card.

Article 13

Land for distribution shall be distributed in the following order of priority:

1. Present tiller: Present tillers are those people cultivating land belonging to another person.

2. Parents, spouse or children of war dead who will directly cultivate the land, if they have submitted an application.

3. Soldiers, civil servants and cadre when discharged or retired who will directly cultivate the land, if they have submitted an application.

4. Soldiers, civil servants and cadre who had to abandon cultivation because of the war, if they have submitted an application in order for their families to directly cultivate the land.

5. Farm laborers who will directly cultivate the land, if they have submitted an application.

In any case, land distributed added to the land already owned cannot exceed the area fixed in Article 12.

Article 14

Persons receiving land are exempted from registration tax, stamp tax, land administration fees and all other fees relating to the transfer of land, and shall be exempted from any tax related to the distributed land in the first year.

Article 15

Persons receiving distributed land must directly cultivate the land themselves.

For a period of fifteen years starting from the date he becomes owner, the person receiving land distributed under this law cannot transfer ownership, or agree to establish real right on the land received except in case of prior official authorization. A person (or his spouse) who has sold distributed land will not be given land a second time.

Article 16

Any farmer who has received expropriated land under Ordinance 57 or former French-owned land and has not completed purchase payments to the Government shall be exempted from payment of the balance due. Persons who have paid over 50 percent of the purchase price will not be subject to Article 15, paragraph 2 of this law.

Chapter V

PUNITIVE MEASURES

Article 17

Any person acting to prevent implementation of this law will be sentenced from six months to three years imprisonment or fined from VN\$ 20,000 to VN\$ 200,000 or both.

Article 18

Any landlord as determined in Article 5, paragraph 1 who refuses to directly cultivate his land shall have his entire property expropriated without compensation.

Article 19

Any farmer violating Article 15 by not directly cultivating the land will be expropriated without compensation. The land shall be redistributed to other farmers under the provisions of this law.

Article 20

Any lawsuit that occurs in the implementation of this law will be under the jurisdiction of the Land Court, composed of professional judges.

Any violation of provisions regarding penal law will be under jurisdiction of the Civil Court.

Chapter VI

COMMON PROVISIONS

Article 21

Regulations for implementation of this law shall be fixed by Decree.

Article 22

Any provisions contrary to this law are cancelled.

This law will be promulgated according to emergency procedures and published in the Official Gazette of the Republic of Viet-Nam.

APPENDIX B

SAMPLE SELECTION
AND INTERVIEW METHODS

Most of the first three and one-half months in-country was spent drafting, translating, pre-testing, editing and printing three basic interview forms for use in the field. Standard interview forms were used for two reasons. First, the detailed nature of the economic information desired made it imperative to write most of the responses down during the interview, despite its disadvantage of introducing a more formal atmosphere into the discussion. Second, with my wife and I conducting most of the interviews separately in order to obtain a larger sample, the forms were necessary to insure comparability of our separate sets of interview responses.

In translating preliminary English drafts into Vietnamese we received invaluable assistance from Mr. Nguyen-van-Hieu and Mr. Le-Tin of the Control Data Corporation, who were especially helpful with the more technical terms.

Ten pre-test interviews were conducted in An-Phu-Tay Village, Binh-Chanh District, Gia-Dinh Province, chosen mostly for its proximity to our residence in Cholon. After much editing and rewriting, sufficient copies were mimeographed for our project.

It would have been helpful to have spent more time pre-testing and rewriting the forms before committing them to the printer. But our research time was limited, and we spent as many weeks in the preparation phase as we dared. We continued to identify errors, omissions and unrealistic or poorly-phrased (for rural Vietnamese comprehension) questions during subsequent field interviews. With only two people conducting the interviews, however, we were able to maintain sufficient control while using the forms mostly as a topic guide and a record of responses, rewording questions to achieve communication and making the necessary corrections as we went along.

Our field operating procedure was to contact the USAID province advisor for land reform and, after making courtesy calls on interested American advisory officials, to rely on him and a letter from the Directorate General of Land Affairs to introduce us to the Vietnamese Province Land Affairs Service chief. From the latter we obtained a list of all landlords who had applied for compensation payments for land expropriated in the village under study. We stratified these according to the number of hectares lost and drew a sample of 10 for each village out a hat, weighting the sample so that each stratum was represented in roughly the same proportion as its share of the total hectarage expropriated. This procedure reduced the sample bias toward the numerically greater small landlord group and gives a fairer representation of the piaster amounts of compensation involved, the disposition of which was our chief interest.

Either the USAID land reform advisor or someone from the Province Land Affairs Service introduced us to the chiefs of the district and the village where we wished to conduct our interviews. The Village Office was a source of current population, agricultural and land reform data. The village chief passed us on to the chiefs of the hamlets chosen for research based on security assessments by the district and village chiefs. After the first village we limited ourselves to those hamlets secure enough for us to enter unescorted on a routine, daily basis.

The establishment of close rapport with and the elimination of suspicion among the village residents were high on our list of priority activities. We found that the presence of my wife, who is Vietnamese, as my research assistant was helpful in this regard, especially among the women, who often seemed suspicious of a lone American male. On the other hand, my appearance also seemed to dispel fears that my wife was a government tax agent. The reaction seemed to be that we were an unlikely team for either government to send to the field, and that only true students would be working as we were. We thus made it a point to be seen and to make our initial introduction together, although we normally conducted our interviews separately.

From each hamlet chief we obtained a list of all household numbers in his hamlet, making it clear that we were not taking names. We drew these numbers out of a hat until we obtained a number of rice farmers proportional to the hamlet's share of village population, for a total of 15 farmers in the village. We then asked the hamlet chief to show us the location of each house we had drawn; and this normally resulted in short visits to each house, complete with introductions by the hamlet chief (a valuable aid to later rapport), and explanations of how they were selected and of their anonymity in our study.

There was always great interest in our method of drawing lots out of a hat. It elicited expressions of approval of the fairness of our research efforts and of the fact that we would take the trouble to interview even the most out-of-the-way, poor and illiterate farmers, if we happened to draw their numbers. Accordingly, we often took the extra time to perform the drawing in the presence of the hamlet chief and his deputies, or in some fairly public place, asking the observers to take turns drawing the numbers.

What we actually drew were 15 **sets** of 3 farmers each, to give us a total of 45 farmers. For comparative purposes we desired to interview 15 present tenants, 15 LTTT title-recipients and 15 original owner-cultivators in each village. Our practice was to interview each of the 15 farmers whose lots we had drawn, to determine his tenure status, and then to ask him to show us the houses of one neighboring farmer in each of the other two categories. This procedure introduced a random element in our selection process while enabling us to interview an equal number of each category. The hamlet chief could usually tell us which households were farmers and which were not (even then his memory was not always accurate), but it was a rare chief who could look at his family register and remember for certain whether each household was a tenant, a new owner, or an old owner.

In addition to the farmers and former landlords, we interviewed ten hamlet chiefs, village officials, merchants, resident school-teachers and other village leaders to elicit their opinions and observations about the matters under study. There was no attempt to be random in this group of interviews.

One problem was the lack of interviewee availability, which was especially acute during the first two months in the field due to the harvest season and Lunar New Year (**Tet**) preparations. We intentionally adopted a low-key approach, making it clear that we did not wish to take the farmer away from pressing work requirements or other commitments and responsibilities, since government delegations usually took the opposite attitude, and as a result we often had to make several trips back before we caught the respondent at home with a couple of hours to spare. In our first and fourth villages, we were occasionally able to make advance appointments that were of some help (though many were forgotten by people who are not accustomed to making appointments); but we were cautioned against this practice as an unnecessary risk in our second and third villages, which were somewhat less "secure." The interviews averaged between two and three hours each.

APPENDIX C

STATISTICAL TABLES

Table A-1

LAND OWNERSHIP DISTRIBUTION IN THE SOUTHERN REGION, 1955, INCLUDING LANDLESS TENANTS AND OWNERS, REPUBLIC OF VIETNAM

(1) Size Category (n) (hectares)	(2) Number of Owners & Landless Tenants	(3) Percent of owners & tenants $(X_n - X_{n-1})$	(4) Cumulative % of owners & tenants (X_n)	(5) Area Owned (hectares)	(6) Percent of area $(Y_n - Y_{n-1})$	(7) Cumulative % of area (Y_n)	(8) $(Y_n + Y_{n-1})$ from col.(7)	(9) $(X_n - X_{n-1}) \times (Y_n + Y_{n-1}) =$ columns (3)x(8)
1. 0	222,110[1]	46.70[1]	46.70	0	0	0	0	0
2. 0.1-4.9	183,670	38.62	85.32	360,000	16.44	16.44	16.44	634.9
3. 5.0-9.9	37,110	7.80	93.12	284,000	12.97	29.41	45.85	357.6
4. 10.0-49.9	26,840	5.64	98.76	526,000	24.02	53.43	82.84	467.2
5. 50.0-99.9	3,550	0.75	99.51	273,000	12.47	65.90	119.33	89.5
6. 100.0 - up	2,330	0.49	100.00	747,000	34.11	100.01	165.91	81.3
TOTALS	475,610	100.00		2,190,000	100.01			1630.5

Gini Index = 1.0 - .1631 = .8369   Average owned per person = 4.60 hectares

[1] Estimated as 46.7% of all farmers (see pp. 76 and 77, above) and assuming an insignificant number of landowners did not farm at all.

SOURCE: Same as Table 3-3.

Table A-2

LAND OWNERSHIP DISTRIBUTION IN THE SOUTHERN REGION, 1966, INCLUDING LANDLESS TENANTS AND OWNERS
REPUBLIC OF VIETNAM

(1) Size Category (n) (hectares)	(2) Number of Owners & Landless Tenants	(3) Percent of owners & tenants $(X_n - X_{n-1})$	(4) Cumulative % of owners & tenants (X_n)	(5) Area owned (hectares)	(6) Percent of area $(Y_n - Y_{n-1})$	(7) Cumulative % of area (Y_n)	(8) $(Y_n + Y_{n-1})$ from col.(7)	(9) $(X - X_{n-1})$x $(Y_n + Y_{n-1})$ = Column(8) (3)x(8)
1. 0	134,115[1]	42.00*	42.00	0	0	0	0	0
2. 0.1-0.4	24,185	7.57	49.57	6,046	0.62	0.62	0.62	4.7
3. 0.5-0.9	24,972	7.82	57.39	18,729	1.92	2.54	3.16	24.7
4. 1.0-2.9	68,001	21.30	78.69	136,003	13.94	16.48	19.02	405.1
5. 3.0-4.9	27,681	8.67	87.36	110,722	11.35	27.83	44.31	384.2
6. 5.0-9.9	22,850	7.16	94.52	171,378	17.56	45.39	73.22	524.3
7. 10.0-19.9	10,592	3.32	97.84	158,869	16.28	61.67	107.06	355.4
8. 20.0-29.9	2,931	0.92	98.76	73,261	7.51	69.18	130.85	120.4
9. 30.0-49.9	2,043	0.64	99.40	81,710	8.37	77.55	146.73	93.9
10. 50.0-99.9	1,389	0.43	99.83	104,140	10.67	88.22	165.77	71.3
11. 100.0-114.9	143	0.04	99.87	15,443	1.58	89.80	178.02	7.1
12. 115.0- up	419	0.13	100.00	99,449	10.19	99.99	189.79	24.7
TOTALS	319,321	100.00		975,750	99.99			2015.8

Gini Index = 1.0 - .2016 = .7984

Average owned per person = 3.06 hectares

[1]Estimated as 42.0% of all farmers (see page 76 and 77, above) and assuming an insignificant number of landowners did not farm at all.

SOURCE: Same as Table 3-4.

Table A-3

SIZE DISTRIBUTION OF OPERATING FARMS IN THE SOUTHERN REGION, 1968
REPUBLIC OF VIETNAM

(1) Size Category (n) (hectares)	(2) Number of Farmers	(3) Percent of Farmers $(X_n - X_{n-1})$	(4) Cumulative % of Farmers (X_n)	(5) Area Farmed (hectares)	(6) Percent of Area $(Y_n - Y_{n-1})$	(7) Cumulative % of Area (Y_n)	(8) $(Y_n + Y_{n-1})$ from col.(7)	(9) $(X_n - X_{n-1}) \times (Y_n + Y_{n-1}) =$ Columns (3)x(8)
1. 0.1-0.4	46	10.5	10.5	12	1.0	1.0	1.0	10.5
2. 0.5-0.9	68	15.5	25.9	41	3.3	4.3	5.3	82.2
3. 1.0-1.4	99	22.5	48.4	104	8.3	12.6	16.9	380.3
4. 1.5-1.9	33	7.5	55.9	53	4.2	16.8	29.4	220.5
5. 2.0-2.9	78	17.7	73.6	162	12.9	29.7	46.5	823.1
6. 3.0-3.9	39	8.9	82.5	121	9.6	39.3	69.0	614.1
7. 4.0-4.9	21	4.8	87.3	86	6.9	46.2	85.5	410.4
8. 5.0-7.4	29	6.6	93.9	166	13.2	59.4	105.6	697.0
9. 7.5-9.9	10	2.3	96.2	82	6.5	65.9	125.3	288.2
10. 10.0-19.9	8	1.8	98.0	100	8.0	73.9	139.8	251.6
11. 20.0-29.9	4	0.9	98.9	88	7.0	80.9	154.8	139.3
12. 30.0-49.9	2	0.5	99.4	63	5.0	85.9	166.8	83.4
13. 50.0-99.9	3	0.2	100.1	176	14.0	99.9	185.8	130.1
TOTALS	440	100.2		1254	99.9			4130.7

Gini Index = 1.0 - .4131 = .5869   Average per farmer = 2.85 hectares

SOURCE: Hamlet Resident Survey, Land Reform in Vietnam, Working Papers, Stanford Research Institute, 1968 Vol. IV, Part 2, Table 289, "Operating Farm Size."

Table A-4a

OWNERSHIP OF RICE LAND IN KHANH HAU VILLAGE, 1958, BEFORE ORDINANCE 57

(1)	(2)	(3)	(4)	(5)	(6)	(7)	(8)	(9)
Area of holdings (n) (hectares)	No. of land-owners	% of total land-owners	Cumula-tive % of total land-owners	No. of ha.	% of total ha.	Cumula-tive % of total ha.(Y_n)	From Col. 7 $(Y_n + Y_{n-1})$	Col. 3 times Col. 8
1. 0.1-2	60	46.2	46.2	52.23	5.6	5.6	5.6	258.7
2. 2-3.9	25	19.2	65.4	70.82	7.6	13.2	18.8	361.0
3. 4-5.9	14	10.8	76.2	69.71	7.5	20.7	33.9	366.1
4. 6-7.9	11	8.5	84.7	75.71	8.2	28.9	49.6	421.6
5. 8-9.9	6	4.6	89.3	54.03	5.8	34.7	63.6	292.6
6. 10-100	13	10.0	99.3	279.55	30.2	64.9	99.6	996.0
7. 100+	1	0.8	100.1	323.86	35.0	99.9	164.8	131.8
TOTAL	130	100.1		925.91	99.9			2827.8

Gini Index = 1.0 - .2828 = .717   Average holding = 7.12 ha.

Note: Includes communal and pagoda land.

SOURCE: 1958 tax rolls, Village of Khanh Hau, as reported in Hendry, _Khanh Hau_, p. 33, with minor recalculations to separate largest landowner.

Table A-4b

DISTRIBUTION OF RICELAND OWNERSHIP AFTER ORDINANCE 57, KHANH HAU VILLAGE, 1958

	(1)	(2)	(3)	(4)	(5)	(6)	(7)	(8)	(9)
	Area of holdings (n) (hectares)	No. of land-owners	% of total land-owners	Cumula-tive % of total land-owners	No. of ha.	% of total ha.	Cumula-tive % of total ha.(Y_n)	From Col. 7 ($Y_n + Y_{n-1}$)	Col. 3 times Col. 8
1.	0.1-2	168	60.2	60.2	168.6	18.2	18.2	18.2	1095.6
2.	2-3.9	61	21.9	82.1	163.1	17.6	35.8	54.0	1182.6
3.	4-5.9	19	6.8	88.9	92.6	10.0	45.8	81.6	554.9
4.	6-7.9	11	3.9	92.8	75.7	8.2	54.0	99.8	389.2
5.	8-9.9	6	2.2	95.0	54.0	5.8	59.8	113.8	250.4
6.	10-100	14	5.0	100.0	371.9	40.2	100.0	159.8	799.0
7.	100+	0	0	100.0	0	0	100.0	200.0	0
	TOTAL	279	100.0		925.9	100.0			4271.7

Gini Index = 1.0 - .427 = .573
Decline from Table 5-5a = -20.1%

Average holding = 3.32 hectares

SOURCE: Calculated from Hendry, Khanh Hau, Table 3.1 and 3.4, pp. 33 and 39.

Table A-5a

DISTRIBUTION OF PRIVATELY OWNED RICELAND IN KHANH HAU BEFORE THE LTTT PROGRAM, 1970

(1) Ownership Stratum (n) (hectares)	(2) No. of land-owners	(3) % of total owners	(4) Cumulative % of total owners	(5) Hectarage owned	(6) % of total area	(7) Cumulative % of total area (Y_n)	(8) From Col. 7 ($Y_n + Y_{n-1}$)	(9) Col. 3 times Col. 8
1. .01-.49	27	9.4	9.4	7.55	0.8	0.8	0.8	7.5
2. .50-.99	45	15.6	25.0	34.83	3.6	4.4	5.2	81.1
3. 1.00-1.49	50	17.4	42.4	62.40	6.4	10.8	15.2	264.5
4. 1.50-1.99	40	13.9	56.3	67.09	6.9	17.7	28.5	396.2
5. 2.00-2.99	47	16.3	72.6	113.40	11.6	29.3	47.0	766.1
6. 3.00-3.99	26	9.0	81.6	88.53	9.1	38.4	67.7	609.3
7. 4.00-4.99	10	3.5	85.1	45.30	4.6	43.0	81.4	284.9
8. 5.00-7.49	22	7.6	92.7	140.65	14.4	57.4	100.4	763.0
9. 7.50-9.99	9	3.1	95.8	77.95	8.0	65.4	122.8	380.7
10. 10.00-19.99	7	2.4	98.2	84.67	8.7	74.1	139.5	334.8
11. 20.00-29.99	1	0.3	98.5	28.98	3.0	77.1	151.2	45.4
12. 30.00-49.99	2	0.7	99.2	74.00	7.6	84.7	161.8	113.3
13. 50.00+	2	0.7	99.9	150.01	15.4	100.1	184.8	129.4
TOTALS	288	99.9		975.36	100.1			4176.2

Gini Index = 1.0 - .418 = .582   Average holding = 3.39 hectares

SOURCE: 1970 Land Tax Register, Village office.

Table A-5b

DISTRIBUTION OF PRIVATELY OWNED RICELAND IN KHANH HAU AFTER THE LTTT PROGRAM, 1972

(1) Ownership Stratum (n) (hectares)	(2) No. of land-owners	(3) % of total owners	(4) Cumulative % of total owners	(5) Hectarage owned	(6) % of total area	(7) Cumulative % of total area (Y_n)	(8) From Col. 7 ($Y_n + Y_{n-1}$)	(9) Col. 3 times Col. 8
1. .01-.49	37	7.8	7.8	10.87	1.1	1.1	1.1	8.58
2. .50-.99	86	18.1	25.9	58.01	6.1	7.2	8.3	150.23
3. 1.00-1.49	150	31.6	57.5	180.85	18.9	26.1	33.3	1052.28
4. 1.50-1.99	58	12.2	69.7	96.66	10.1	36.2	62.3	760.06
5. 2.00-2.99	61	12.9	82.6	144.01	15.1	51.3	87.5	1128.75
6. 3.00-3.99	40	8.4	91.0	129.81	13.6	64.9	116.2	976.08
7. 4.00-4.99	10	2.1	93.0	45.39	4.7	69.6	134.5	282.45
8. 5.00-7.49	19	4.0	97.1	111.12	11.6	81.2	150.8	603.20
9. 7.50-9.99	6	1.3	98.4	51.52	5.4	86.6	167.8	218.14
10. 10.00-19.99	6	1.3	99.7	77.57	8.1	94.7	181.3	235.69
11. 20.00- up	1	0.2	99.9	50.01	5.2	99.9	194.6	38.92
TOTALS	474	99.9		955.82	99.9			5454.38

Average holding = 2.02 hectares

Gini Index = 1.0 - .545 = .455
Decline in GI from 1970 to 1972 = -21.8% (owners only)
Decline in GI from 1957 to 1972 = -36.5% (owners only)

SOURCE: 1970 Land Tax Register and preliminary LTTT Program records (as of Sept. 1972), Village Office. The data has been adjusted to compensate for 34 unidentified cases of multiple titles distributed to the same tenant for different plots of land.

Table A-6

DISTRIBUTION OF RICELAND OWNERSHIP IN KHANH HAU
AMONG OWNERS AND TENANTS, BEFORE AND AFTER ORDINANCE 57, 1958

a. Before Ord. 57:

Ownership Stratum (n) (hectares) (1)	No. of owners & tenants (2)	% of total owners & tenants (3)	Cumulative % of total owners & tenants (4)	Cumulative % of total area (Y_n) (5)	From Col. 5 $(Y_n + Y_{n-1})$ (6)	Col. 3 times Col. 6 (7)
1. 0	267	67.3	67.3	0	0	0
2. 0.1-2	60	15.1	82.4	5.6	5.6	84.56
3. 2-3.9	25	6.3	88.7	13.2	18.8	118.44
4. 4-5.9	14	3.5	92.2	20.7	33.9	118.65
5. 6-7.9	11	2.8	95.0	28.9	49.6	138.88
6. 8-9.9	6	1.5	96.5	34.7	63.6	95.40
7. 10-100	13	3.3	99.8	64.9	99.6	328.68
8. 100+	1	0.3	100.1	99.9	164.8	49.44
TOTALS	397	100.1				934.05

Gini Index = 1.0 - .093 = .907   Average holding owned = 2.33 hectares

b. After Ord. 57:

Ownership Stratum (n) (hectares) (1)	No. of owners & tenants (2)	% of total owners & tenants (3)	Cumulative % of total owners & tenants (4)	Cumulative % of total area (Y_n) (5)	From Col. 5 $(Y_n + Y_{n-1})$ (6)	Col. 3 times Col. 6 (7)
1. 0	118	29.7	29.7	0	0	0
2. .1-2	168	42.3	72.0	18.2	18.2	769.86
3. 2-3.9	61	15.4	87.4	35.8	54.0	831.60
4. 4-5.9	19	4.8	92.2	45.8	81.6	391.68
5. 6-7.9	11	2.8	95.0	54.0	99.8	279.44
6. 8-9.9	6	1.5	96.5	59.8	113.8	170.70
7. 10-100	14	3.5	100.0	100.0	159.8	559.30
8. 100+	0	0	100.0	100.0	200.0	0
TOTALS	397	100.0				3002.58

Gini Index = 1.0 - .300 = .700
Decline in GI from Table 5-7a = -22.8%   Average holding owned = 2.33 hectares

SOURCE: Calculated from Hendry, Khanh Hau, Tables 3.1, 3.4 and 3.5, pp. 33, 39 and 45.
Column (5) is from Table A-4a and b, above.

Table A-7a

DISTRIBUTION OF PRIVATELY OWNED RICELAND IN KHANH HAU VILLAGE
AMONG OWNERS AND TENANTS, BEFORE LTTT PROGRAM, 1970

1) With Remaining Tenants Estimated as 55:

	(1)	(2)	(3)	(4)	(5)	(6)	(7)
	Ownership Stratum	Number of Owners & Tenants	Percentage of total Owners & Tenants	Cumulative Percentage of total Owners & Tenants	Cumulative Percentage of total area(Y_n)	From Col.5 (Y_n+Y_{n-1})	Col.3 times Col.6
(n)	(hectares)						
1.	0	256	47.1	47.1	0	0	0
2.	.01-.49	27	5.0	52.1	0.8	0.8	4.0
3.	.50-.99	45	8.3	60.4	4.4	5.2	43.2
4.	1.00-1.49	50	9.2	69.6	10.8	15.2	139.8
5.	1.50-1.99	50	7.4	77.0	17.7	28.5	210.9
6.	2.00-2.99	47	8.6	85.6	29.3	47.0	404.2
7.	3.00-3.99	26	4.8	90.4	38.4	67.7	325.0
8.	4.00-4.99	10	1.8	92.2	43.0	81.4	146.5
9.	5.00-7.49	22	4.0	96.2	57.4	100.4	401.6
10.	7.50-9.99	9	1.7	97.9	65.4	122.8	208.8
11.	10.00-19.99	7	1.3	99.2	74.1	139.5	181.4
12.	20.00- up	5	0.9	100.1	100.1	174.2	156.8
	TOTALS	544	100.1				2222.2

Gini Index = 1.0 - .222 = .778   Average holding owned = 1.79 ha.

2) With Remaining Tenants Estimated as 115:

1.	0	316	52.3	52.3	0	0	0
2.	.01-.49	27	4.5	56.8	0.8	0.8	3.6
3.	.50-.99	45	7.5	64.3	4.4	5.2	39.0
4.	1.00-1.49	50	8.3	72.6	10.8	15.2	126.2
5.	1.50-1.99	40	6.6	79.2	17.7	28.5	188.1
6.	2.00-2.99	47	7.8	87.0	29.3	47.0	366.6
7.	3.00-3.99	26	4.3	91.3	38.4	67.7	291.1
8.	4.00-4.99	10	1.7	93.0	43.0	81.4	138.4
9.	5.00-7.49	22	3.6	96.6	57.4	100.4	361.4
10.	7.50-9.99	9	1.5	98.1	65.4	122.8	184.2
11.	10.00-19.99	7	1.2	99.3	74.1	139.5	167.4
12.	20.00-up	5	0.8	100.1	100.1	174.2	139.4
	TOTALS	604	100.1				2005.4

Gini Index = 1.0 - .2005 = .7995   Average holding owned = 1.61 ha.

SOURCE: 1970 Land Tax Register, Village Office.
          Column (5) is from Table A-5a, above.

Table A-7b

DISTRIBUTION OF PRIVATELY OWNED RICELAND IN KHANH HAU VILLAGE
AMONG OWNERS AND TENANTS, AFTER LTTT PROGRAM, 1972

1) With Remaining Tenants Estimated as 55:

	(1)	(2)	(3)	(4)	(5)	(6)	(7)
			Percentage	Cumulative Percentage	Cumulative		
		Number of	of total	of total	Percentage	From	Col.3
	Ownership Stratum	Owners &	Owners &	Owners &	of total	Col.5	times
(n)	(hectares)	Tenants	Tenants	Tenants	area(Y_n)	(Y_n+Y_{n-1})	Col.6
1.	0	70	12.9	12.9	0	0	0
2.	.01-.49	37	6.8	19.7	1.1	1.1	7.5
3.	.50-.99	86	15.8	35.5	7.2	8.3	131.1
4.	1.00-1.49	150	27.6	63.1	26.1	33.3	919.1
5.	1.50-1.99	58	10.7	73.8	36.2	62.3	666.6
6.	2.00-2.99	61	11.2	85.0	51.3	87.5	980.0
7.	3.00-3.99	40	7.4	92.4	64.9	116.2	859.9
8.	4.00-4.99	10	1.8	94.2	69.6	134.5	242.1
9.	5.00-7.49	19	3.5	97.7	81.2	150.8	527.8
10.	7.50-9.99	6	1.1	98.8	86.6	167.8	184.6
11.	10.00-19.99	6	1.1	99.9	94.7	181.3	199.4
12.	20.00- up	1	0.2	100.1	99.9	194.6	38.9
	TOTALS	544	100.1				4757.0

Gini Index = 1.0 - .476 = .524   Average holding owned = 1.76 ha.
Decline in GI between 1970 and 1972 = -32.6% (See Table 5-8a1)
Decline in GI between 1955 and 1972 = -42.2% (See Table 5-7a)

2) With Remaining Tenants Estimated as 115:

1.	0	130	21.5	21.5	0	0	0
2.	.01-.49	37	6.1	27.6	1.1	1.1	6.7
3.	.50-.99	86	14.2	41.8	7.2	8.3	117.0
4.	1.00-1.49	150	24.8	66.6	26.1	33.3	825.8
5.	1.50-1.99	58	9.6	76.2	36.2	62.3	598.1
6.	2.00-2.99	61	10.1	86.3	51.3	87.5	883.8
7.	3.00-3.99	40	6.6	92.9	64.9	116.2	766.9
8.	4.00-4.99	10	1.7	94.6	69.6	134.5	228.7
9.	5.00-7.49	19	3.1	97.7	81.2	150.8	467.5
10.	7.50-9.99	6	1.0	98.7	86.6	167.8	167.8
11.	10.00-19.99	6	1.0	99.7	94.7	181.3	181.3
12.	20.00- up	1	0.2	99.9	99.9	194.6	38.9
	TOTALS	604	99.9				4282.5

Gini Index = 1.0 - .428 = .572   Average Holding owned = 1.58 ha.
Decline in GI between 1970 and 1972 = -28.5% (See Table 5-8a2)
Decline in GI between 1955 and 1972 = -37.2% (See Table 5-7a)

SOURCES: 1970 Land Tax Register and preliminary LTTT Program records (as of
Sept. 1972), Village Office. Column (5) is from Table A-5b, above.
The data has been adjusted to compensate for 34 unidentified cases
of multiple titles, for different small plots of land, distributed
to the same former tenant.

Table A-8a

OWNERSHIP DISTRIBUTION OF PRIVATELY OWNED RICELAND IN LONG BINH DIEN VILLAGE, BEFORE THE LTTT PROGRAM, INCLUDING OWNERS ONLY

(1) Ownership Stratum (n) (hectares)	(2) Number of land-owners	(3) % of total owners	(4) Cumulative percentage of total owners	(5) Hectarage Owned	(6) % of total area	(7) Cumulative percentage of total area (Y_n)	(8) From Col. 7 ($Y_n + Y_{n-1}$)	(9) Col. 3 times Col. 8
1. .01-.49	48	15.9	15.9	13.83	1.4	1.4	1.4	22.3
2. .50-.99	42	14.0	29.9	31.70	3.2	4.6	6.0	84.0
3. 1.00-1.49	42	14.0	43.9	50.98	5.1	9.7	14.3	200.2
4. 1.50-1.99	28	9.3	53.2	48.46	4.8	14.5	24.2	225.1
5. 2.00-2.99	44	14.6	67.8	107.12	10.7	25.2	39.7	579.6
6. 3.00-3.99	31	10.3	78.1	106.94	10.6	35.8	61.0	628.3
7. 4.00-4.99	15	5.0	83.1	68.32	6.8	42.6	78.4	392.0
8. 5.00-7.49	24	8.0	91.1	149.11	14.8	57.4	100.0	800.0
9. 7.50-9.99	5	1.7	92.8	39.69	3.9	61.3	118.7	201.8
10. 10.00-19.99	17	5.6	98.4	222.49	22.1	83.4	114.7	810.3
11. 20.00- up	5	1.7	100.1	166.23	16.5	99.9	183.3	311.6
TOTALS	301	100.1		1004.87	99.9			4255.2

Gini Index = 1.0 - .426 = .574   Average size of holding owned = 3.34 hectares

SOURCE: 1970 Land Tax Register, LBD Village Office

Table A-8b

OWNERSHIP DISTRIBUTION OF PRIVATELY OWNED RICELAND IN LONG BINH DIEN VILLAGE
AFTER THE LTTT PROGRAM, INCLUDING OWNERS ONLY

(1) Ownership Stratum (n) (hectares)	(2) Number of land-owners	(3) % of total owners	(4) Cumulative percentage of total owners	(5) Hectarage Owned	(6) % of total area	(7) Cumulative percentage of total area (Y_n)	(8) From Col. 7 $(Y_n + Y_{n-1})$	(9) Col. 3 times Col. 8
1. .01-.49	84	12.6	12.6	23.59	2.4	2.4	2.4	30.2
2. .50-.99	105	15.7	28.3	72.77	7.3	9.7	12.1	190.0
3. 1.00-1.49	296	44.4	72.7	348.38	35.2	44.9	54.6	2424.2
4. 1.50-1.99	67	10.0	82.7	112.27	11.3	56.2	101.1	1011.0
5. 2.00-2.99	62	9.3	92.0	146.37	14.8	71.0	127.2	1183.0
6. 3.00-3.99	19	2.8	94.8	63.47	6.4	77.4	148.4	415.5
7. 4.00-4.99	11	1.6	96.4	50.56	5.1	82.5	159.9	255.8
8. 5.00-7.49	17	2.5	98.9	104.97	10.6	93.1	175.6	439.0
9. 7.50-9.99	3	0.4	99.3	24.79	2.5	95.6	188.7	75.5
10. 10.00- up	3	0.4	99.7	43.70	4.4	100.0	195.6	78.2
TOTALS	667	99.7		990.87	100.0			6102.4

Gini Index = 1.0 - .610 = .390   Average size of holding owned = 1.49 hectares
Decline in GI between 1970 and 1972 = -32.1% (See Table A-8a)

SOURCE: 1970 Land Tax Register and preliminary LTTT redistribution records as of Feb. 1972, LBD Village Office. Estimated adjustments have been made in the data to compensate for 87 cases where the same tenant received more than one LTTT title (for different parcels of land).

Table A-9

OWNERSHIP DISTRIBUTION OF PRIVATELY OWNED RICELAND IN LONG BINH DIEN
AMONG OWNERS AND TENANTS, BEFORE AND AFTER LTTT PROGRAM, 1970-1972
(With Remaining Tenants Estimated as 136)

A. **Before LTTT:**

(1)		(2)	(3)	(4) Cumulative	(5)	(6)	(7)
		Number of	Percentage of total	Percentage of total	Cumulative Percentage	From	Col. 3 times
Ownership Stratum		Owners &	Owners &	Owners &	of total	Col.5	
(n)	(hectares)	Tenants	Tenants	Tenants	area(Y_n)	($Y_n + Y_{n-1}$)	Col. 6
1.	0	567	65.3	65.3	0	0	0
2.	.01-.49	48	5.5	70.8	1.4	1.4	7.7
3.	.50-.99	42	4.8	75.6	4.6	6.0	28.8
4.	1.00-1.49	42	4.8	80.4	9.7	14.3	68.6
5.	1.50-1.99	28	3.2	83.6	14.5	24.2	77.4
6.	2.00-2.99	44	5.1	88.7	25.2	39.7	202.5
7.	3.00-3.99	31	3.6	92.3	35.8	61.0	219.6
8.	4.00-4.99	15	1.7	94.0	42.6	78.4	133.3
9.	5.00-7.49	24	2.8	96.8	57.4	100.0	280.0
10.	7.50-9.99	5	0.6	97.4	61.3	118.7	71.2
11.	10.00-19.99	17	2.0	99.4	83.4	144.7	289.4
12.	20.00- up	5	0.6	100.0	99.9	183.3	110.0
	TOTALS	868	100.0				1488.5

Gini Index = 1.0 - .149 = .851 Average holding owned = 1.16 ha.

B. **After LTTT:**

1.	0	201	23.2	23.2	0	0	0
2.	.01-.49	84	9.7	32.9	2.4	2.4	23.3
3.	.50-.99	105	12.1	45.0	9.7	12.1	146.4
4.	1.00-1.49	296	34.1	79.1	44.9	54.6	1861.9
5.	1.50-1.99	67	7.7	86.8	56.2	101.1	778.5
6.	2.00-2.99	62	7.1	93.9	71.0	127.2	903.1
7.	3.00-3.99	19	2.2	96.1	77.4	148.4	326.5
8.	4.00-4.99	11	1.3	97.4	82.5	159.9	207.9
9.	5.00-7.49	17	2.0	99.4	93.1	175.6	351.2
10.	7.50-9.99	3	0.3	99.7	95.6	188.7	56.6
11.	10.00- up	3	0.3	100.0	100.0	195.6	58.7
	TOTALS	868	100.0				4714.1

Gini Index = 1.0 - .471 = .529 Average holding owned = 1.14 ha.
Decline in GI due to LTTT Program = -37.8% (counting both tenants and
owners)

SOURCE: 1970 Land Tax Register and preliminary LTTT redistribution records
as of Feb. 1972, LBD Village Office. Adjustments have been made
to compensate for 87 cases of multiple LTTT-title distribution
(for more than one parcel of land to each tenant). Column (5) is
from Table A-8a and b, above.

Table A-10a

OWNERSHIP DISTRIBUTION OF PRIVATELY OWNED LAND IN PHU THU VILLAGE,
BEFORE THE LTTT PROGRAM, 1970, INCLUDING OWNERS ONLY

(1) Ownership Stratum (n) (hectares)	(2) Number of land-owners	(3) % of total owners	(4) Cumulative percentage of total owners	(5) Hectarage Owned	(6) % of total area	(7) Cumulative percentage of total area (Y_n)	(8) From Col. 7 $(Y_n + Y_{n-1})$	(9) Col. 3 times Col. 8
1. .01-.49	79	17.5	17.5	24.29	1.7	1.7	1.7	29.8
2. .50-.99	73	16.2	33.7	53.05	3.8	5.5	7.2	116.6
3. 1.00-1.49	62	13.5	47.2	76.80	5.5	11.0	16.5	222.8
4. 1.50-1.99	41	9.1	56.3	71.58	5.1	16.1	27.1	246.6
5. 2.00-2.99	50	11.1	67.4	124.42	8.9	25.0	41.1	456.2
6. 3.00-3.99	37	8.2	75.6	129.36	9.2	34.2	59.2	485.4
7. 4.00-4.99	26	5.8	81.4	114.45	8.2	42.4	76.6	444.3
8. 5.00-7.49	35	7.7	89.1	216.26	15.4	57.8	100.2	771.5
9. 7.50-9.99	22	4.9	94.0	195.93	14.0	71.8	129.6	635.0
10. 10.00-19.99	23	5.1	99.1	285.77	20.4	92.2	164.0	836.4
11. 20.00-up	4	0.9	100.0	109.74	7.8	100.0	192.2	173.0
TOTALS	452	100.0		1401.65	100.0			4417.6

Gini Index = 1.0 - .442 = .558   Average size of holding = 3.10 hectares

SOURCE: Phu Thu Village Land Register, Village Office

Table A-10b

OWNERSHIP DISTRIBUTION OF PRIVATELY OWNED LAND IN PHU THU VILLAGE,
AFTER THE LTTT PROGRAM, 1972, INCLUDING OWNERS ONLY

(1) Ownership Stratum (n) (hectares)	(2) Number of land-owners	(3) % of total owners	(4) Cumulative percentage of total owners	(5) Hectarage owned	(6) % of total area	(7) Cumulative percentage of total area (Y_n)	(8) From Col. 7 $(Y_n + Y_{n-1})$	(9) Col. 3 times Col. 8
1. .01-.49	191	21.9	21.9	51.84	4.1	4.1	4.1	89.8
2. .50-.99	180	20.6	42.5	124.76	9.8	13.9	18.0	370.8
3. 1.00-1.49	245	28.1	70.6	280.15	22.0	35.9	49.8	1399.4
4. 1.50-1.99	102	11.7	82.3	173.84	13.7	49.6	85.5	1000.4
5. 2.00-2.99	69	7.9	90.2	166.43	13.1	62.7	112.3	887.2
6. 3.00-3.99	32	3.7	93.9	107.37	8.4	71.1	133.8	495.1
7. 4.00-4.99	13	1.5	95.4	56.31	4.4	75.5	146.6	219.9
8. 5.00-7.49	24	2.8	98.2	144.88	11.4	86.9	162.4	454.7
9. 7.50-9.99	13	1.5	99.7	116.36	9.1	96.0	182.9	274.4
10. 10.00- up	3	0.3	100.0	50.56	4.0	100.0	196.0	58.8
TOTALS	872	100.0		1272.50	100.0			5250.5

Gini Index = $1.0 - .525 = .475$ Average size of holding = 1.46 hectares

Decline in GI due to LTTT Program = -14.9% (owners only, see Table 5-31a)

SOURCE: Phu Thu Village Land Register, Village Office, as of May 23, 1972. In addition to the land tabulated above, the records indicated that another 126.94 ha. had been expropriated but not yet redistributed, that there were 25 hectares of cong dien and 7.05 ha. of hau dien, or publicly-owned land (cong dien is communal land and hau dien is land that has been given to the village for religious purposes), for a total of 1431.49 hectares.

The data has been adjusted to compensate for the issuance of multiple LTTT titles to the same new owners.

Table A-11

OWNERSHIP DISTRIBUTION OF PRIVATELY OWNED LAND IN PHU THU VILLAGE
AMONG OWNERS AND TENANTS, BEFORE AND AFTER LTTT PROGRAM, 1970-72
(With Remaining Tenants Estimated as 128)

A. Before LTTT:

(1) Ownership Stratum (n) (hectares)	(2) Number of Owners & Tenants	(3) Percentage of total Owners & Tenants	(4) Cumulative Percentage of total Owners & Tenants	(5) Cumulative Percentage of total Area(Y_n)	(6) From Col.5 (Y_n+Y_{n-1})	(7) Col.3 times Col.6
1. 0	593[1]	56.7	56.7	0	0	0
2. .01-.49	79	7.6	64.3	1.7	1.7	12.9
3. .50-.99	73	7.0	71.3	5.5	7.2	50.4
4. 1.00-1.49	62	5.9	77.2	11.0	16.5	97.4
5. 1.50-1.99	41	3.9	81.1	16.1	27.1	105.7
6. 2.00-2.99	50	4.8	85.9	25.0	41.1	197.3
7. 3.00-3.99	37	3.5	89.4	34.2	59.2	207.2
8. 4.00-4.99	26	2.5	91.9	42.4	76.6	191.5
9. 5.00-7.49	35	3.3	95.2	57.8	100.2	330.7
10. 7.50-9.99	22	2.1	97.3	71.8	129.6	272.2
11. 10.00-19.99	23	2.2	99.5	92.2	164.0	360.8
12. 20.00 - up	4	0.4	99.9	100.0	192.2	76.9
Totals	1045	100.0				1903.0

Gini Index = 1.0 - .190 = .810   Average holding owned = 1.34 ha.

B. After LTTT:

1. 0	173[2]	16.6	16.6	0	0	0
2. .01-.49	191	18.3	34.9	4.1	4.1	75.0
3. .50-.99	180	17.2	52.1	13.9	18.0	309.6
4. 1.00-1.49	245	23.4	75.5	35.9	49.8	1165.3
5. 1.50-1.99	102	9.8	85.3	49.6	85.5	837.9
6. 2.00-2.99	69	6.6	91.9	62.7	112.3	741.2
7. 3.00-3.99	32	3.1	95.0	71.1	133.8	414.8
8. 4.00-4.99	13	1.2	96.2	75.5	146.6	175.9
9. 5.00-7.49	24	2.3	98.5	86.9	162.4	373.5
10. 7.50-9.99	13	1.2	99.7	96.0	182.9	219.5
11. 10.00- up	3	0.3	100.0	100.0	196.0	58.8
Totals	1045	100.0				4371.5

Gini Index = 1.0 - .437 = .563   Average holding owned = 1.22 ha.
Decline in GI due to LTTT Program = -30.5% (counting both tenants and
owners)

[1] Includes 465 LTTT-title recipients and an estimated 128 remaining tenants.
[2] Includes 45 completely dispossessed landlords and an estimated 128 remaining tenants.

SOURCE: Phu Thu Village Land Register, Village Office, 1970 and with LTTT
changes posted as of May 23, 1972. See Source note for Table A-10b.
Column (5) is from Table A-10a and b, above.
Post-LTTT data has been adjusted to compensate for the issuance of
multiple LTTT titles (for different small parcels of land) to the
same new owners.

BIBLIOGRAPHY

"Bang Nhan Xet va De Nghi Tu Chinh Du Luat Cai Cach Dien Dia cua Ha Nghi Vien" (Table of Comments and Recommended Amendments for the Lower House Land Reform Bill), Ministry of Land Reform and Agricultural Development, prepared for the Senate Committee on Agriculture, undated.

Bien Ban Phien Hop cua Ha Nghi Vien (Session Minutes of the Lower House), So: 63/69/H/BB/DB, 64-70/69/H/BB/BT, and 125/69/H/BB/BT, Ha Nghi Vien, Viet Nam Cong Hoa (Lower House, Republic of Vietnam), August 25, 26, 28, September 1-5 and 9, 1969, and March 16, 1970. (Mimeographed.)

Bien Ban Phien Hop cua Thuong Nghi Vien (Session Minutes of the Senate), So: 06-07/70-TNV/BB, Thuong Nghi Vien, Viet Nam Cong Hoa (The Senate, Republic of Vietnam), March 2 and 3, 1970.

Bredo, William, "Agrarian Reform in Vietnam: Viet Cong and Government of Vietnam Strategies in Conflict," **Asian Survey**, 10:8; 739-50, August 1970.

Bredo, William, Project Director, **Land Reform in Vietnam, Summary Volume** and **Working Papers** (the latter 4 volumes in 6 parts), Menlo Park, Calif.: Stanford Research Institute, 1968.

Bush, Henry C., "Findings of Survey of 100 Exlandlords, on Payments to be Compensated, and on Uses and Intended Uses of Compensation Money," Memorandum to William Fuller, ADTS/ADLR, USAID, Saigon, from Dr. Bush, CDC, P&R/ADLR, April 16, 1973.

Bush, Henry C., "Further Data on Rent Income, Farm Income Other than Main Crop, and Main Crop Gross Net Income," Memorandum from USAID, ADLR/P&R/CDC, dated 25 June 1971.

Bush, Henry C., **Obstacles to the Land-to-the-Tiller Program in Coastal Central Vietnam**, Saigon: Control Data Corp., June 1973 (Draft).

Bush, Henry C., **Small Landlords Dependence on Rent Income in Vietnam**, Vietnam: Control Data Corp., ADLR, USAID, October 1970.

Bush, Henry C., "Small Landlords Dependence on Rent Income Survey," Memorandum from USAID, ADLR/P&R/CDC, dated 28 May 1971.

Bush, Henry C., **Village Use of Communal Rice Land in Long An Province, Vietnam,** Vietnam: Control Data Corp., ADLR, USAID, January 1971.

Bush, Henry C., Gordon H. Messegee and Roger V. Russell, **The Impact of the Land-to-the-Tiller Program in the Mekong Delta,** Vietnam: Control Data Corp., ADLR, USAID, December 1972.

Buttinger, Joseph, **The Smaller Dragon,** New York: Praeger, 1958.

Buttinger, Joseph, **Vietnam: A Dragon Embattled,** New York: Praeger, 1967.

Callison, C. Stuart, "Land-to-the-Tiller in the Mekong Delta," Ph.D. Dissertation, Cornell University, Ithaca, N.Y., 1976.

Chanda, Nayan, "Vietnam's Battle of the Home Front," **Far Eastern Economic Review,** November 2, 1979, pp. 44-48.

Dac San Kinh Te Nong Nghiep, 1974, (Bulletin of Agricultural Economics, Special Issue), Saigon: Ministry of Agriculture, 1974.

Dore, R. P., **Land Reform in Japan,** London: Oxford University Press, 1959.

Dorner, Peter, **Land Reform & Economic Development,** Baltimore: Penguin Books, Inc., 1972.

Duiker, William J., "Ideology and Nation-Building in the Democratic Republic of Vietnam," **Asian Survey,** University of California Press, May 1977, pp. 413-31.

"Economic Background Data," Joint Economic Office, Saigon: USAID, July 26, 1974.

Eney, Richard H., "Anticipated Use of Landlord Compensation Payments, MR 4," Memorandum from Mr. Eney, Chief, Land Reform Division, CG4/RRO, dated May 7, 1973.

Fall, Bernard B., **The Two Viet-Nams,** New York: Praeger, 1963.

Fitzgerald, Edward T., and Henry C. Bush, **Village Use of Communal Rice Land in Quang Tri, Thua Thien, Quang Nam, Quang Tin and Quang Ngai Provinces, Vietnam,** Saigon: Control Data Corp., December 1970.

Fitzgerald, Dr. Edward T., Dr. Henry C. Bush, Dr. E. Eugene Dayhoff and Vilis Donis, **Land Ownership and Tenancy Among Village and Hamlet Officials in the Delta,** Saigon: Pacification Studies Group, Hq. MACV, March 1970.

Fox, Ray S., **Rice Cost of Production in Vietnam—1968/69 Rice Crop and Preliminary Estimates for 1970,** Saigon: U.S. Agency for International Development, March 1970.

Gini, C., "Variabilita e Mutabilita," **Studi Economico-Guiridici della R. Universita di Cagliari,** anno 3, part 2, 1912.

Gittinger, J. P., **Studies on Land Tenure in Viet Nam,** U.S. Operations Mission to Vietnam, December 1959.

"GVN Tax Performance," attached to Enclosure 3 of letter from Robert S. Ingersoll, Acting Secretary of State, to the Hon. John Sparkman, Chm., Committee on Foreign Relations, U.S. Senate, March 18, 1975.

Hendry, James B., **The Small World of Khanh Hau,** Chicago: Aldine, 1964.

Henry, Yves, **Economie Agricole de l'Indochine,** Hanoi: Imprimerie d'Extreme-Orient, 1932.

Hickey, Gerald C., **Village in Vietnam,** New Haven, Conn.: Yale University Press, 1964.

Hien, Vu Van, **Che-Do Tai-San trong Gia-Dinh Viet-Nam, Tap I** (Property Regimes in the Vietnamese Family, Vol. I), Saigon: Bo Quoc-Gia Giao Duc (Ministry of Education), 1960.

Joint Development Group, **The Postwar Development of the Republic of Vietnam,** New York: Praeger Publishers, 1970.

Kendall, Maurice G., **The Advanced Theory of Statistics,** New York: Hafner Publishing Co., 1943.

Key Indicators of Developing Member Countries of ADB, Asian Development Bank, October 1979.

Khoi, Le Thanh, **Le Viet-Nam,** Paris: Les Editions de Minuit, 1955.

Koo, Anthony Y. C., **The Role of Land Reform in Economic Development: A Case Study of Taiwan,** New York: Praeger, 1968.

Ladejinsky, Wolf, "Agrarian Reform in Free Vietnam," in **Vietnam in World Affairs,** Special Issue, **Studies on National and International Affairs,** Vietnam, 1960.

"Land Reform in RVN," **Viet-Nam Bulletin,** (Vietnam Info Series 27), Washington, D.C.: Embassy of Viet-Nam, March 1970.

Lee, Teng-hui, **Intersectoral Capital Flows in the Economic Development of Taiwan, 1895-1960,** Ithaca, New York: Cornell University Press, 1971.

Leibenstein, Harvey, "Allocative Efficiency vs. 'X-Efficiency,'" **American Economic Review,** 1966, pp. 392-415.

Leibenstein, Harvey, "Bandwagon, Snob, and Veblen Effects in the Theory of Consumers' Demand," **Quarterly Journal of Economics,** 1950, pp. 183-207.

Lewis, W. Arthur, **The Theory of Economic Growth,** New York: Harper & Row, 1970 (originally published by George Allen & Unwin Ltd., London, 1955).

Linh, Le, **Nhung Van de Kinh te Viet Nam** (Vietnam Economic Problems), Saigon: Khai Tri, 1967.

McAlister, John T., Jr., **Viet Nam: The Origins of Revolution,** New York: Knopf, 1969.

Meier, Gerald M., **Leading Issues in Economic Development: Studies in International Poverty,** Oxford University Press, 1970.

Mellor, John W., **The Economics of Agricultural Development,** Ithaca, New York: Cornell University Press, 1966.

Messegee, Gordon H., **Soldiers and the Land to the Tiller Program in Military Region 3 of Vietnam,** Vietnam: Control Data Corp., ADLR, USAID, November 1971.

"Miracle Rice Comes to Vietnam," **Vietnam Bulletin,** Viet-Nam Info Series 15, Agriculture: Miracle Rice (11-69), Washington, D.C.: Embassy of Vietnam.

Mitchell, Edward J., "Land Tenure and Rebellion: A Statistical Analysis of Factors Affecting Government Control in South Vietnam," RAND Memorandum 5181-ARPA, Santa Monica, Calif., June 1967, also summarized in **Asian Survey,** Vol. VII, August 1967, pp. 577-580, reported in **The New York Times,** October 16, 1967, and published as "Inequality and Insurgency:

A Statistical Study of South Vietnam," **World Politics**, Vol. XX, No. 3, April 1968, pp. 421-438.

Morse, Chandler, **et. al., Modernization by Design,** Ithaca, New York: Cornell University Press, 1969.

Newberry, Larry, **Soldiers and the Land-to-the-Tiller Program in Military Region 4 of Vietnam,** Vietnam: Control Data Corp., ADLR, USAID, August 1971.

"New Land Reforms for South Vietnam," **The New York Times,** October 19, 1975.

Nho, Ta Van, "Dinh-Nghia Danh-tu Cai-cach Dien-dia" (The Meaning of Land Reform), in Nha Cai-Cach Dien Dia (Land Reform Service), **Nhung Bai Giang ve Cai-Cach Dien Dia** (Lectures on Land Reform), Bo Dien Tho va Cai Cach Dien Dia (Ministry of Land and Land Reform), Saigon, 1955.

Nien Giam Thong Ke Nong Nghiep, 1969, and **1970,** (Agricultural Statistics Yearbook), Saigon: Agricultural Economics and Statistical Service, 1970 and 1971.

Nien Giam Thong Ke Vietnam, 1971 (Viet Nam Statistical Yearbook), Saigon: National Institute of Statistics, 1972.

Nguyet San Thong Ke Nong Nghiep, So 3, 1972, (Dac Biet) (Monthly Bulletin of Agricultural Statistics, No. 3, 1972, Special Issue), Saigon: Agricultural Economics and Statistics Service, 1972.

Paige, Jeffery M., "Inequality and Insurgency in Vietnam, a re-Analysis," **World Politics,** Vol. 23, October 1970, pp. 24-37.

Paranzino, Dennis, "Inequality and Insurgency in Vietnam, a Further Re-Analysis," **World Politics,** Vol. 24, July 1972, pp. 565-78.

Phuc Trinh ve cuoc Kiem Tra Canh Nong tai Viet Nam, 1960-61 (Report of the Agricultural Census of Vietnam), Saigon: Agricultural Economics and Statistics Service, 1964.

Pike, Douglas, **Viet Cong,** Cambridge, Mass.: M.I.T. Press, 1969.

Pike, Douglas, "Vietnam in 1977: More of the Same," **Asian Survey,** University of California Press, January 1978, pp. 68-75.

Prosterman, Roy L., "Land-to-the-Tiller in South Vietnam: the Tables Turn," **Asian Survey,** 10:8; 751-64, August 1970.

Race, Jeffrey, "The Battle Over Land," **Far Eastern Economic Review,** August 20, 1970, pp. 19-22.

Race, Jeffrey, **War Comes to Long An,** Berkeley: University of California Press, 1972.

Rose, Ed, "Highlights of Trip to Chau Doc 10-11 April 73," Cable Can Tho 0061 from AM CONSUL/CAN THO to USAID/ADLR/FSLB, Saigon, April 14, 1973.

Rose, Ed, "Highlights of Visit to An Giang 4-6 April 73," Cable Can Tho 0033 from AM CONSUL/CAN THO to USAID/ADLR/FSLB, Saigon, April 9, 1973.

Russett, Bruce M., "Inequality and Instability, The Relation of Land Tenure to Politics," **World Politics,** April 1964, pp. 442-54.

Russett, Bruce M., Hayward R. Alker, Jr., Karl W. Deutsch and Harold D. Lasswell, **World Handbook of Political and Social Indicators,** New Haven, Conn.: Yale University Press, 1964.

Sacks, I. Milton, "Marxism in Vietnam," in Frank N. Trager (ed.), **Marxism in Southeast Asia,** Stanford, Calif.: Stanford University Press, 1959.

Salter, MacDonald, "The Broadening Base of Land Reform in South Vietnam," **Asian Survey,** 10:8; 724-37, August 1970.

Salter, MacDonald, **Land Reform in South Vietnam,** Spring Review Country Paper, Agency for International Development, Washington, D.C., June 1970.

Sang, Ho Thoi, **Kinh Te Viet Nam** (Vietnam Economy), Lecture notes, Saigon University, Saigon, 1967-8 (Mimeographed).

Sansom, Robert L., **The Economics of Insurgency in the Mekong Delta of Vietnam,** Cambridge, Mass.: M.I.T. Press, 1970.

Sherper, Keith W., and Phi Ngoc Huyen, "Grievances and Land-to-the-Tiller," U.S. Agency for International Development and Directorate General for Land Affairs, RVN, February 15, 1973 (Mimeographed).

Tai, Hung-chao, **Land Reform and Politics, A Comparative Analysis,** Berkeley: University of California Press, 1974.

Tai Lieu Giai Thich Luat Nguoi Cay Co Ruong (Explanations of the Land-to-the-Tiller Law), Ministry of Information, undated pamphlet.

Tang, H.S., and S.C. Hsieh, "Land Reform and Agricultural Development in Taiwan," **The Malayan Economic Review**, Vol. VI, No. 1, April 1961, pp. 49-54.

"Terminal Project Appraisal Report" for Land Reform in Vietnam, Agency for International Development, Dept. of State, Washington, D.C., October 7, 1975.

Thompson, Virginia, **French Indo-China**, London: The Macmillan Co., 1937 (Reprinted by Octagon Books, New York, 1968).

Thong Ke Nguyet San (Monthly Bulletin of Statistics), Saigon: National Institute of Statistics, 1972 and 1973.

Tuma, Elais H., **Twenty-Six Centuries of Agrarian Reform**, Berkeley: University of California Press, 1965.

"Vietnam," **Far Eastern Economic Review, Asia 1979 Yearbook**, pp. 316-23.

"Vietnam Land-to-the-Tiller Plan Unprecedented," **Vietnam Bulletin**, Vol. V, No. 15, Embassy of Vietnam, Washington, D.C., April 12, 1971.

Warriner, Doreen, **Land Reform in Principle and Practice**, London: Oxford University Press, 1969.

Woodruff, Lloyd W., **The Study of a Vietnamese Rural Community—Administrative Activities**, 2 Vols., Saigon: Michigan State University Vietnam Advisory Group, 1960.

Yang, Martin M.C., **Socio-Economic Results of Land Reform in Taiwan**, Honolulu: East-West Center Press, 1970.

INDEX